NCLE
from ANOTHER WORLD

III

Hotondoshindeiru
A Man Who Survived

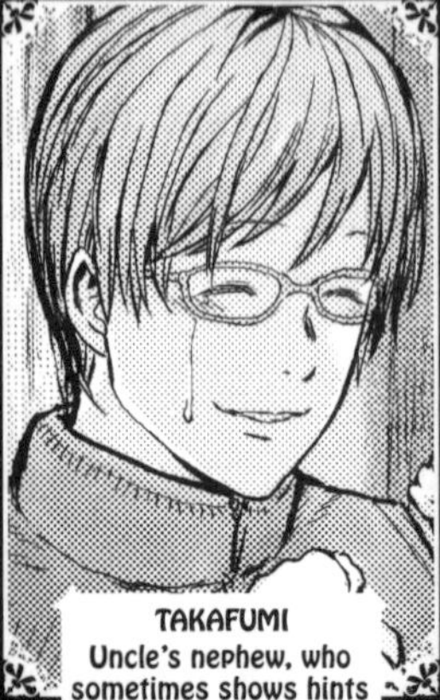

TAKAFUMI
Uncle's nephew, who sometimes shows hints of his inner darkness.

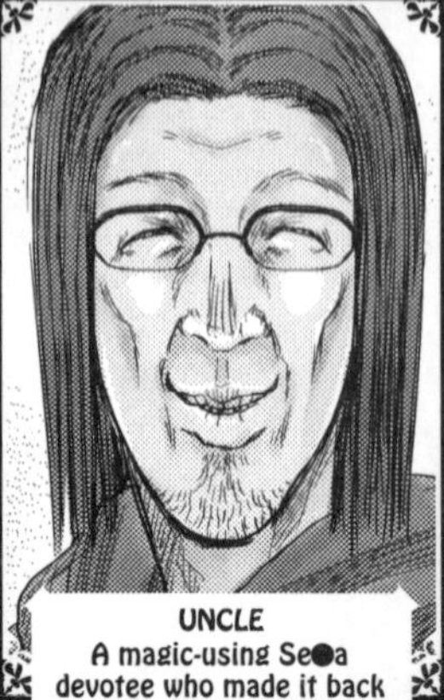

UNCLE
A magic-using Se●a devotee who made it back from another world.

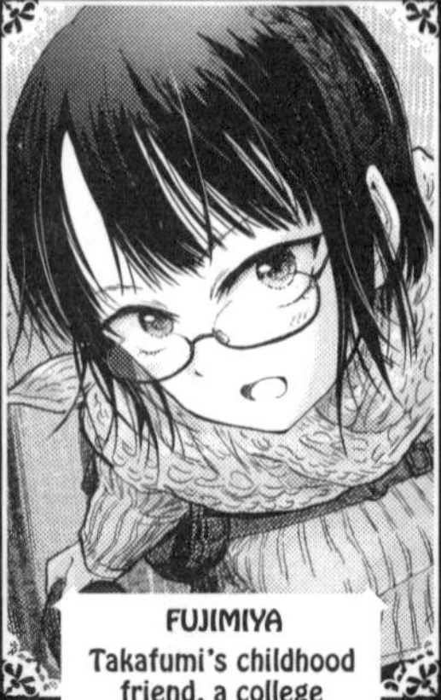

FUJIMIYA
Takafumi's childhood friend, a college student who's into him.

THE STORY SO FAR

The uncle is back after spending years in another world. He lives with his nephew Takafumi. Together with Fujimiya (the girl of the group), they were hanging out like normal on a day in June 2018. When Uncle showed them an otherworld flashback video to illustrate a point, they heard ex-shut-in Mabel mention that Uncle was transported to their world from "Japanbahamal."

CONTENTS

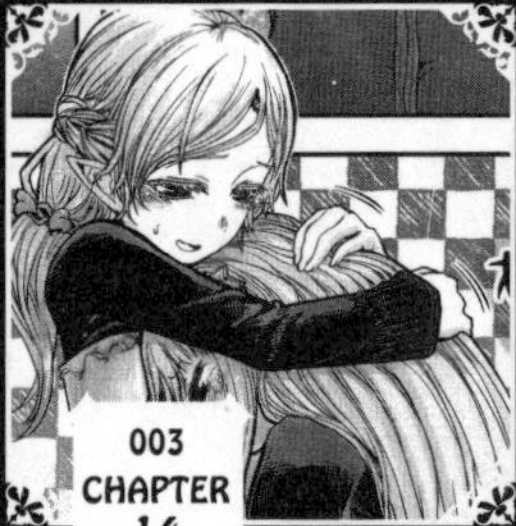

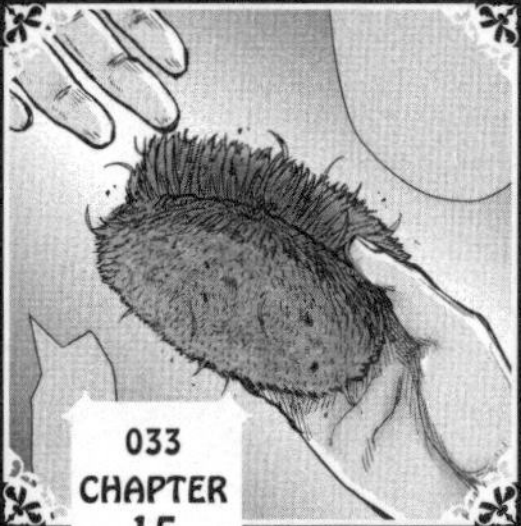

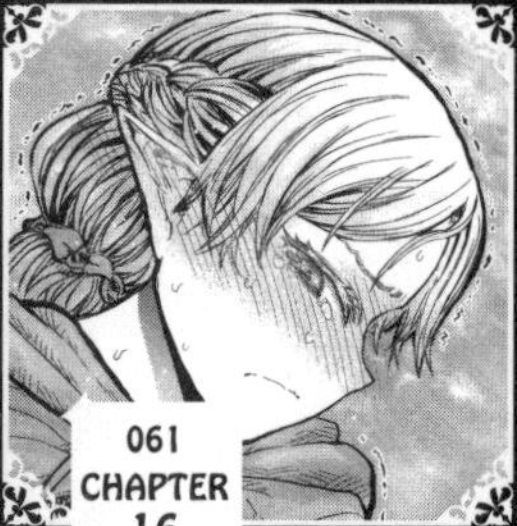

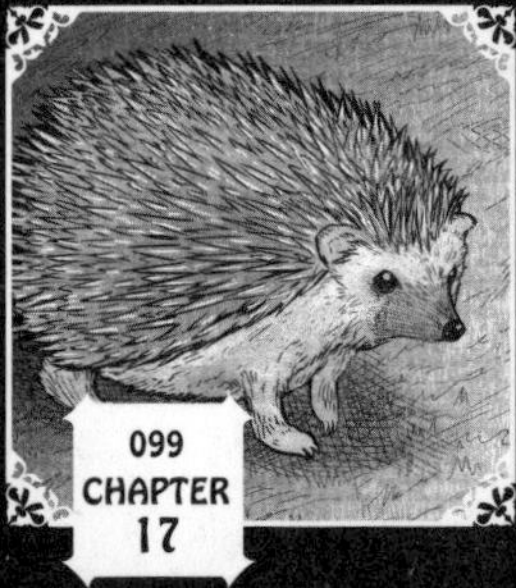

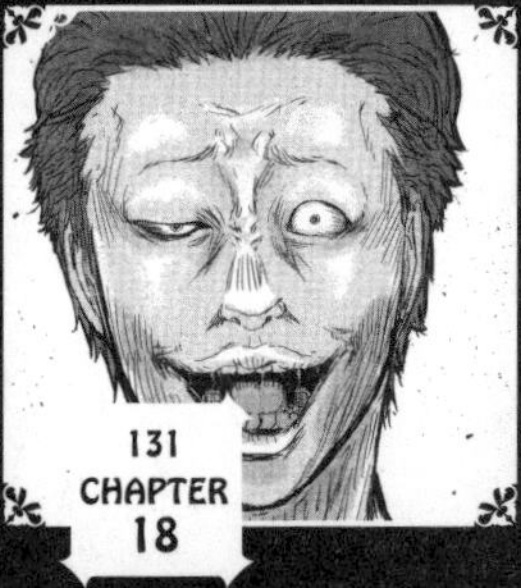

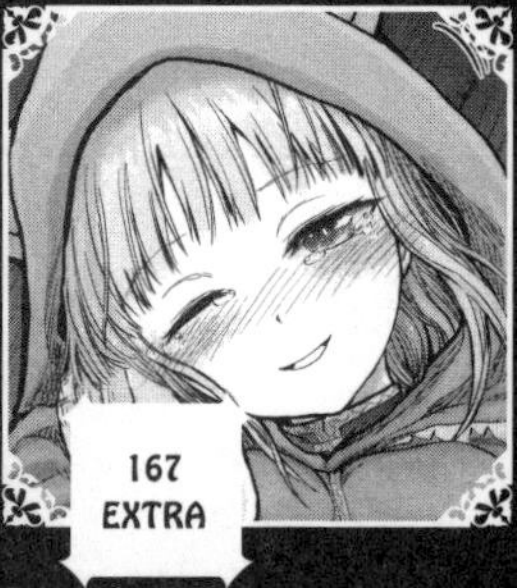

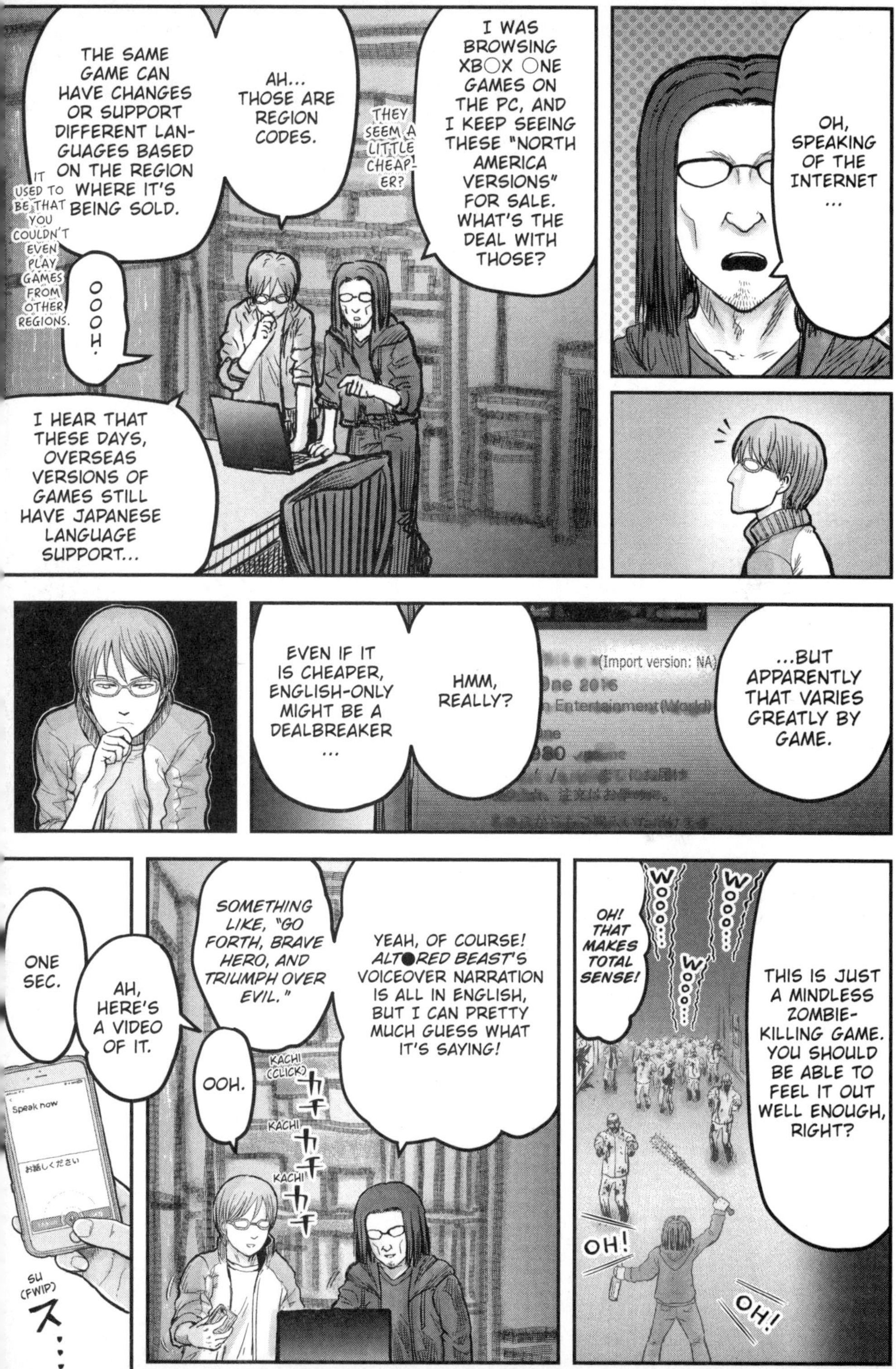
OH, SPEAKING OF THE INTERNET…
I WAS BROWSING XB○X ○NE GAMES ON THE PC, AND I KEEP SEEING THESE "NORTH AMERICA VERSIONS" FOR SALE. WHAT'S THE DEAL WITH THOSE?
THEY SEEM A LITTLE CHEAPER?
AH… THOSE ARE REGION CODES.
THE SAME GAME CAN HAVE CHANGES OR SUPPORT DIFFERENT LANGUAGES BASED ON THE REGION WHERE IT'S BEING SOLD.
IT USED TO BE THAT YOU COULDN'T EVEN PLAY GAMES FROM OTHER REGIONS.
OOOOH.
I HEAR THAT THESE DAYS, OVERSEAS VERSIONS OF GAMES STILL HAVE JAPANESE LANGUAGE SUPPORT…
…BUT APPARENTLY THAT VARIES GREATLY BY GAME.
(Import version: NA)
HMM, REALLY?
EVEN IF IT IS CHEAPER, ENGLISH-ONLY MIGHT BE A DEALBREAKER…
THIS IS JUST A MINDLESS ZOMBIE-KILLING GAME. YOU SHOULD BE ABLE TO FEEL IT OUT WELL ENOUGH, RIGHT?
WOOOO…
WOOOO…
OH! THAT MAKES TOTAL SENSE!
WOOOO…
OH!
OH!
YEAH, OF COURSE! ALT●RED BEAST'S VOICEOVER NARRATION IS ALL IN ENGLISH, BUT I CAN PRETTY MUCH GUESS WHAT IT'S SAYING!
SOMETHING LIKE, "GO FORTH, BRAVE HERO, AND TRIUMPH OVER EVIL."
OOH.
KACHI (CLICK) カチ
KACHI カチ
KACHI カチ
AH, HERE'S A VIDEO OF IT.
ONE SEC.
Speak now
お話しください
SU (FWIP) ス…

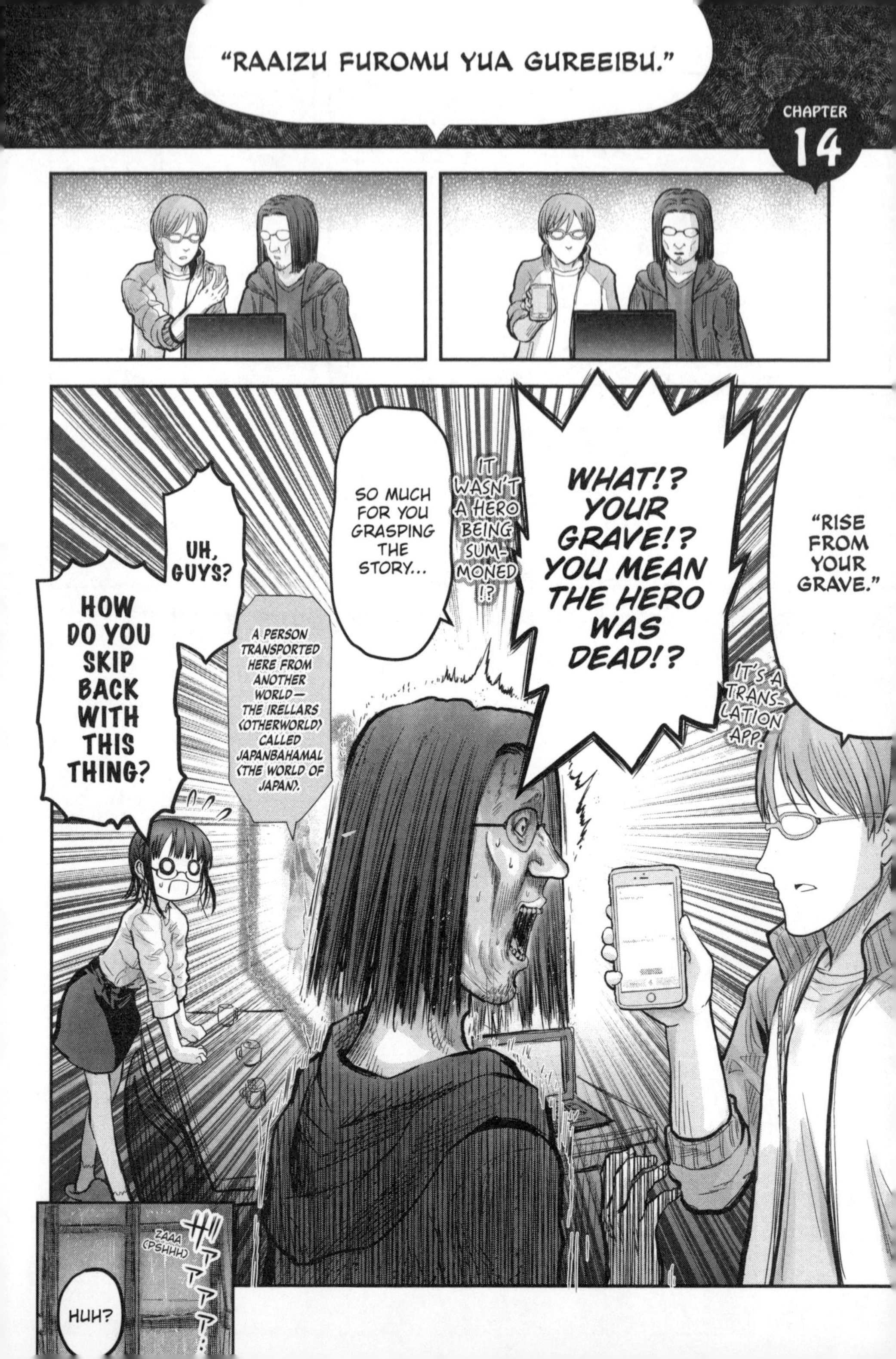
"RAAIZU FUROMU YUA GUREEIBU."
CHAPTER 14
"RISE FROM YOUR GRAVE."
IT'S A TRANSLATION APP.
WHAT!? YOUR GRAVE!? YOU MEAN THE HERO WAS DEAD!?
IT WASN'T A HERO BEING SUMMONED!?
SO MUCH FOR YOU GRASPING THE STORY...
A PERSON TRANSPORTED HERE FROM ANOTHER WORLD—THE IRELLARS (OTHERWORLD) CALLED JAPANBAHAMAL (THE WORLD OF JAPAN).
UH, GUYS?
HOW DO YOU SKIP BACK WITH THIS THING?
ZAAA (PSHHH)
HUH?

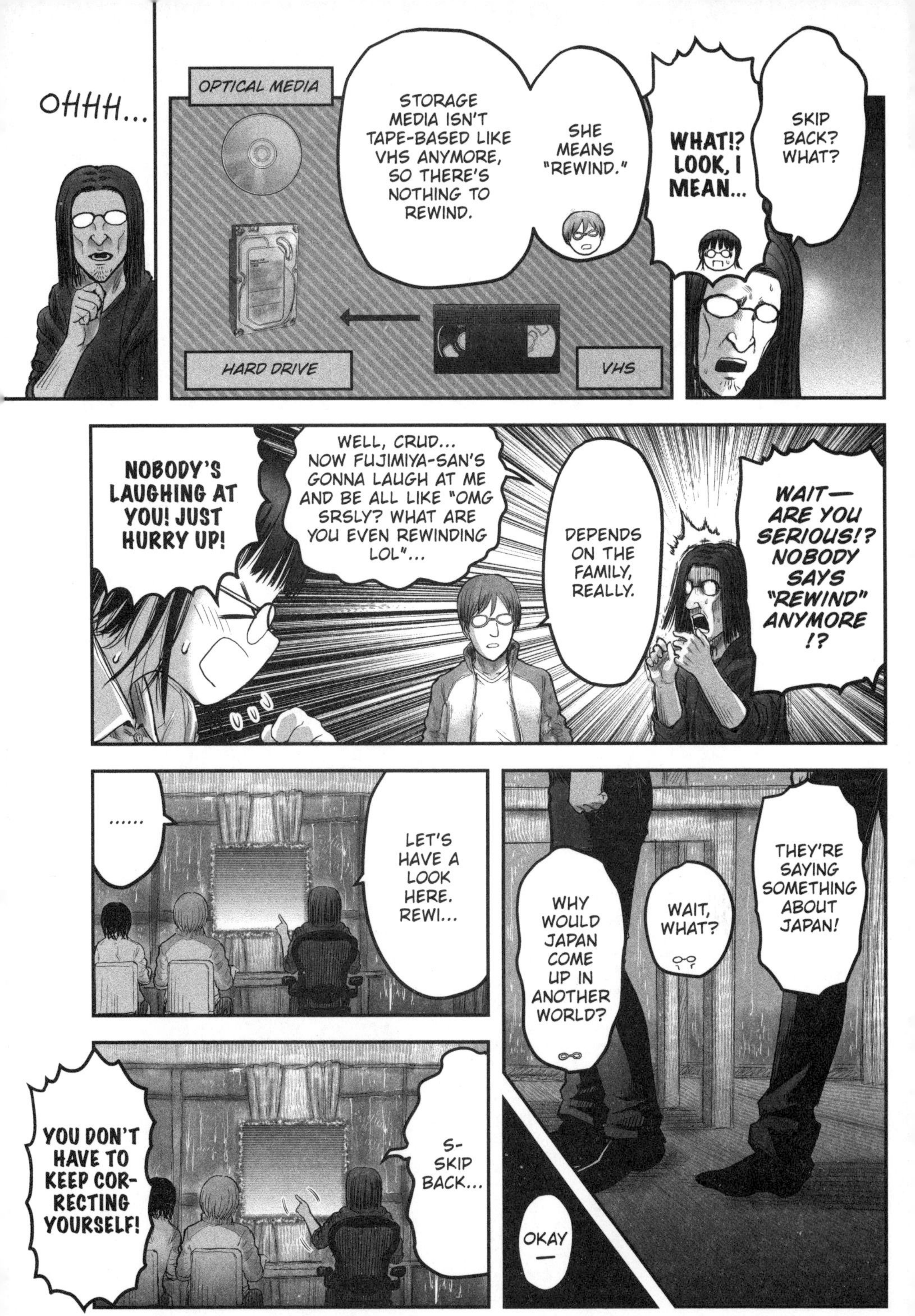
SKIP BACK? WHAT?
WHAT!? LOOK, I MEAN...
SHE MEANS "REWIND."
STORAGE MEDIA ISN'T TAPE-BASED LIKE VHS ANYMORE, SO THERE'S NOTHING TO REWIND.
OPTICAL MEDIA
VHS
HARD DRIVE
OHHH...
WAIT— ARE YOU SERIOUS!? NOBODY SAYS "REWIND" ANYMORE!?
DEPENDS ON THE FAMILY, REALLY.
WELL, CRUD... NOW FUJIMIYA-SAN'S GONNA LAUGH AT ME AND BE ALL LIKE "OMG SRSLY? WHAT ARE YOU EVEN REWINDING LOL"...
NOBODY'S LAUGHING AT YOU! JUST HURRY UP!
THEY'RE SAYING SOMETHING ABOUT JAPAN!
WAIT, WHAT?
WHY WOULD JAPAN COME UP IN ANOTHER WORLD?
OKAY—
LET'S HAVE A LOOK HERE. REWI...
......
S-SKIP BACK...
YOU DON'T HAVE TO KEEP COR-RECTING YOURSELF!

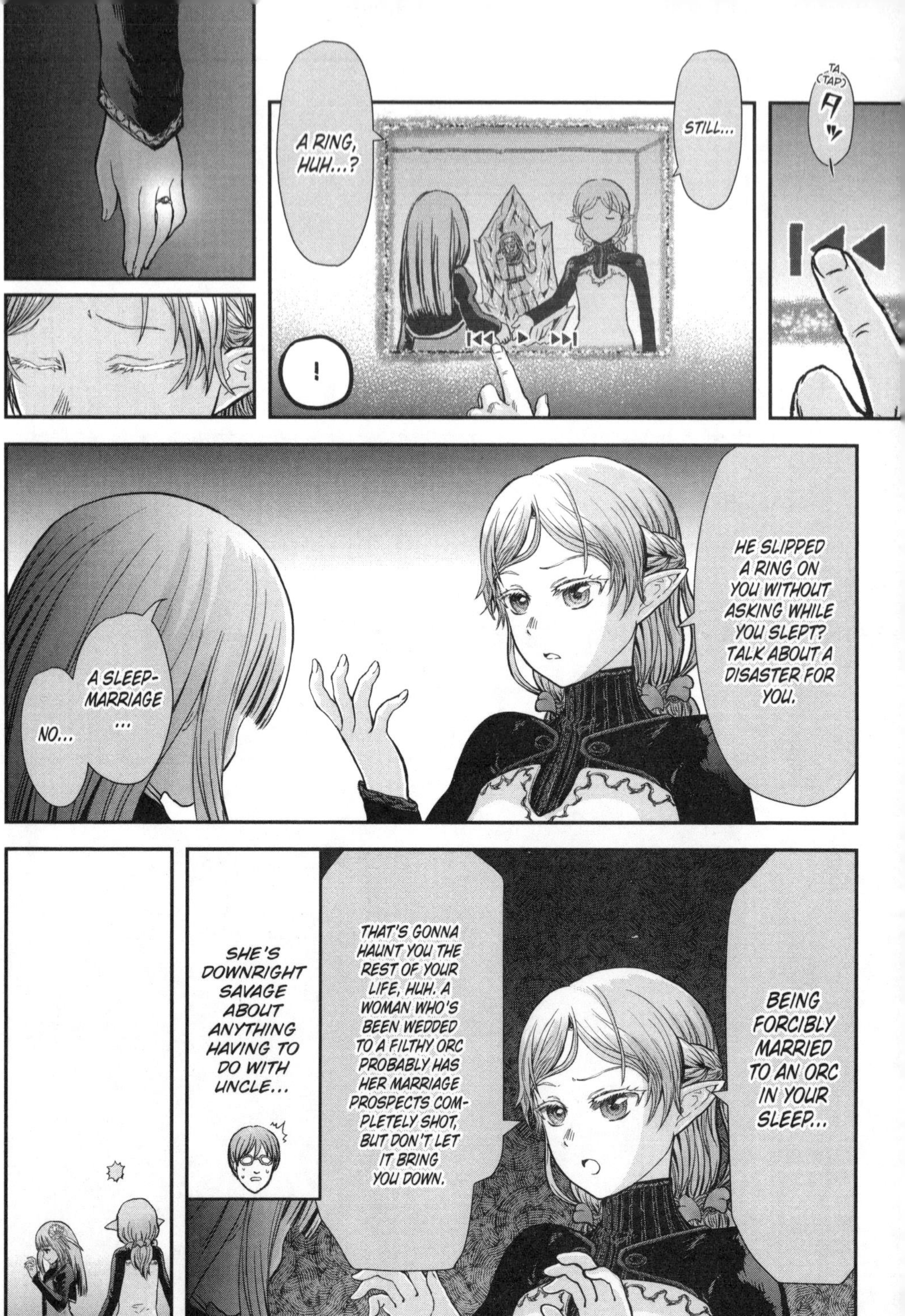
TA (TAP)
STILL...
A RING, HUH...?
!
HE SLIPPED A RING ON YOU WITHOUT ASKING WHILE YOU SLEPT? TALK ABOUT A DISASTER FOR YOU.
A SLEEP-MARRIAGE...
NO...
BEING FORCIBLY MARRIED TO AN ORC IN YOUR SLEEP...
THAT'S GONNA HAUNT YOU THE REST OF YOUR LIFE, HUH. A WOMAN WHO'S BEEN WEDDED TO A FILTHY ORC PROBABLY HAS HER MARRIAGE PROSPECTS COMPLETELY SHOT, BUT DON'T LET IT BRING YOU DOWN.
SHE'S DOWNRIGHT SAVAGE ABOUT ANYTHING HAVING TO DO WITH UNCLE...

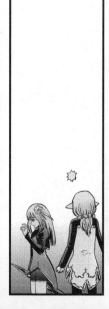

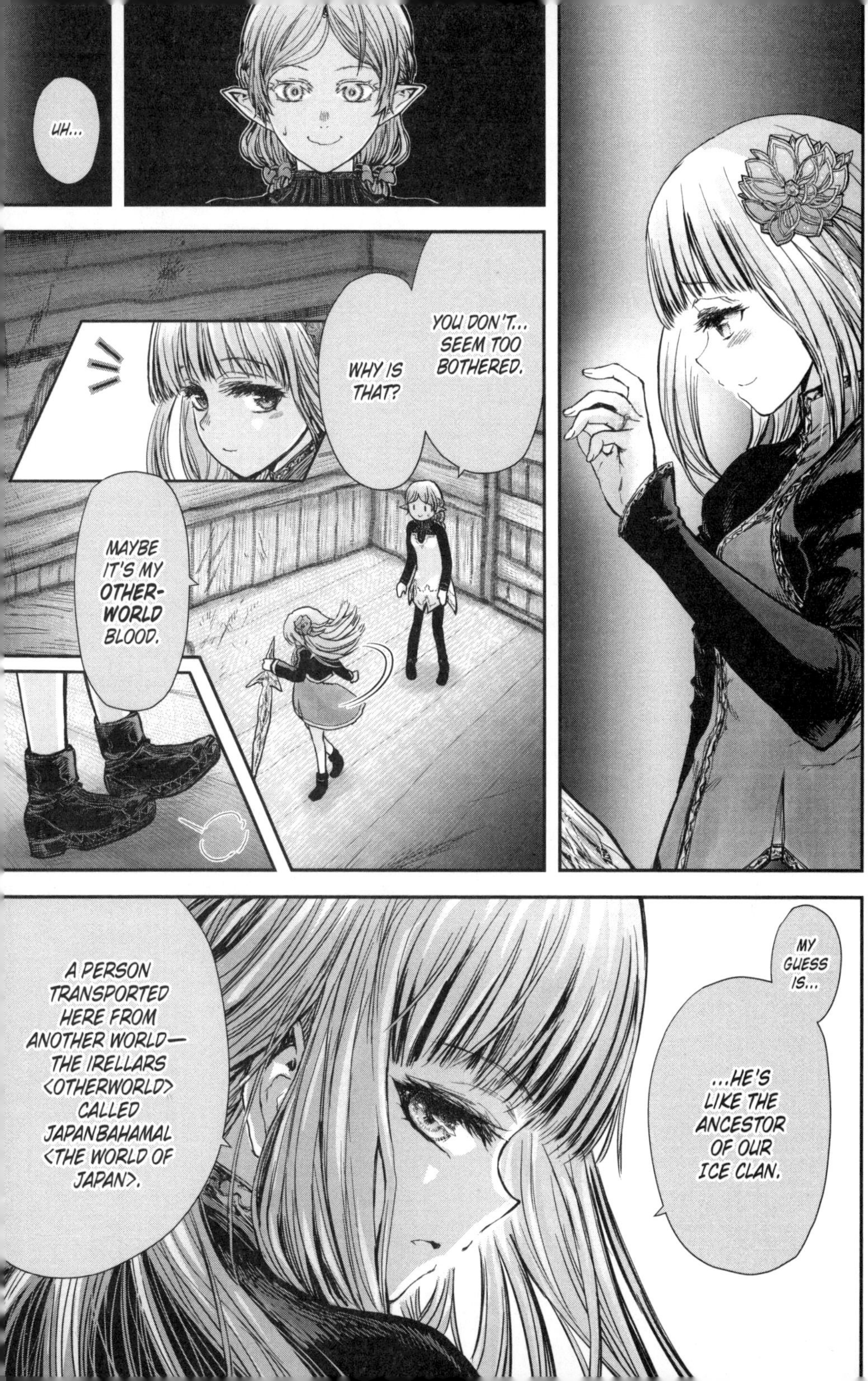
UH...
YOU DON'T... SEEM TOO BOTHERED.
WHY IS THAT?
MAYBE IT'S MY OTHER-WORLD BLOOD.
MY GUESS IS...
...HE'S LIKE THE ANCESTOR OF OUR ICE CLAN.
A PERSON TRANSPORTED HERE FROM ANOTHER WORLD—THE IRELLARS <OTHERWORLD> CALLED JAPANBAHAMAL <THE WORLD OF JAPAN>.

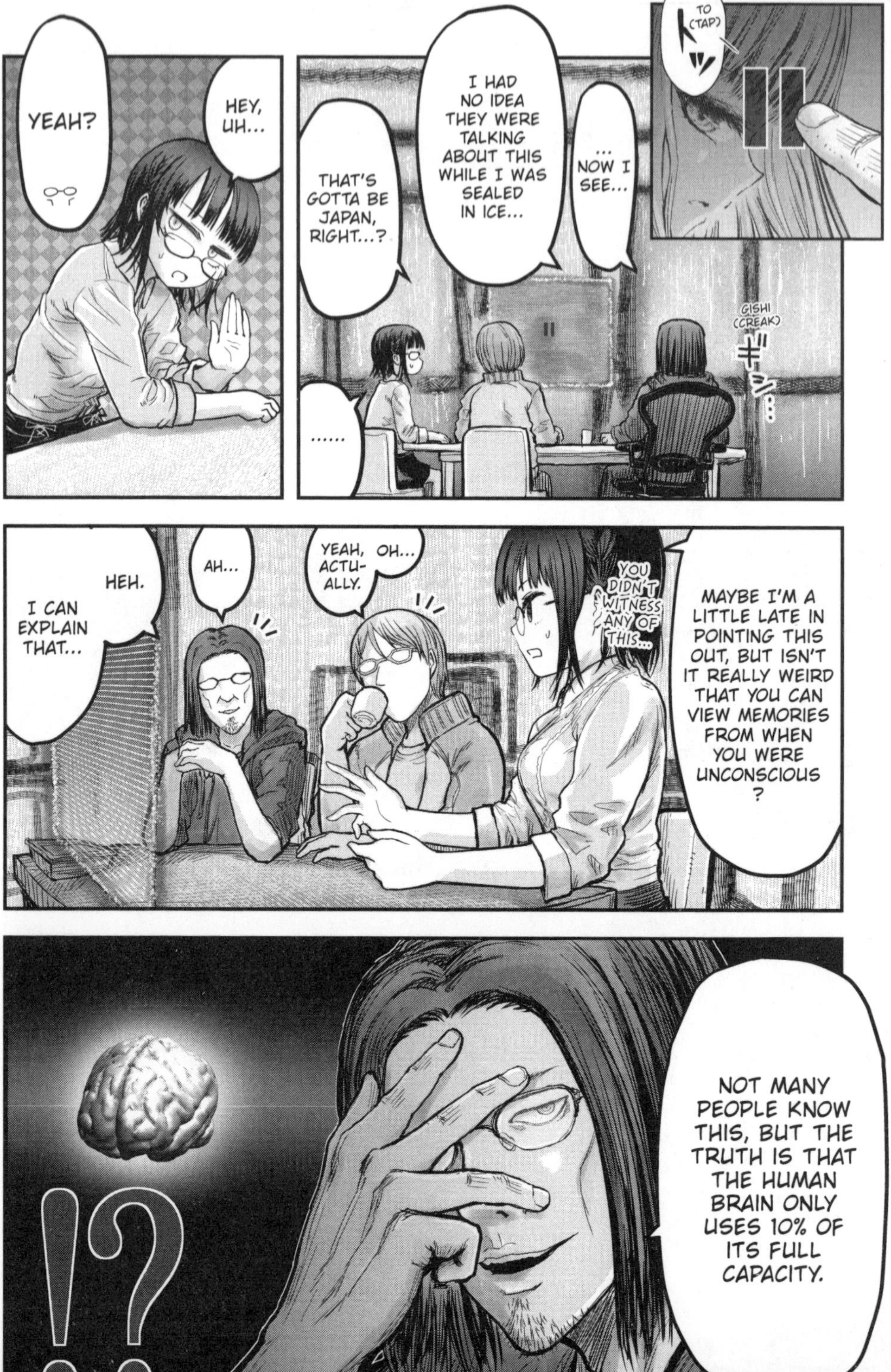
トッ
TO (TAP)
... NOW I SEE...
I HAD NO IDEA THEY WERE TALKING ABOUT THIS WHILE I WAS SEALED IN ICE...
THAT'S GOTTA BE JAPAN, RIGHT...?
ギシッ…
GISHI (CREAK)
......
HEY, UH...
YEAH?
MAYBE I'M A LITTLE LATE IN POINTING THIS OUT, BUT ISN'T IT REALLY WEIRD THAT YOU CAN VIEW MEMORIES FROM WHEN YOU WERE UNCONSCIOUS?
YOU DIDN'T WITNESS ANY OF THIS...
OH...
YEAH, ACTUALLY.
AH...
HEH.
I CAN EXPLAIN THAT...
NOT MANY PEOPLE KNOW THIS, BUT THE TRUTH IS THAT THE HUMAN BRAIN ONLY USES 10% OF ITS FULL CAPACITY.
!?

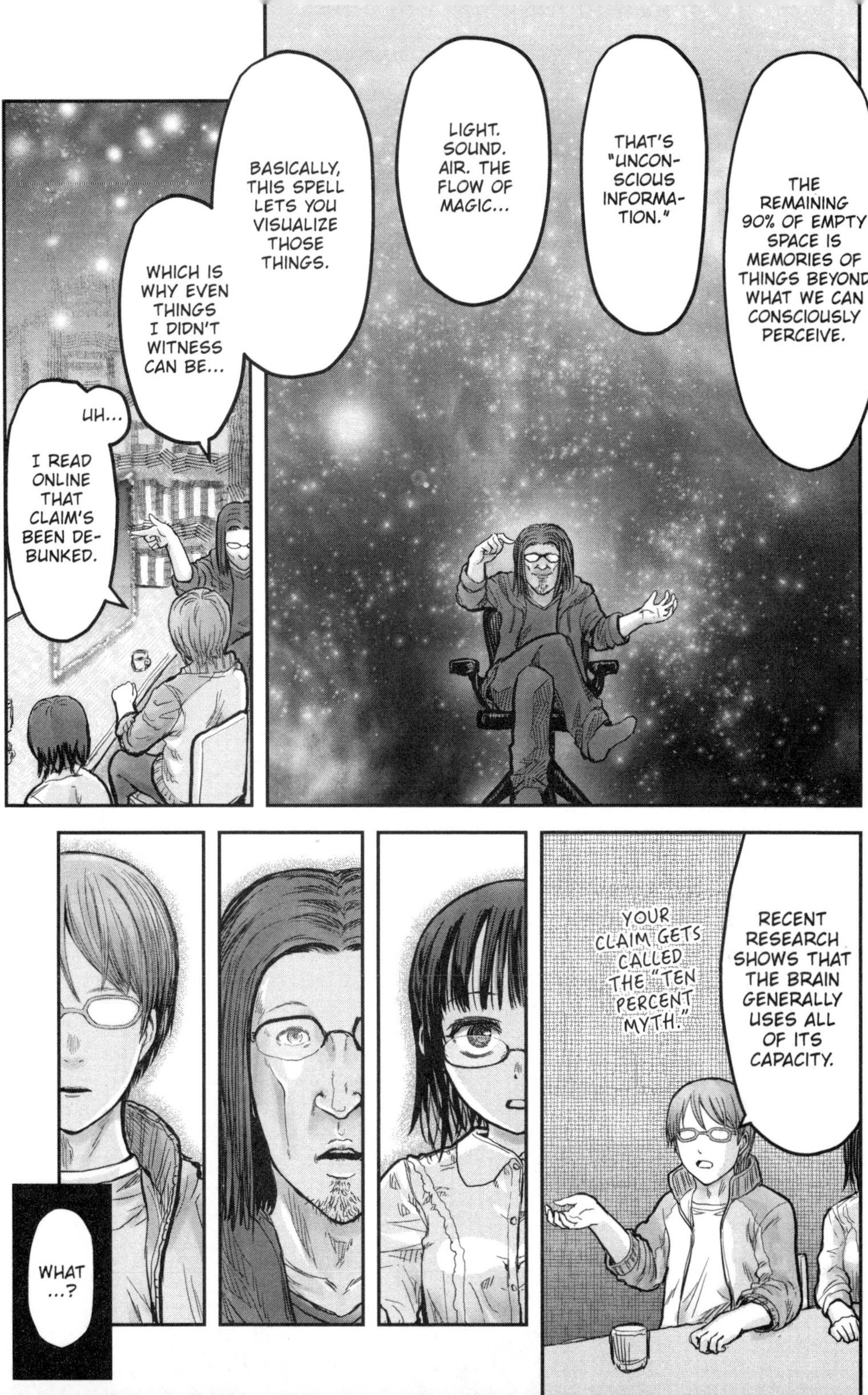
THE REMAINING 90% OF EMPTY SPACE IS MEMORIES OF THINGS BEYOND WHAT WE CAN CONSCIOUSLY PERCEIVE.
THAT'S "UNCONSCIOUS INFORMATION."
LIGHT. SOUND. AIR. THE FLOW OF MAGIC...
BASICALLY, THIS SPELL LETS YOU VISUALIZE THOSE THINGS.
WHICH IS WHY EVEN THINGS I DIDN'T WITNESS CAN BE...
UH...
I READ ONLINE THAT CLAIM'S BEEN DEBUNKED.
RECENT RESEARCH SHOWS THAT THE BRAIN GENERALLY USES ALL OF ITS CAPACITY.
YOUR CLAIM GETS CALLED THE "TEN PERCENT MYTH."
WHAT ...?

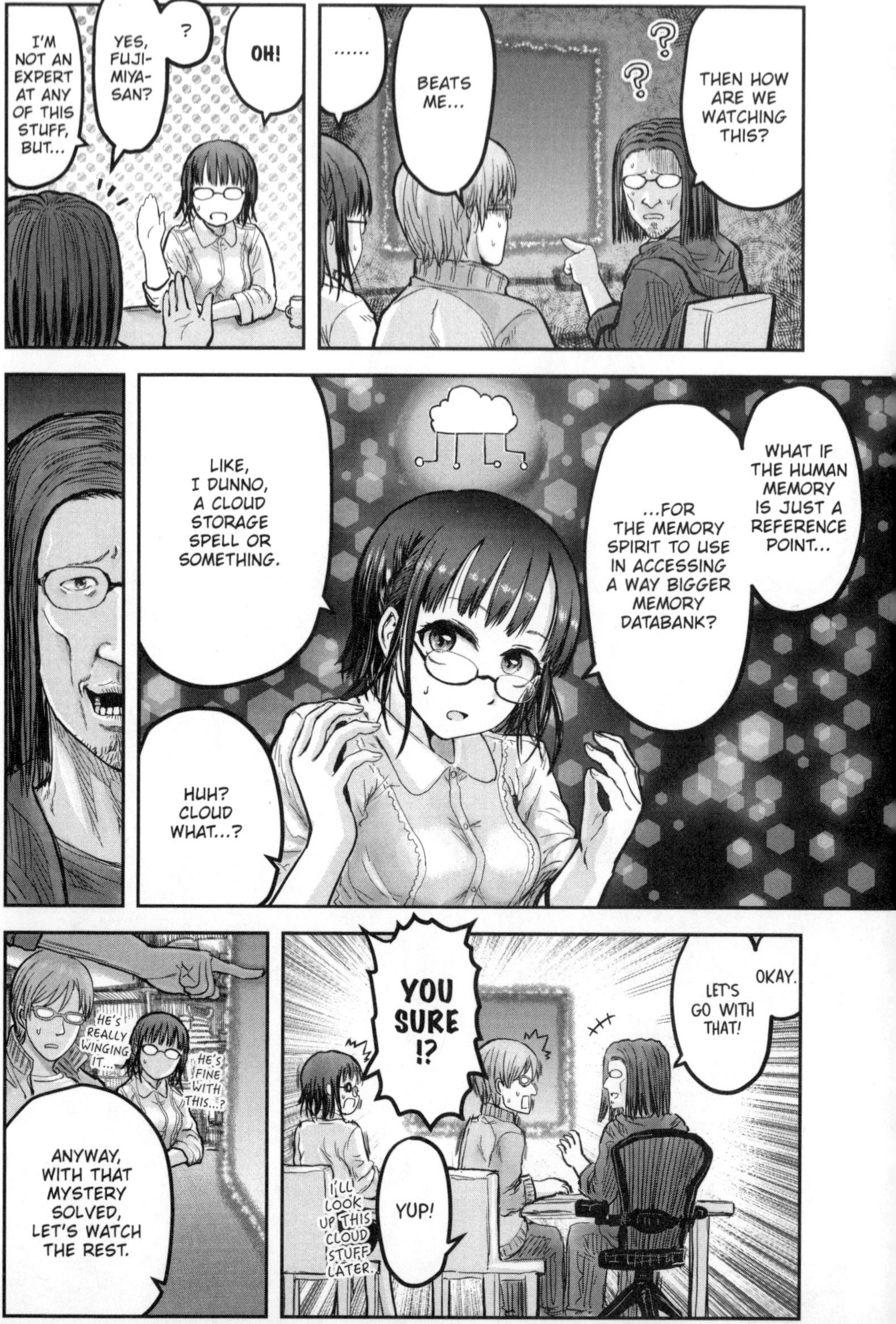
THEN HOW ARE WE WATCHING THIS?
BEATS ME...
......
OH!
?
YES, FUJIMIYA-SAN?
I'M NOT AN EXPERT AT ANY OF THIS STUFF, BUT...
WHAT IF THE HUMAN MEMORY IS JUST A REFERENCE POINT...
...FOR THE MEMORY SPIRIT TO USE IN ACCESSING A WAY BIGGER MEMORY DATABANK?
LIKE, I DUNNO, A CLOUD STORAGE SPELL OR SOMETHING.
HUH? CLOUD WHAT...?
OKAY.
LET'S GO WITH THAT!
YOU SURE!?
YUP!
I'LL LOOK UP THIS CLOUD STUFF LATER.
HE'S REALLY WINGING IT...
HE'S FINE WITH THIS...?
ANYWAY, WITH THAT MYSTERY SOLVED, LET'S WATCH THE REST.

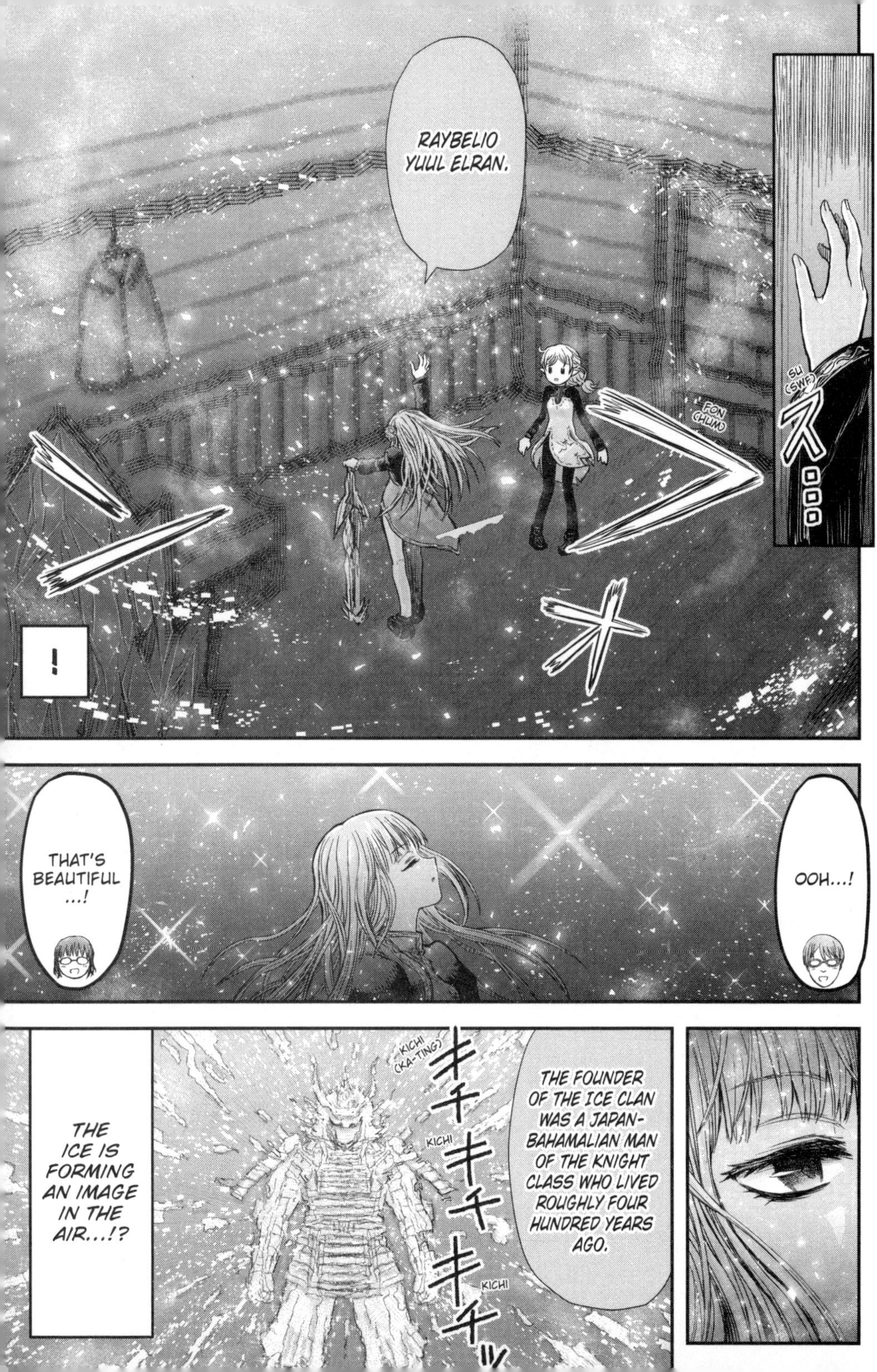
SU (SWF)
RAYBELIO YUUL ELRAN.
FON (HUM)
!
OOH...!
THAT'S BEAUTIFUL ...!
THE FOUNDER OF THE ICE CLAN WAS A JAPAN-BAHAMALIAN MAN OF THE KNIGHT CLASS WHO LIVED ROUGHLY FOUR HUNDRED YEARS AGO.
KICHI (KA-TING)
KICHI
KICHI
THE ICE IS FORMING AN IMAGE IN THE AIR...!?

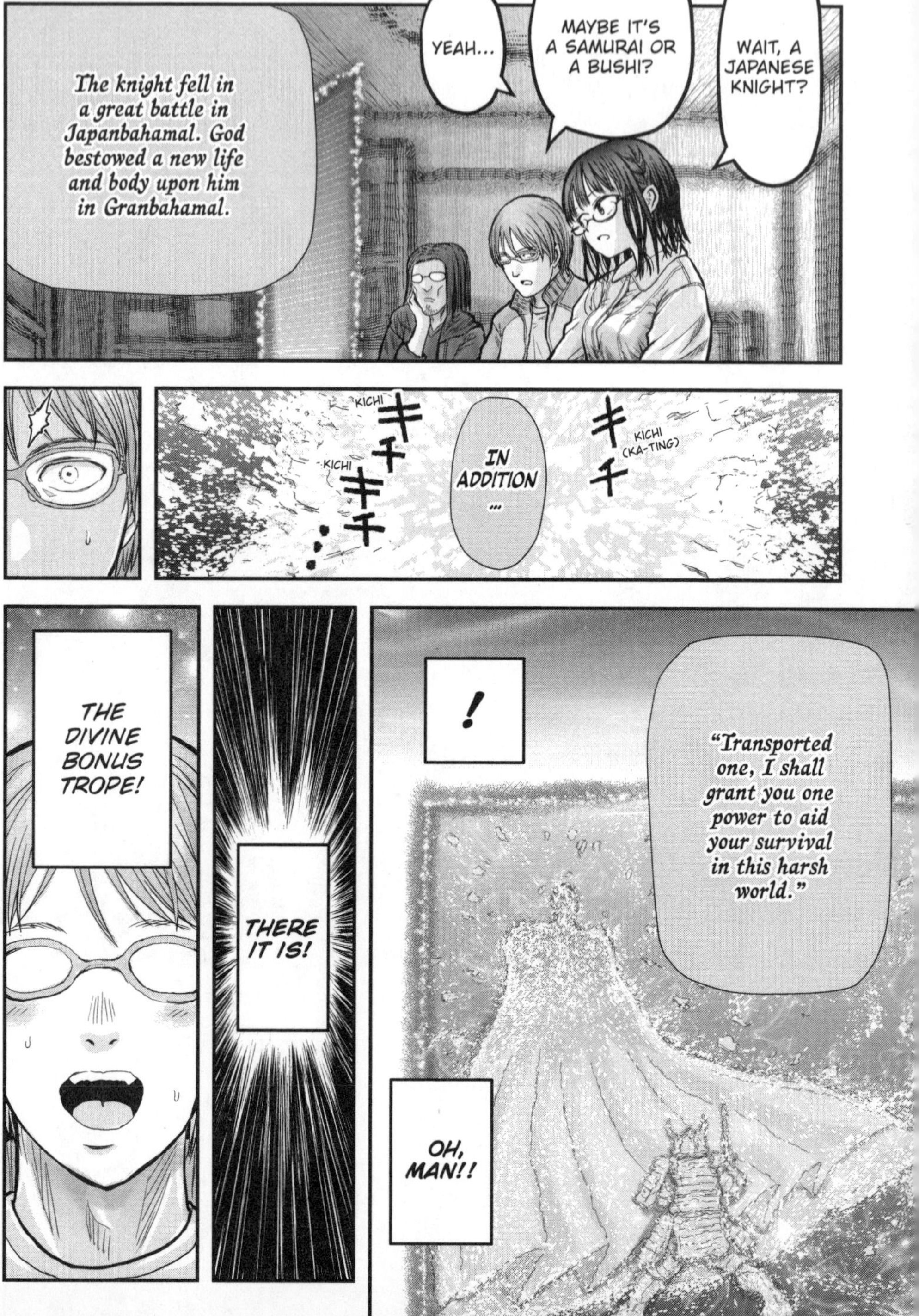

WAIT, A JAPANESE KNIGHT?
MAYBE IT'S A SAMURAI OR A BUSHI?
YEAH...
The knight fell in a great battle in Japanbahamal. God bestowed a new life and body upon him in Granbahamal.
KICHI (KA-TING)
IN ADDITION ...
KICHI
KICHI
"Transported one, I shall grant you one power to aid your survival in this harsh world."
!
OH, MAN!!
THERE IT IS!
THE DIVINE BONUS TROPE!

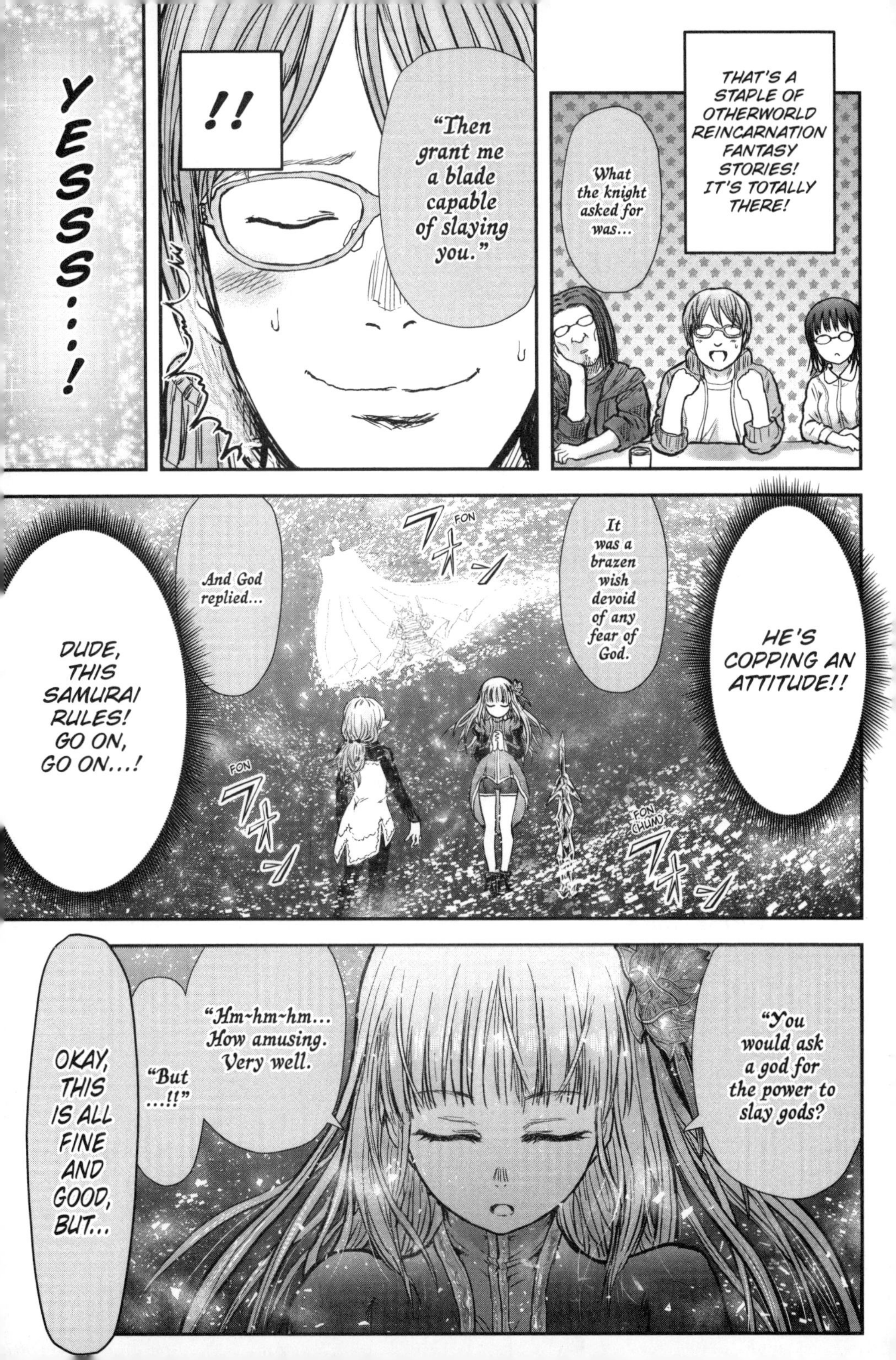
THAT'S A STAPLE OF OTHERWORLD REINCARNATION FANTASY STORIES! IT'S TOTALLY THERE!
What the knight asked for was...
"Then grant me a blade capable of slaying you."
!!
YESSS...!
HE'S COPPING AN ATTITUDE!!
It was a brazen wish devoid of any fear of God.
FON
FON (HUM)
And God replied...
FON
DUDE, THIS SAMURAI RULES! GO ON, GO ON...!
"You would ask a god for the power to slay gods?
"Hm~hm~hm... How amusing. Very well.
"But ...!!"
OKAY, THIS IS ALL FINE AND GOOD, BUT...

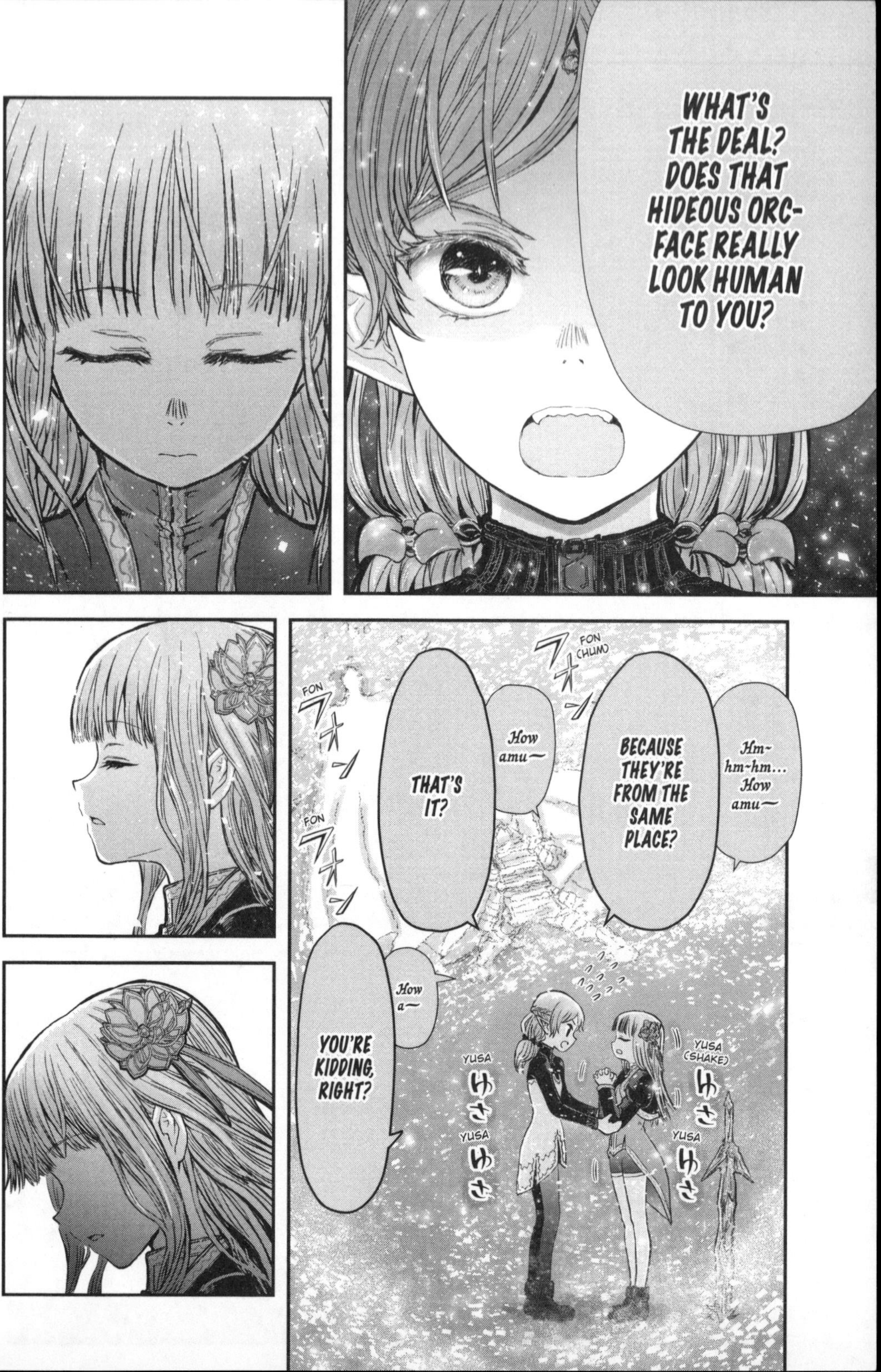
WHAT'S THE DEAL? DOES THAT HIDEOUS ORC-FACE REALLY LOOK HUMAN TO YOU?
Hm-hm-hm... How amu~
BECAUSE THEY'RE FROM THE SAME PLACE?
FON (HUM) フォン
How amu~
THAT'S IT?
FON フォン
FON フォン
How a~
YOU'RE KIDDING, RIGHT?
YUSA (SHAKE) ゆさ
YUSA ゆさ
YUSA ゆさ
YUSA ゆさ

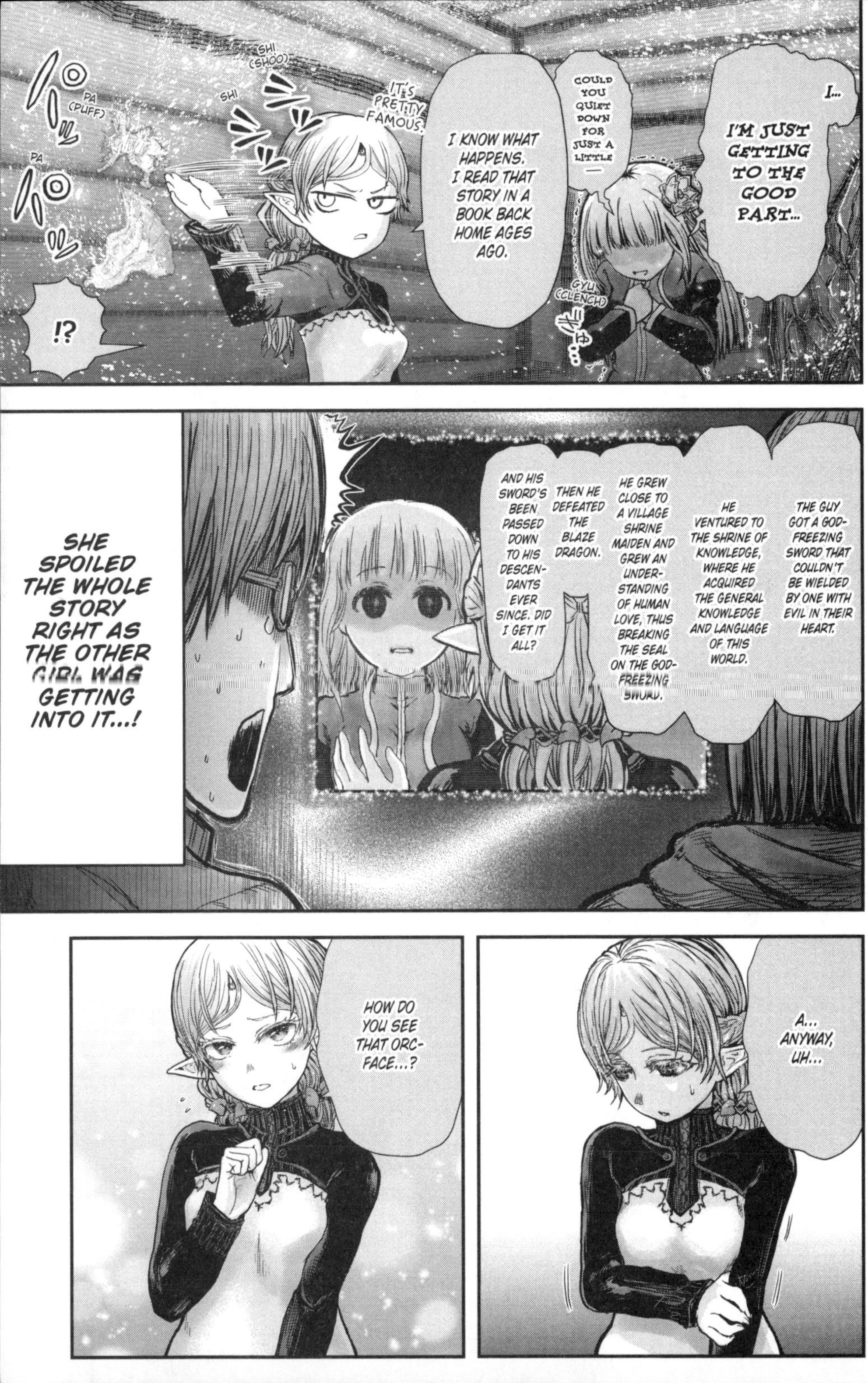
I...
I'M JUST GETTING TO THE GOOD PART...
COULD YOU QUIET DOWN FOR JUST A LITTLE—
GYU (CLENCH)
I KNOW WHAT HAPPENS. I READ THAT STORY IN A BOOK BACK HOME AGES AGO.
IT'S PRETTY FAMOUS.
SHI SHI (SHOO)
PA PA (PUFF)
!?
THE GUY GOT A GOD-FREEZING SWORD THAT COULDN'T BE WIELDED BY ONE WITH EVIL IN THEIR HEART.
HE VENTURED TO THE SHRINE OF KNOWLEDGE, WHERE HE ACQUIRED THE GENERAL KNOWLEDGE AND LANGUAGE OF THIS WORLD.
HE GREW CLOSE TO A VILLAGE SHRINE MAIDEN AND GREW AN UNDER-STANDING OF HUMAN LOVE, THUS BREAKING THE SEAL ON THE GOD-FREEZING SWORD.
THEN HE DEFEATED THE BLAZE DRAGON.
AND HIS SWORD'S BEEN PASSED DOWN TO HIS DESCEN-DANTS EVER SINCE. DID I GET IT ALL?
SHE SPOILED THE WHOLE STORY RIGHT AS THE OTHER GIRL WAS GETTING INTO IT...!
A... ANYWAY, UH...
HOW DO YOU SEE THAT ORC-FACE...?

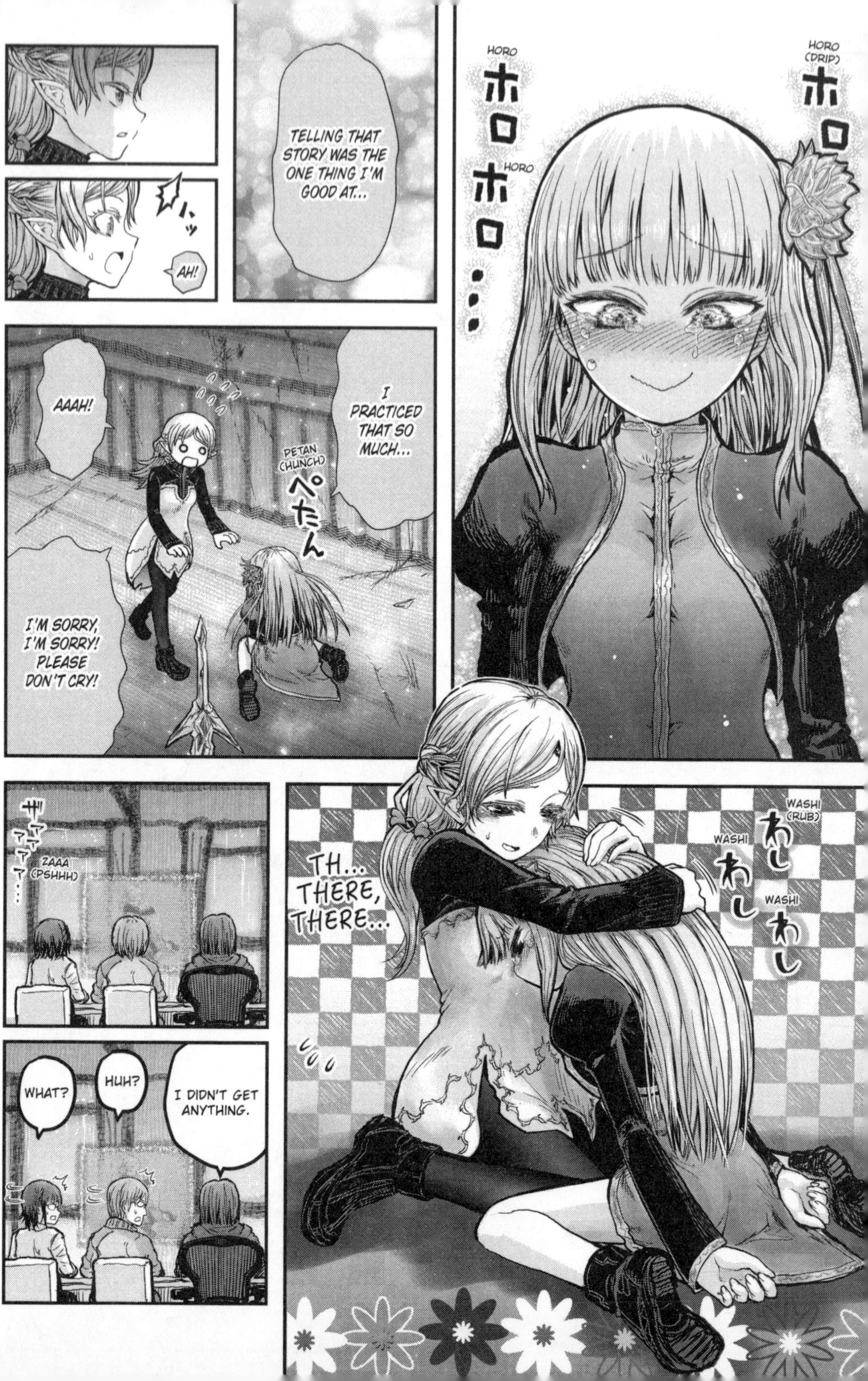
HORO (DRIP)
ホロ
HORO
ホロ
HORO
ホロ...
TELLING THAT STORY WAS THE ONE THING I'M GOOD AT...
ハッ
AH!
I PRACTICED THAT SO MUCH...
PETAN (HUNCH)
ぺたん
AAAH!
I'M SORRY, I'M SORRY! PLEASE DON'T CRY!
WASHI (RUB)
わし
WASHI
わし
WASHI
わし
TH... THERE, THERE...
ザアアアア...
ZAAA (PSHHH)
I DIDN'T GET ANYTHING.
HUH?
WHAT?

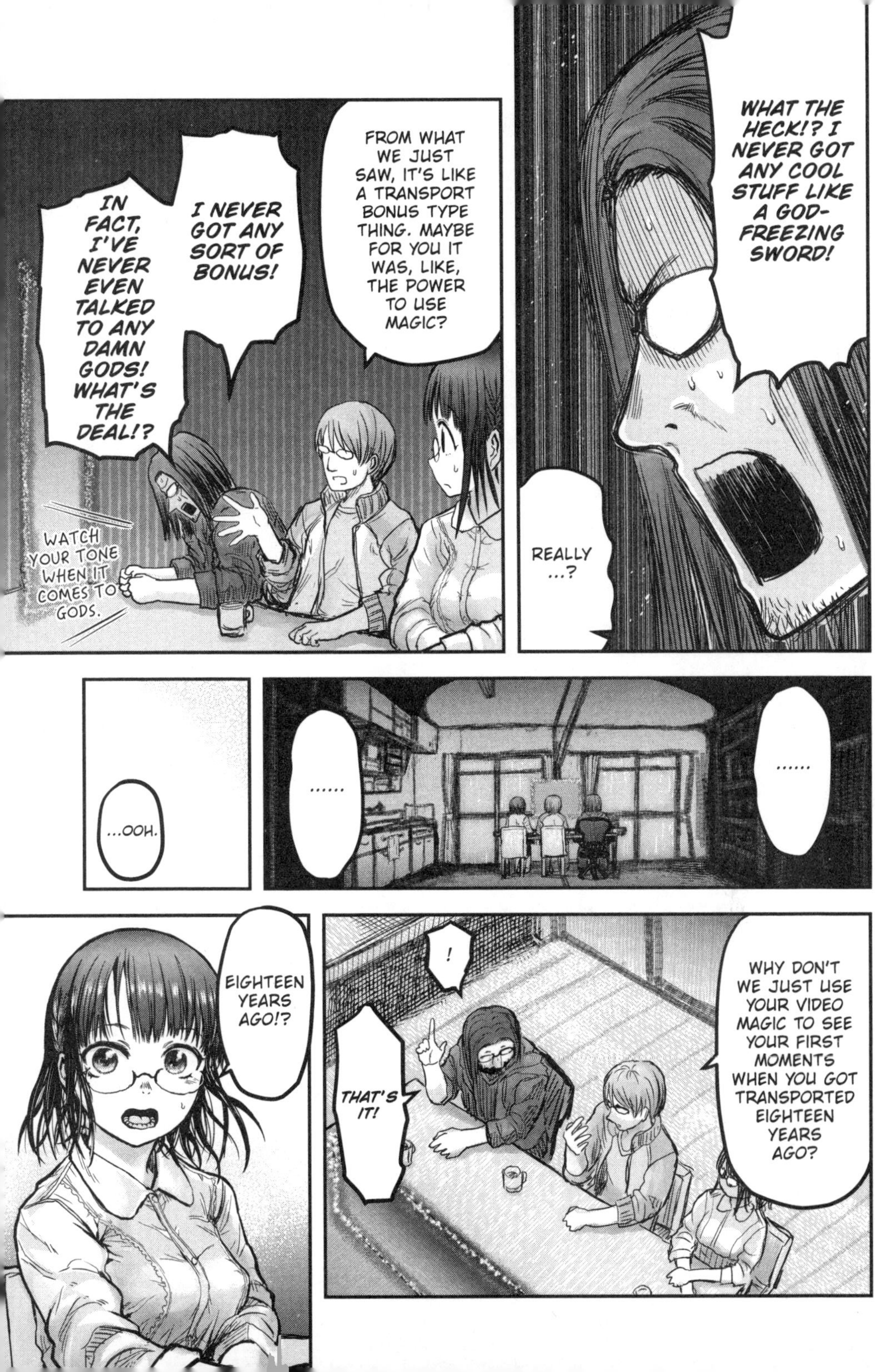

WHAT THE HECK!? I NEVER GOT ANY COOL STUFF LIKE A GOD-FREEZING SWORD!
REALLY ...?
FROM WHAT WE JUST SAW, IT'S LIKE A TRANSPORT BONUS TYPE THING. MAYBE FOR YOU IT WAS, LIKE, THE POWER TO USE MAGIC?
I NEVER GOT ANY SORT OF BONUS!
IN FACT, I'VE NEVER EVEN TALKED TO ANY DAMN GODS! WHAT'S THE DEAL!?
WATCH YOUR TONE WHEN IT COMES TO GODS.
......
......
...OOH.
WHY DON'T WE JUST USE YOUR VIDEO MAGIC TO SEE YOUR FIRST MOMENTS WHEN YOU GOT TRANSPORTED EIGHTEEN YEARS AGO?
!
THAT'S IT!
EIGHTEEN YEARS AGO!?

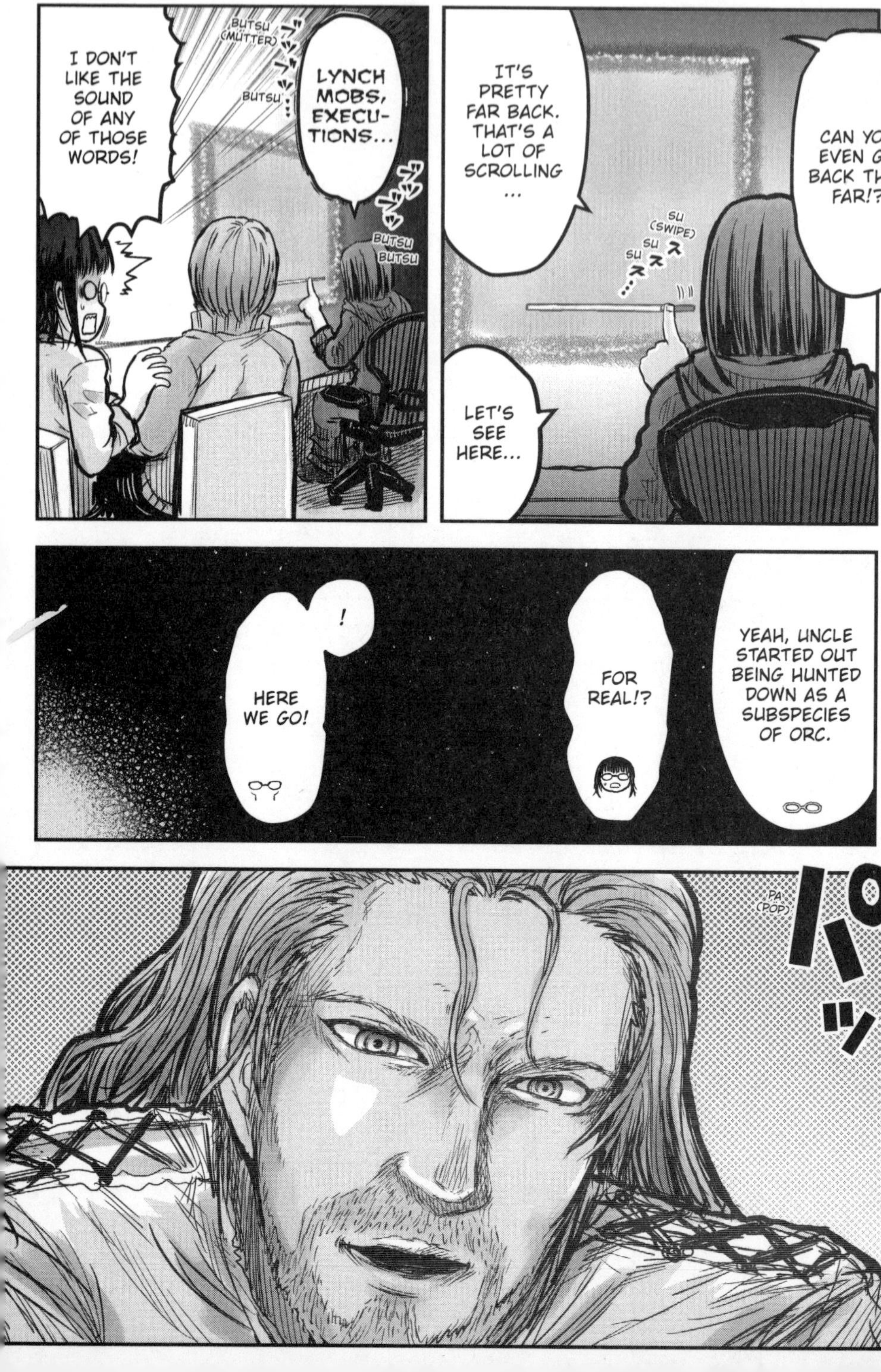
CAN YOU EVEN GO BACK THAT FAR!?
IT'S PRETTY FAR BACK. THAT'S A LOT OF SCROLLING ...
SU (SWIPE) SU SU...
LET'S SEE HERE...
LYNCH MOBS, EXECUTIONS...
BUTSU (MUTTER) BUTSU
BUTSU BUTSU
I DON'T LIKE THE SOUND OF ANY OF THOSE WORDS!
YEAH, UNCLE STARTED OUT BEING HUNTED DOWN AS A SUBSPECIES OF ORC.
FOR REAL!?
!
HERE WE GO!
PA (POP)

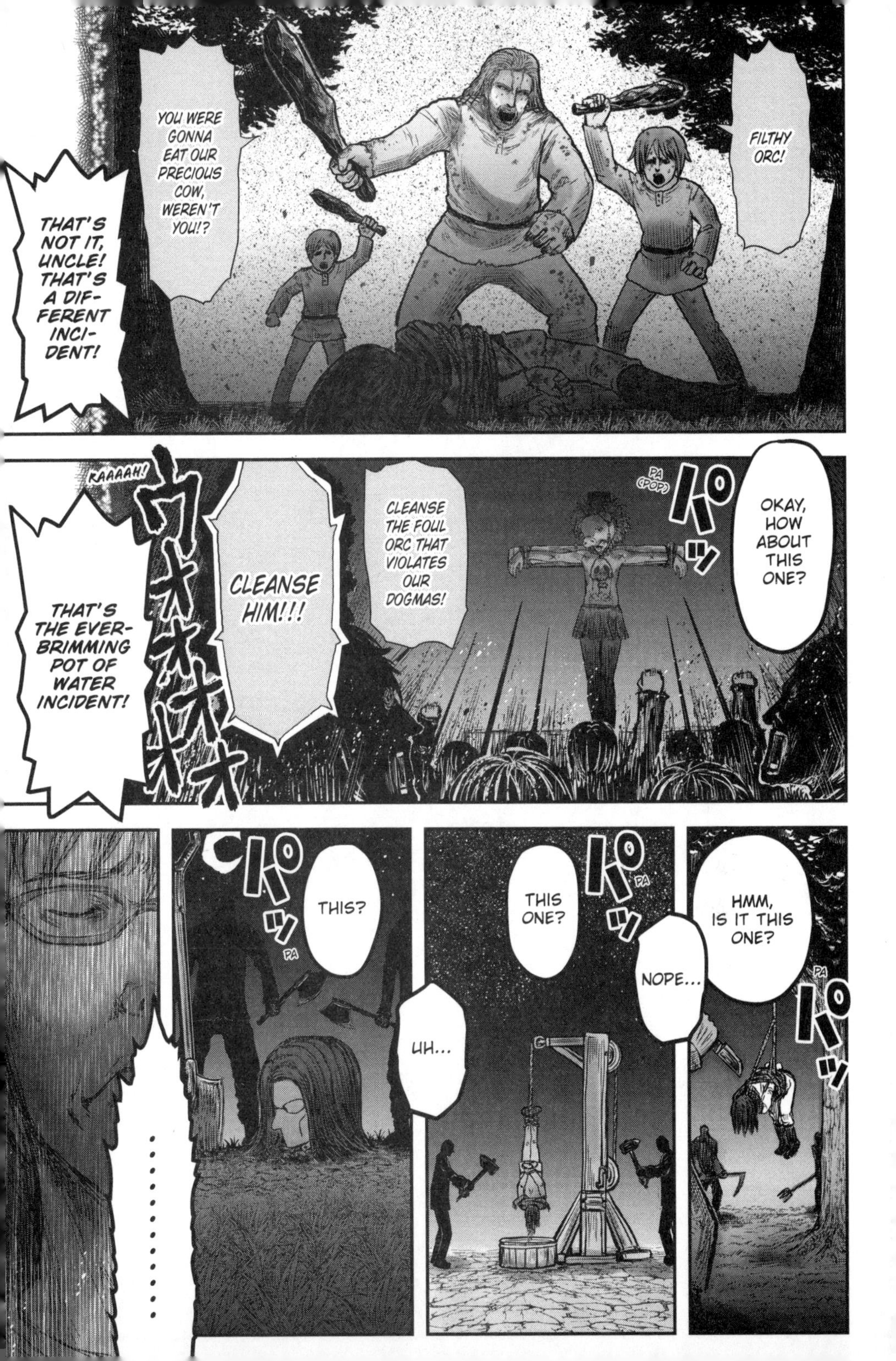

FILTHY ORC!
YOU WERE GONNA EAT OUR PRECIOUS COW, WEREN'T YOU!?
THAT'S NOT IT, UNCLE! THAT'S A DIF-FERENT INCI-DENT!
OKAY, HOW ABOUT THIS ONE?
PA (POP)
パッ
CLEANSE THE FOUL ORC THAT VIOLATES OUR DOGMAS!
CLEANSE HIM!!!
KRAAAAH!
ウオオオオオ
THAT'S THE EVER-BRIMMING POT OF WATER INCIDENT!
HMM, IS IT THIS ONE?
PA
パッ
NOPE...
THIS ONE?
PA
パッ
UH...
THIS?
PA
パッ
......

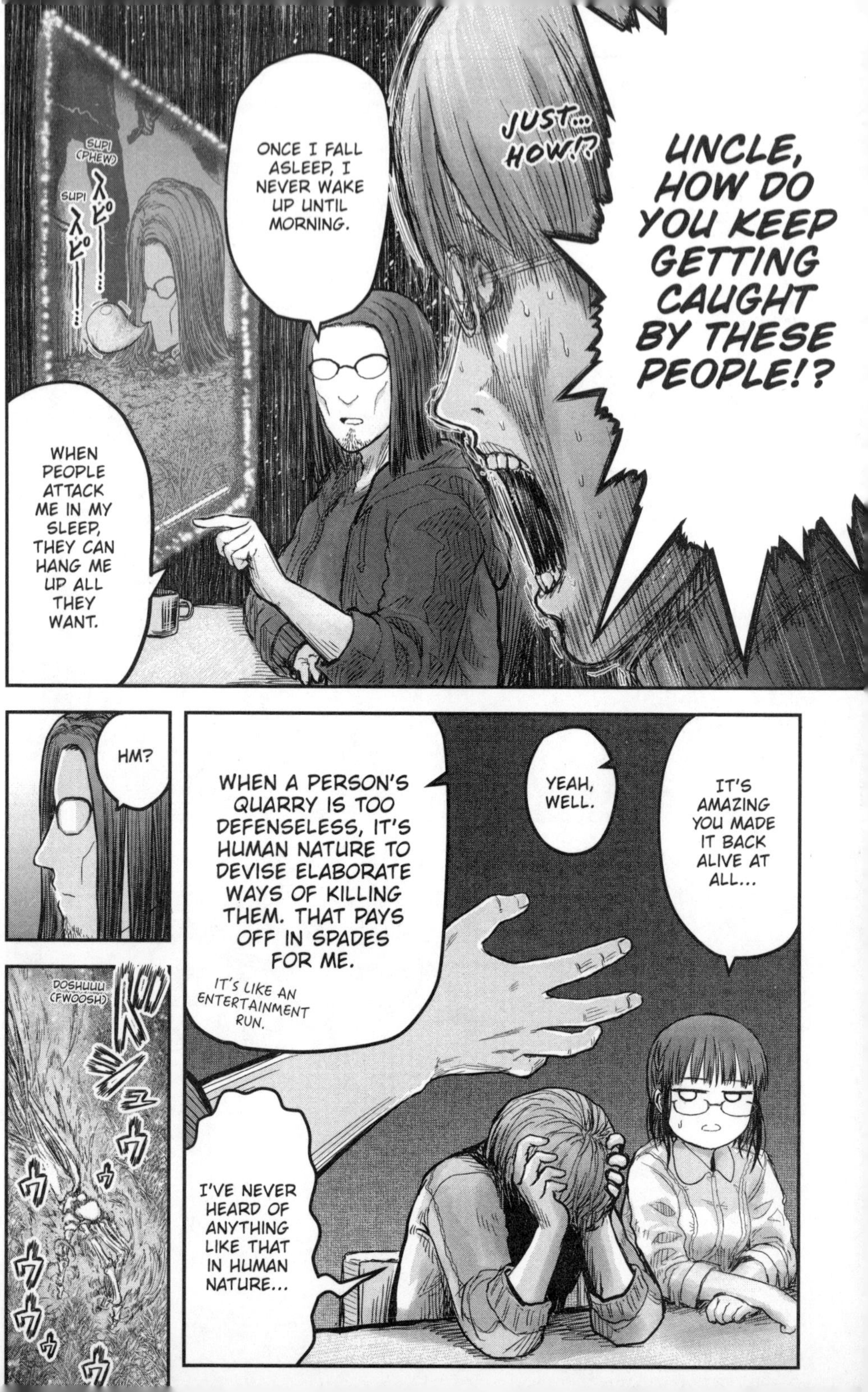
UNCLE, HOW DO YOU KEEP GETTING CAUGHT BY THESE PEOPLE!?
JUST... HOW!?
ONCE I FALL ASLEEP, I NEVER WAKE UP UNTIL MORNING.
SUPI (PHEW)
SUPI
WHEN PEOPLE ATTACK ME IN MY SLEEP, THEY CAN HANG ME UP ALL THEY WANT.
IT'S AMAZING YOU MADE IT BACK ALIVE AT ALL...
YEAH, WELL.
WHEN A PERSON'S QUARRY IS TOO DEFENSELESS, IT'S HUMAN NATURE TO DEVISE ELABORATE WAYS OF KILLING THEM. THAT PAYS OFF IN SPADES FOR ME.
IT'S LIKE AN ENTERTAINMENT RUN.
I'VE NEVER HEARD OF ANYTHING LIKE THAT IN HUMAN NATURE...
HM?
DOSHUUU (FWOOSH)

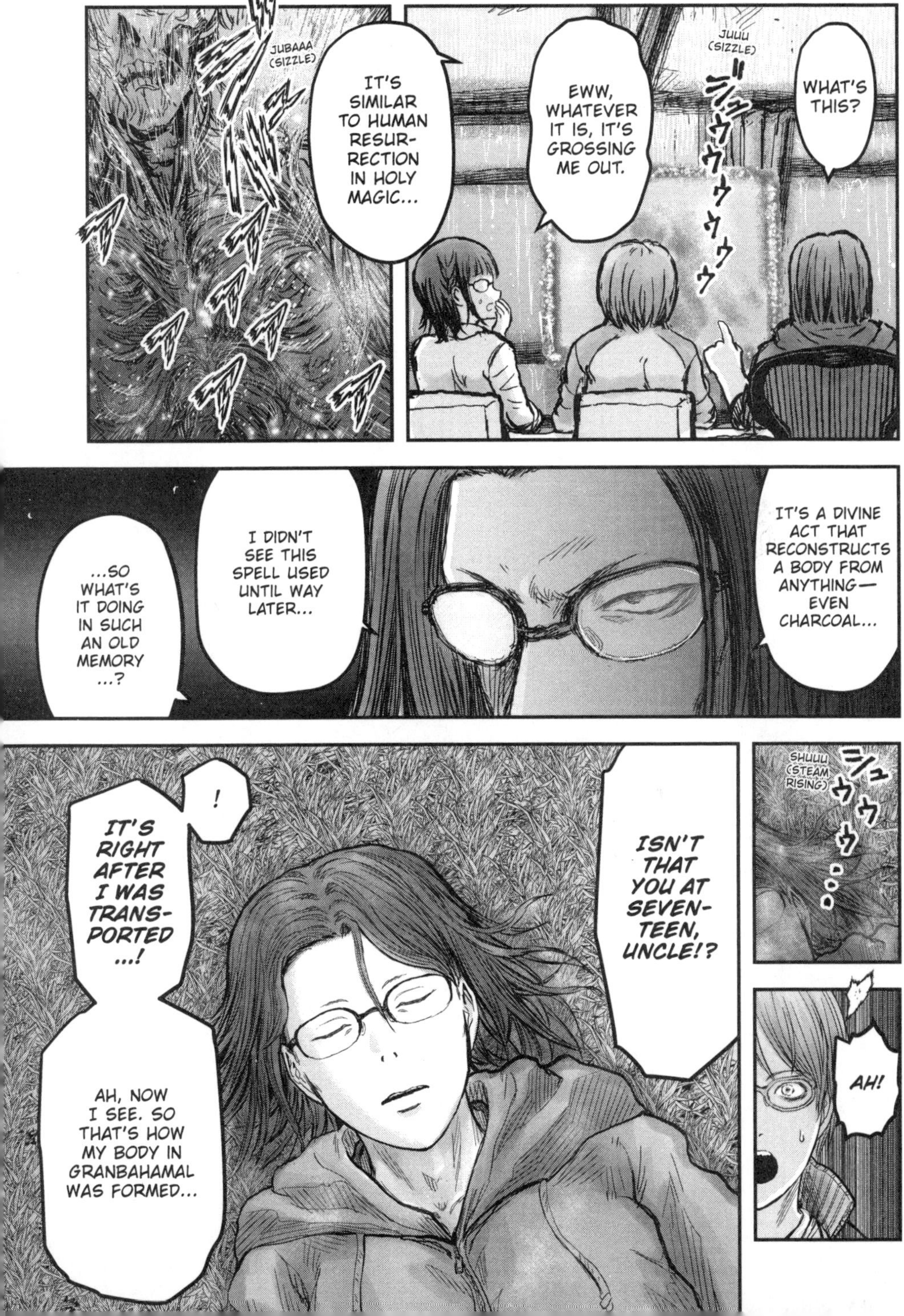
WHAT'S THIS?
JUUU (SIZZLE)
EWW, WHATEVER IT IS, IT'S GROSSING ME OUT.
IT'S SIMILAR TO HUMAN RESURRECTION IN HOLY MAGIC...
JUBAAA (SIZZLE)
IT'S A DIVINE ACT THAT RECONSTRUCTS A BODY FROM ANYTHING—EVEN CHARCOAL...
I DIDN'T SEE THIS SPELL USED UNTIL WAY LATER...
...SO WHAT'S IT DOING IN SUCH AN OLD MEMORY...?
SHUUU (STEAM RISING)
AH!
ISN'T THAT YOU AT SEVENTEEN, UNCLE!?
!
IT'S RIGHT AFTER I WAS TRANSPORTED...!
AH, NOW I SEE. SO THAT'S HOW MY BODY IN GRANBAHAMAL WAS FORMED...

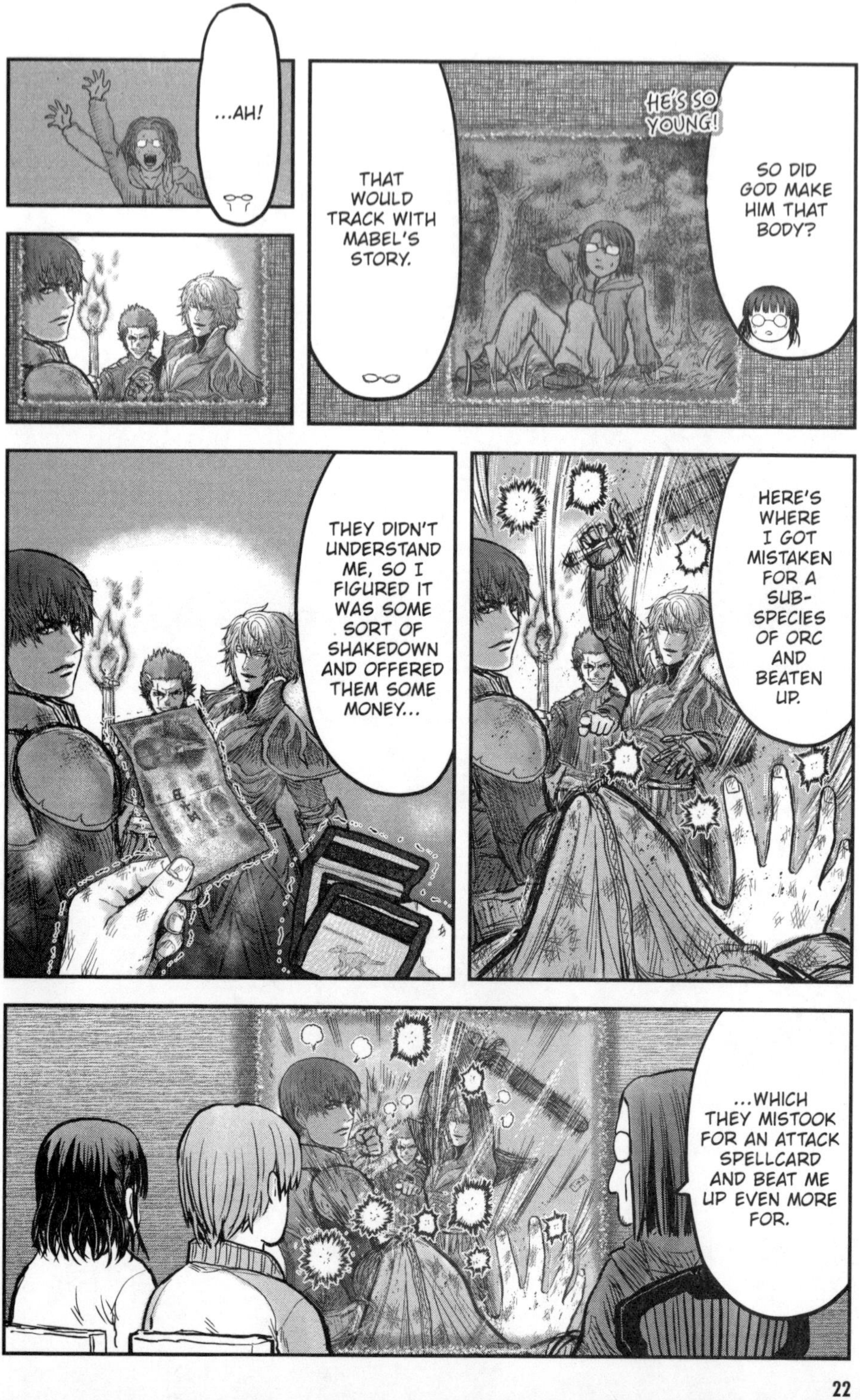
HE'S SO YOUNG!
SO DID GOD MAKE HIM THAT BODY?
THAT WOULD TRACK WITH MABEL'S STORY.
...AH!
HERE'S WHERE I GOT MISTAKEN FOR A SUB-SPECIES OF ORC AND BEATEN UP.
THEY DIDN'T UNDERSTAND ME, SO I FIGURED IT WAS SOME SORT OF SHAKEDOWN AND OFFERED THEM SOME MONEY...
...WHICH THEY MISTOOK FOR AN ATTACK SPELLCARD AND BEAT ME UP EVEN MORE FOR.

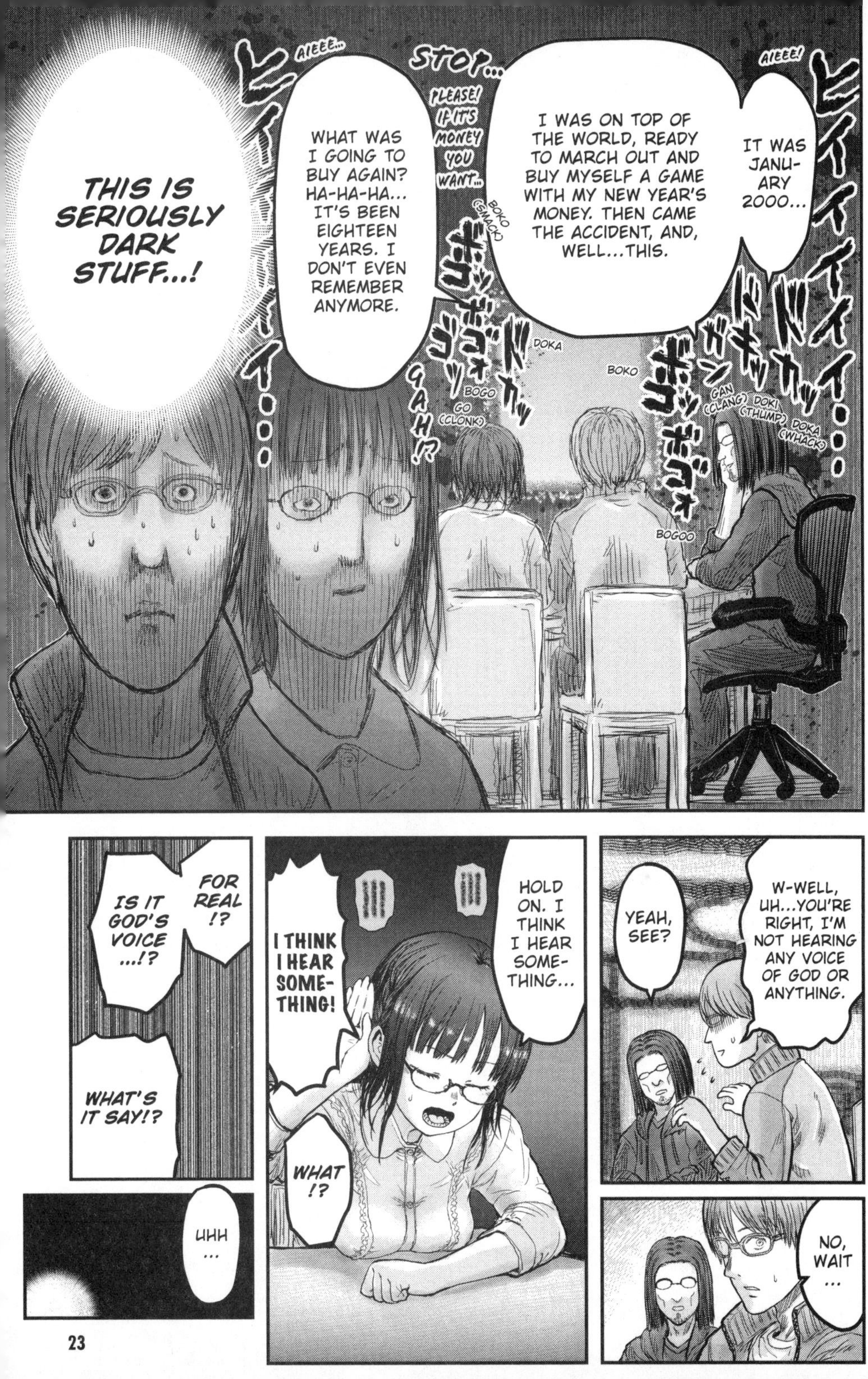

AIEEE!
IT WAS JANUARY 2000...
GAN (CLANG)
DOKI (THUMP)
DOKA (WHACK)
BOGOO
BOKO
I WAS ON TOP OF THE WORLD, READY TO MARCH OUT AND BUY MYSELF A GAME WITH MY NEW YEAR'S MONEY. THEN CAME THE ACCIDENT, AND, WELL...THIS.
STOP...
PLEASE! IF IT'S MONEY YOU WANT...
BOKO (SMACK)
DOKA
BOGO
GO (CLONK)
GAH!?
WHAT WAS I GOING TO BUY AGAIN? HA-HA-HA... IT'S BEEN EIGHTEEN YEARS. I DON'T EVEN REMEMBER ANYMORE.
AIEEE...
THIS IS SERIOUSLY DARK STUFF...!
W-WELL, UH...YOU'RE RIGHT, I'M NOT HEARING ANY VOICE OF GOD OR ANYTHING.
YEAH, SEE?
NO, WAIT...
HOLD ON. I THINK I HEAR SOMETHING...
I THINK I HEAR SOMETHING!
WHAT!?
FOR REAL!?
IS IT GOD'S VOICE...!?
WHAT'S IT SAY!?
UHH...

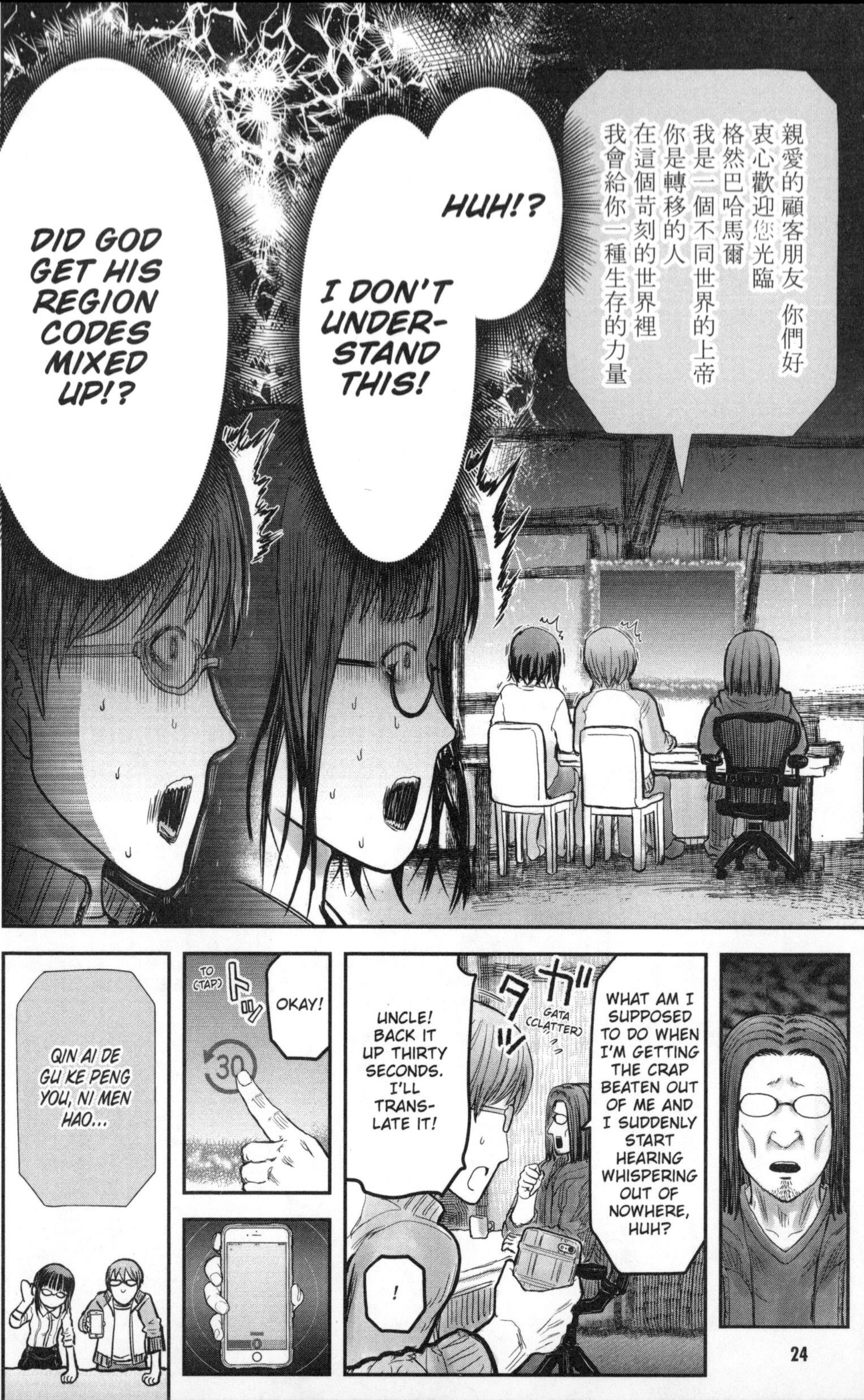
親愛的顧客朋友 你們好
衷心歡迎您光臨
格然巴哈馬爾
我是一個不同世界的上帝
你是轉移的人
在這個苛刻的世界裡
我會給你一種生存的力量
HUH!?
I DON'T UNDER-STAND THIS!
DID GOD GET HIS REGION CODES MIXED UP!?
WHAT AM I SUPPOSED TO DO WHEN I'M GETTING THE CRAP BEATEN OUT OF ME AND I SUDDENLY START HEARING WHISPERING OUT OF NOWHERE, HUH?
GATA (CLATTER)
UNCLE! BACK IT UP THIRTY SECONDS. I'LL TRANS-LATE IT!
!
OKAY!
TO (TAP)
30
QIN AI DE GU KE PENG YOU, NI MEN HAO...

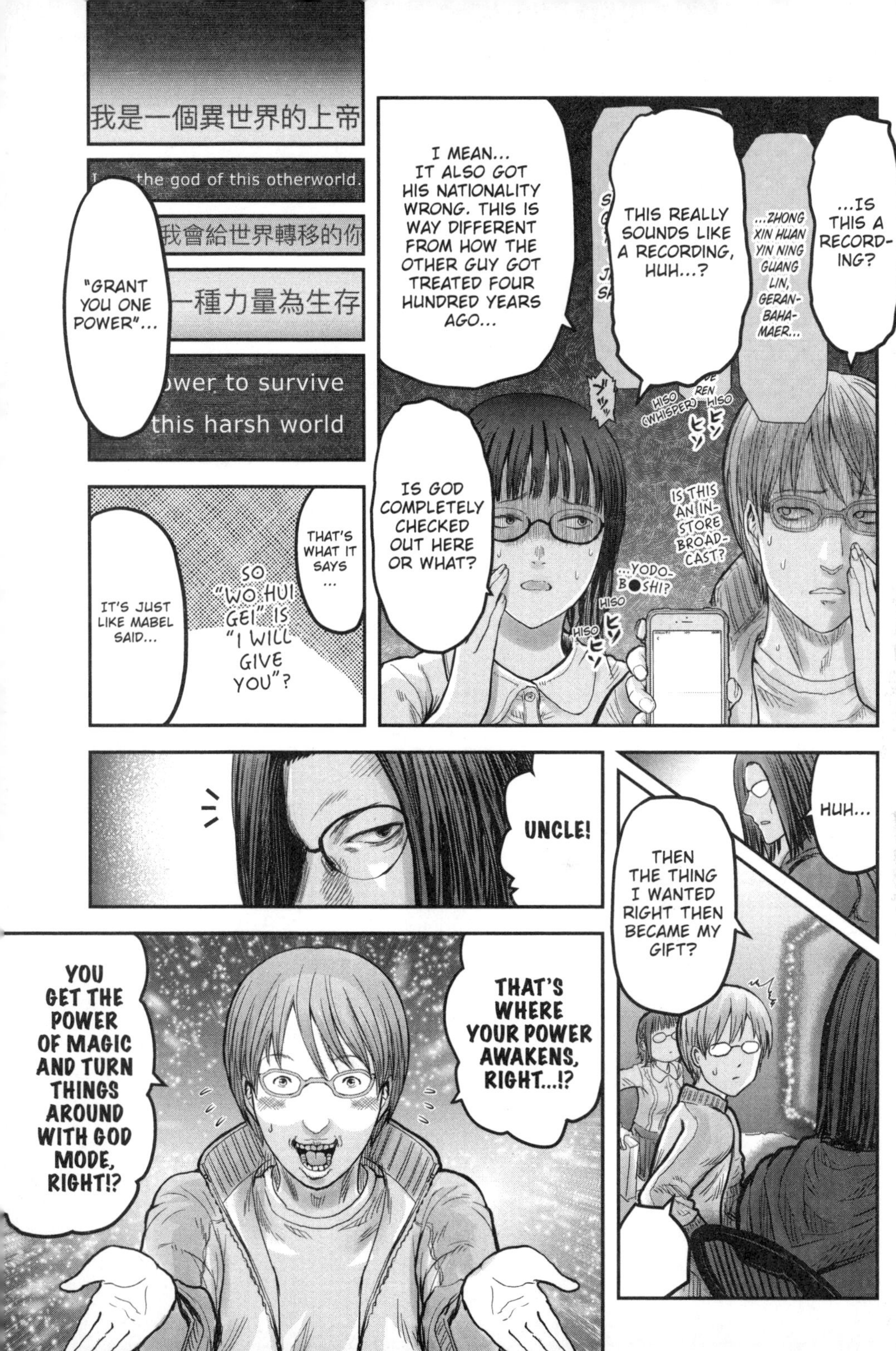
...IS THIS A RECORDING?
...ZHONG XIN HUAN YIN NING GUANG LIN, GERAN-BAHA-MAER...
THIS REALLY SOUNDS LIKE A RECORDING, HUH...?
I MEAN... IT ALSO GOT HIS NATIONALITY WRONG. THIS IS WAY DIFFERENT FROM HOW THE OTHER GUY GOT TREATED FOUR HUNDRED YEARS AGO...
HISO (WHISPER)
HISO
IS THIS AN IN-STORE BROAD-CAST?
IS GOD COMPLETELY CHECKED OUT HERE OR WHAT?
...YODO-B●SHI?
HISO
HISO
我是一個異世界的上帝
the god of this otherworld.
我會給世界轉移的你
一種力量為生存
ower to survive
this harsh world
"GRANT YOU ONE POWER"...
THAT'S WHAT IT SAYS...
SO "WO HUI GEI" IS "I WILL GIVE YOU"?
IT'S JUST LIKE MABEL SAID...
HUH...
THEN THE THING I WANTED RIGHT THEN BECAME MY GIFT?
UNCLE!
THAT'S WHERE YOUR POWER AWAKENS, RIGHT...!?
YOU GET THE POWER OF MAGIC AND TURN THINGS AROUND WITH GOD MODE, RIGHT!?

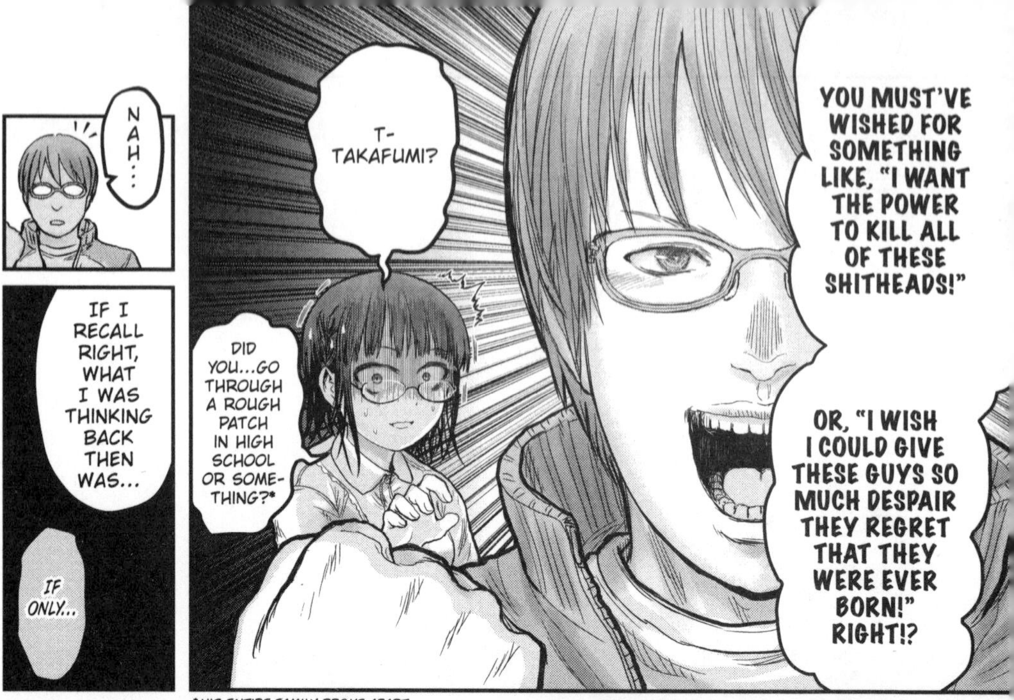
YOU MUST'VE WISHED FOR SOMETHING LIKE, "I WANT THE POWER TO KILL ALL OF THESE SHITHEADS!"
OR, "I WISH I COULD GIVE THESE GUYS SO MUCH DESPAIR THEY REGRET THAT THEY WERE EVER BORN!" RIGHT!?
T-TAKAFUMI?
DID YOU...GO THROUGH A ROUGH PATCH IN HIGH SCHOOL OR SOME-THING?*
NAH...
IF I RECALL RIGHT, WHAT I WAS THINKING BACK THEN WAS...
IF ONLY...

*HIS ENTIRE FAMILY BROKE APART

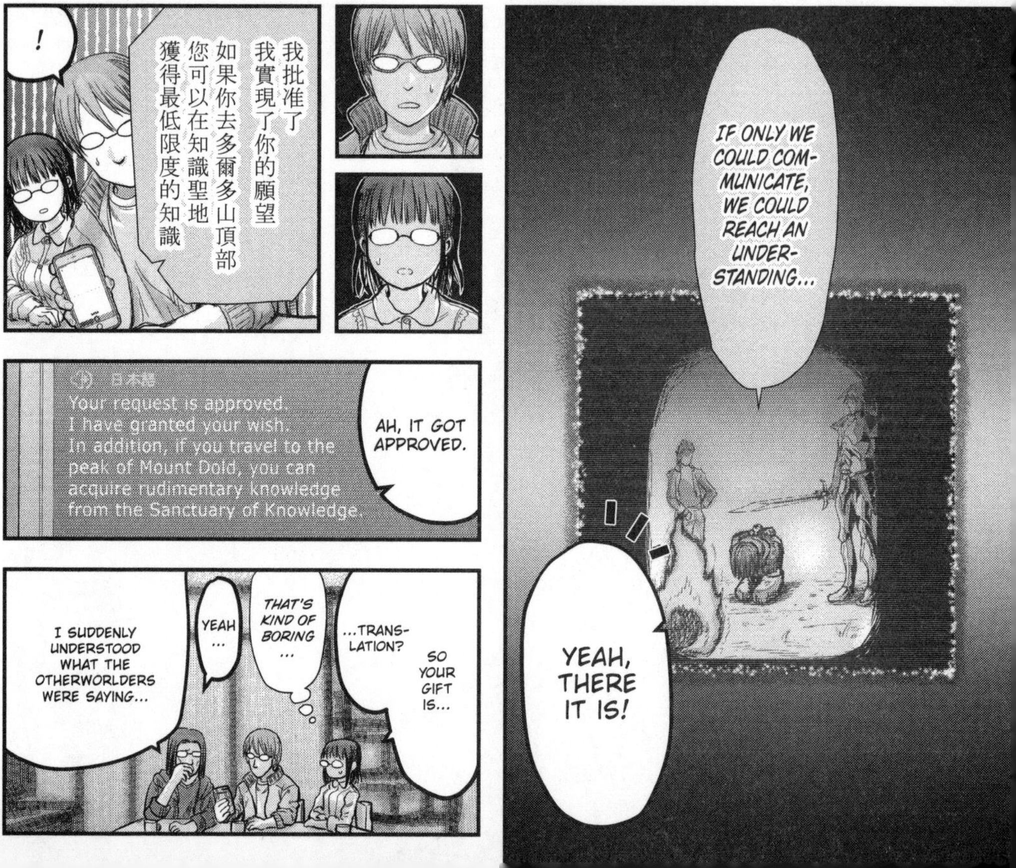
IF ONLY WE COULD COM-MUNICATE, WE COULD REACH AN UNDER-STANDING...
YEAH, THERE IT IS!
我批准了
我實現了你的願望
如果你去多爾多山頂部
您可以在知識聖地
獲得最低限度的知識
!
日本語
Your request is approved.
I have granted your wish.
In addition, if you travel to the peak of Mount Dold, you can acquire rudimentary knowledge from the Sanctuary of Knowledge.
AH, IT GOT APPROVED.
SO YOUR GIFT IS...
...TRANS-LATION?
THAT'S KIND OF BORING...
YEAH...
I SUDDENLY UNDERSTOOD WHAT THE OTHERWORLDERS WERE SAYING...

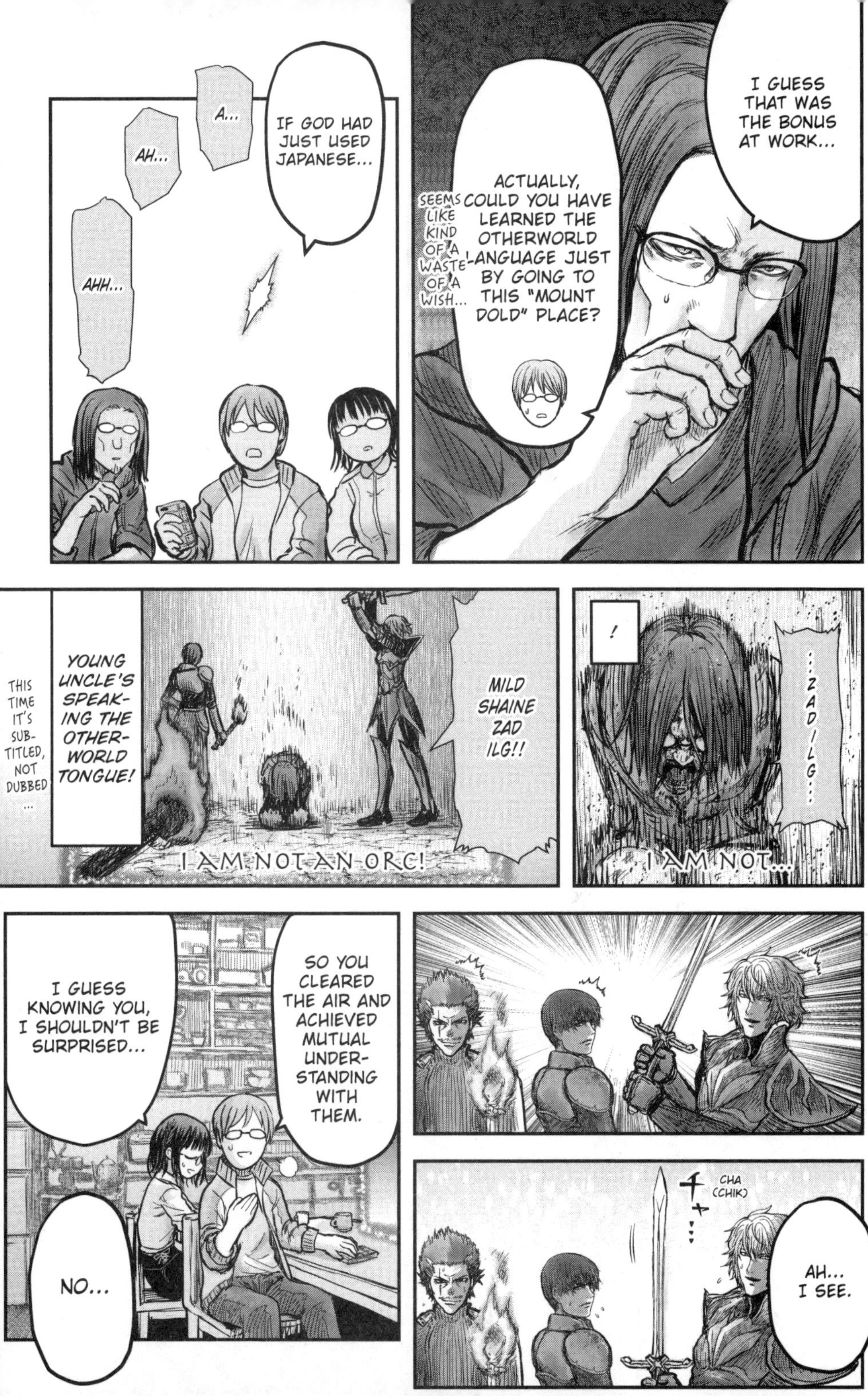
I GUESS THAT WAS THE BONUS AT WORK...
ACTUALLY, COULD YOU HAVE LEARNED THE OTHERWORLD LANGUAGE JUST BY GOING TO THIS "MOUNT DOLD" PLACE?
SEEMS LIKE KIND OF A WASTE OF A WISH...
IF GOD HAD JUST USED JAPANESE...
A...
AH...
AHH...
!
...ZAD ILG...
I AM NOT...
MILD SHAINE ZAD ILG!!
YOUNG UNCLE'S SPEAK-ING THE OTHER-WORLD TONGUE!
THIS TIME IT'S SUB-TITLED, NOT DUBBED...
I AM NOT AN ORC!
チャ
CHA (CHIK)
AH... I SEE.
SO YOU CLEARED THE AIR AND ACHIEVED MUTUAL UNDER-STANDING WITH THEM.
I GUESS KNOWING YOU, I SHOULDN'T BE SURPRISED...
NO...

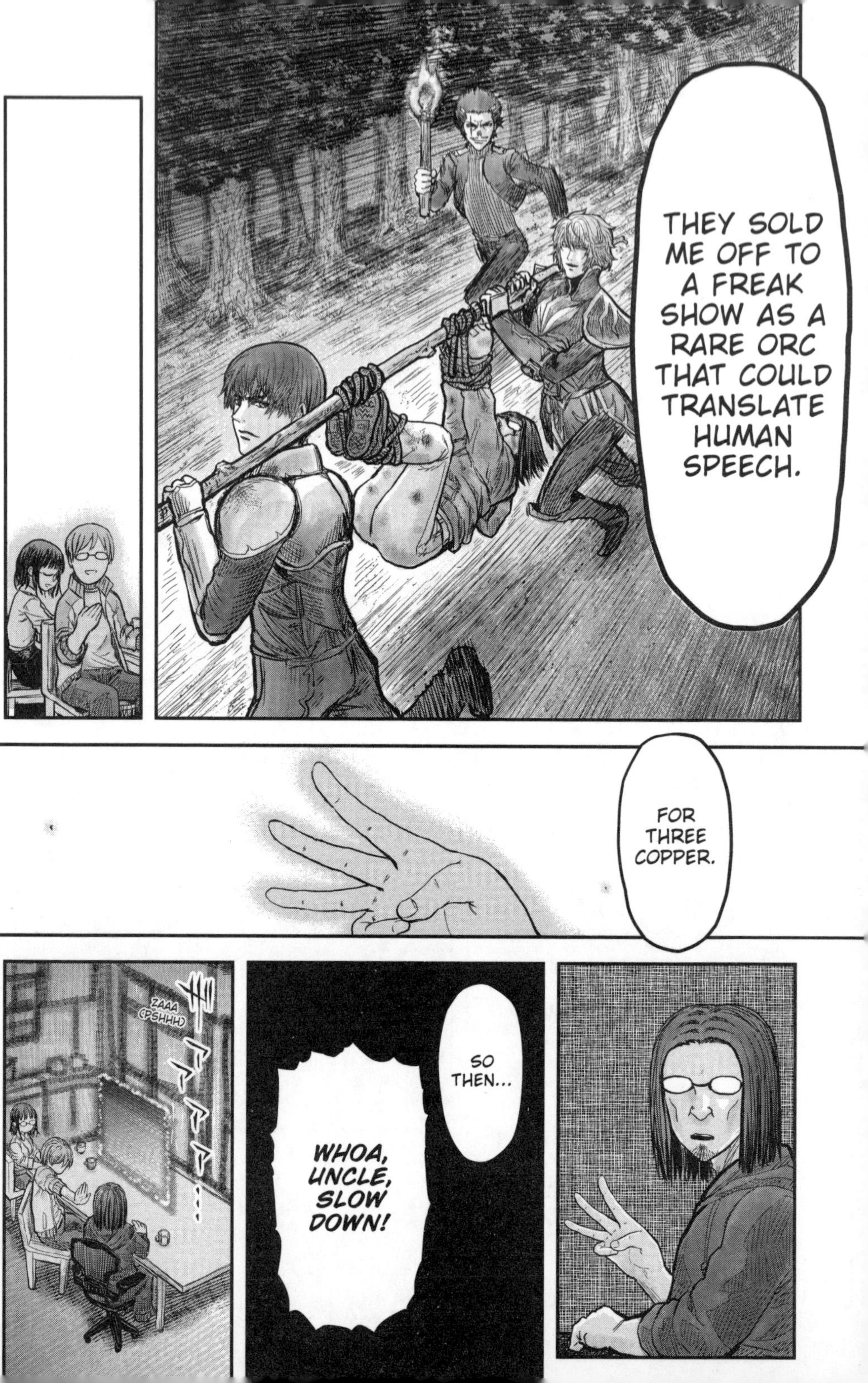
THEY SOLD ME OFF TO A FREAK SHOW AS A RARE ORC THAT COULD TRANSLATE HUMAN SPEECH.
FOR THREE COPPER.
SO THEN...
WHOA, UNCLE, SLOW DOWN!
ZAAA (PSHHH)

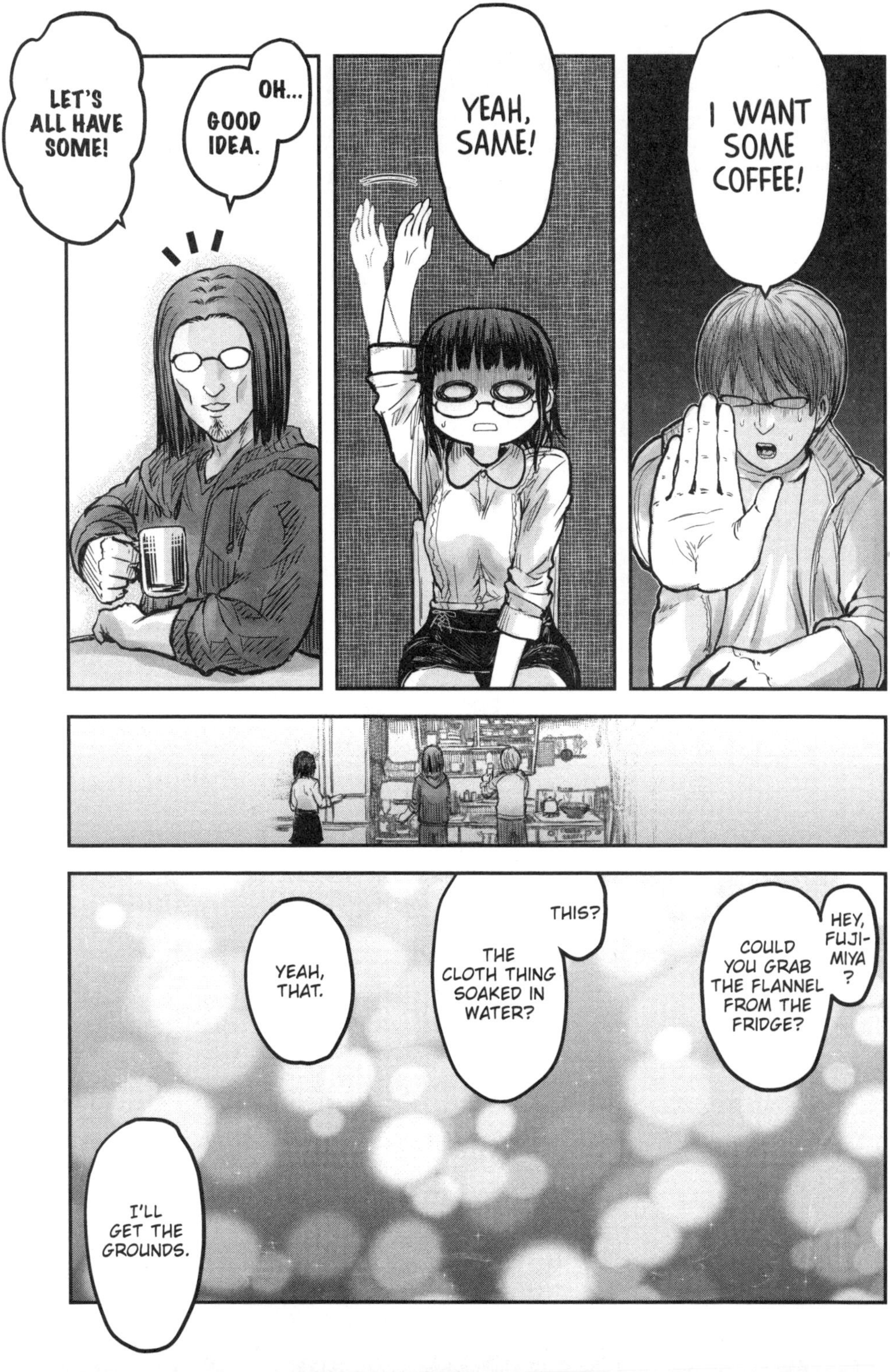
I WANT SOME COFFEE!
YEAH, SAME!
OH... GOOD IDEA.
LET'S ALL HAVE SOME!
HEY, FUJI-MIYA?
COULD YOU GRAB THE FLANNEL FROM THE FRIDGE?
THIS?
THE CLOTH THING SOAKED IN WATER?
YEAH, THAT.
I'LL GET THE GROUNDS.

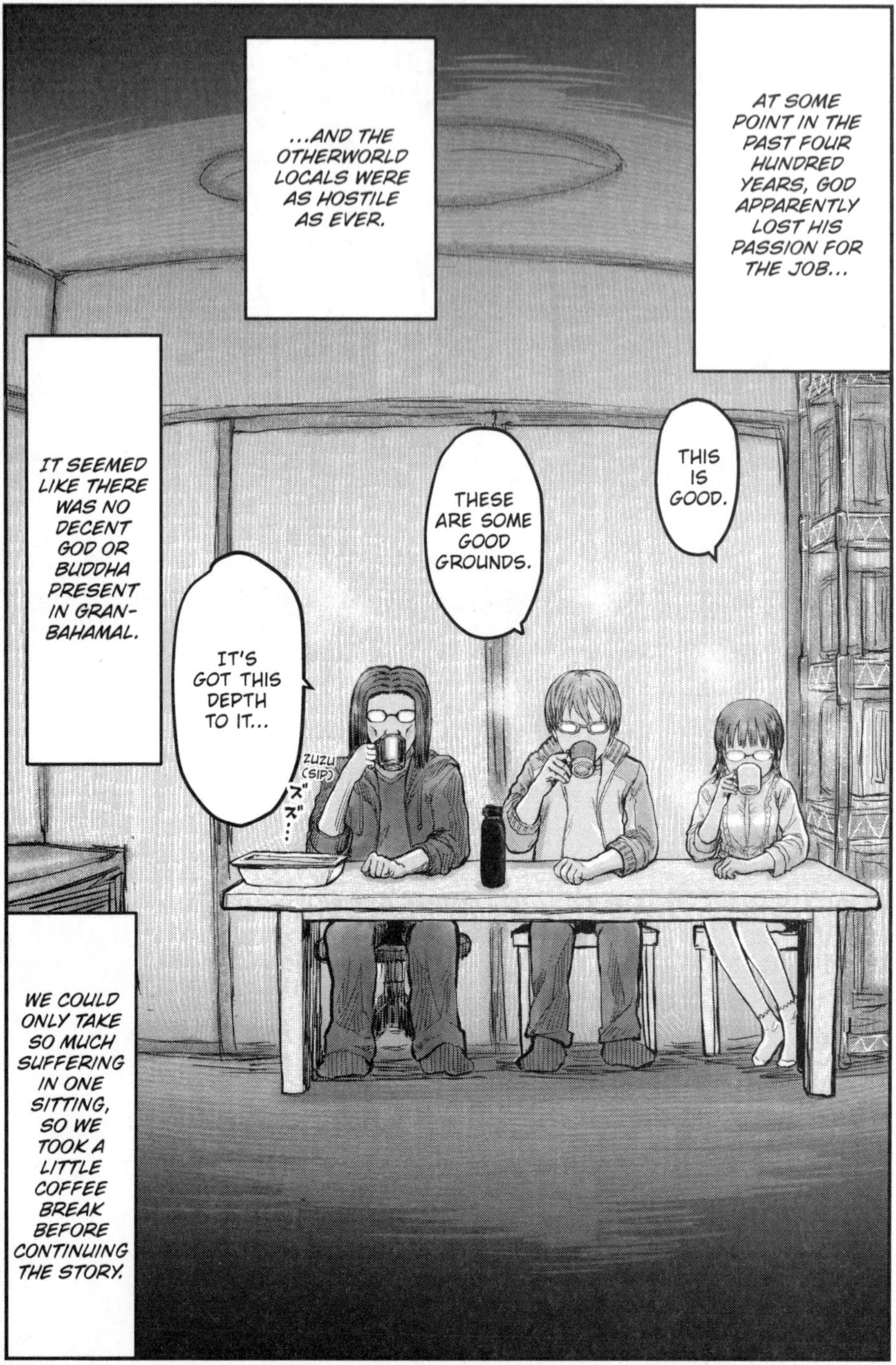
AT SOME POINT IN THE PAST FOUR HUNDRED YEARS, GOD APPARENTLY LOST HIS PASSION FOR THE JOB...
...AND THE OTHERWORLD LOCALS WERE AS HOSTILE AS EVER.
IT SEEMED LIKE THERE WAS NO DECENT GOD OR BUDDHA PRESENT IN GRAN-BAHAMAL.
THIS IS GOOD.
THESE ARE SOME GOOD GROUNDS.
IT'S GOT THIS DEPTH TO IT...
ZUZU (SIP)
ズズ...
WE COULD ONLY TAKE SO MUCH SUFFERING IN ONE SITTING, SO WE TOOK A LITTLE COFFEE BREAK BEFORE CONTINUING THE STORY.

Cloud Storage

A service which leases hard drive space for storing data online.

UNCLE from ANOTHER WORLD

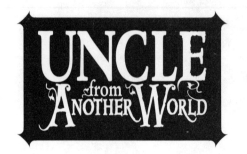

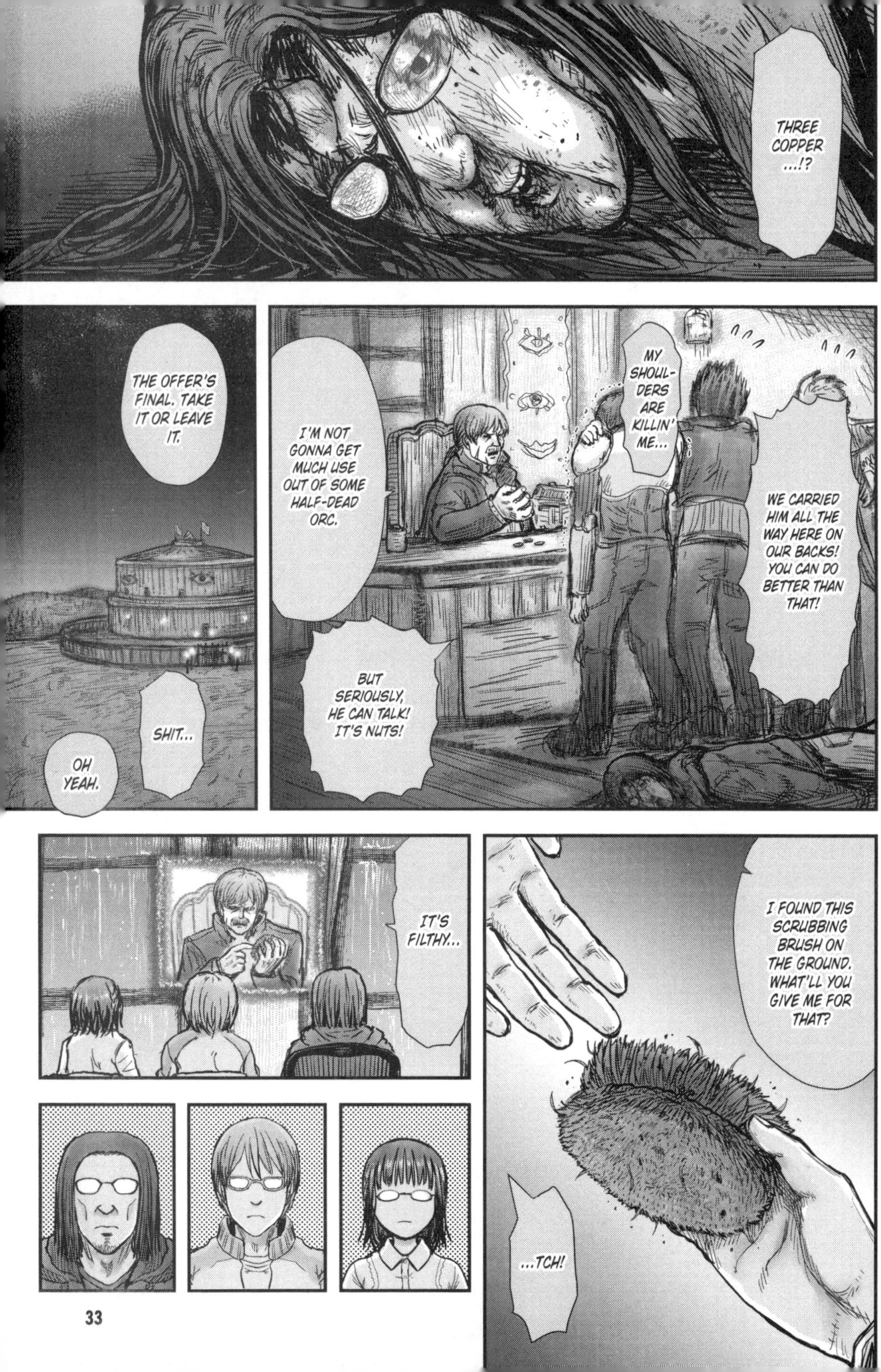
THREE COPPER ...!?
MY SHOULDERS ARE KILLIN' ME...
WE CARRIED HIM ALL THE WAY HERE ON OUR BACKS! YOU CAN DO BETTER THAN THAT!
I'M NOT GONNA GET MUCH USE OUT OF SOME HALF-DEAD ORC.
BUT SERIOUSLY, HE CAN TALK! IT'S NUTS!
THE OFFER'S FINAL. TAKE IT OR LEAVE IT.
SHIT...
OH YEAH.
I FOUND THIS SCRUBBING BRUSH ON THE GROUND. WHAT'LL YOU GIVE ME FOR THAT?
...TCH!
IT'S FILTHY...

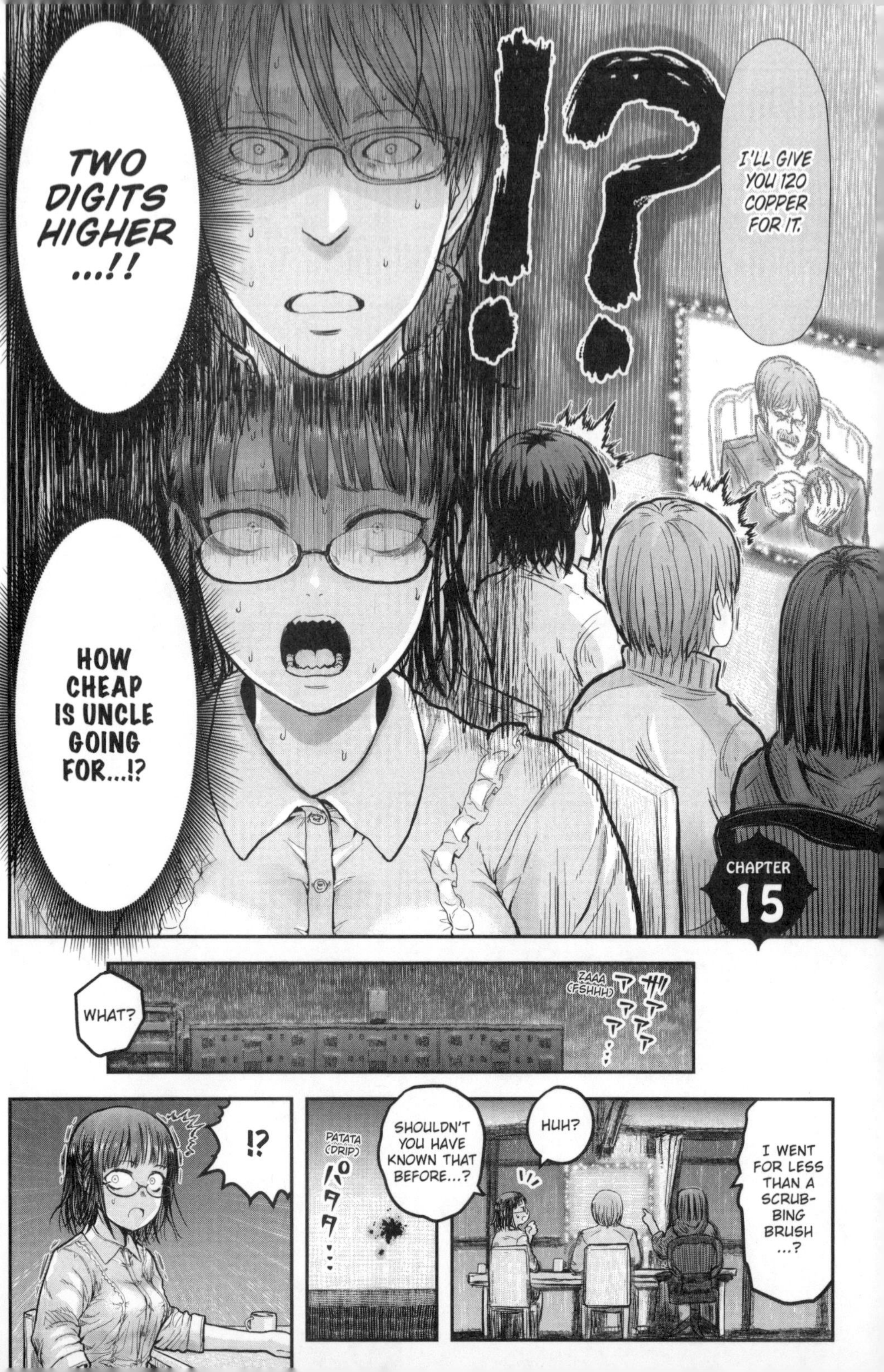
I'LL GIVE YOU 120 COPPER FOR IT.
!?
TWO DIGITS HIGHER ...!!
HOW CHEAP IS UNCLE GOING FOR...!?
CHAPTER 15
ZAAA (FSHHH)
WHAT?
I WENT FOR LESS THAN A SCRUB-BING BRUSH ...?
HUH?
SHOULDN'T YOU HAVE KNOWN THAT BEFORE...?
PATATA (DRIP)
!?

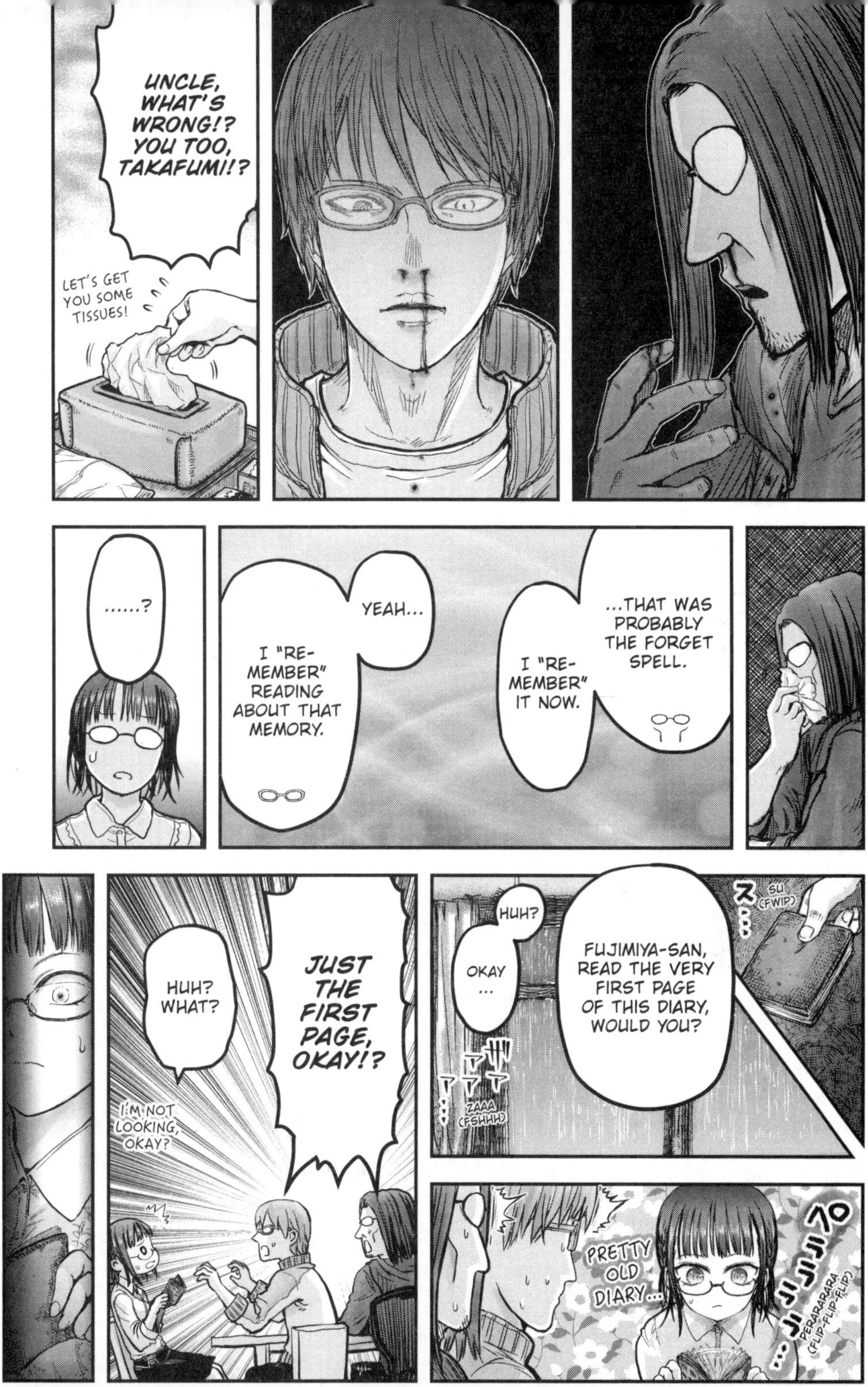
UNCLE, WHAT'S WRONG!? YOU TOO, TAKAFUMI!?
LET'S GET YOU SOME TISSUES!
...THAT WAS PROBABLY THE FORGET SPELL.
I "RE-MEMBER" IT NOW.
YEAH...
I "RE-MEMBER" READING ABOUT THAT MEMORY.
......?
SU (FWIP)
FUJIMIYA-SAN, READ THE VERY FIRST PAGE OF THIS DIARY, WOULD YOU?
HUH?
OKAY...
ZAAA (FSHHH)
PERARARARA (FLIP-FLIP-FLIP)
PRETTY OLD DIARY...
JUST THE FIRST PAGE, OKAY!?
HUH? WHAT?
I'M NOT LOOKING, OKAY?

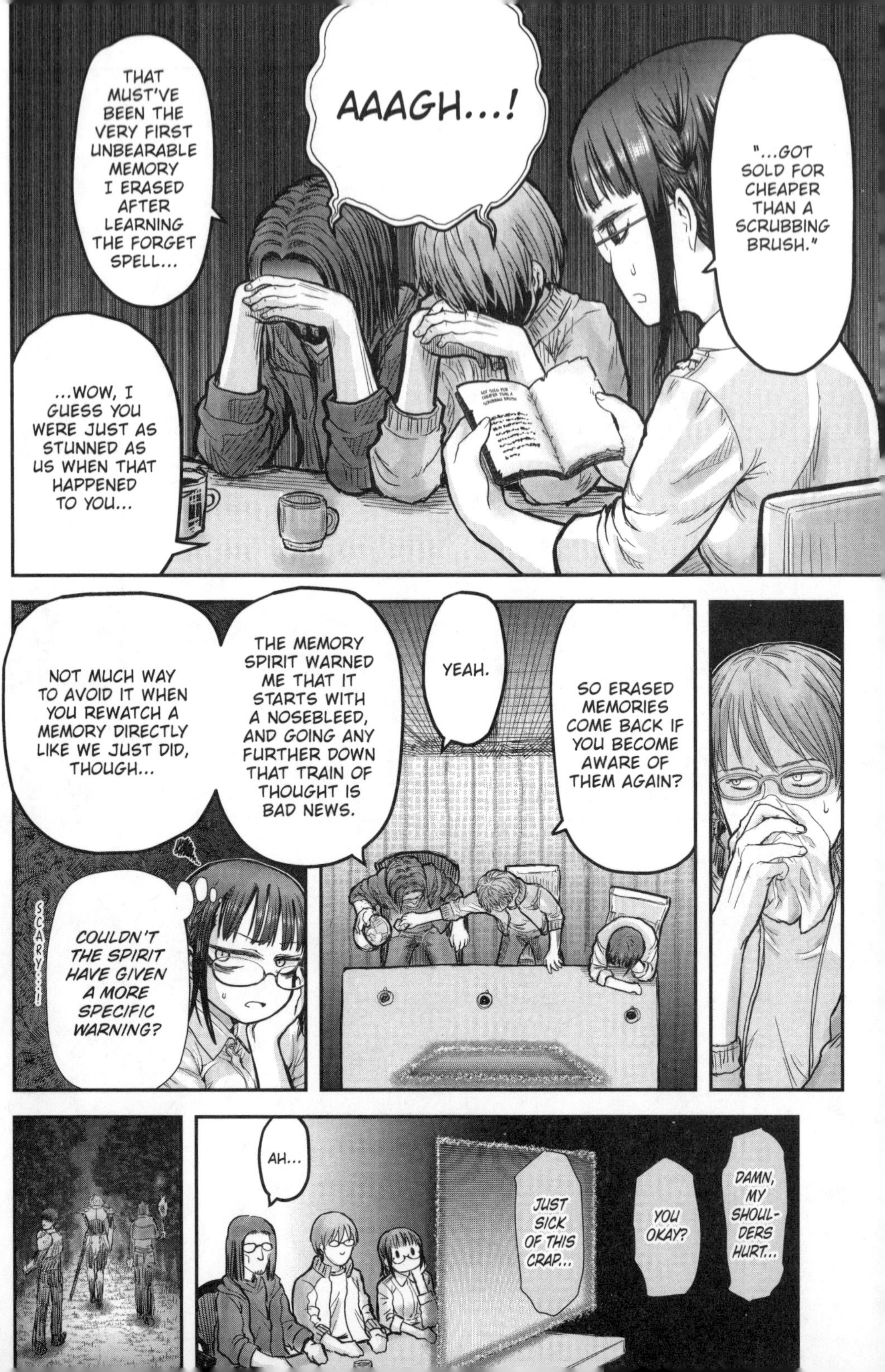
"...GOT SOLD FOR CHEAPER THAN A SCRUBBING BRUSH."
AAAGH...!
THAT MUST'VE BEEN THE VERY FIRST UNBEARABLE MEMORY I ERASED AFTER LEARNING THE FORGET SPELL...
...WOW, I GUESS YOU WERE JUST AS STUNNED AS US WHEN THAT HAPPENED TO YOU...
SO ERASED MEMORIES COME BACK IF YOU BECOME AWARE OF THEM AGAIN?
YEAH.
THE MEMORY SPIRIT WARNED ME THAT IT STARTS WITH A NOSEBLEED, AND GOING ANY FURTHER DOWN THAT TRAIN OF THOUGHT IS BAD NEWS.
NOT MUCH WAY TO AVOID IT WHEN YOU REWATCH A MEMORY DIRECTLY LIKE WE JUST DID, THOUGH...
SCARY...!
COULDN'T THE SPIRIT HAVE GIVEN A MORE SPECIFIC WARNING?
DAMN, MY SHOUL-DERS HURT...
YOU OKAY?
JUST SICK OF THIS CRAP...
AH...

CAN! HA HA HA

P!!
(TWEET)

P!!
(TWEET)

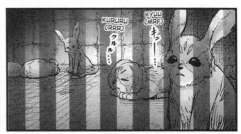

KURURU
(RRR)

KYUU
(MRF)

A PEN...!

AND SO I GOT THROWN INTO A PEN IN A FREAK SHOW'S BASEMENT.

I'M GONNA SKIP AHEAD A WEEK HERE.

WHAT?

WHY?

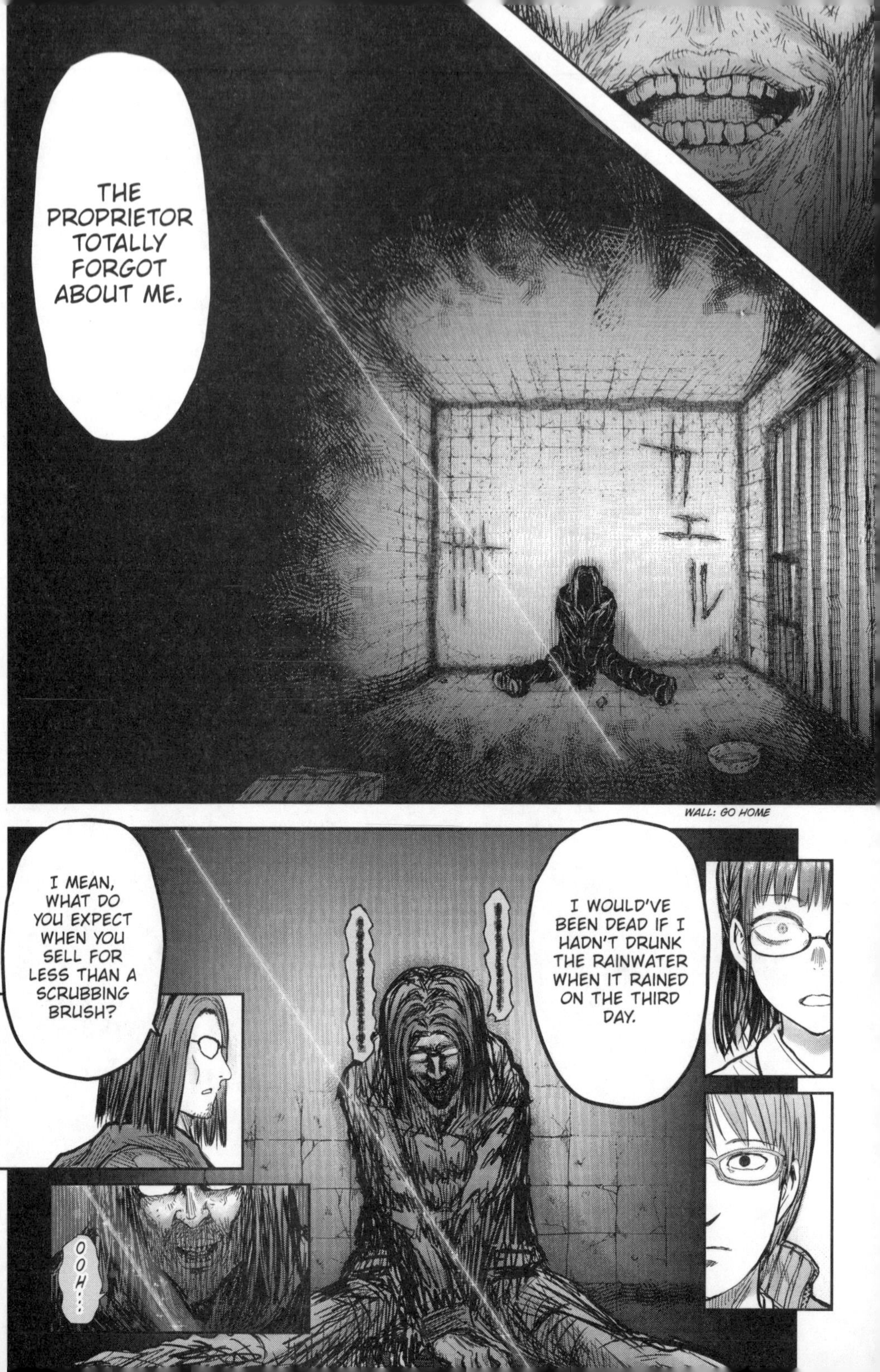
THE PROPRIETOR TOTALLY FORGOT ABOUT ME.
WALL: GO HOME
I WOULD'VE BEEN DEAD IF I HADN'T DRUNK THE RAINWATER WHEN IT RAINED ON THE THIRD DAY.
I MEAN, WHAT DO YOU EXPECT WHEN YOU SELL FOR LESS THAN A SCRUBBING BRUSH?
OOH...

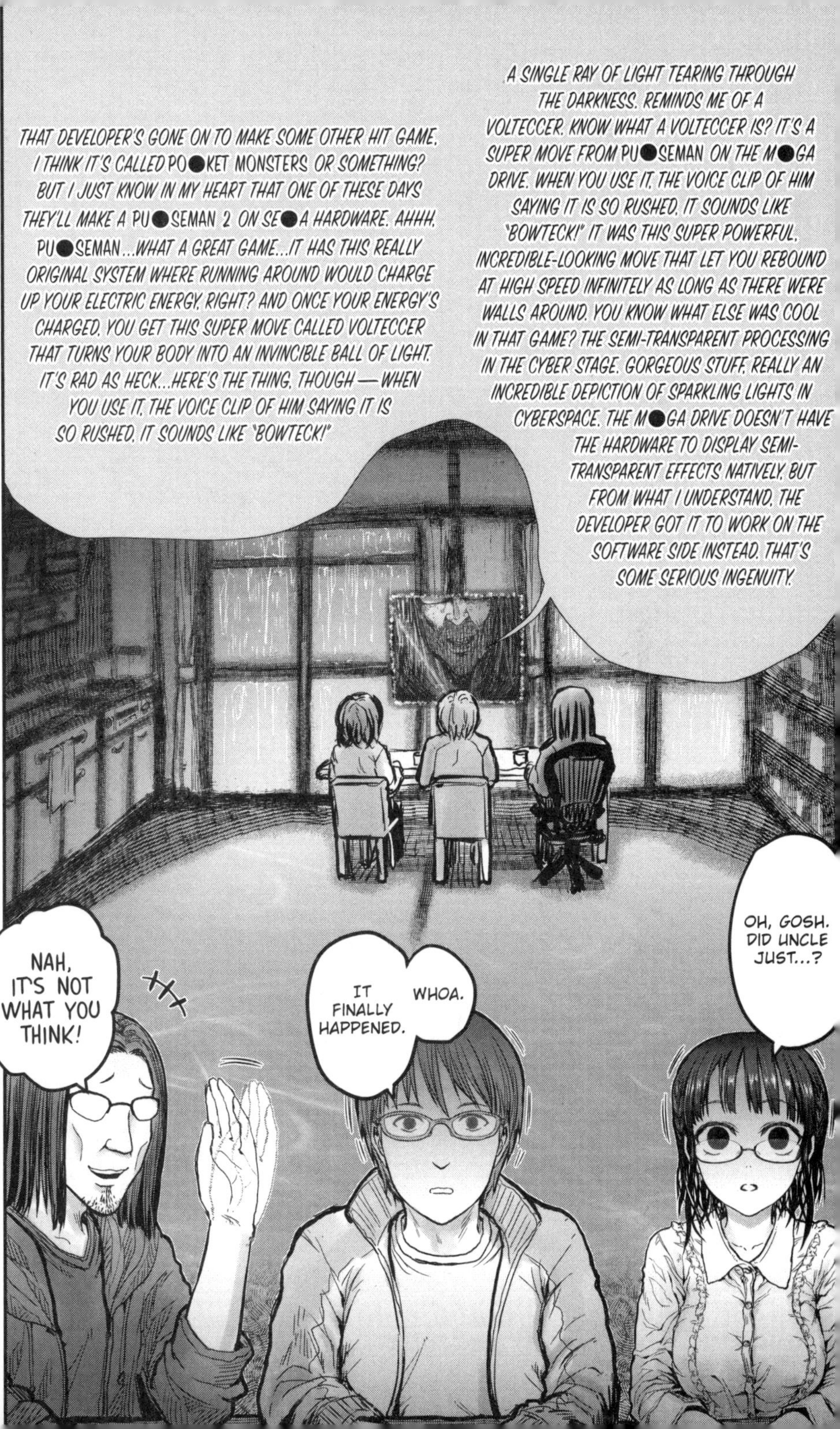
A SINGLE RAY OF LIGHT TEARING THROUGH THE DARKNESS. REMINDS ME OF A VOLTECCER. KNOW WHAT A VOLTECCER IS? IT'S A SUPER MOVE FROM PU●SEMAN ON THE M●GA DRIVE. WHEN YOU USE IT, THE VOICE CLIP OF HIM SAYING IT IS SO RUSHED, IT SOUNDS LIKE "BOWTECK!" IT WAS THIS SUPER POWERFUL, INCREDIBLE-LOOKING MOVE THAT LET YOU REBOUND AT HIGH SPEED INFINITELY AS LONG AS THERE WERE WALLS AROUND. YOU KNOW WHAT ELSE WAS COOL IN THAT GAME? THE SEMI-TRANSPARENT PROCESSING IN THE CYBER STAGE. GORGEOUS STUFF, REALLY AN INCREDIBLE DEPICTION OF SPARKLING LIGHTS IN CYBERSPACE. THE M●GA DRIVE DOESN'T HAVE THE HARDWARE TO DISPLAY SEMI-TRANSPARENT EFFECTS NATIVELY, BUT FROM WHAT I UNDERSTAND, THE DEVELOPER GOT IT TO WORK ON THE SOFTWARE SIDE INSTEAD. THAT'S SOME SERIOUS INGENUITY.
THAT DEVELOPER'S GONE ON TO MAKE SOME OTHER HIT GAME. I THINK IT'S CALLED PO●KET MONSTERS OR SOMETHING? BUT I JUST KNOW IN MY HEART THAT ONE OF THESE DAYS THEY'LL MAKE A PU●SEMAN 2 ON SE●A HARDWARE. AHHH, PU●SEMAN...WHAT A GREAT GAME...IT HAS THIS REALLY ORIGINAL SYSTEM WHERE RUNNING AROUND WOULD CHARGE UP YOUR ELECTRIC ENERGY, RIGHT? AND ONCE YOUR ENERGY'S CHARGED, YOU GET THIS SUPER MOVE CALLED VOLTECCER THAT TURNS YOUR BODY INTO AN INVINCIBLE BALL OF LIGHT. IT'S RAD AS HECK...HERE'S THE THING, THOUGH—WHEN YOU USE IT, THE VOICE CLIP OF HIM SAYING IT IS SO RUSHED, IT SOUNDS LIKE "BOWTECK!"
OH, GOSH. DID UNCLE JUST...?
WHOA.
IT FINALLY HAPPENED.
NAH, IT'S NOT WHAT YOU THINK!

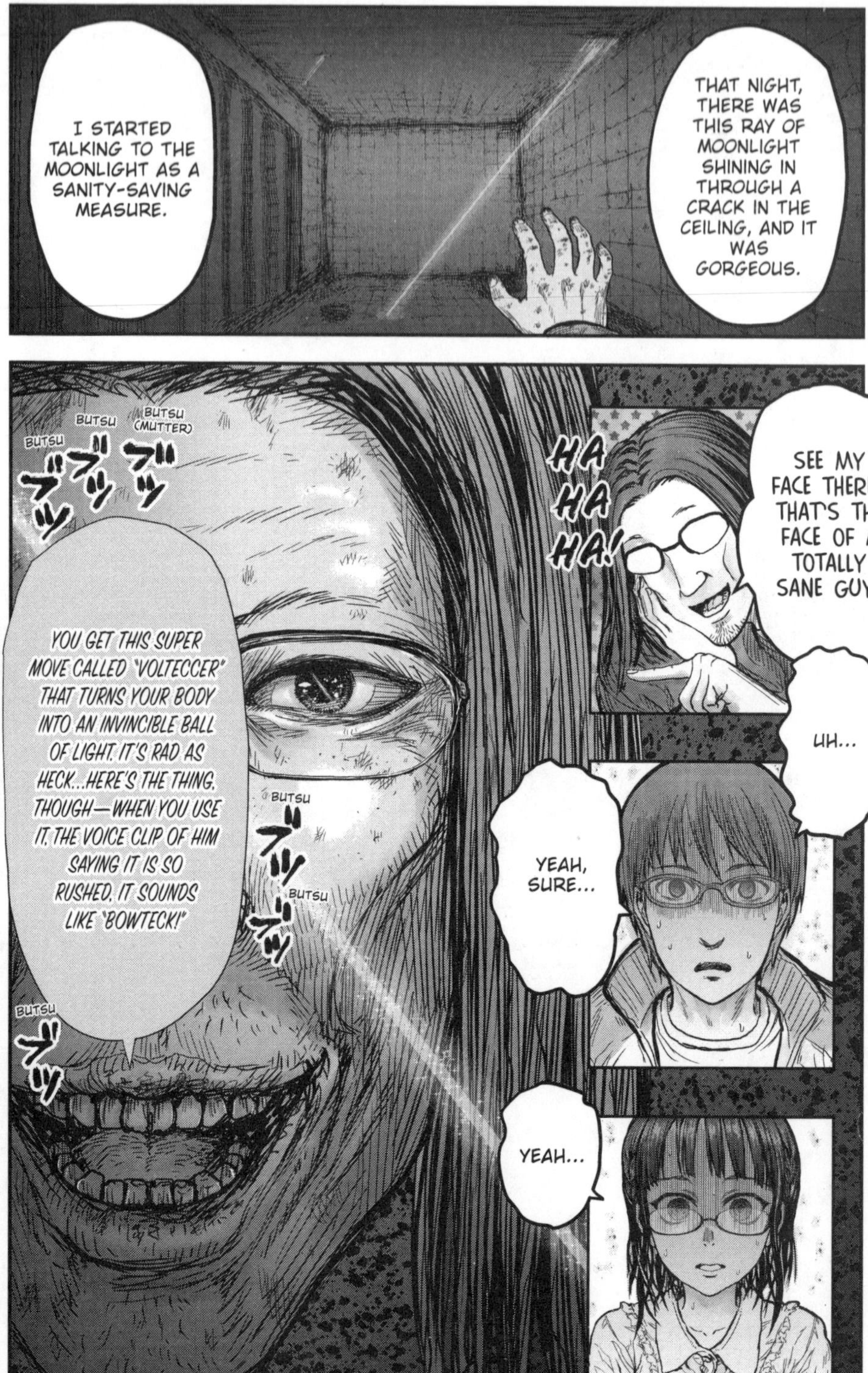
THAT NIGHT, THERE WAS THIS RAY OF MOONLIGHT SHINING IN THROUGH A CRACK IN THE CEILING, AND IT WAS GORGEOUS.
I STARTED TALKING TO THE MOONLIGHT AS A SANITY-SAVING MEASURE.
HA HA HA!
SEE MY FACE THERE? THAT'S THE FACE OF A TOTALLY SANE GUY!
UH...
YEAH, SURE...
YEAH...
BUTSU (MUTTER)
ブツ
BUTSU
ブツ
BUTSU
ブツ
YOU GET THIS SUPER MOVE CALLED "VOLTECCER" THAT TURNS YOUR BODY INTO AN INVINCIBLE BALL OF LIGHT. IT'S RAD AS HECK...HERE'S THE THING, THOUGH—WHEN YOU USE IT, THE VOICE CLIP OF HIM SAYING IT IS SO RUSHED, IT SOUNDS LIKE "BOWTECK!"
BUTSU
ブツ
BUTSU
ブツ
BUTSU
ブツ

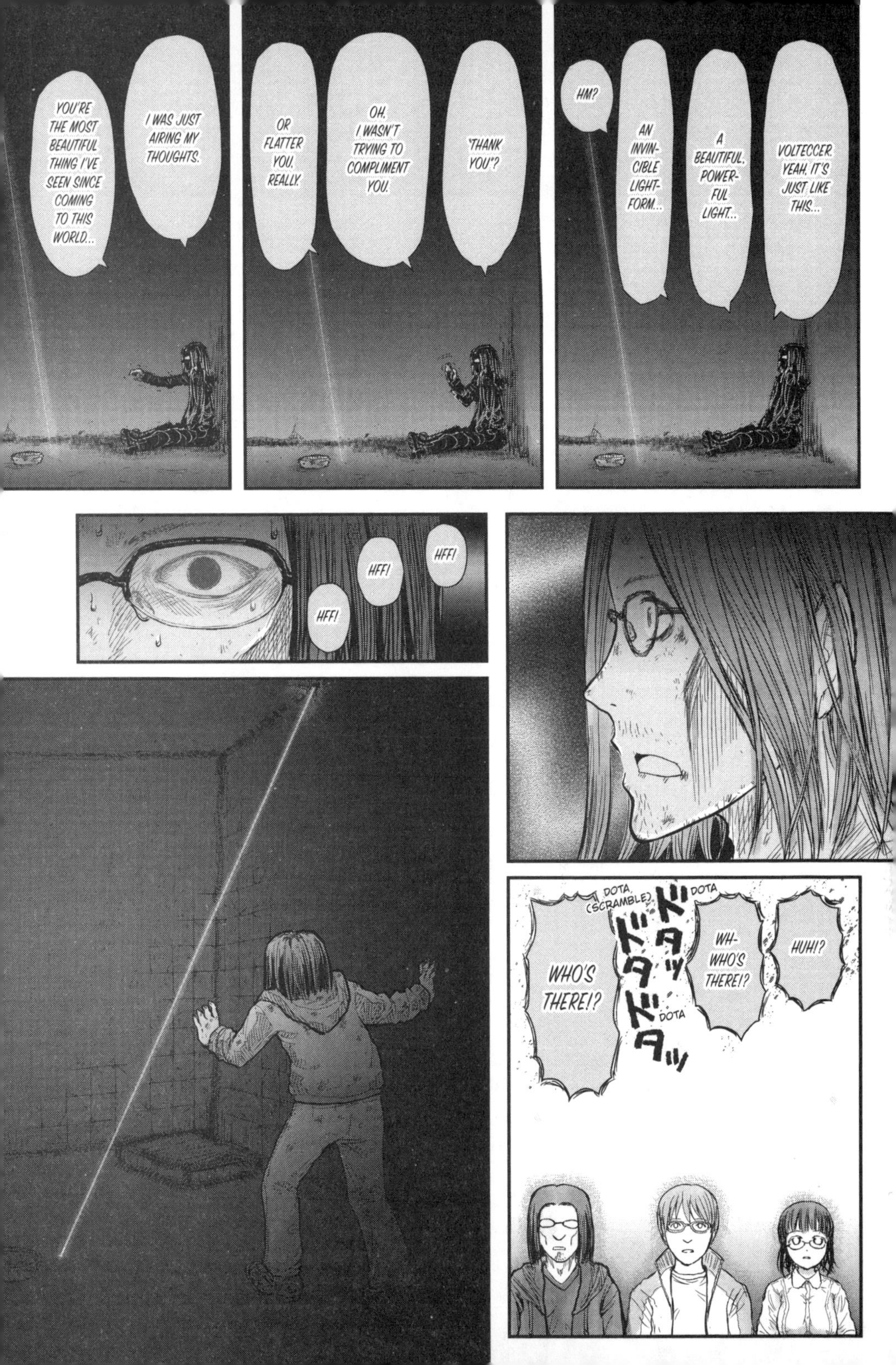

HM?
AN INVINCIBLE LIGHT-FORM...
A BEAUTIFUL, POWERFUL LIGHT...
VOLTECCER. YEAH, IT'S JUST LIKE THIS...
"THANK YOU"?
OH, I WASN'T TRYING TO COMPLIMENT YOU.
OR FLATTER YOU, REALLY.
I WAS JUST AIRING MY THOUGHTS.
YOU'RE THE MOST BEAUTIFUL THING I'VE SEEN SINCE COMING TO THIS WORLD...
HFF!
HFF!
HFF!
HUH!?
WH-WHO'S THERE!?
DOTA
ドタッ
DOTA (SCRAMBLE)
DOTA
ドタッドタッ
WHO'S THERE!?

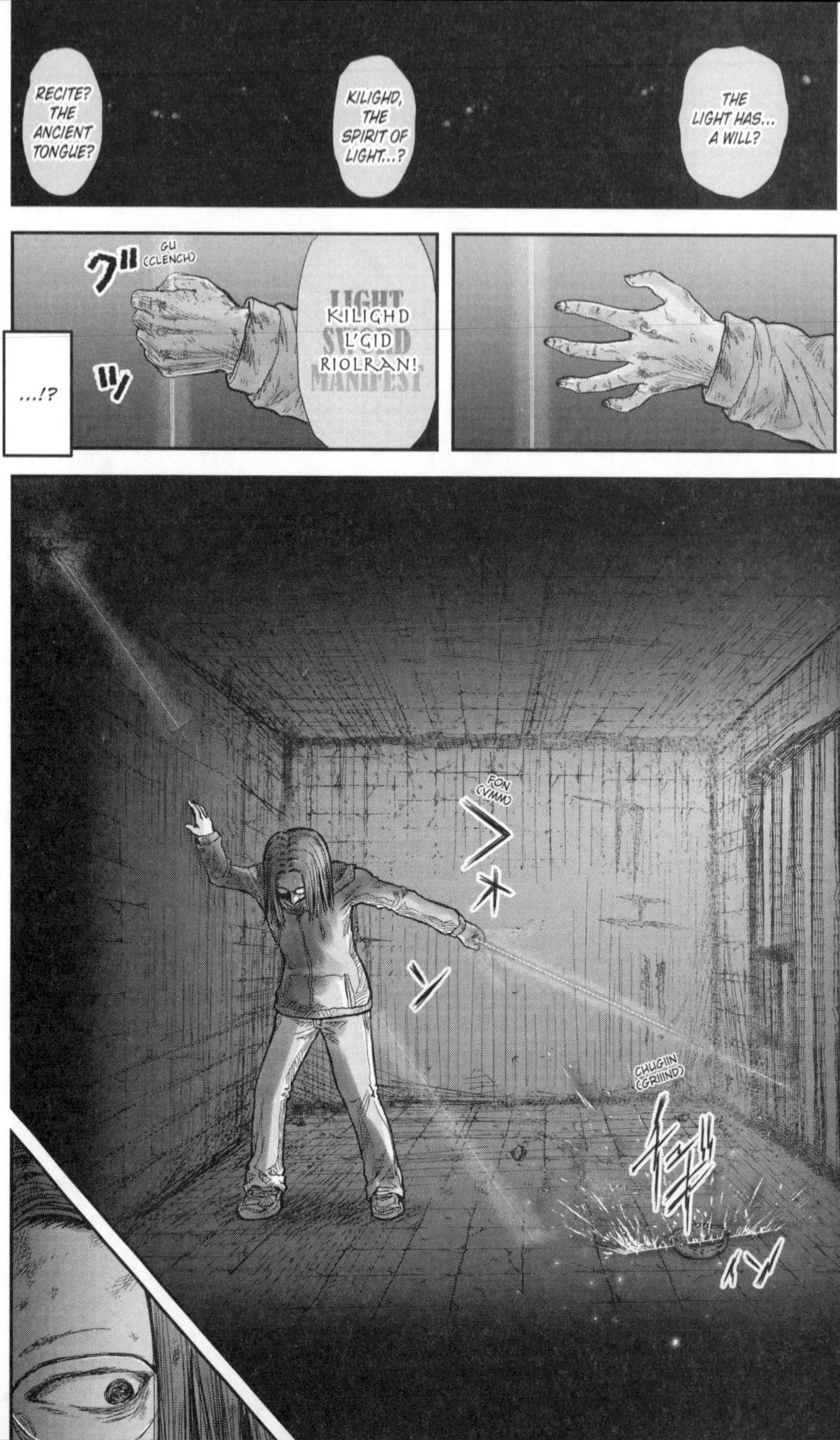
THE LIGHT HAS... A WILL?
KILIGHD, THE SPIRIT OF LIGHT...?
RECITE? THE ANCIENT TONGUE?
KILIGHD L'GID RIOLRAN!
GU (CLENCH)
...!?
FON (VMM)
CHUGIIN (GRIIIND)

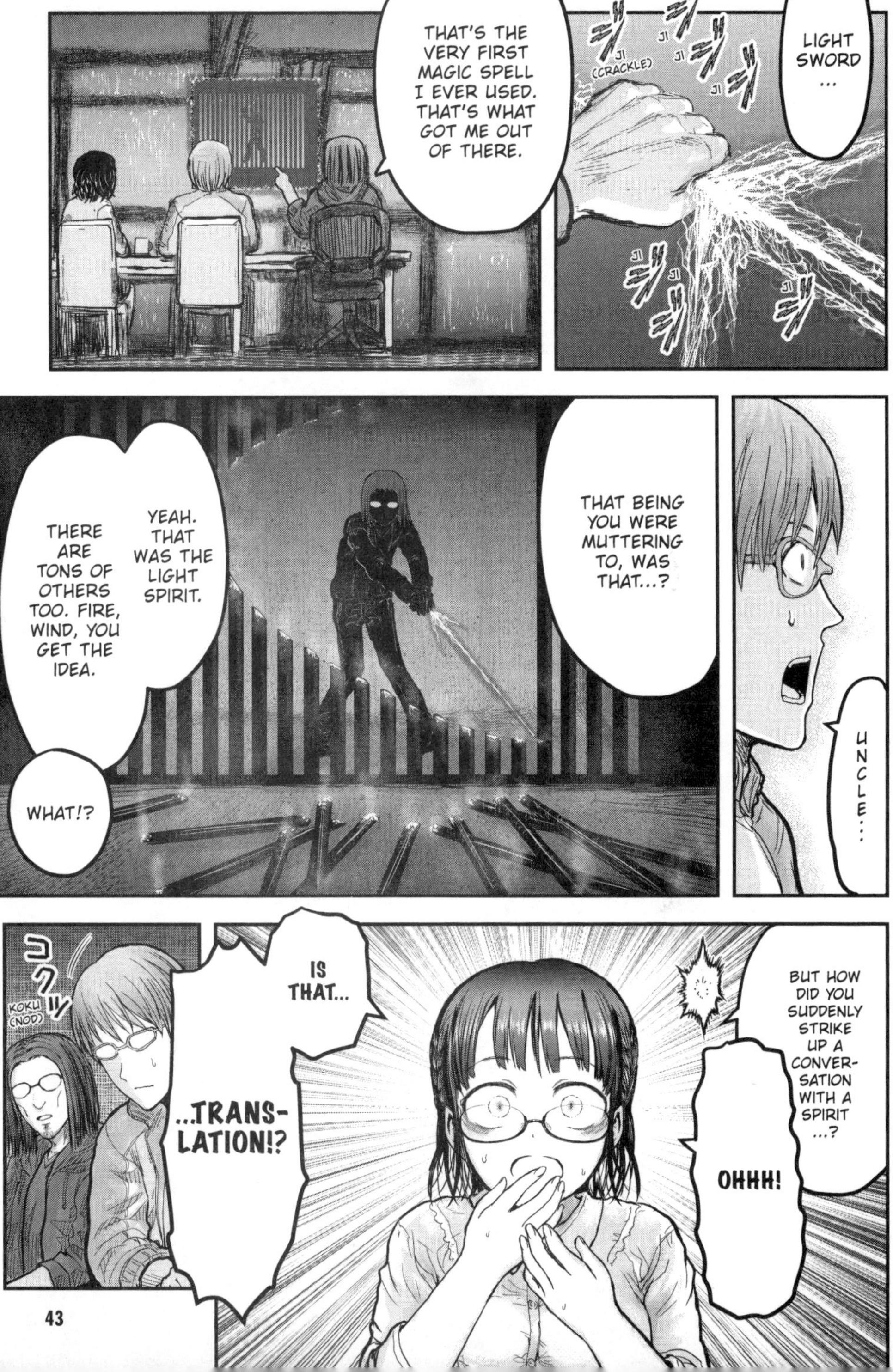

LIGHT SWORD ...
JI JI JI JI (CRACKLE)
JI JI JI
THAT'S THE VERY FIRST MAGIC SPELL I EVER USED. THAT'S WHAT GOT ME OUT OF THERE.
UNCLE...
THAT BEING YOU WERE MUTTERING TO, WAS THAT...?
YEAH. THAT WAS THE LIGHT SPIRIT.
THERE ARE TONS OF OTHERS TOO. FIRE, WIND, YOU GET THE IDEA.
WHAT!?
BUT HOW DID YOU SUDDENLY STRIKE UP A CONVERSATION WITH A SPIRIT ...?
OHHH!
IS THAT...
...TRANSLATION!?
KOKU (NOD)

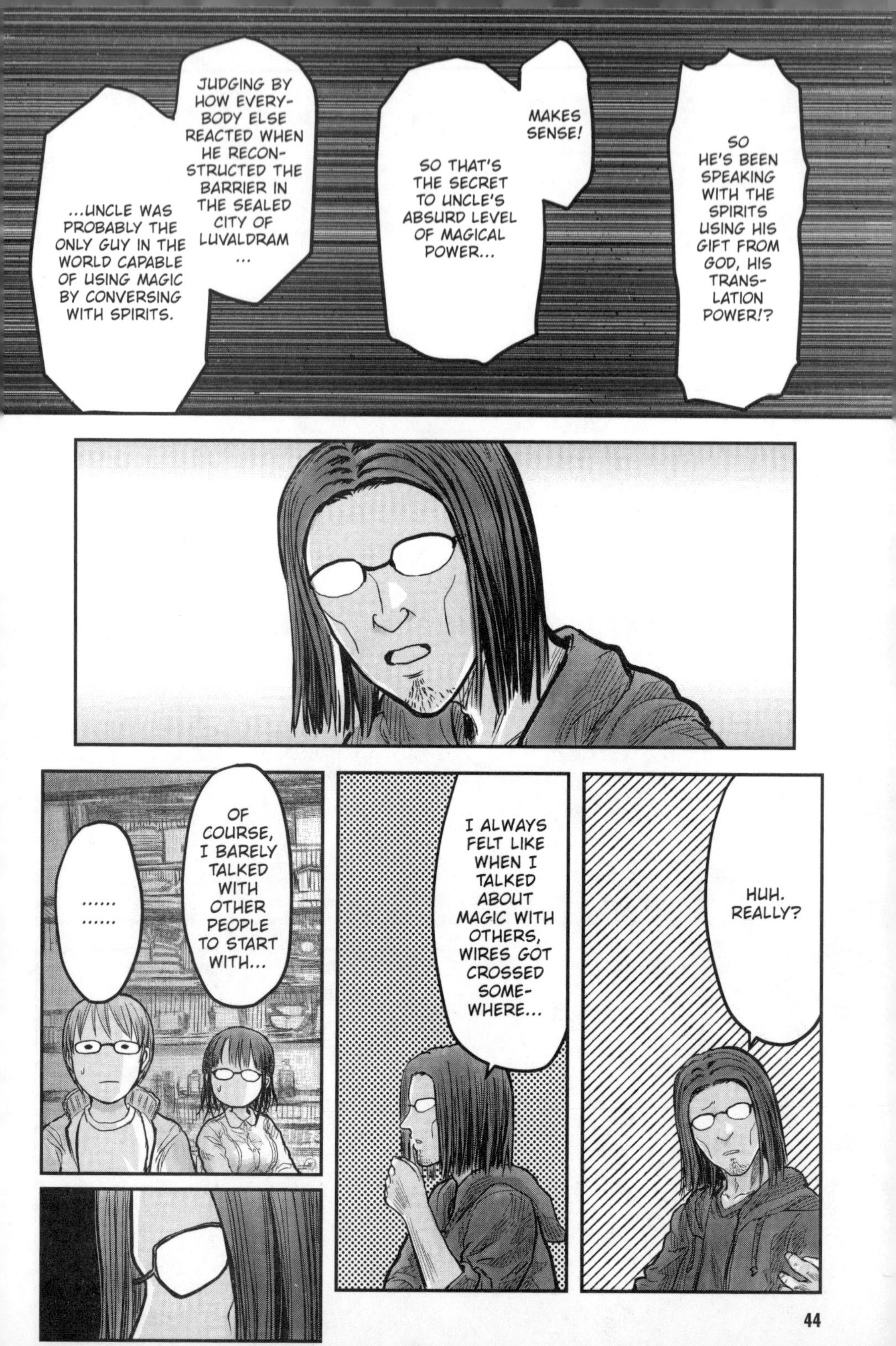
SO HE'S BEEN SPEAKING WITH THE SPIRITS USING HIS GIFT FROM GOD, HIS TRANS-LATION POWER!?
MAKES SENSE!
SO THAT'S THE SECRET TO UNCLE'S ABSURD LEVEL OF MAGICAL POWER...
JUDGING BY HOW EVERY-BODY ELSE REACTED WHEN HE RECON-STRUCTED THE BARRIER IN THE SEALED CITY OF LUVALDRAM ...
...UNCLE WAS PROBABLY THE ONLY GUY IN THE WORLD CAPABLE OF USING MAGIC BY CONVERSING WITH SPIRITS.
HUH. REALLY?
I ALWAYS FELT LIKE WHEN I TALKED ABOUT MAGIC WITH OTHERS, WIRES GOT CROSSED SOME-WHERE...
OF COURSE, I BARELY TALKED WITH OTHER PEOPLE TO START WITH...
....

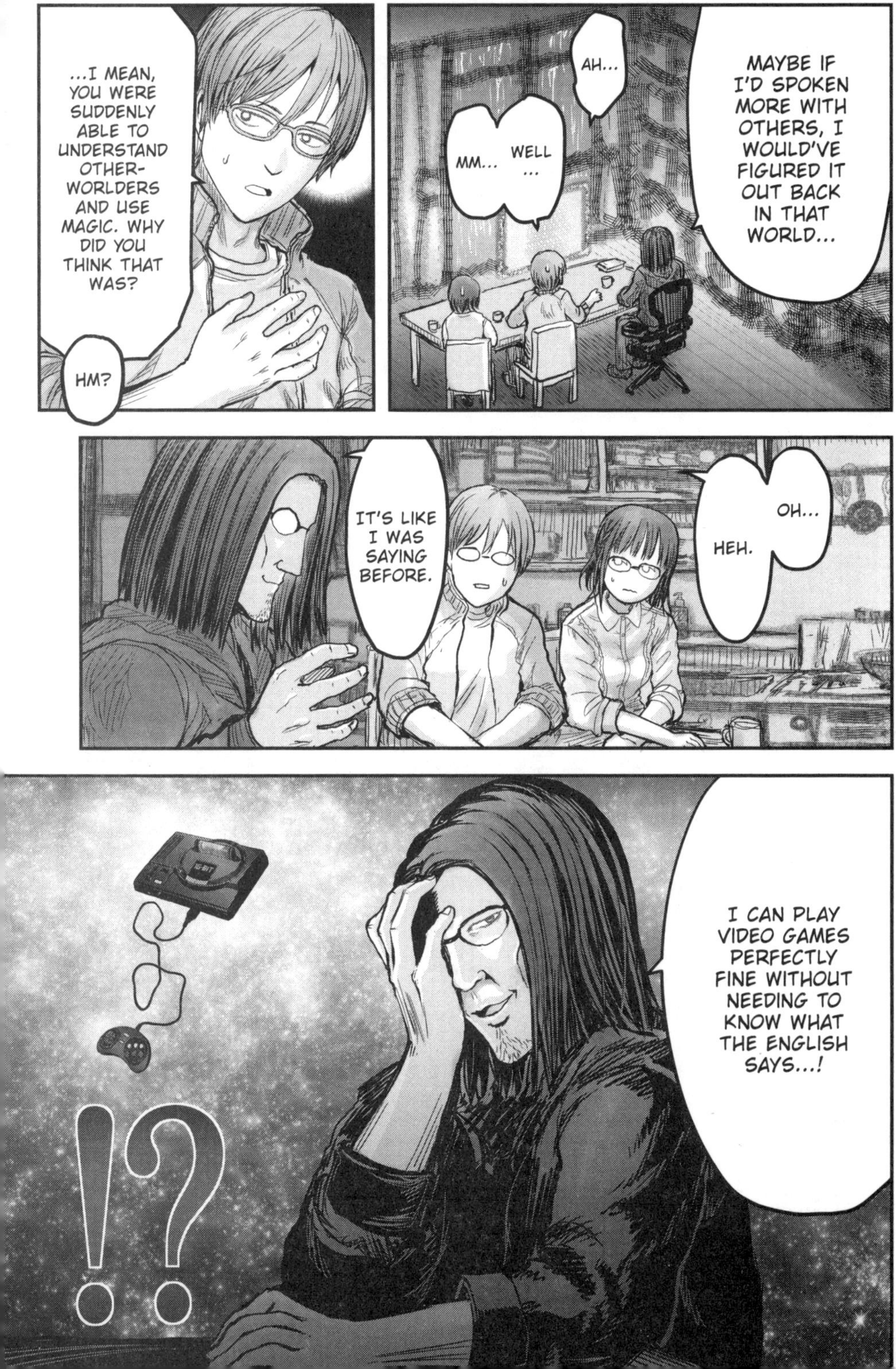
MAYBE IF I'D SPOKEN MORE WITH OTHERS, I WOULD'VE FIGURED IT OUT BACK IN THAT WORLD...
AH...
WELL...
MM...
...I MEAN, YOU WERE SUDDENLY ABLE TO UNDERSTAND OTHER-WORLDERS AND USE MAGIC. WHY DID YOU THINK THAT WAS?
HM?
OH... HEH.
IT'S LIKE I WAS SAYING BEFORE.
I CAN PLAY VIDEO GAMES PERFECTLY FINE WITHOUT NEEDING TO KNOW WHAT THE ENGLISH SAYS...!
!?

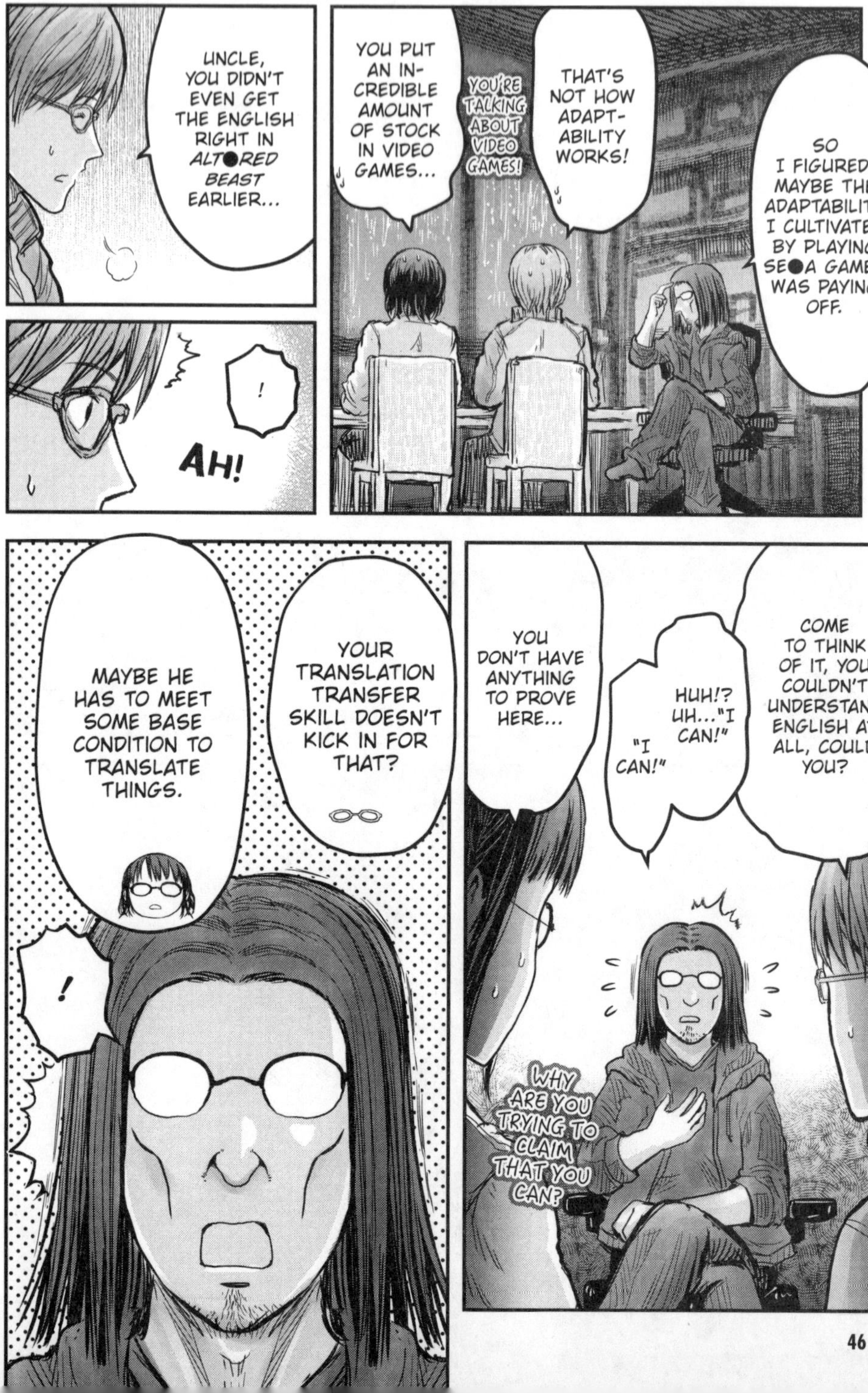
SO I FIGURED, MAYBE THE ADAPTABILITY I CULTIVATED BY PLAYING SE●A GAMES WAS PAYING OFF.
THAT'S NOT HOW ADAPT-ABILITY WORKS!
YOU'RE TALKING ABOUT VIDEO GAMES!
YOU PUT AN IN-CREDIBLE AMOUNT OF STOCK IN VIDEO GAMES...
UNCLE, YOU DIDN'T EVEN GET THE ENGLISH RIGHT IN ALT●RED BEAST EARLIER...
!
AH!
COME TO THINK OF IT, YOU COULDN'T UNDERSTAND ENGLISH AT ALL, COULD YOU?
HUH!? UH..."I CAN!"
"I CAN!"
YOU DON'T HAVE ANYTHING TO PROVE HERE...
WHY ARE YOU TRYING TO CLAIM THAT YOU CAN?
YOUR TRANSLATION TRANSFER SKILL DOESN'T KICK IN FOR THAT?
MAYBE HE HAS TO MEET SOME BASE CONDITION TO TRANSLATE THINGS.
!

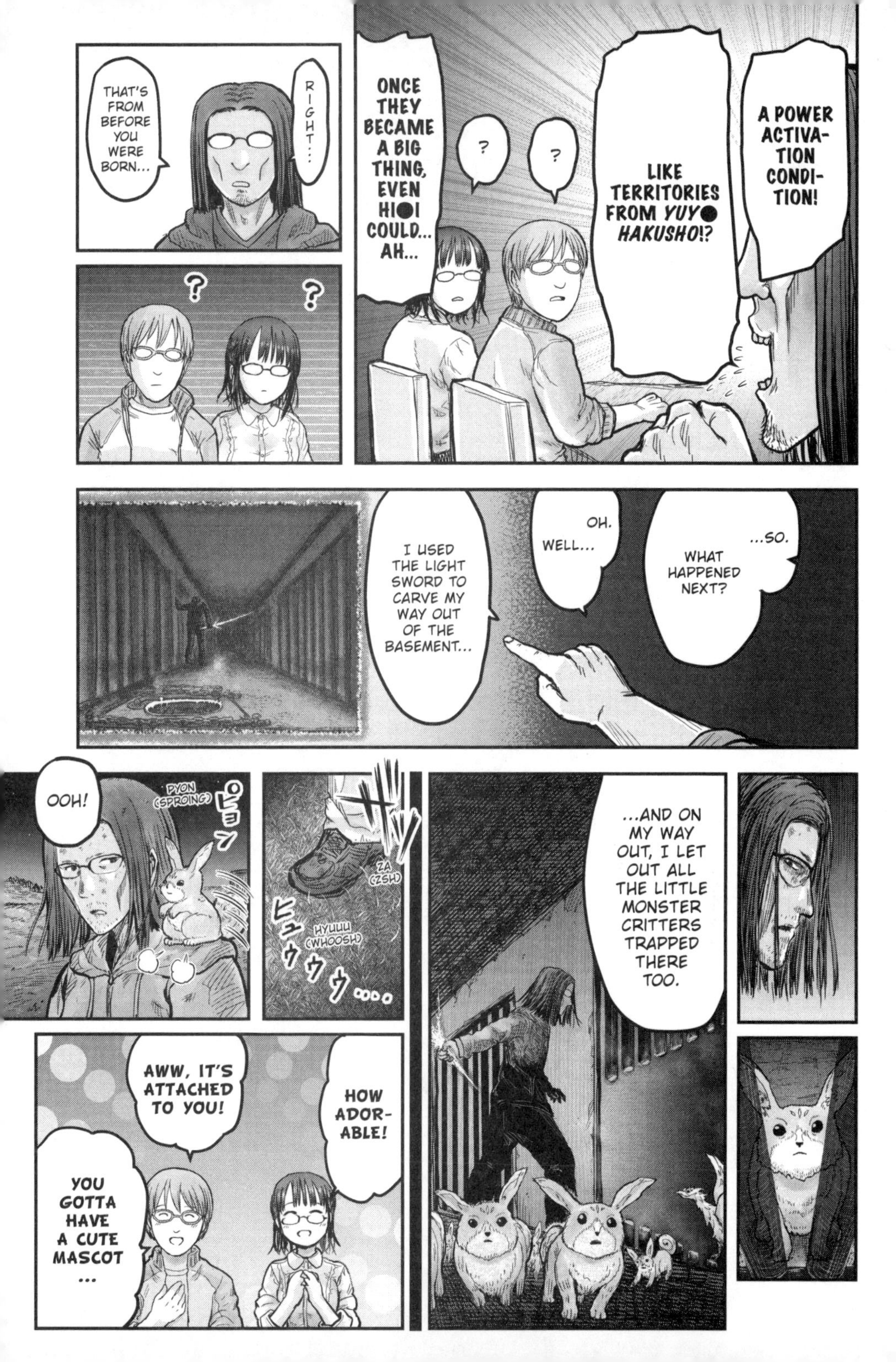
A POWER ACTIVATION CONDITION!
LIKE TERRITORIES FROM *YUYU● HAKUSHO*!?
?
?
ONCE THEY BECAME A BIG THING, EVEN HI●I COULD... AH...
RIGHT...
THAT'S FROM BEFORE YOU WERE BORN...
?
?
...SO.
WHAT HAPPENED NEXT?
OH. WELL...
I USED THE LIGHT SWORD TO CARVE MY WAY OUT OF THE BASEMENT...
...AND ON MY WAY OUT, I LET OUT ALL THE LITTLE MONSTER CRITTERS TRAPPED THERE TOO.
ZA (ZSHD)
HYUUU (WHOOSH)
PYON (SPROING)
OOH!
HOW ADORABLE!
AWW, IT'S ATTACHED TO YOU!
YOU GOTTA HAVE A CUTE MASCOT...

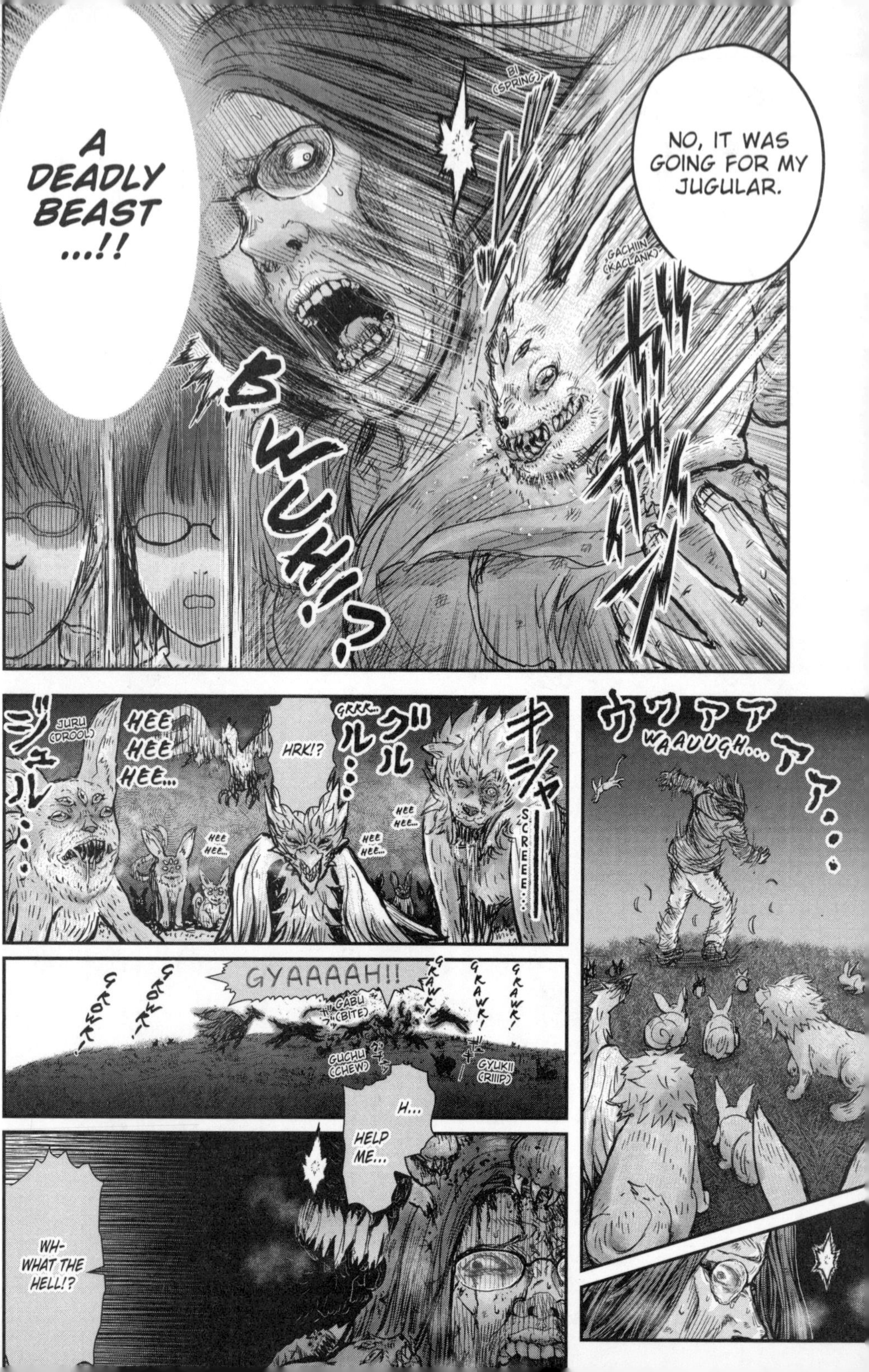

NO, IT WAS GOING FOR MY JUGULAR.
BI (SPRING)
GACHIIN (KACLANK)
A DEADLY BEAST ...!!
BWUH!?
WAAUGH...
SCREEEE...
GRRR...
HRK!?
HEE HEE...
HEE HEE...
HEE HEE...
HEE HEE HEE...
JURU (DROOL)
GRAWR!
GRAWR!
GRAWR!
GYAAAAH!!
GABU (BITE)
GYUKI (RIIIP)
GUCHU (CHEW)
GROWL!
GROWL!
H...
HELP ME...
WH- WHAT THE HELL!?

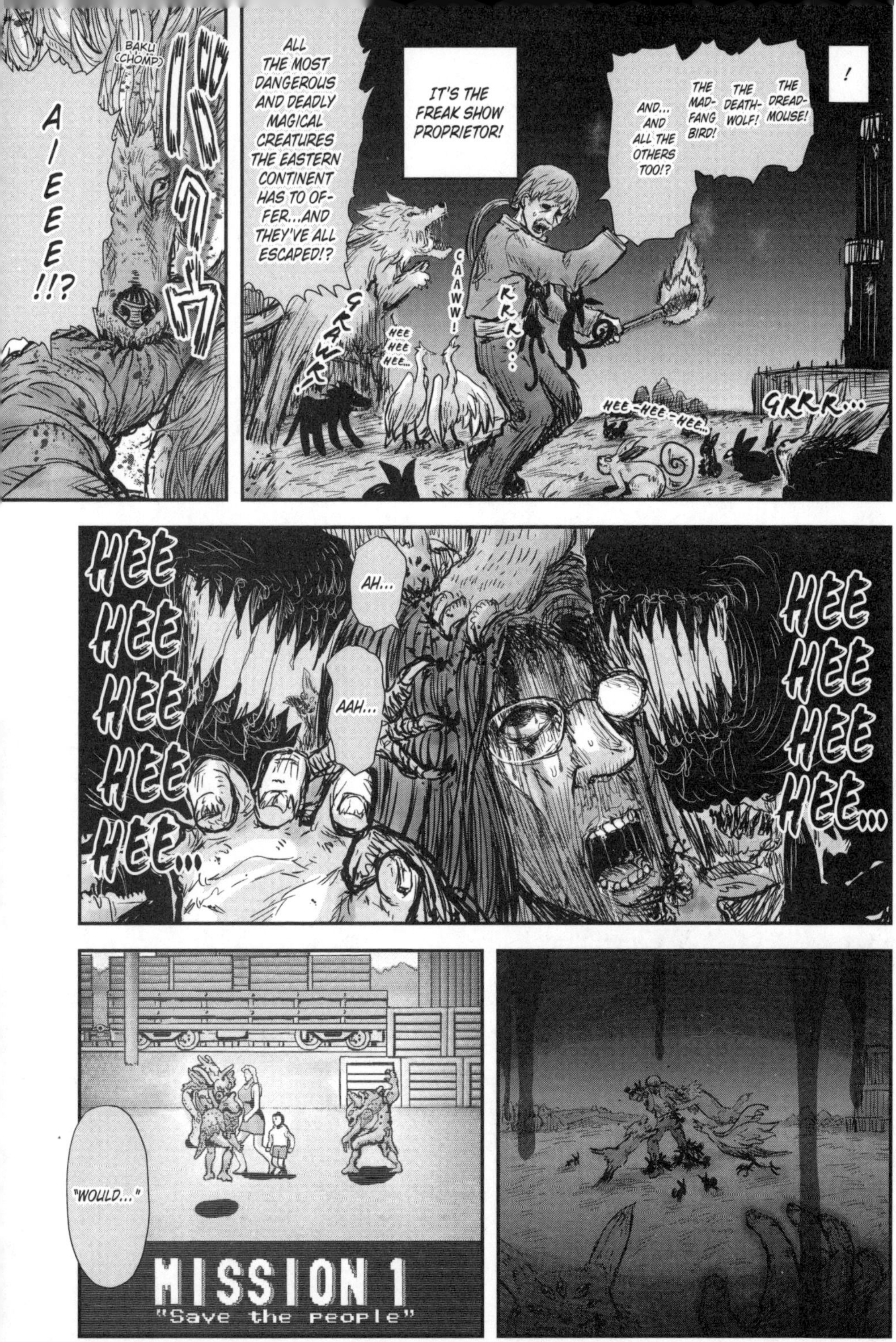
!
THE DREAD-MOUSE!
THE DEATH-WOLF!
THE MAD-FANG BIRD!
AND... AND ALL THE OTHERS TOO!?
IT'S THE FREAK SHOW PROPRIETOR!
ALL THE MOST DANGEROUS AND DEADLY MAGICAL CREATURES THE EASTERN CONTINENT HAS TO OFFER...AND THEY'VE ALL ESCAPED!?
GRRR...
HEE-HEE-HEE...
KRRR...
CAAWW!
HEE HEE HEE...
GRAWK!
BAKU (CHOMP)
AIEEEE!!?
HEE HEE HEE HEE HEE...
AH...
AAH...
HEE HEE HEE HEE HEE...
"WOULD..."
MISSION 1
"Save the people"

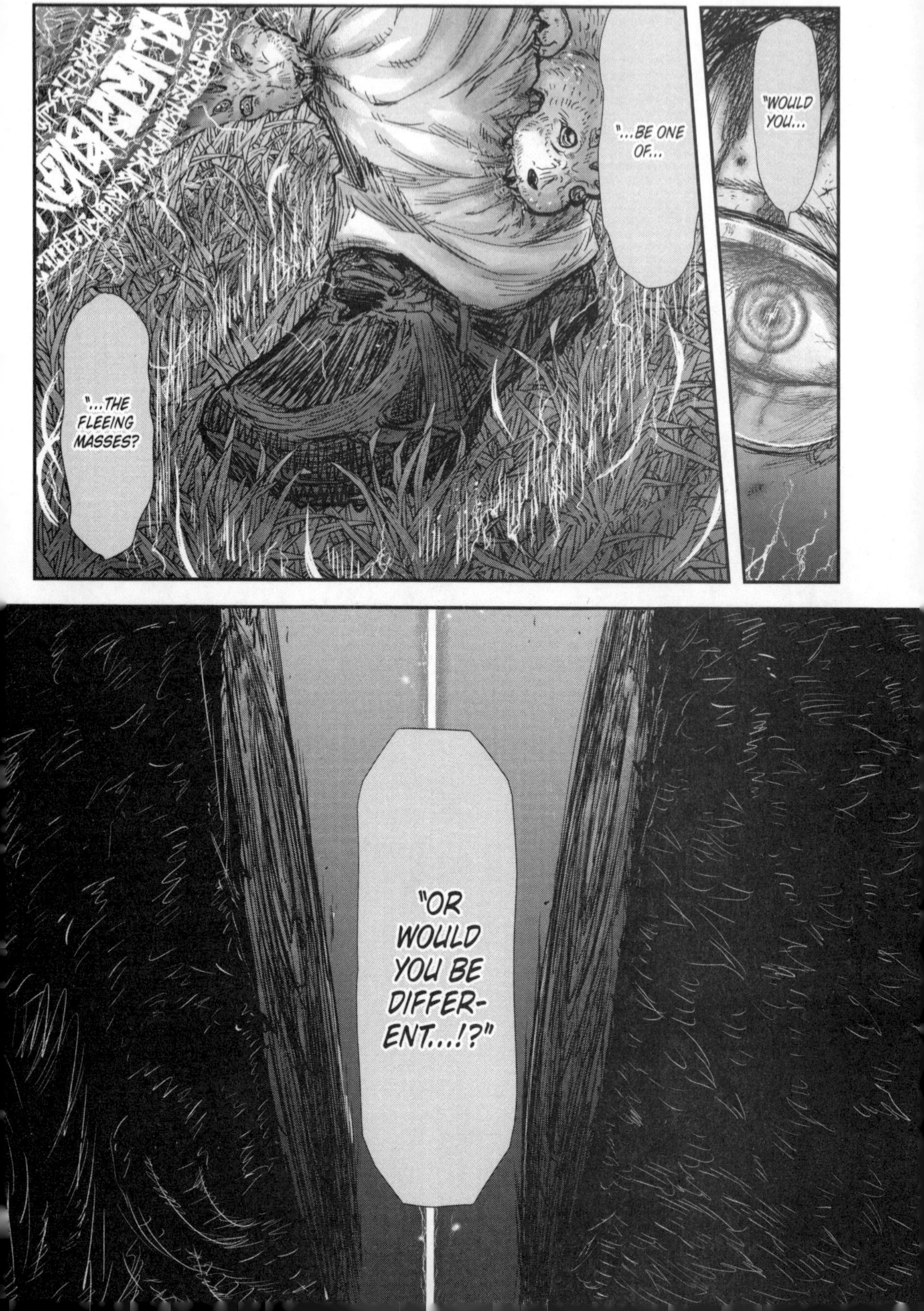
"WOULD YOU...
"...BE ONE OF...
"...THE FLEEING MASSES?
"OR WOULD YOU BE DIFFER-ENT...!?"

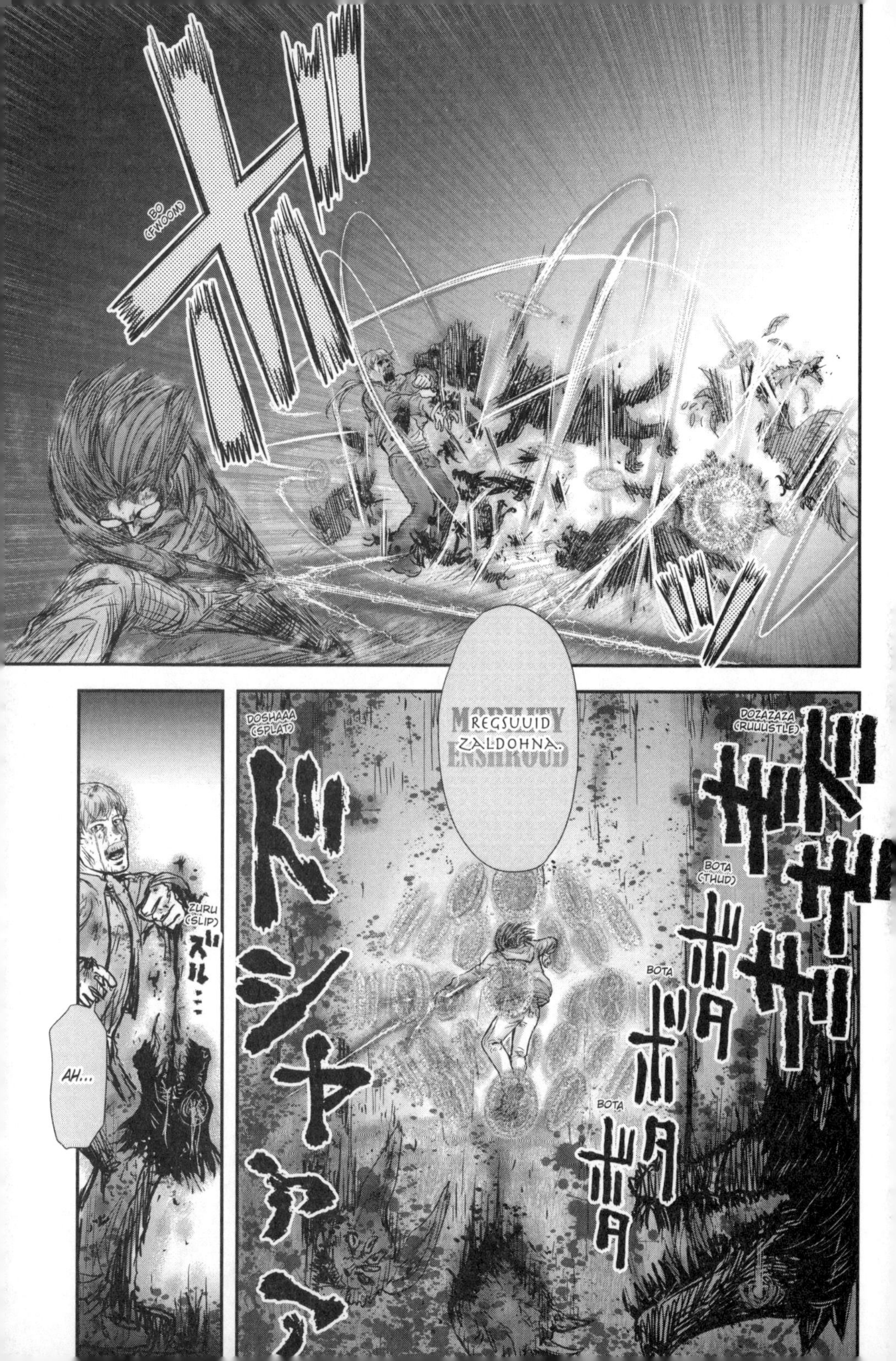
BO (FWOOM)
DOZAZAZA (RUUUSTLE)
REGSUUID ZALDOHNA.
ENSHROUD
BOTA (THUD)
BOTA
BOTA
DOSHAAA (SPLAT)
ZURU (SLIP)
AH...

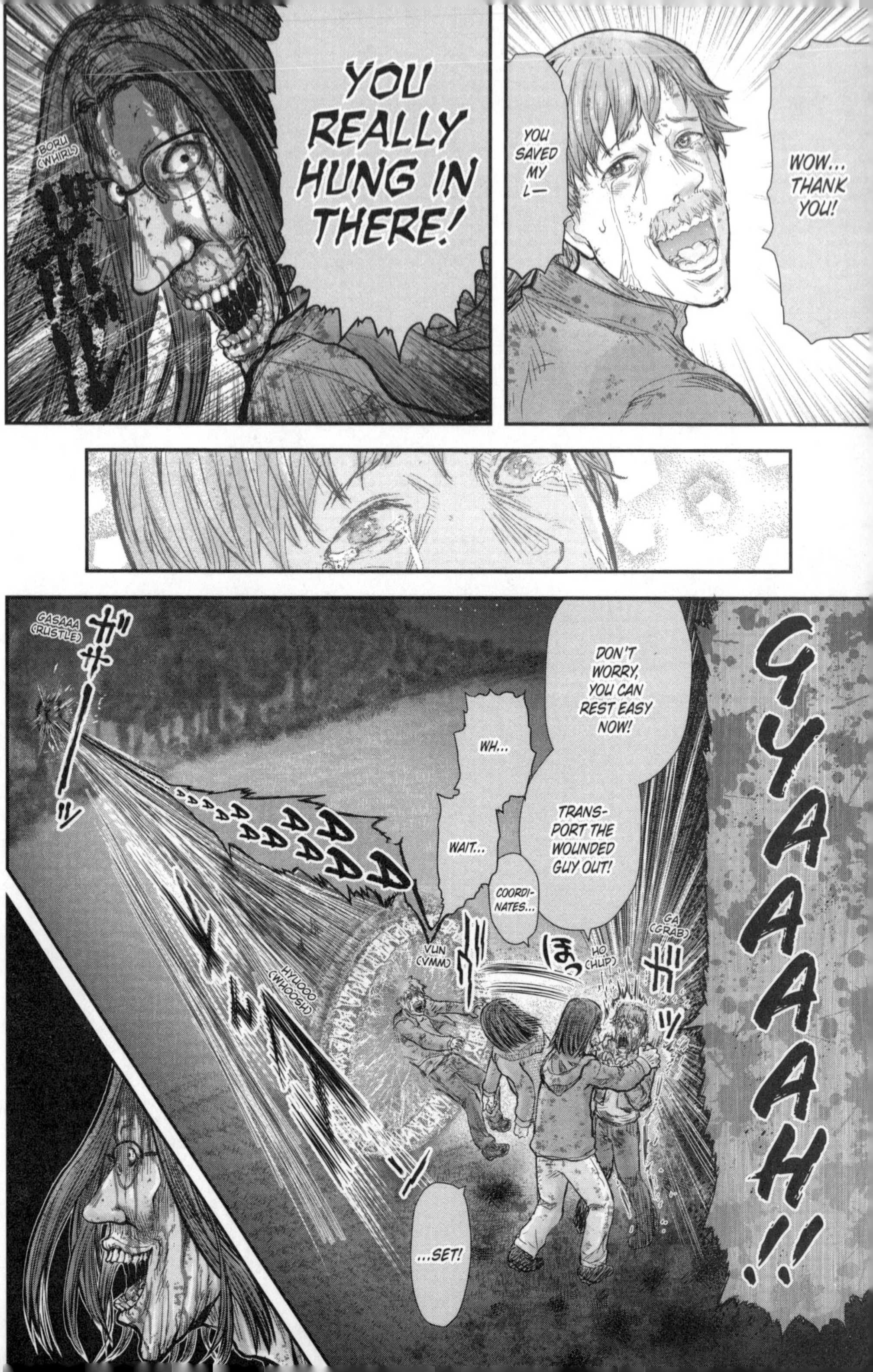
WOW... THANK YOU!
YOU SAVED MY L—
BORU (WHIRL)
YOU REALLY HUNG IN THERE!
GYAAAAAH!!
DON'T WORRY, YOU CAN REST EASY NOW!
TRANS-PORT THE WOUNDED GUY OUT!
GA (GRAB)
ほっ
HO (HUP)
WH...
WAIT...
COORDI-NATES...
VUN (VMM)
GASAAA (RUSTLE)
HYUOOO (WHOOSH)
...SET!

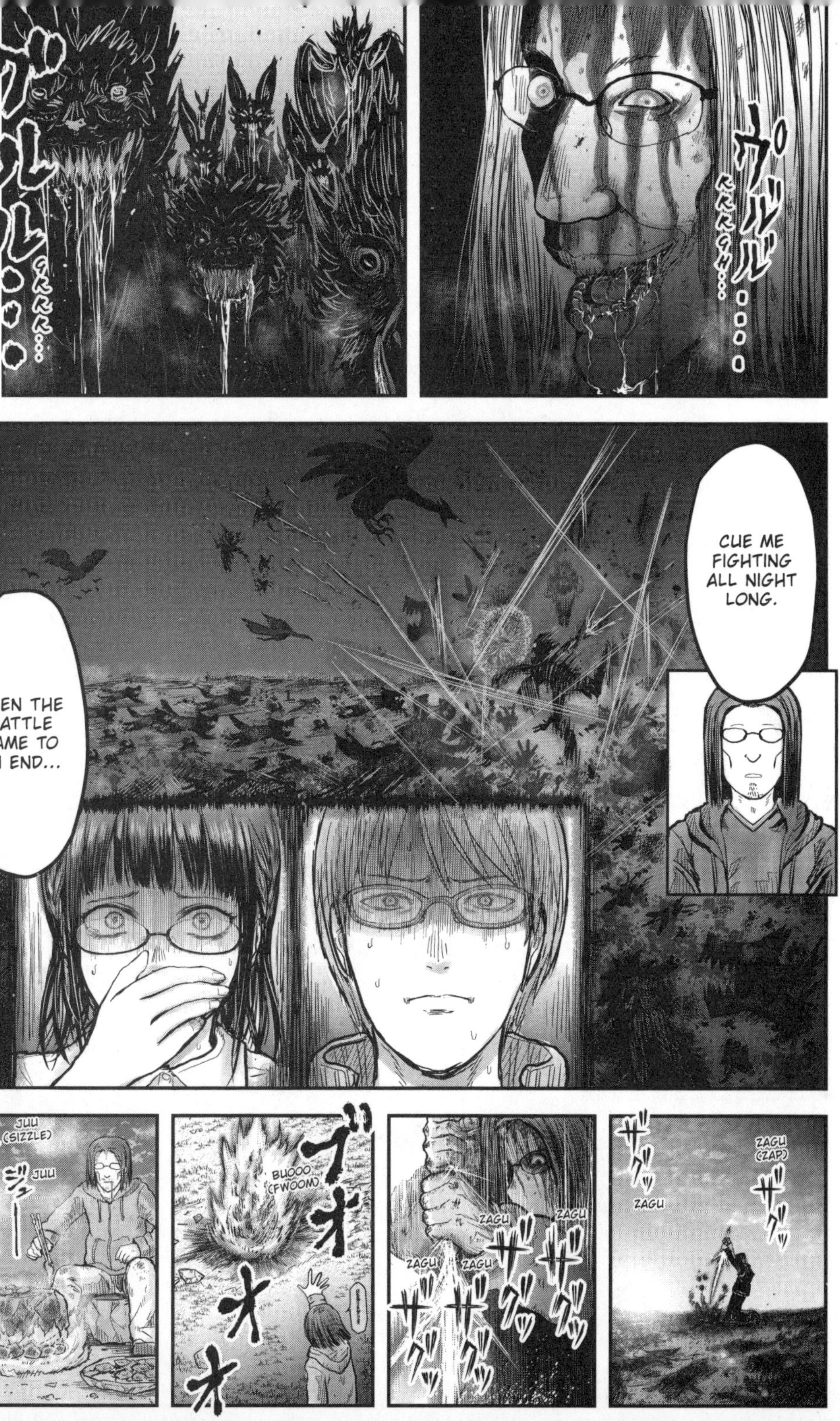
ヴルルル…
RRRRGH...
グルル…
GRRR...
CUE ME FIGHTING ALL NIGHT LONG.
THEN THE BATTLE CAME TO AN END...
ザクッ ザクッ
ZAGU (ZAP)
ZAGU
ZAGU
ZAGU
ZAGU
ZAGU
ザクッ ザクッ ザクッ ザクッ
ゴオオオ
BUOOO (FWOOM)
!
ジュー
JUU (SIZZLE)
ジュー
JUU

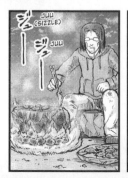

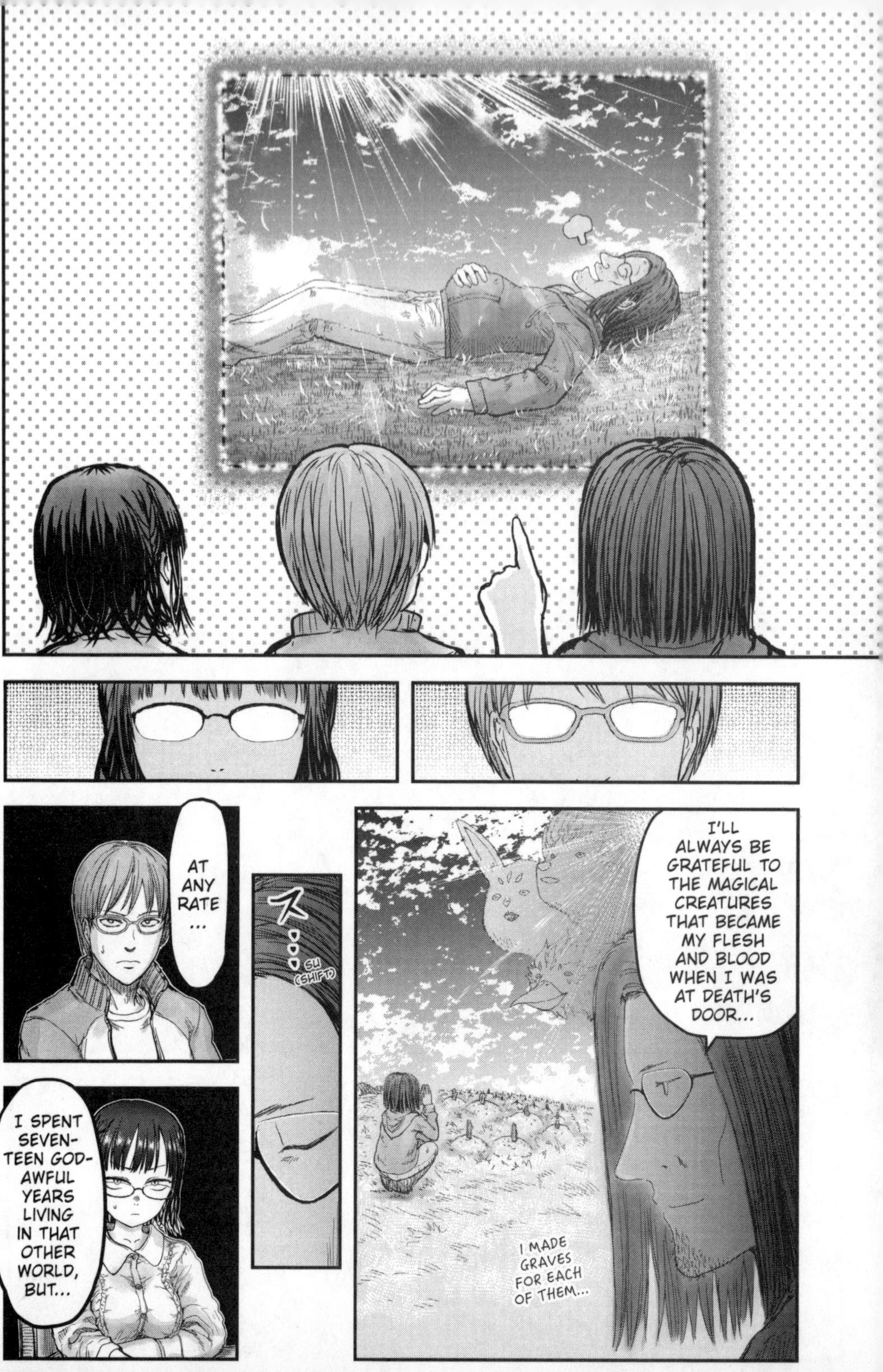
I'LL ALWAYS BE GRATEFUL TO THE MAGICAL CREATURES THAT BECAME MY FLESH AND BLOOD WHEN I WAS AT DEATH'S DOOR...
I MADE GRAVES FOR EACH OF THEM...
ス
SU (SHIFT)
AT ANY RATE...
I SPENT SEVENTEEN GOD-AWFUL YEARS LIVING IN THAT OTHER WORLD, BUT...

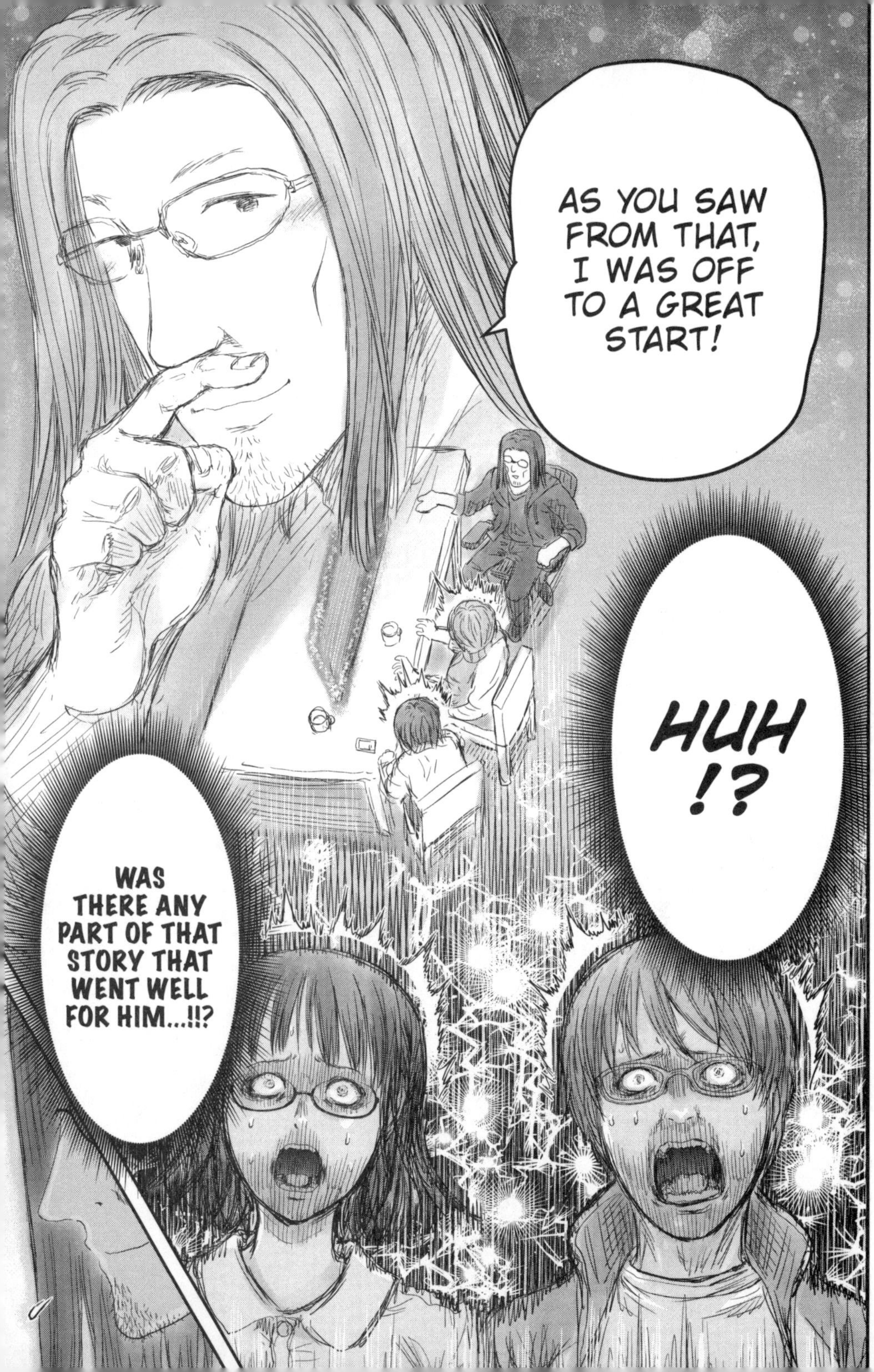
AS YOU SAW FROM THAT, I WAS OFF TO A GREAT START!
HUH !?
WAS THERE ANY PART OF THAT STORY THAT WENT WELL FOR HIM...!!?

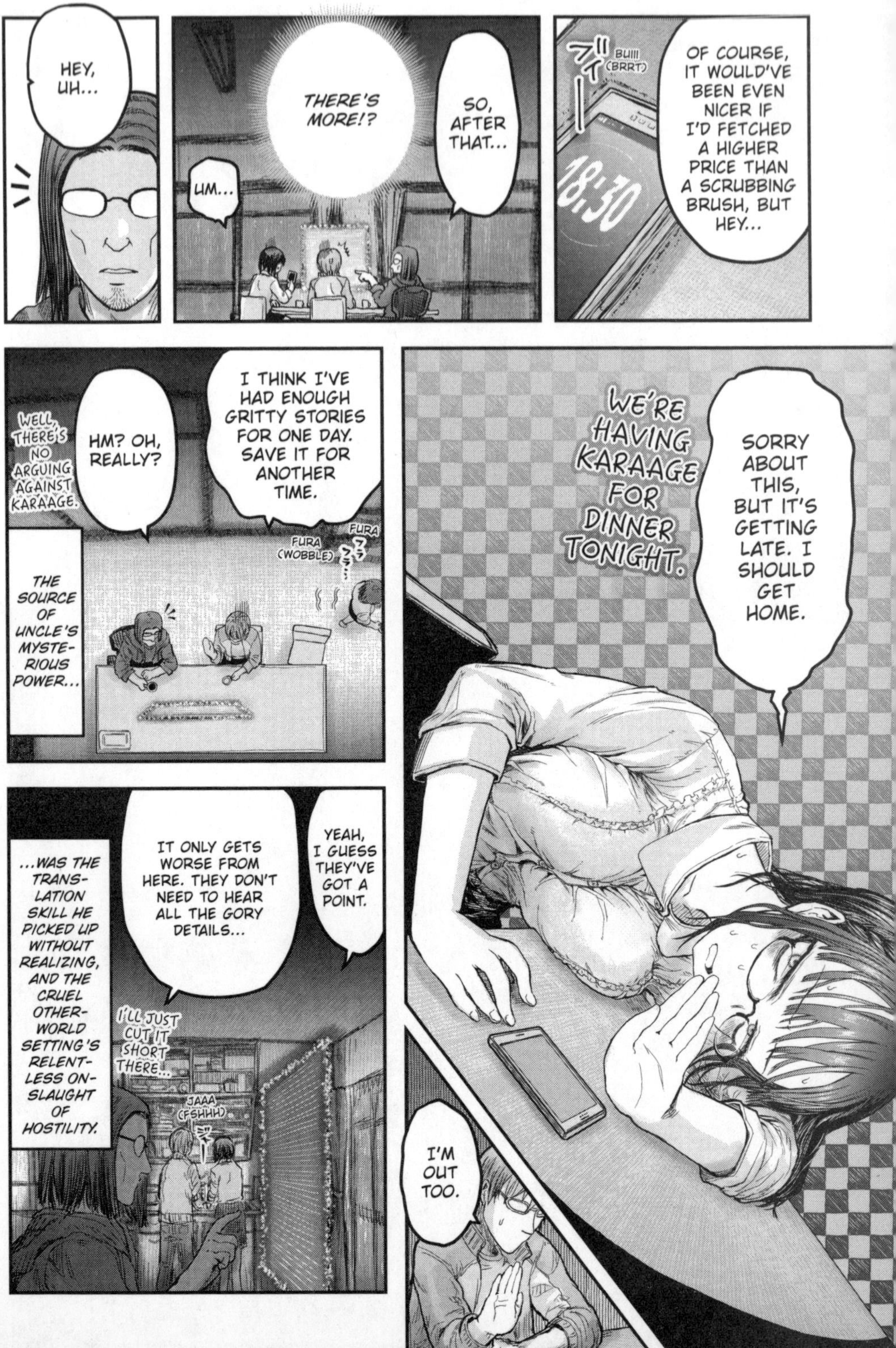
BUIII (BRRT)
18:30
OF COURSE, IT WOULD'VE BEEN EVEN NICER IF I'D FETCHED A HIGHER PRICE THAN A SCRUBBING BRUSH, BUT HEY...
SO, AFTER THAT...
THERE'S MORE!?
UM...
HEY, UH...
SORRY ABOUT THIS, BUT IT'S GETTING LATE. I SHOULD GET HOME.
WE'RE HAVING KARAAGE FOR DINNER TONIGHT.
I'M OUT TOO.
I THINK I'VE HAD ENOUGH GRITTY STORIES FOR ONE DAY. SAVE IT FOR ANOTHER TIME.
HM? OH, REALLY?
WELL, THERE'S NO ARGUING AGAINST KARAAGE.
FURA FURA (WOBBLE)
THE SOURCE OF UNCLE'S MYSTERIOUS POWER...
YEAH, I GUESS THEY'VE GOT A POINT.
IT ONLY GETS WORSE FROM HERE. THEY DON'T NEED TO HEAR ALL THE GORY DETAILS...
...WAS THE TRANSLATION SKILL HE PICKED UP WITHOUT REALIZING, AND THE CRUEL OTHERWORLD SETTING'S RELENTLESS ONSLAUGHT OF HOSTILITY.
I'LL JUST CUT IT SHORT THERE...
JAAA (FSHHH)

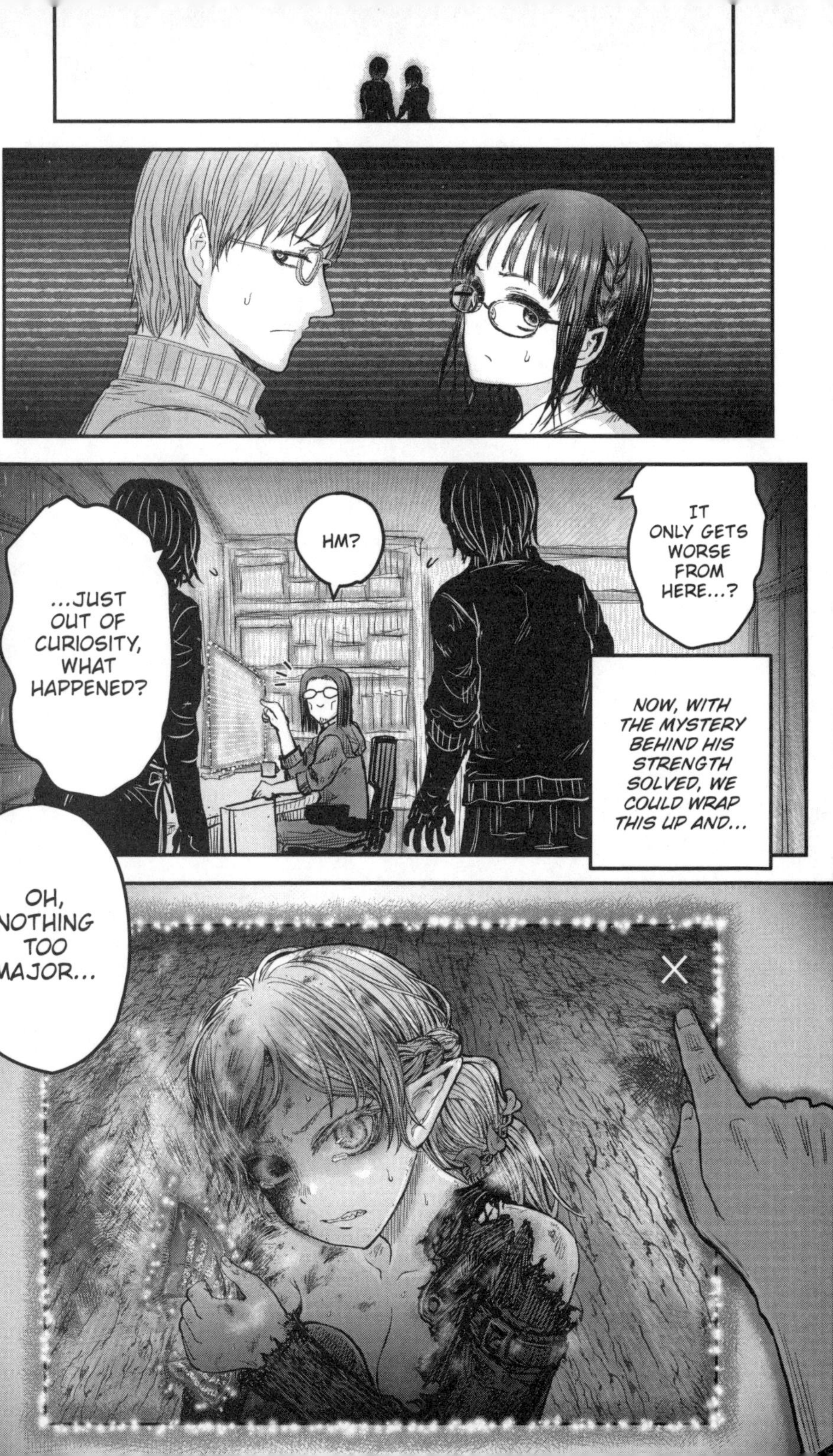
IT ONLY GETS WORSE FROM HERE...?
NOW, WITH THE MYSTERY BEHIND HIS STRENGTH SOLVED, WE COULD WRAP THIS UP AND...
HM?
...JUST OUT OF CURIOSITY, WHAT HAPPENED?
OH, NOTHING TOO MAJOR...

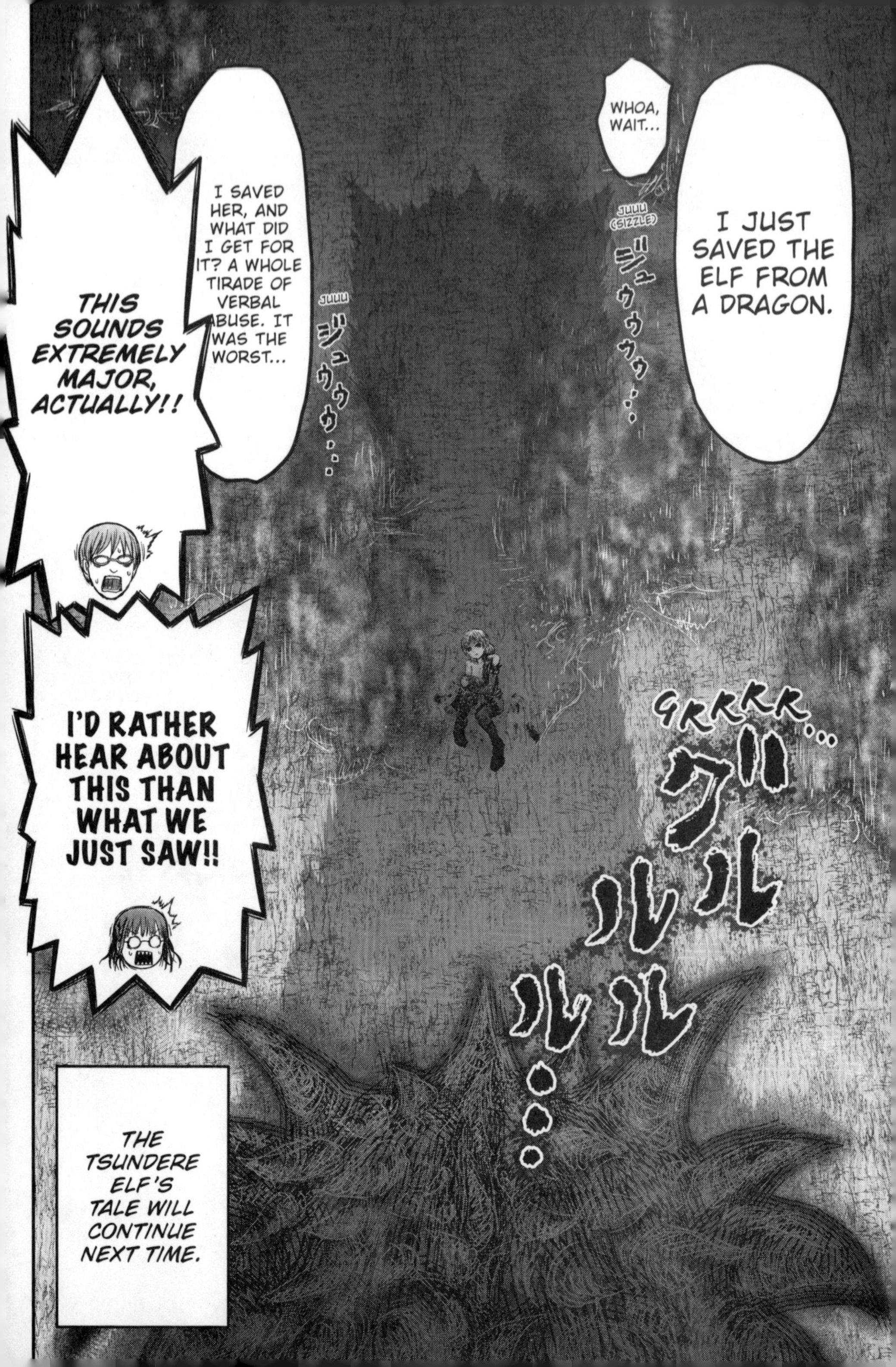

I JUST SAVED THE ELF FROM A DRAGON.
WHOA, WAIT...
JUUU (SIZZLE)
ジュウウウウ・・
I SAVED HER, AND WHAT DID I GET FOR IT? A WHOLE TIRADE OF VERBAL ABUSE. IT WAS THE WORST...
JUUU
ジュウウウ・・
THIS SOUNDS EXTREMELY MAJOR, ACTUALLY!!
I'D RATHER HEAR ABOUT THIS THAN WHAT WE JUST SAW!!
GRRRR...
グルルルルル・・・
THE TSUNDERE ELF'S TALE WILL CONTINUE NEXT TIME.

Rule of Threes

In survival, the generally accepted knowledge is that in adverse conditions, humans can survive up to three days without drinking water, after which point they will perish.
Other commonly associated statements: People can survive up to three weeks without food, and up to three months in solitude.

TIPS

UNCLE from ANOTHER WORLD

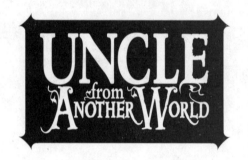

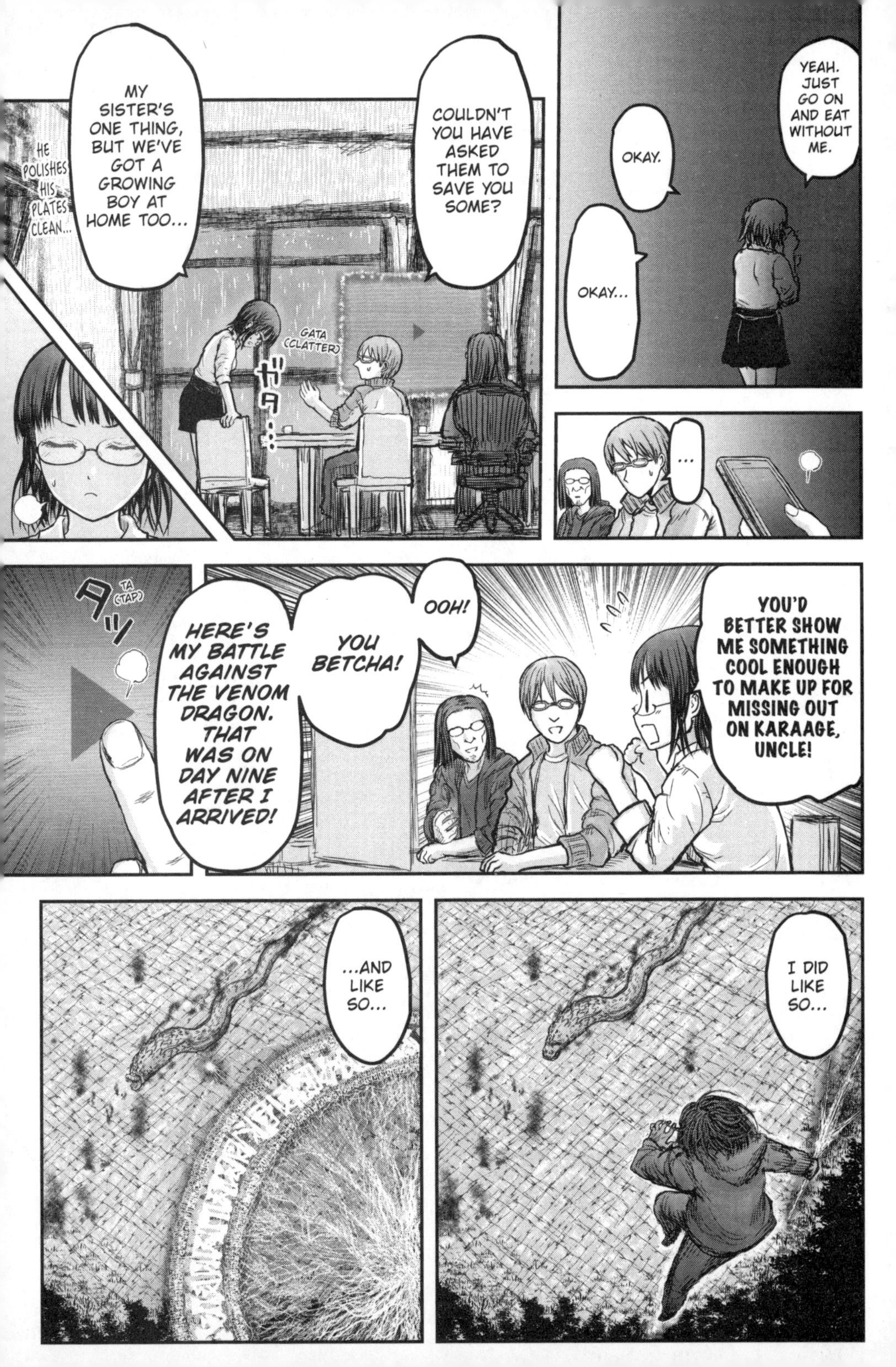
YEAH. JUST GO ON AND EAT WITHOUT ME.
OKAY.
OKAY...
...
COULDN'T YOU HAVE ASKED THEM TO SAVE YOU SOME?
MY SISTER'S ONE THING, BUT WE'VE GOT A GROWING BOY AT HOME TOO...
HE POLISHES HIS PLATES CLEAN...
GATA (CLATTER)
ガタ
YOU'D BETTER SHOW ME SOMETHING COOL ENOUGH TO MAKE UP FOR MISSING OUT ON KARAAGE, UNCLE!
OOH!
YOU BETCHA!
HERE'S MY BATTLE AGAINST THE VENOM DRAGON. THAT WAS ON DAY NINE AFTER I ARRIVED!
TA (TAP)
タッ
I DID LIKE SO...
...AND LIKE SO...

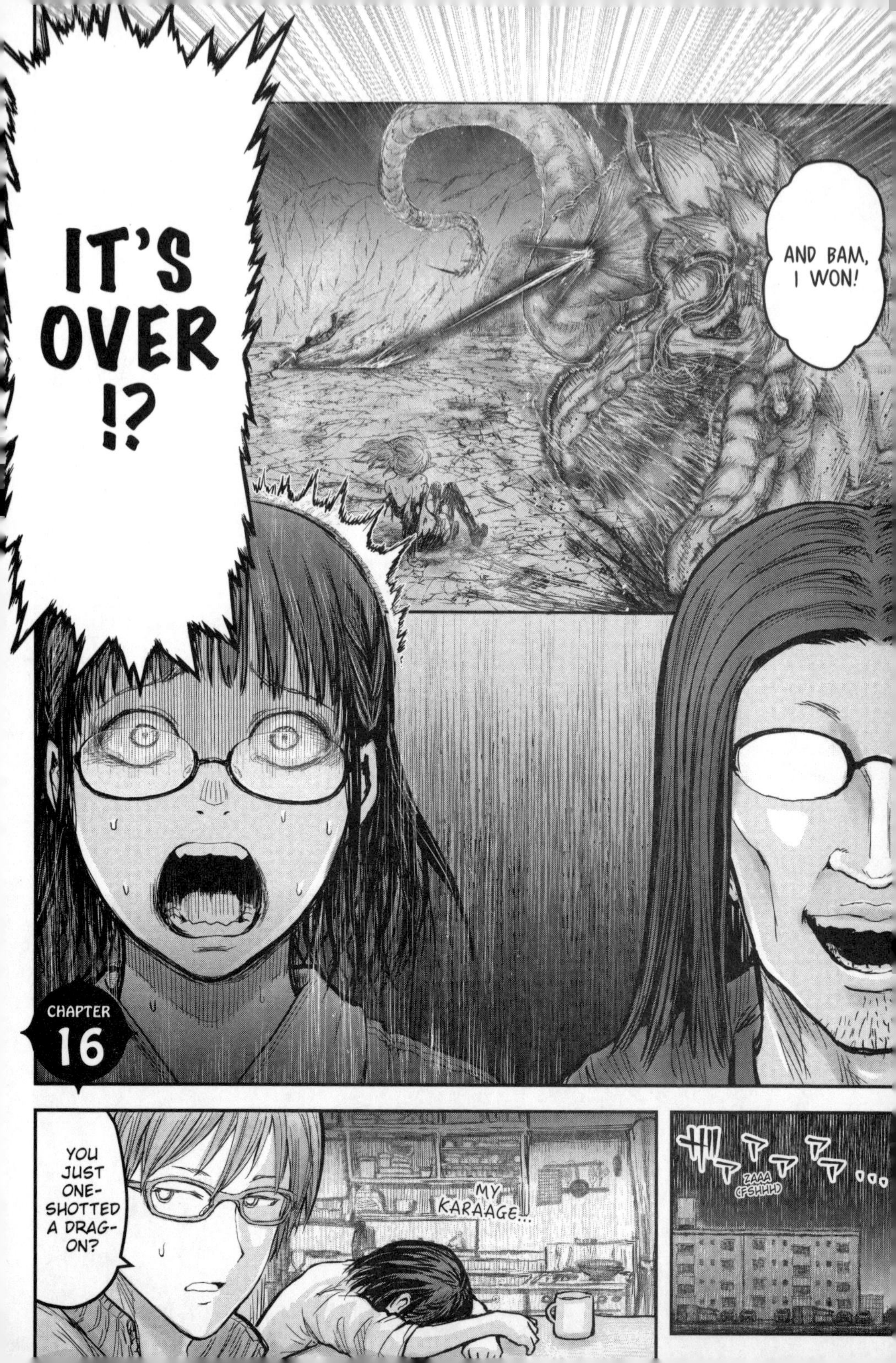
AND BAM, I WON!
IT'S OVER!?
CHAPTER 16
ZAAA (FSHHH)
MY KARAAGE...
YOU JUST ONE-SHOTTED A DRAGON?

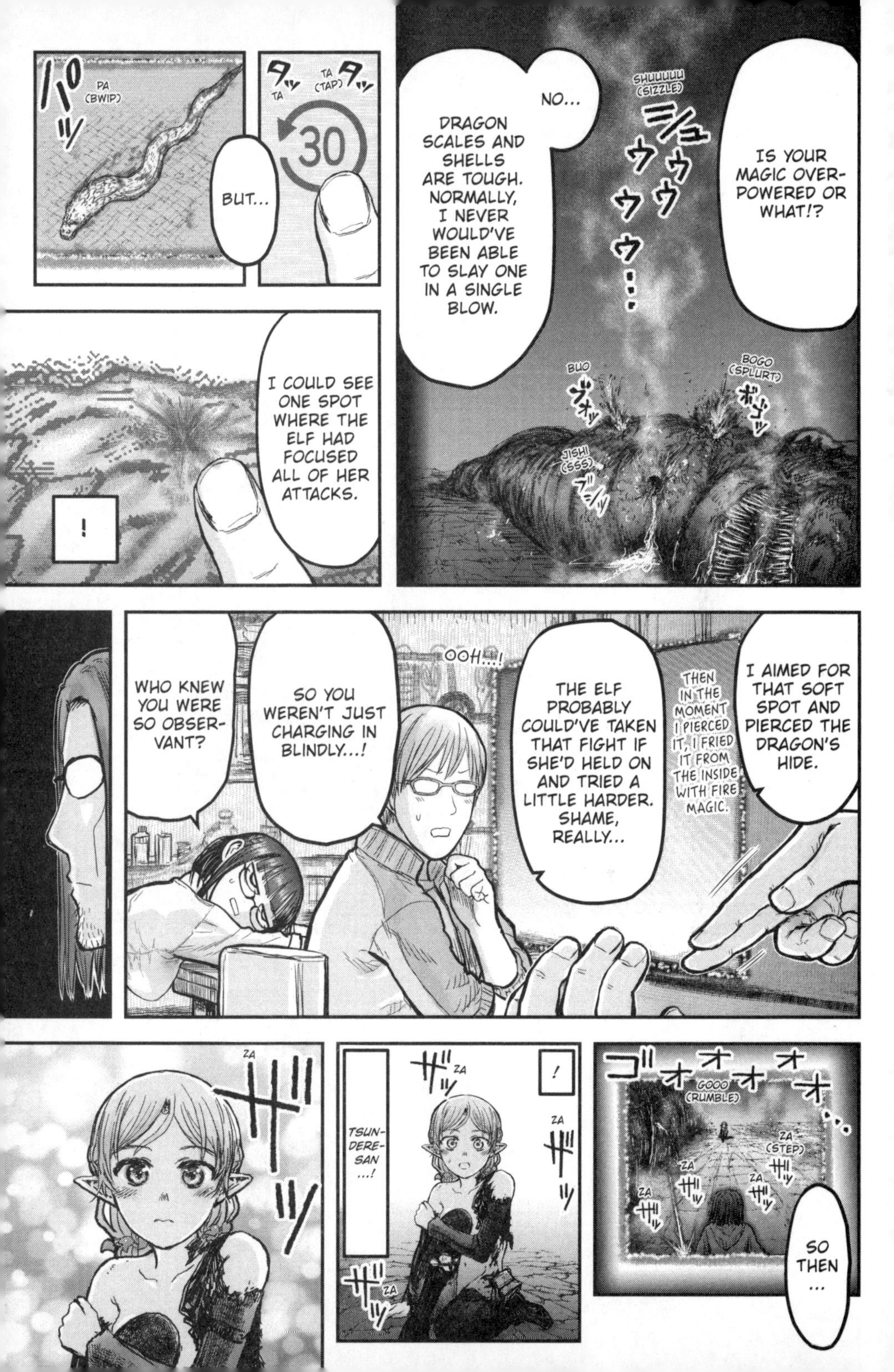

IS YOUR MAGIC OVER-POWERED OR WHAT!?
SHUUUUU (SIZZLE)
シュウウウウウ…
NO…
DRAGON SCALES AND SHELLS ARE TOUGH. NORMALLY, I NEVER WOULD'VE BEEN ABLE TO SLAY ONE IN A SINGLE BLOW.
BOGO (SPLURT)
ボゴッ
BUO
ブオッ
JISHI (SSS)
ジシッ
TA (TAP) タッ
TA タッ
30
BUT…
PA (BWIP)
パッ
I COULD SEE ONE SPOT WHERE THE ELF HAD FOCUSED ALL OF HER ATTACKS.
!
I AIMED FOR THAT SOFT SPOT AND PIERCED THE DRAGON'S HIDE.
THEN IN THE MOMENT I PIERCED IT, I FRIED IT FROM THE INSIDE WITH FIRE MAGIC.
THE ELF PROBABLY COULD'VE TAKEN THAT FIGHT IF SHE'D HELD ON AND TRIED A LITTLE HARDER. SHAME, REALLY…
OOH…!
SO YOU WEREN'T JUST CHARGING IN BLINDLY…!
WHO KNEW YOU WERE SO OBSER-VANT?
ゴオオオオ…
GOOO (RUMBLE)
ZA (STEP)
ザッ
ZA ザッ
ZA ザッ
ZA ザッ
SO THEN…
!
ZA ザッ
ZA ザッ
TSUN-DERE-SAN…!
ZA ザッ
ZA ザッ

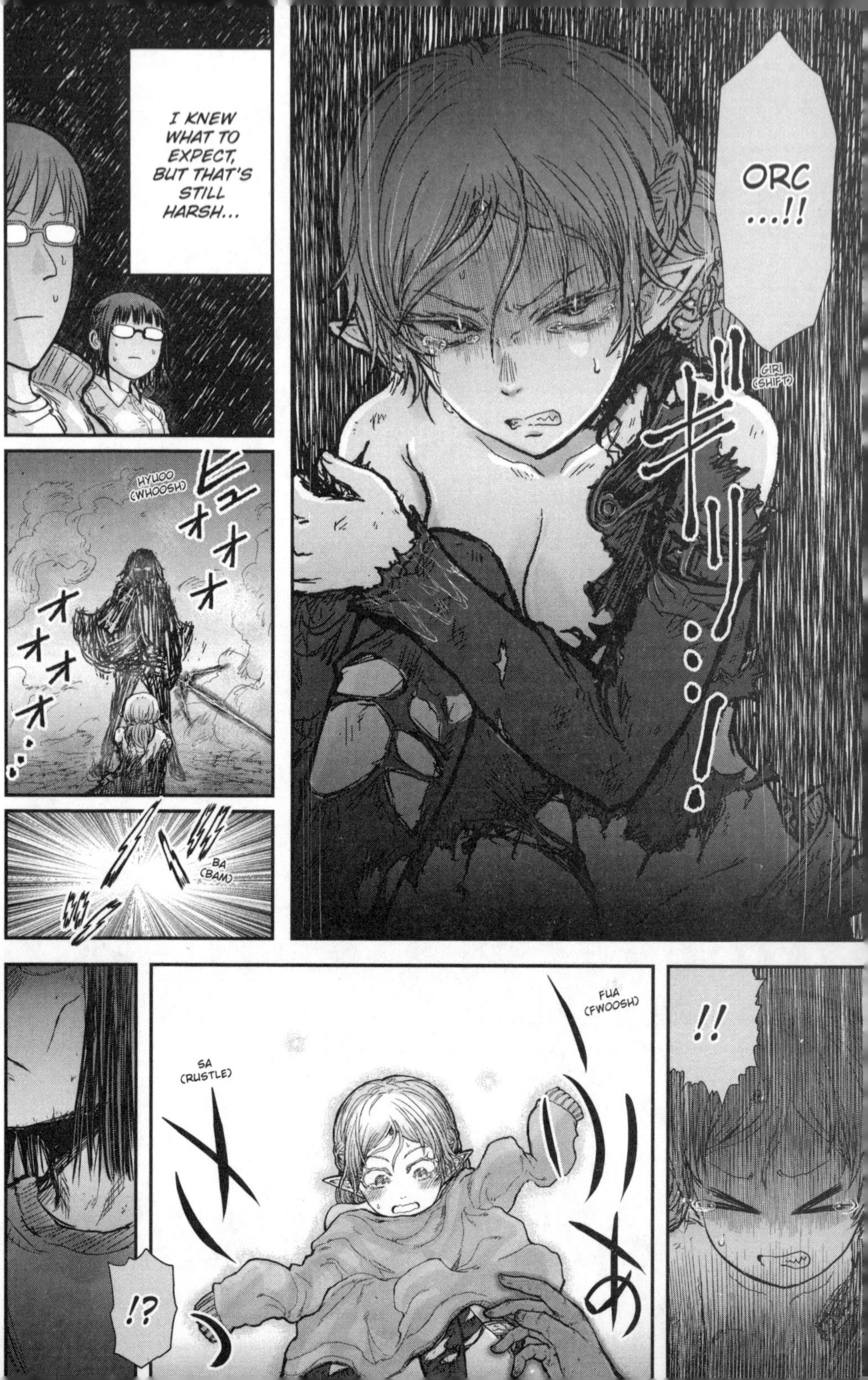
ORC ...!!
GIRI (SHIFT)
I KNEW WHAT TO EXPECT, BUT THAT'S STILL HARSH...
HYUOO (WHOOSH)
BA (BAM)
!!
FUA (FWOOSH)
SA (RUSTLE)
!?

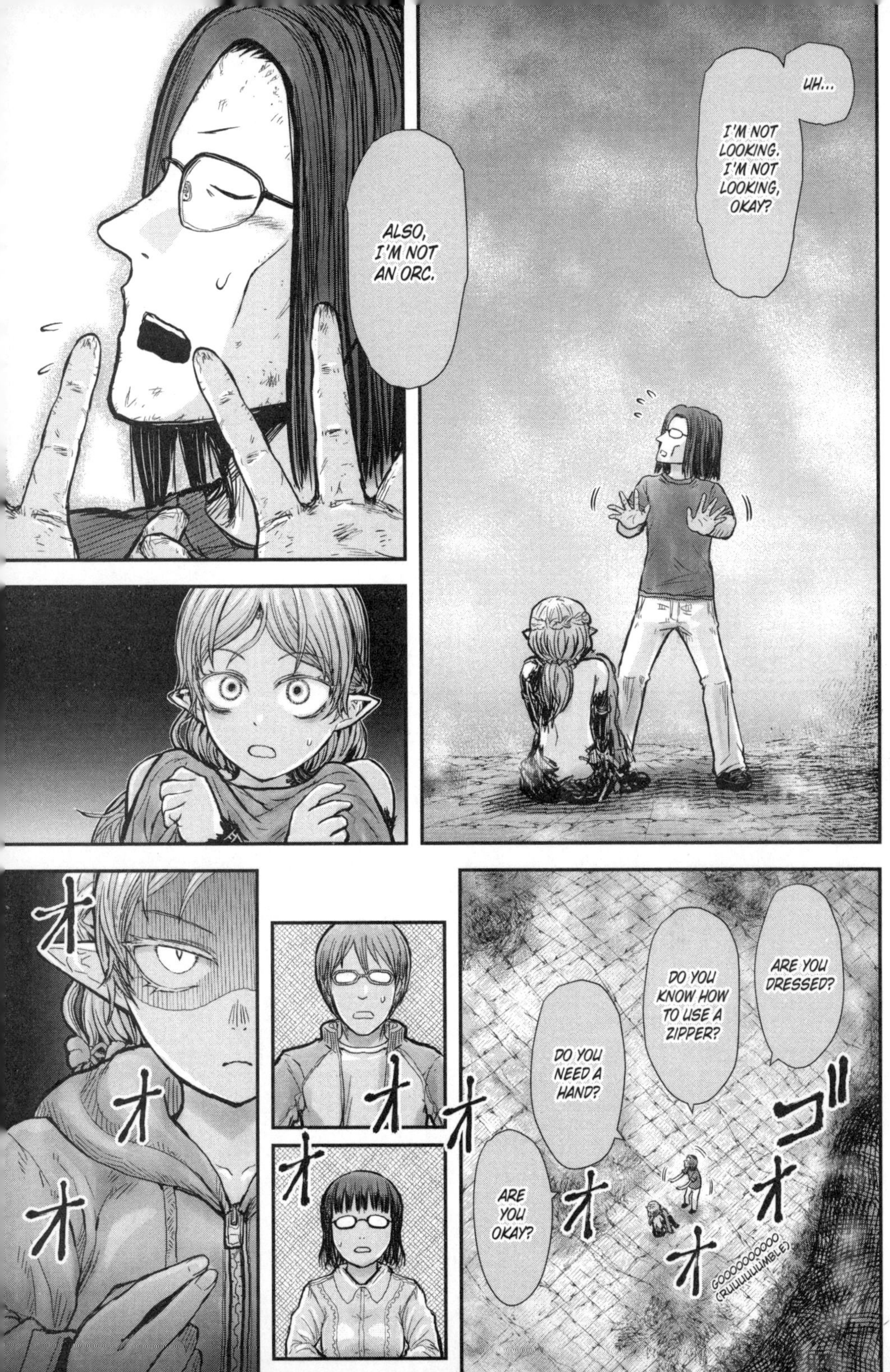
UH...
I'M NOT LOOKING. I'M NOT LOOKING, OKAY?
ALSO, I'M NOT AN ORC.
ARE YOU DRESSED?
DO YOU KNOW HOW TO USE A ZIPPER?
DO YOU NEED A HAND?
ARE YOU OKAY?
ゴオオオ
GOOOOOOOOOO (RUUUUUUMBLE)
オオオオオオ

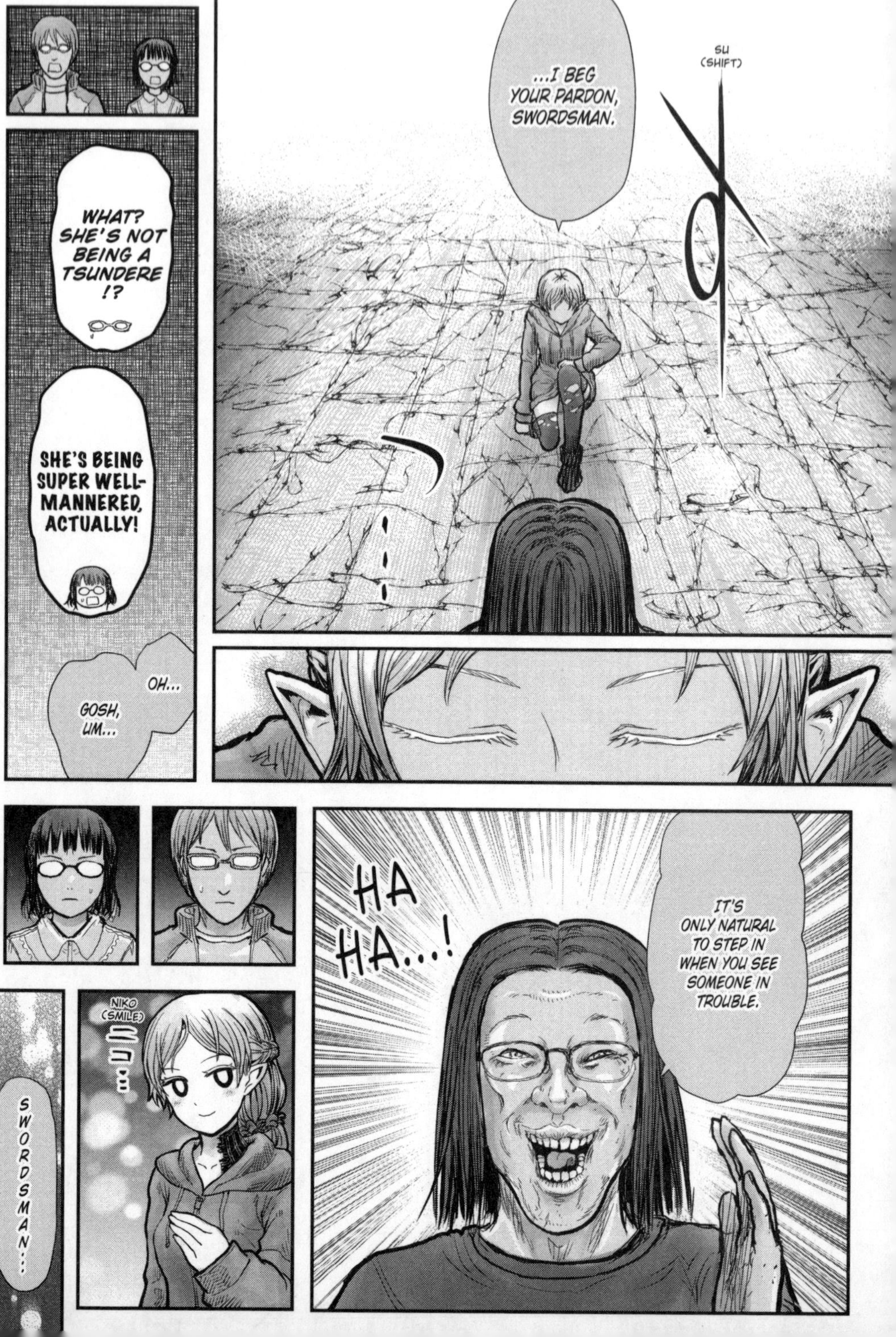
SU (SHIFT)
...I BEG YOUR PARDON, SWORDSMAN.
...
WHAT? SHE'S NOT BEING A TSUNDERE!?
SHE'S BEING SUPER WELL-MANNERED, ACTUALLY!
OH...
GOSH, UM...
HA HA...!
IT'S ONLY NATURAL TO STEP IN WHEN YOU SEE SOMEONE IN TROUBLE.
NIKO (SMILE)
SWORDSMAN...

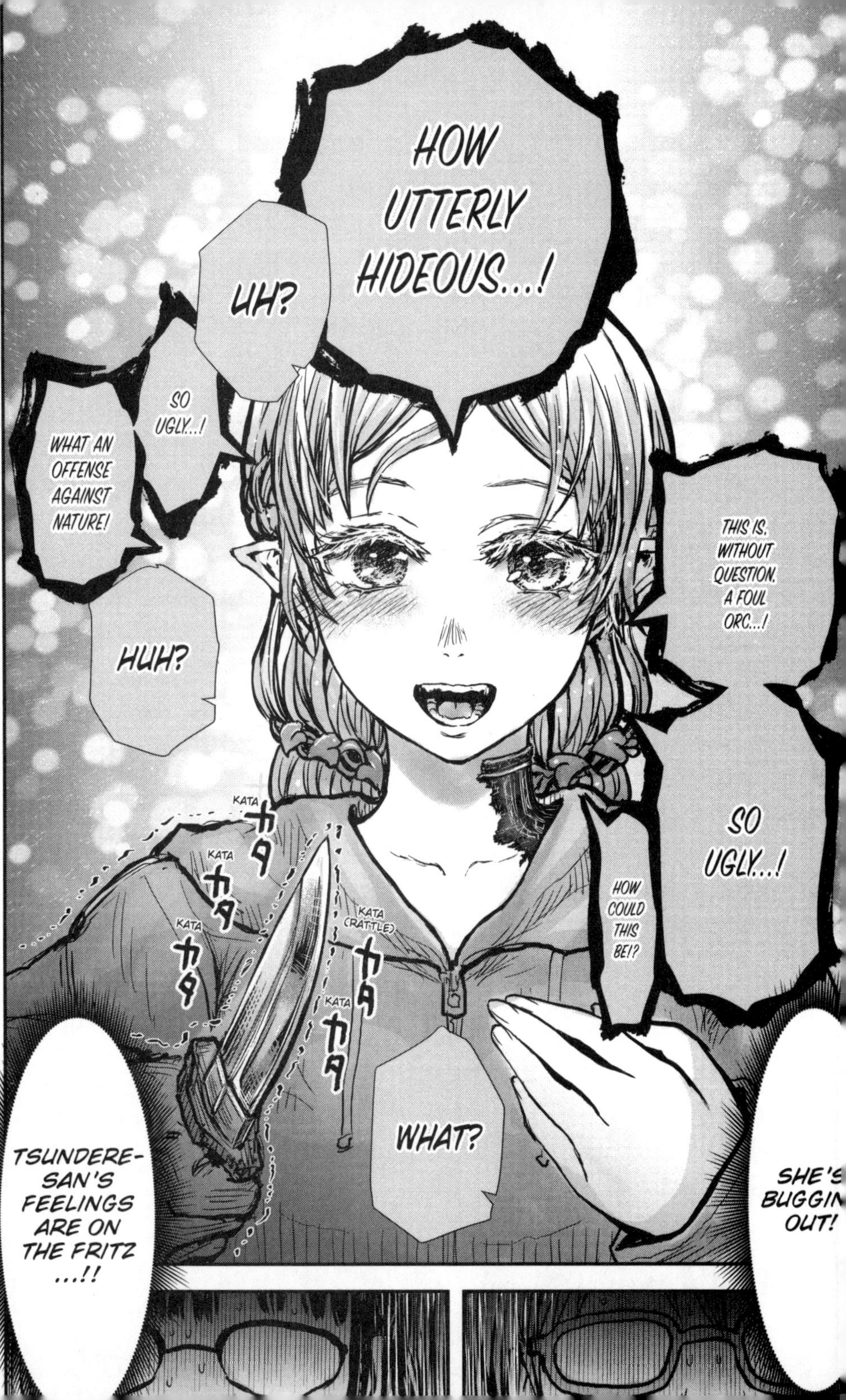

HOW UTTERLY HIDEOUS...!
UH?
SO UGLY...!
WHAT AN OFFENSE AGAINST NATURE!
HUH?
THIS IS, WITHOUT QUESTION, A FOUL ORC...!
SO UGLY...!
HOW COULD THIS BE!?
WHAT?
KATA (RATTLE) カタ
KATA カタ
KATA カタ
KATA カタ
KATA カタ
SHE'S BUGGIN OUT!
TSUNDERE-SAN'S FEELINGS ARE ON THE FRITZ ...!!

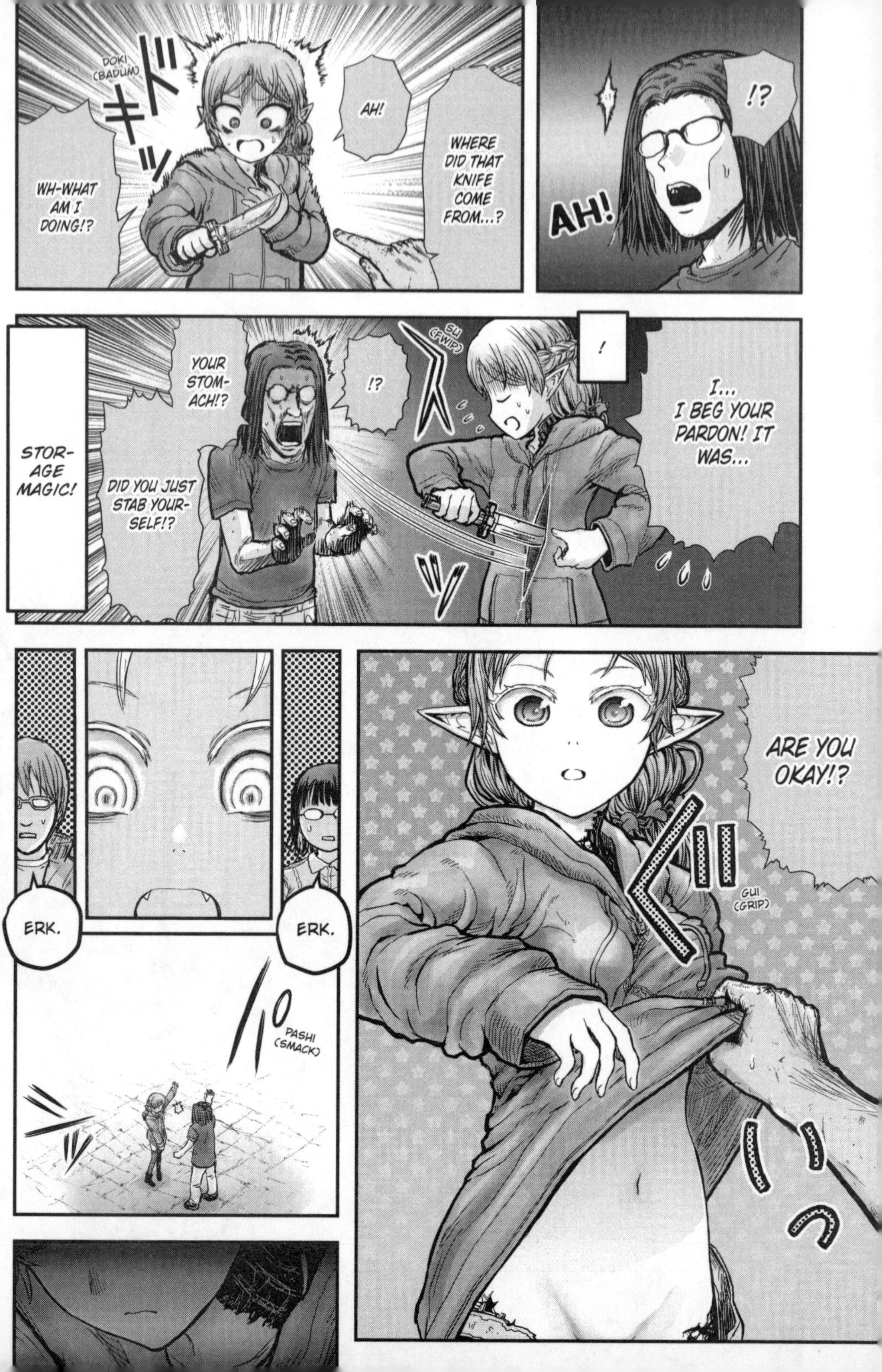

!?
AH!
AH!
WHERE DID THAT KNIFE COME FROM...?
DOKI (BADUM)
WH-WHAT AM I DOING!?
!
I... I BEG YOUR PARDON! IT WAS...
SU (FWIP)
!?
YOUR STOM-ACH!?
DID YOU JUST STAB YOUR-SELF!?
STOR-AGE MAGIC!
ARE YOU OKAY!?
GUI (GRIP)
ERK.
ERK.
PASHI (SMACK)

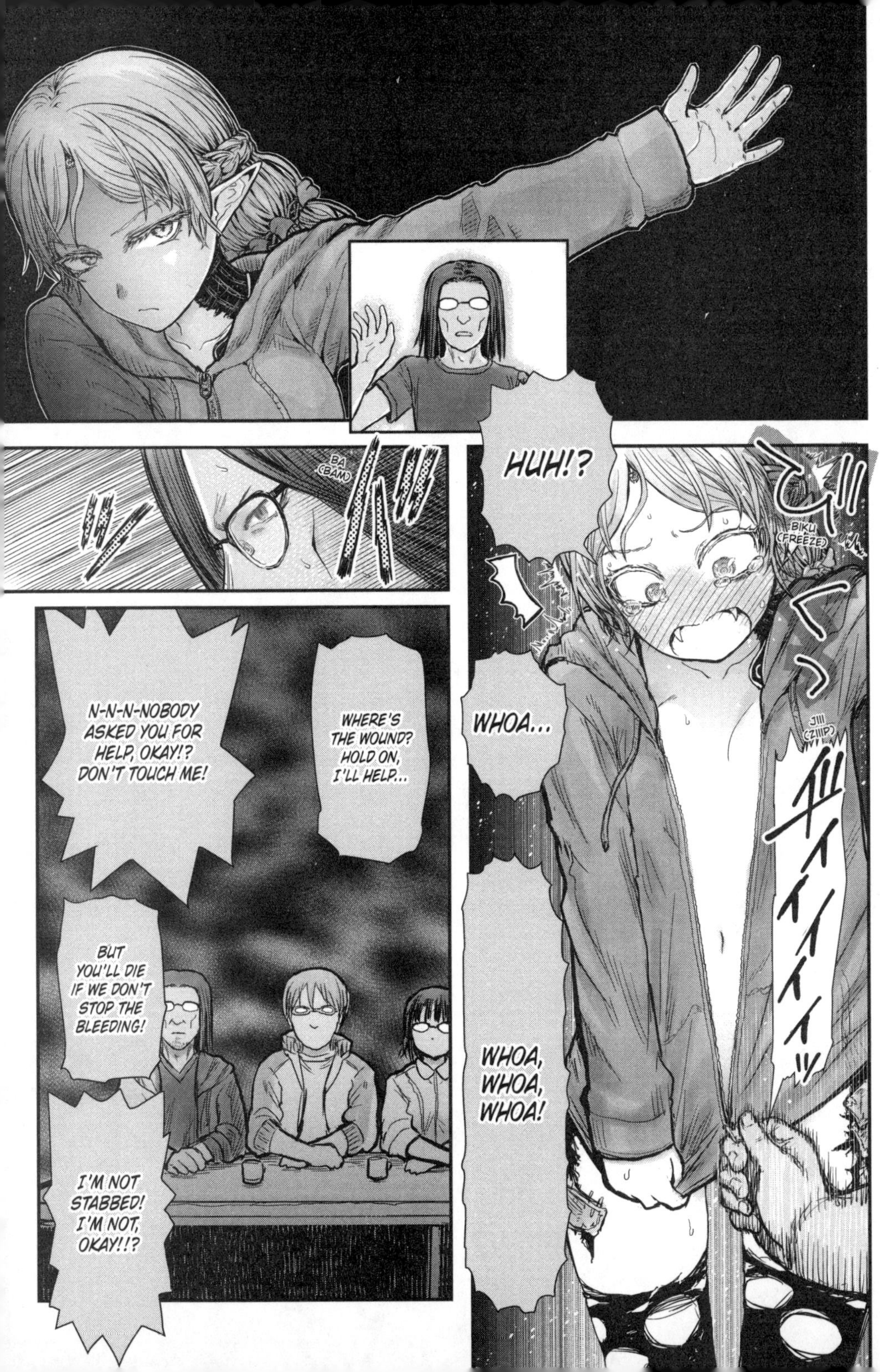

HUH!?
BIKU (FREEZE)
WHOA...
JIII (ZIIIP)
WHOA, WHOA, WHOA!
BA (BAM)
WHERE'S THE WOUND? HOLD ON, I'LL HELP...
N-N-N-NOBODY ASKED YOU FOR HELP, OKAY!? DON'T TOUCH ME!
BUT YOU'LL DIE IF WE DON'T STOP THE BLEEDING!
I'M NOT STABBED! I'M NOT, OKAY!!?

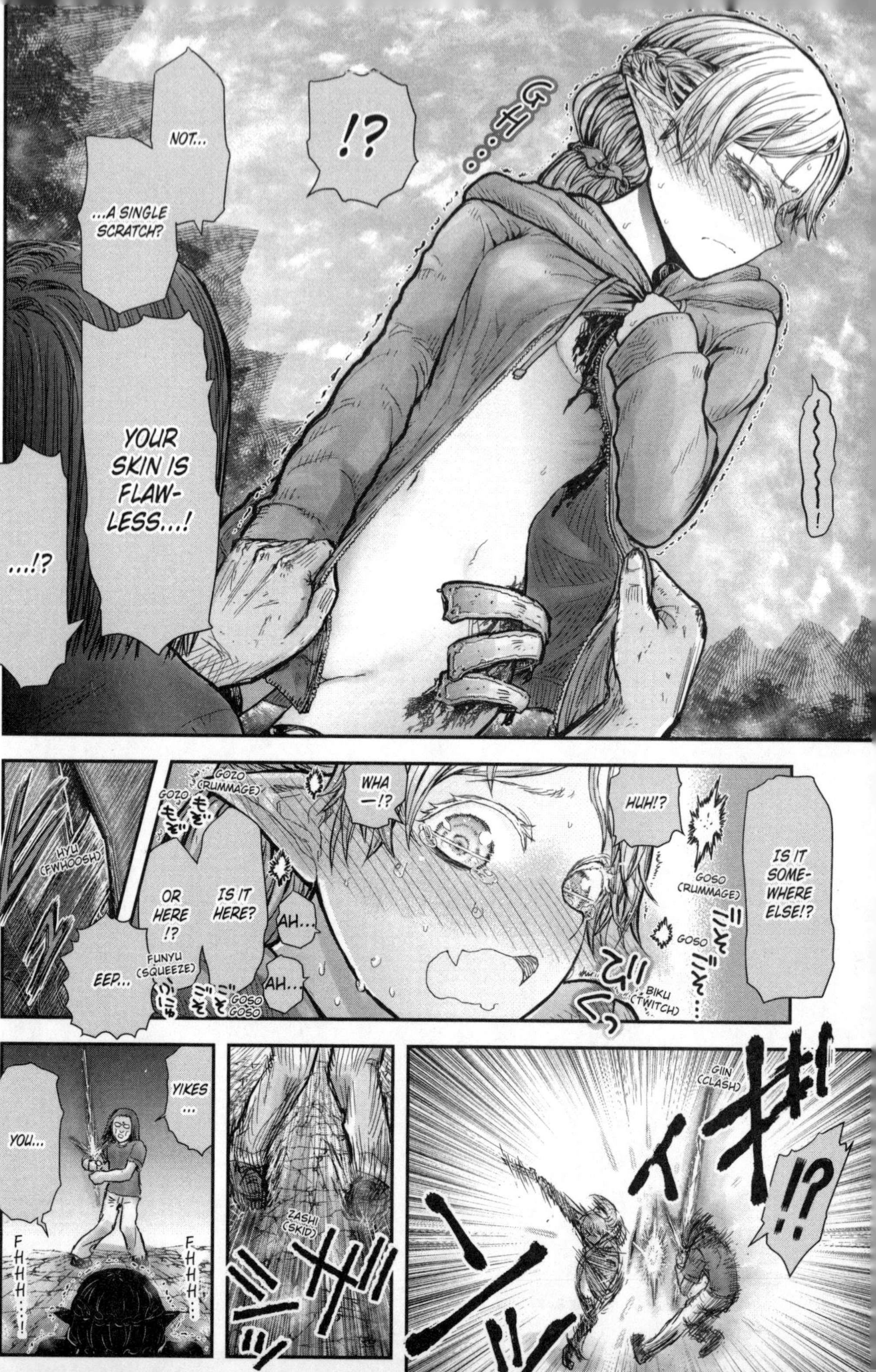
......!
!?
NOT...
...A SINGLE SCRATCH?
YOUR SKIN IS FLAWLESS...!
...!?
IS IT SOMEWHERE ELSE!?
GOSO (RUMMAGE)
GOSO
BIKU (TWITCH)
HUH!?
WHA—!?
GOZO GOZO (RUMMAGE)
IS IT HERE?
OR HERE!?
AH...
AH...
GOSO GOSO
FUNYU (SQUEEZE)
EEP...
HYU (FWHOOSH)
GIIN (CLASH)
!!?
ZASHI (SKID)
YIKES...
YOU...
FHHH...!
FHHH...!

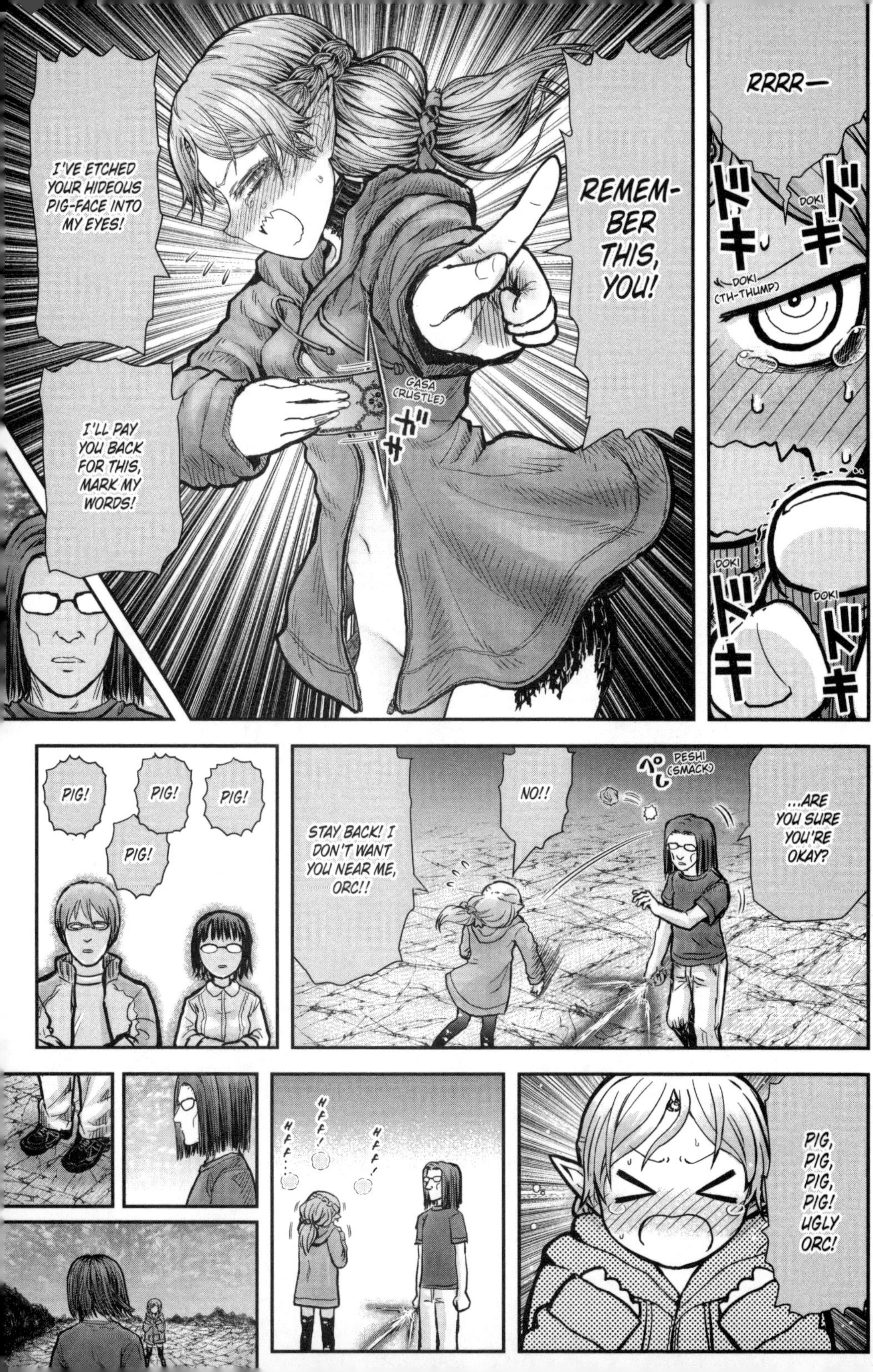
RRRR—
ドキ
DOKI
ドキ
DOKI (TH-THUMP)
ドキ
DOKI
ドキ
DOKI
REMEMBER THIS, YOU!
I'VE ETCHED YOUR HIDEOUS PIG-FACE INTO MY EYES!
ガサ
GASA (RUSTLE)
I'LL PAY YOU BACK FOR THIS, MARK MY WORDS!
...ARE YOU SURE YOU'RE OKAY?
ぺし
PESHI (SMACK)
NO!!
STAY BACK! I DON'T WANT YOU NEAR ME, ORC!!
PIG!
PIG!
PIG!
PIG!
PIG, PIG, PIG, PIG! UGLY ORC!
HFF!
HFF!
HFF...

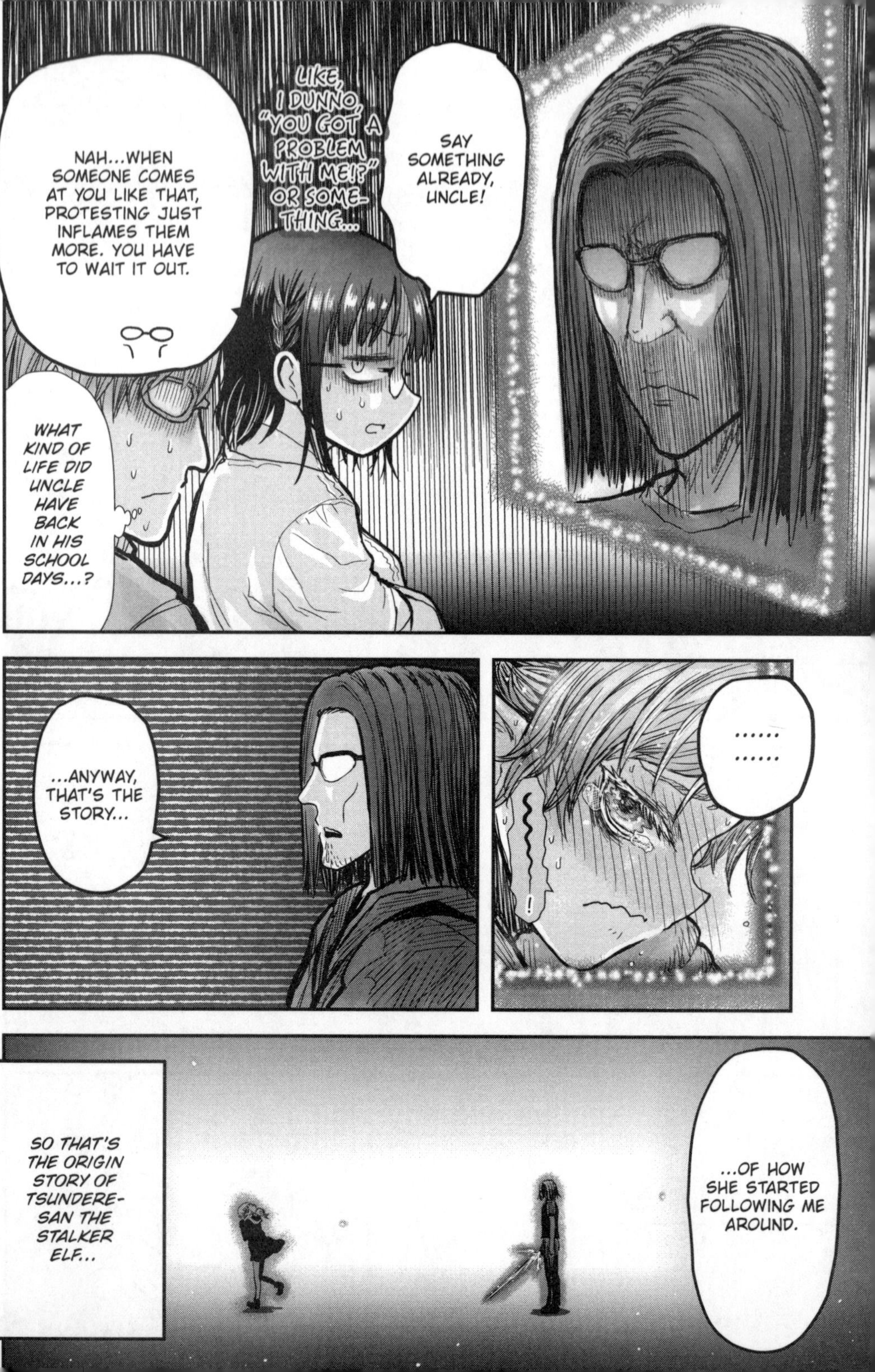
SAY SOMETHING ALREADY, UNCLE!
LIKE, I DUNNO, "YOU GOT A PROBLEM WITH ME!?" OR SOME-THING...
NAH...WHEN SOMEONE COMES AT YOU LIKE THAT, PROTESTING JUST INFLAMES THEM MORE. YOU HAVE TO WAIT IT OUT.
WHAT KIND OF LIFE DID UNCLE HAVE BACK IN HIS SCHOOL DAYS...?
....
...ANYWAY, THAT'S THE STORY...
...OF HOW SHE STARTED FOLLOWING ME AROUND.
SO THAT'S THE ORIGIN STORY OF TSUNDERE-SAN THE STALKER ELF...

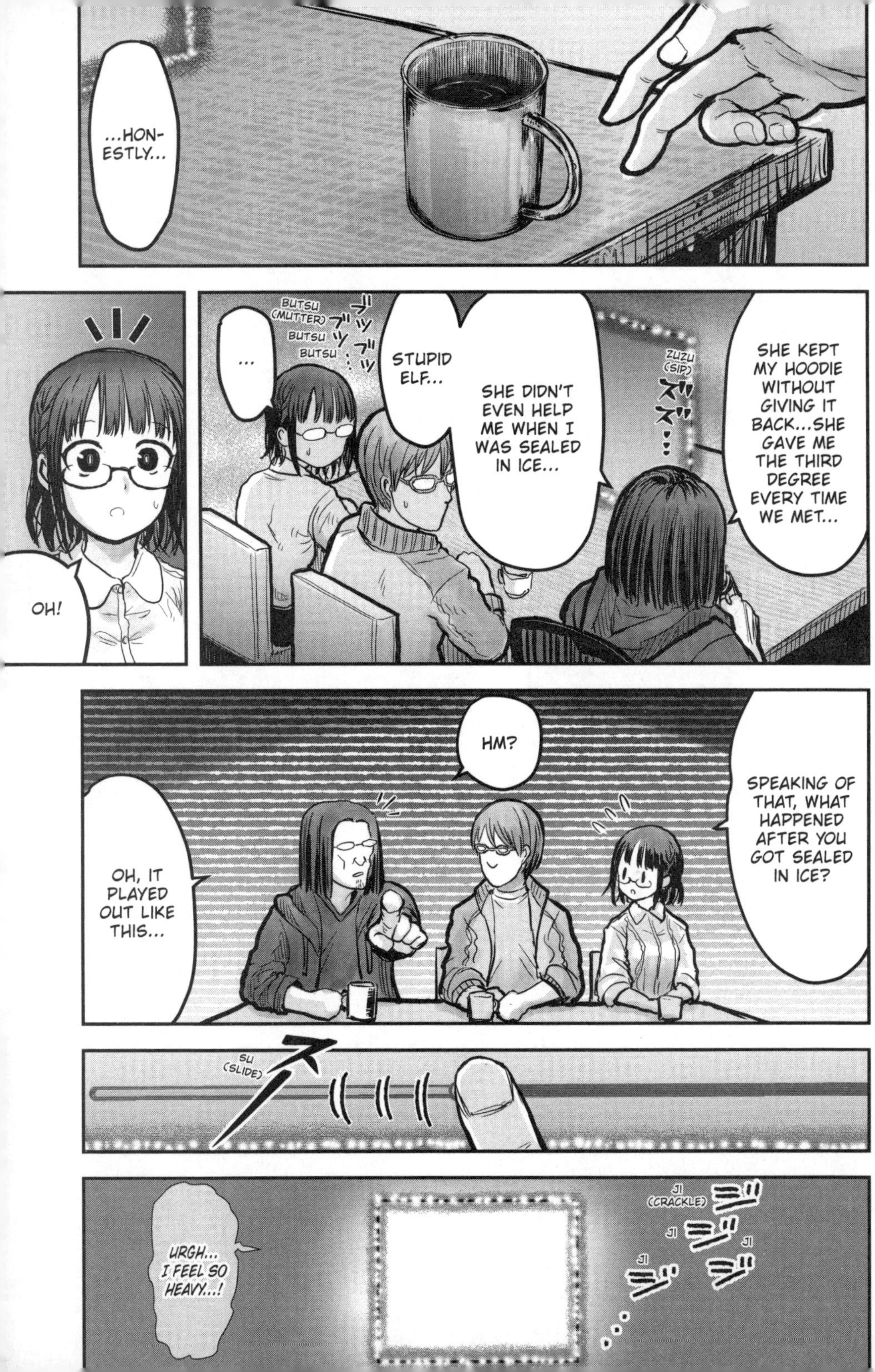
...HON-ESTLY...
SHE KEPT MY HOODIE WITHOUT GIVING IT BACK...SHE GAVE ME THE THIRD DEGREE EVERY TIME WE MET...
ZUZU (SIP)
SHE DIDN'T EVEN HELP ME WHEN I WAS SEALED IN ICE...
STUPID ELF...
BUTSU (MUTTER) BUTSU BUTSU
...
OH!
SPEAKING OF THAT, WHAT HAPPENED AFTER YOU GOT SEALED IN ICE?
HM?
OH, IT PLAYED OUT LIKE THIS...
SU (SLIDE)
JI (CRACKLE) JI JI JI
URGH... I FEEL SO HEAVY...!

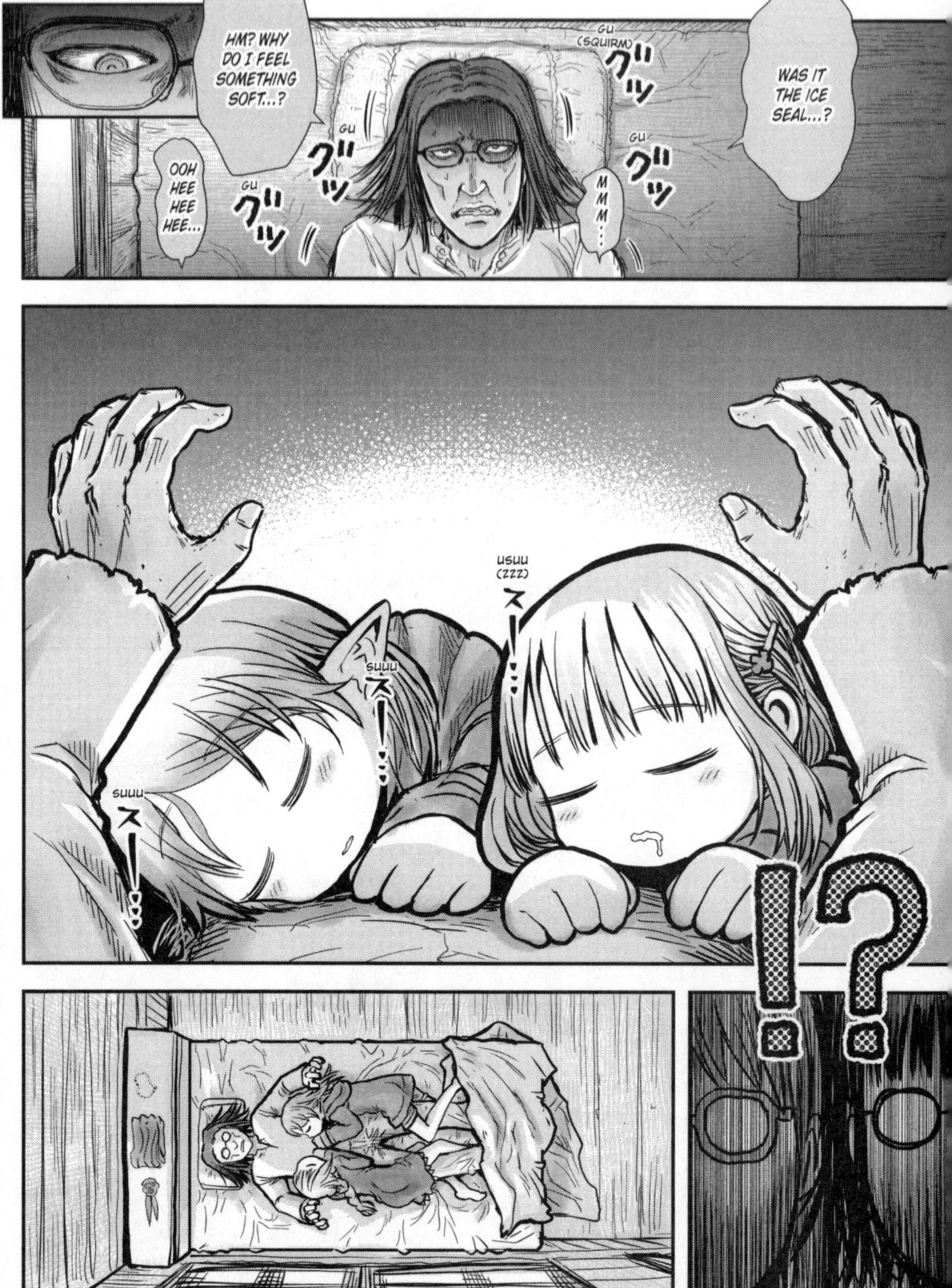
WAS IT THE ICE SEAL...?
GU (SQUIRM) グッ
GU グッ
MMM...
HM? WHY DO I FEEL SOMETHING SOFT...?
GU グッ
OOH HEE HEE HEE...
GU グッ
USUU (ZZZ) スー
SUUU スー
SUUU スー
!?

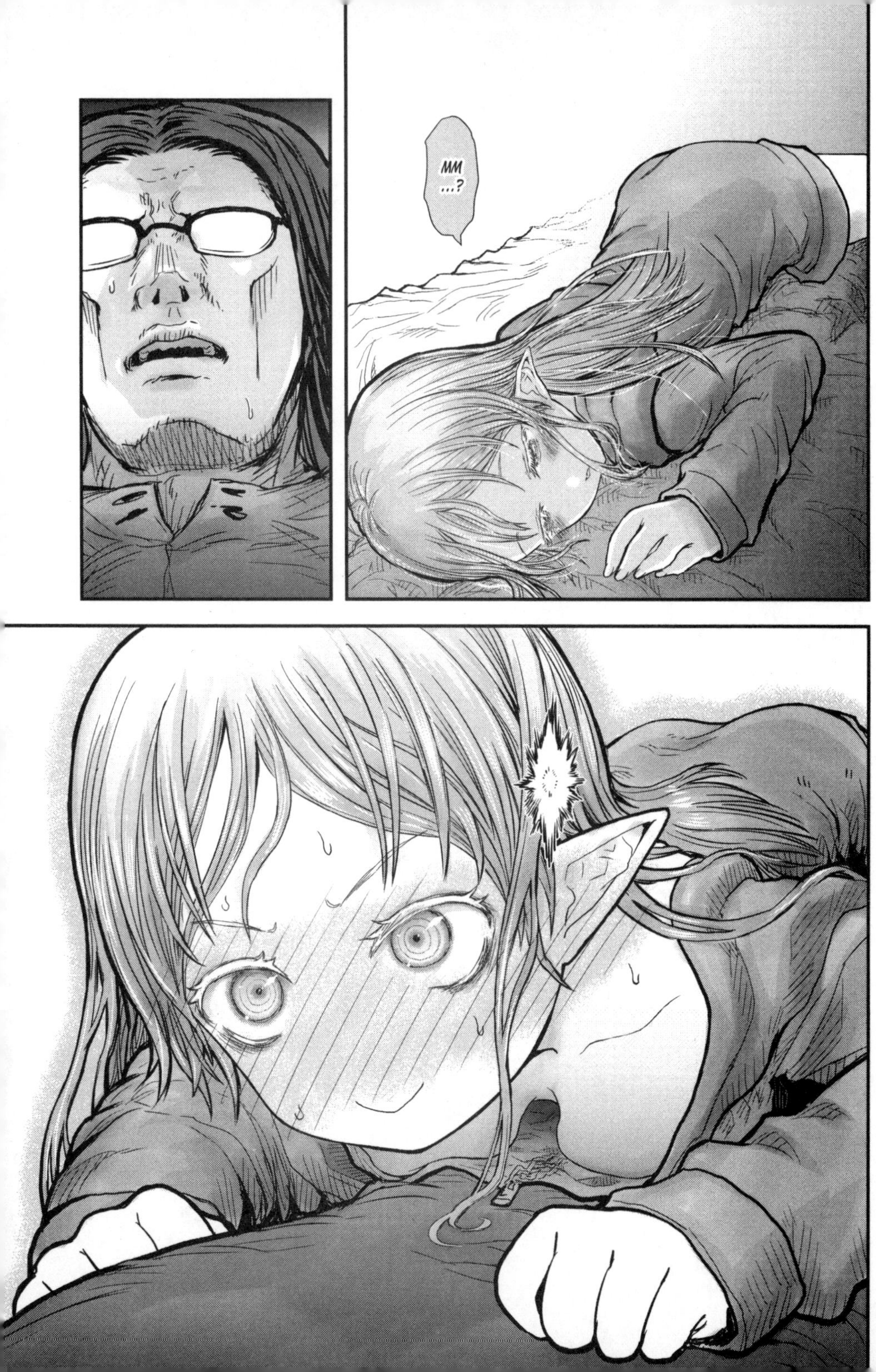
MM ...?

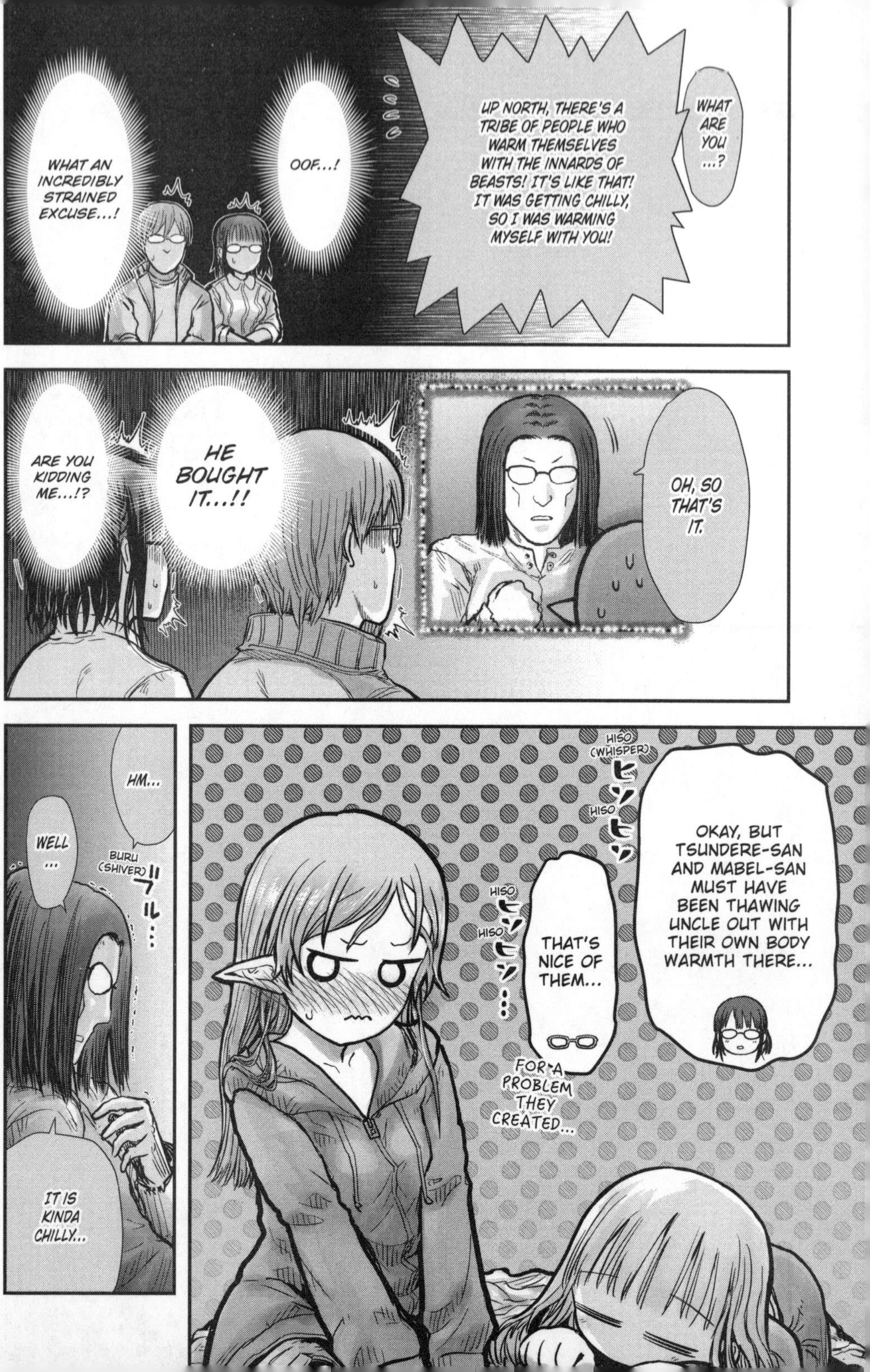
WHAT ARE YOU ...?
UP NORTH, THERE'S A TRIBE OF PEOPLE WHO WARM THEMSELVES WITH THE INNARDS OF BEASTS! IT'S LIKE THAT! IT WAS GETTING CHILLY, SO I WAS WARMING MYSELF WITH YOU!
OOF...!
WHAT AN INCREDIBLY STRAINED EXCUSE...!
OH, SO THAT'S IT.
HE BOUGHT IT...!!
ARE YOU KIDDING ME...!?
OKAY, BUT TSUNDERE-SAN AND MABEL-SAN MUST HAVE BEEN THAWING UNCLE OUT WITH THEIR OWN BODY WARMTH THERE...
HISO (WHISPER)
HISO
HISO
HISO
THAT'S NICE OF THEM...
FOR A PROBLEM THEY CREATED...
HM...
WELL ...
BURU (SHIVER)
IT IS KINDA CHILLY...

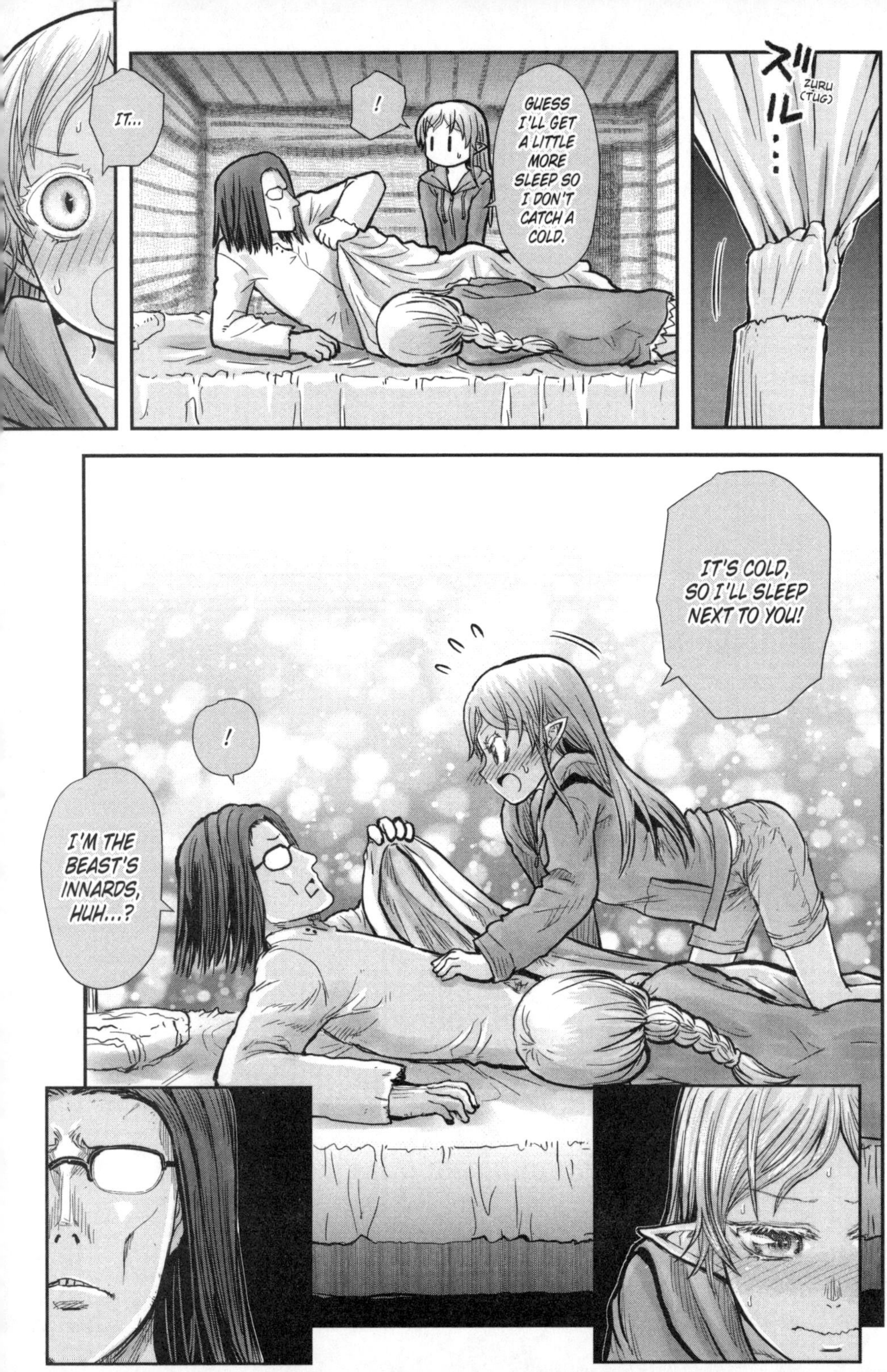
ZURU (TUG)
GUESS I'LL GET A LITTLE MORE SLEEP SO I DON'T CATCH A COLD.
!
IT...
IT'S COLD, SO I'LL SLEEP NEXT TO YOU!
!
I'M THE BEAST'S INNARDS, HUH...?

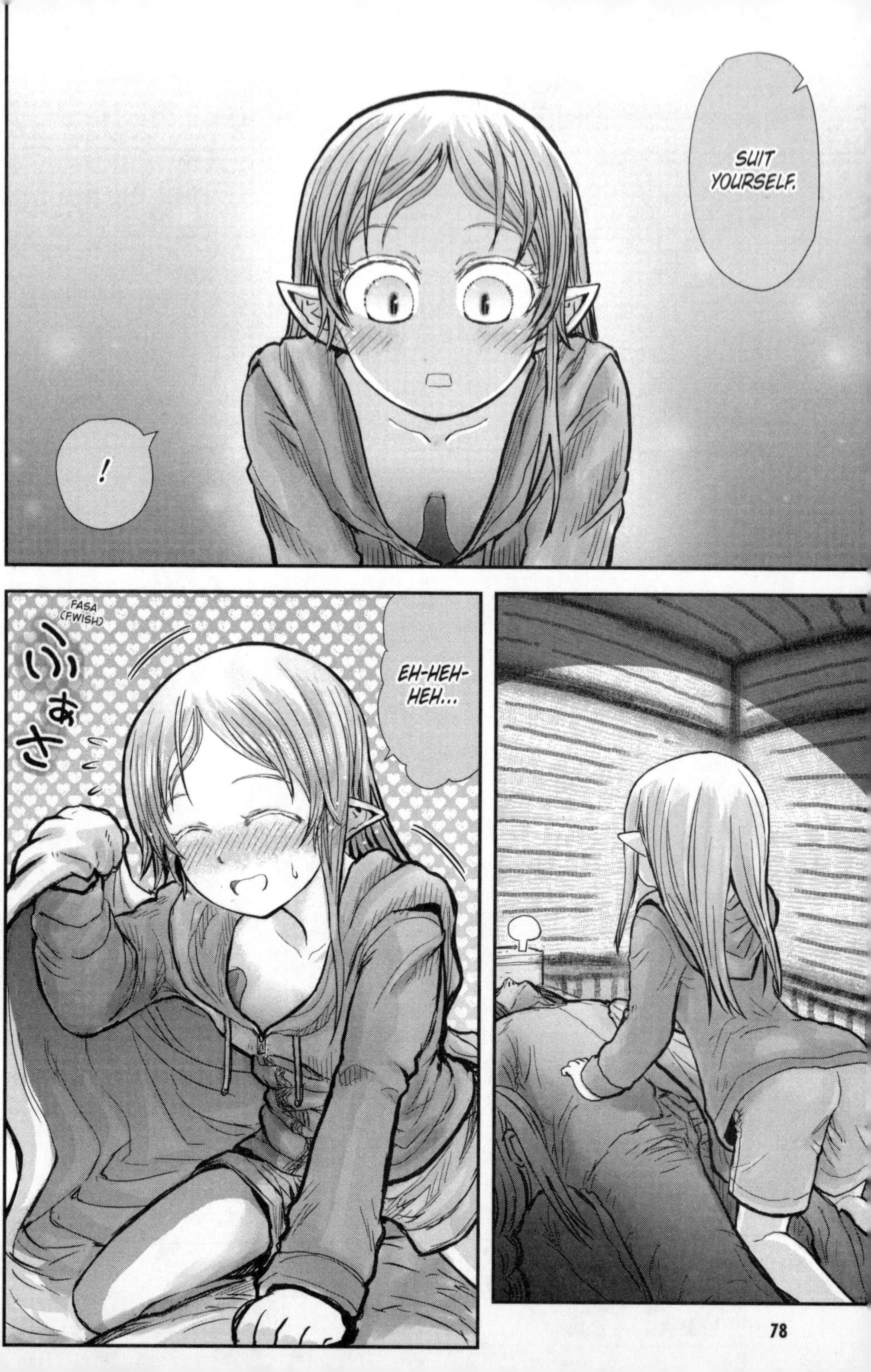
SUIT YOURSELF.
!
EH-HEH-HEH...
ふぁさ
FASA (FWISH)

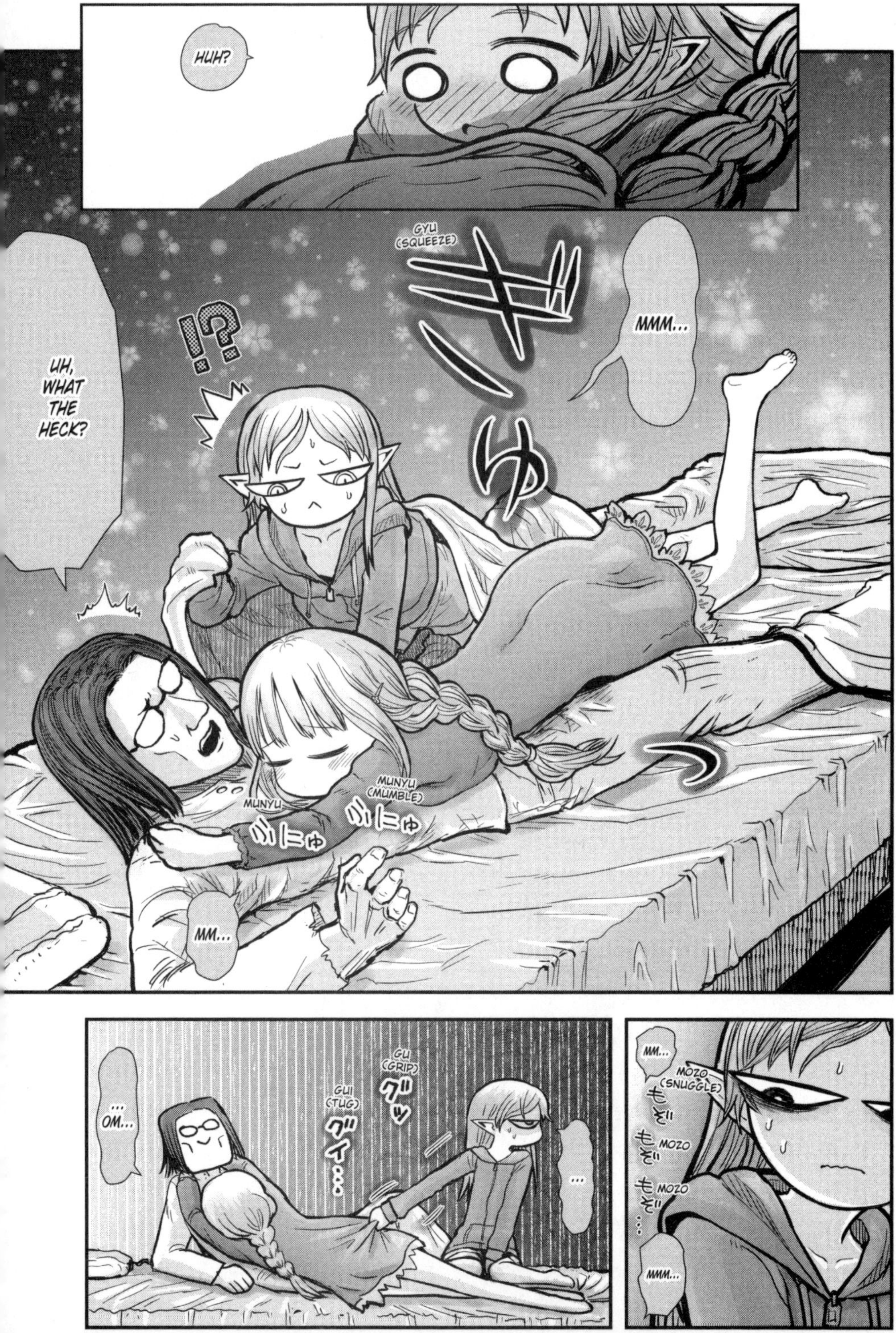
HUH?
MMM...
GYU (SQUEEZE)
ぎゅ
!?
UH, WHAT THE HECK?
MUNYU (MUMBLE)
ふにゅ
MUNYU
ふにゅ
MM...
MM...
MOZO (SNUGGLE)
もぞ
MOZO
もぞ
MOZO
もぞ...
MMM...
...
GU (GRIP)
グッ
GUI (TUG)
グイ...
... OM...

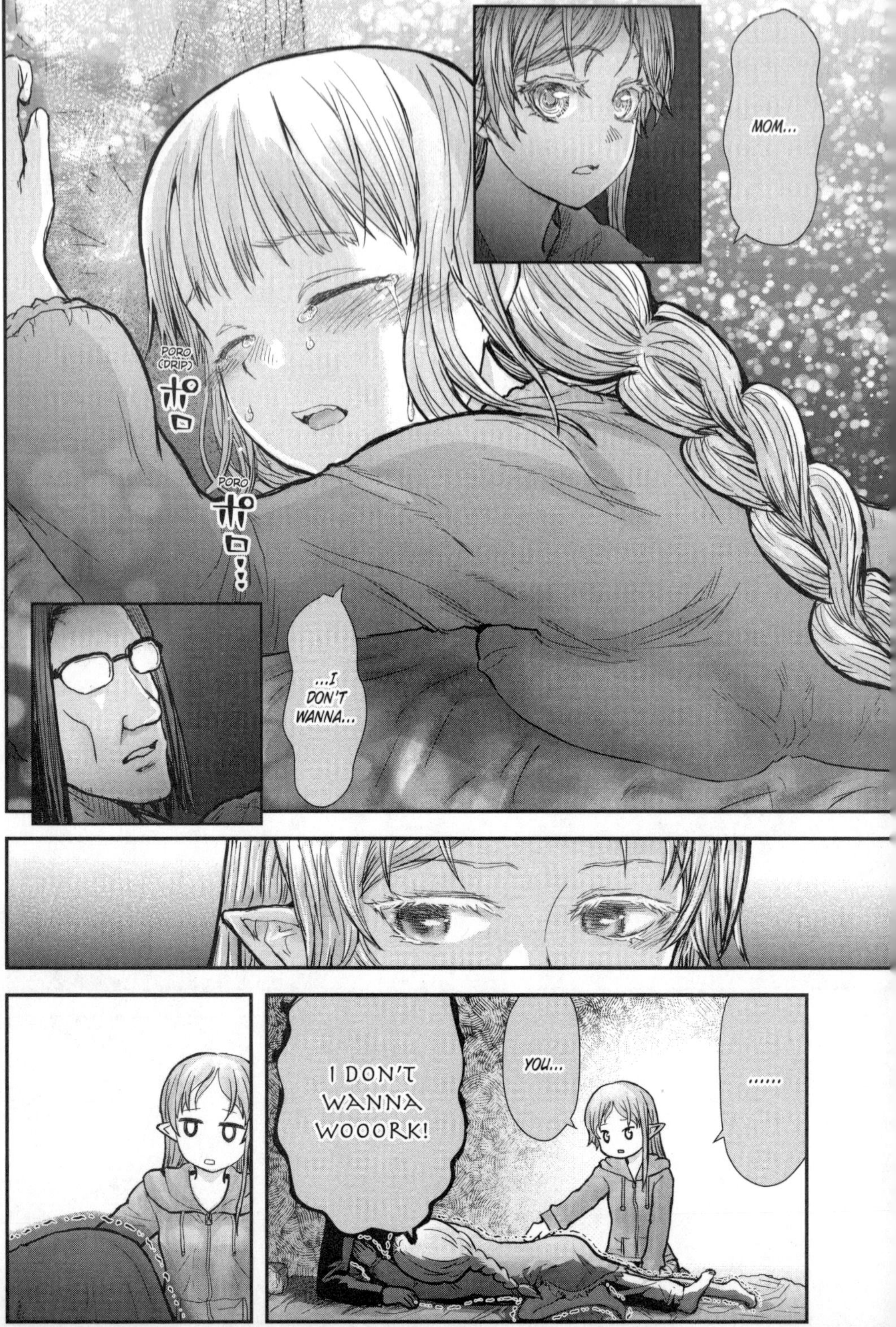
MOM...
PORO (DRIP)
ポロ
PORO
ポロ...
...I DON'T WANNA...
......
YOU...
I DON'T WANNA WOOORK!

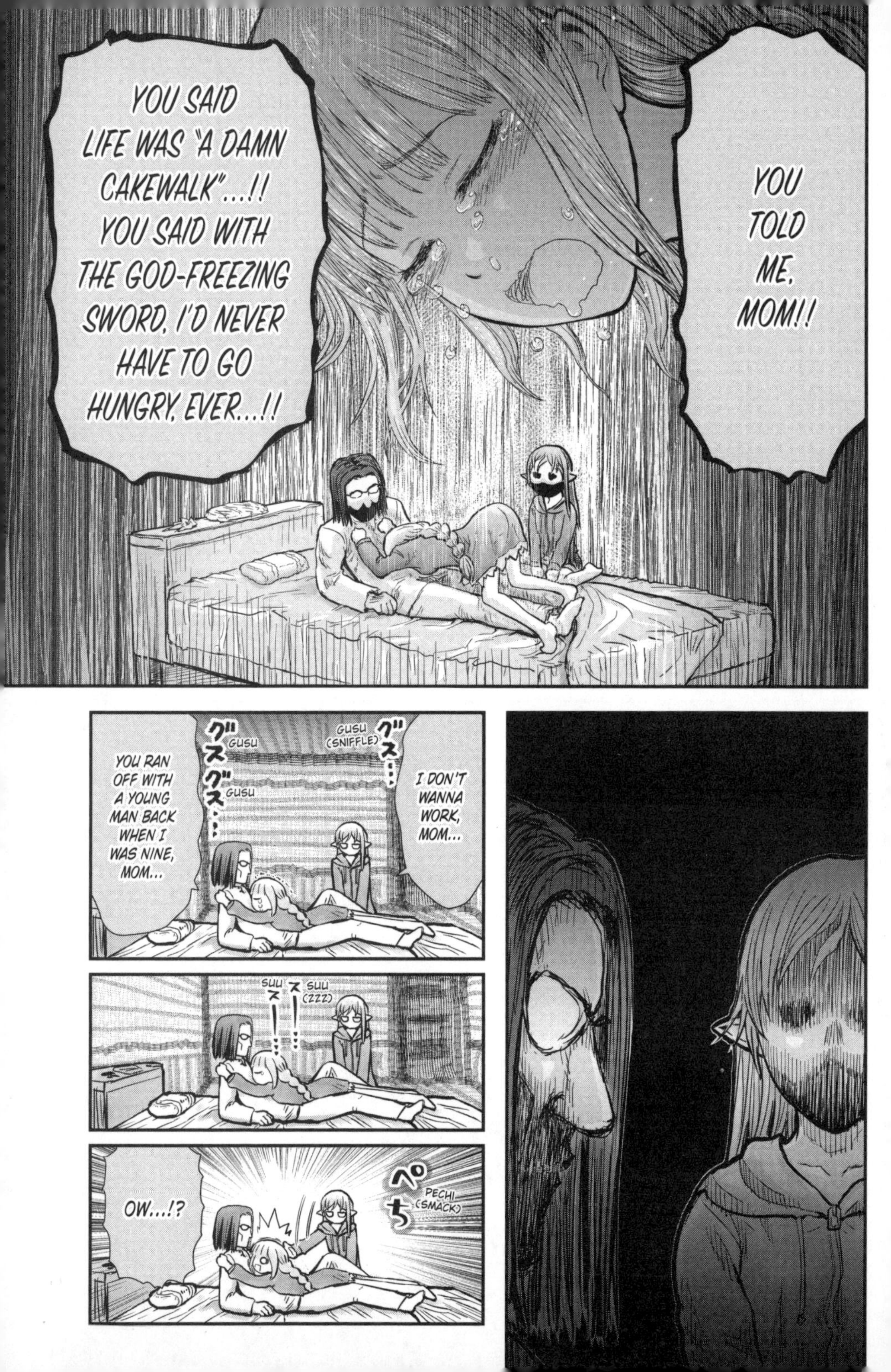
YOU TOLD ME, MOM!!
YOU SAID LIFE WAS "A DAMN CAKEWALK"...!! YOU SAID WITH THE GOD-FREEZING SWORD, I'D NEVER HAVE TO GO HUNGRY, EVER...!!
グス… GUSU (SNIFFLE)
I DON'T WANNA WORK, MOM...
グスグス… GUSU GUSU
YOU RAN OFF WITH A YOUNG MAN BACK WHEN I WAS NINE, MOM...
スー…スー… SUU SUU (ZZZ)
ぺち PECHI (SMACK)
OW...!?

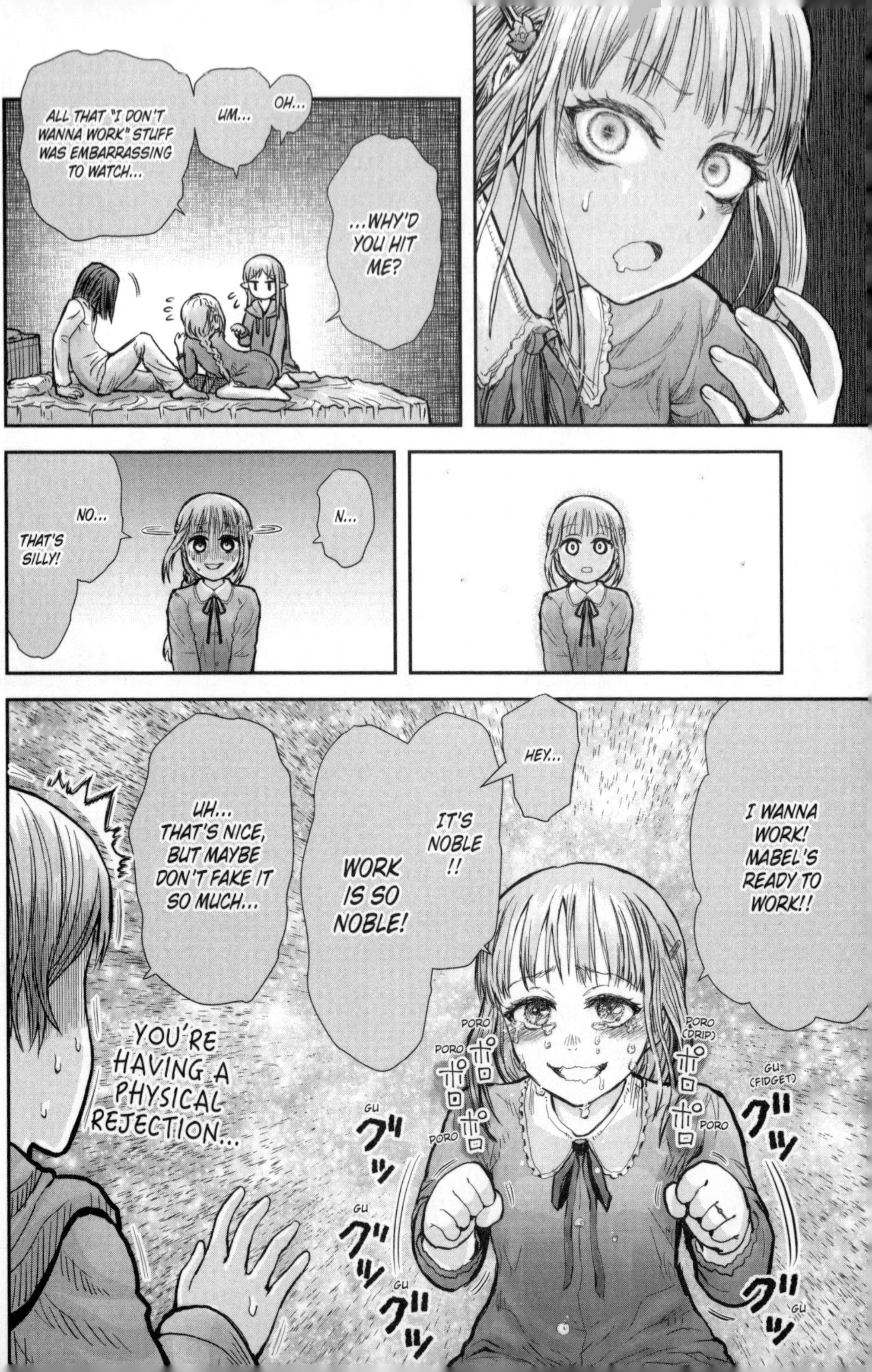
...WHY'D YOU HIT ME?
OH...
UM...
ALL THAT "I DON'T WANNA WORK" STUFF WAS EMBARRASSING TO WATCH...
N...
NO...
THAT'S SILLY!
I WANNA WORK! MABEL'S READY TO WORK!!
HEY...
IT'S NOBLE!!
WORK IS SO NOBLE!
UH... THAT'S NICE, BUT MAYBE DON'T FAKE IT SO MUCH...
ポロ PORO (DRIP)
ポロ PORO
ポロ PORO
ポロ PORO
グッ GU (FIDGET)
グッ GU
グッ GU
グッ GU
グッ GU
YOU'RE HAVING A PHYSICAL REJECTION...

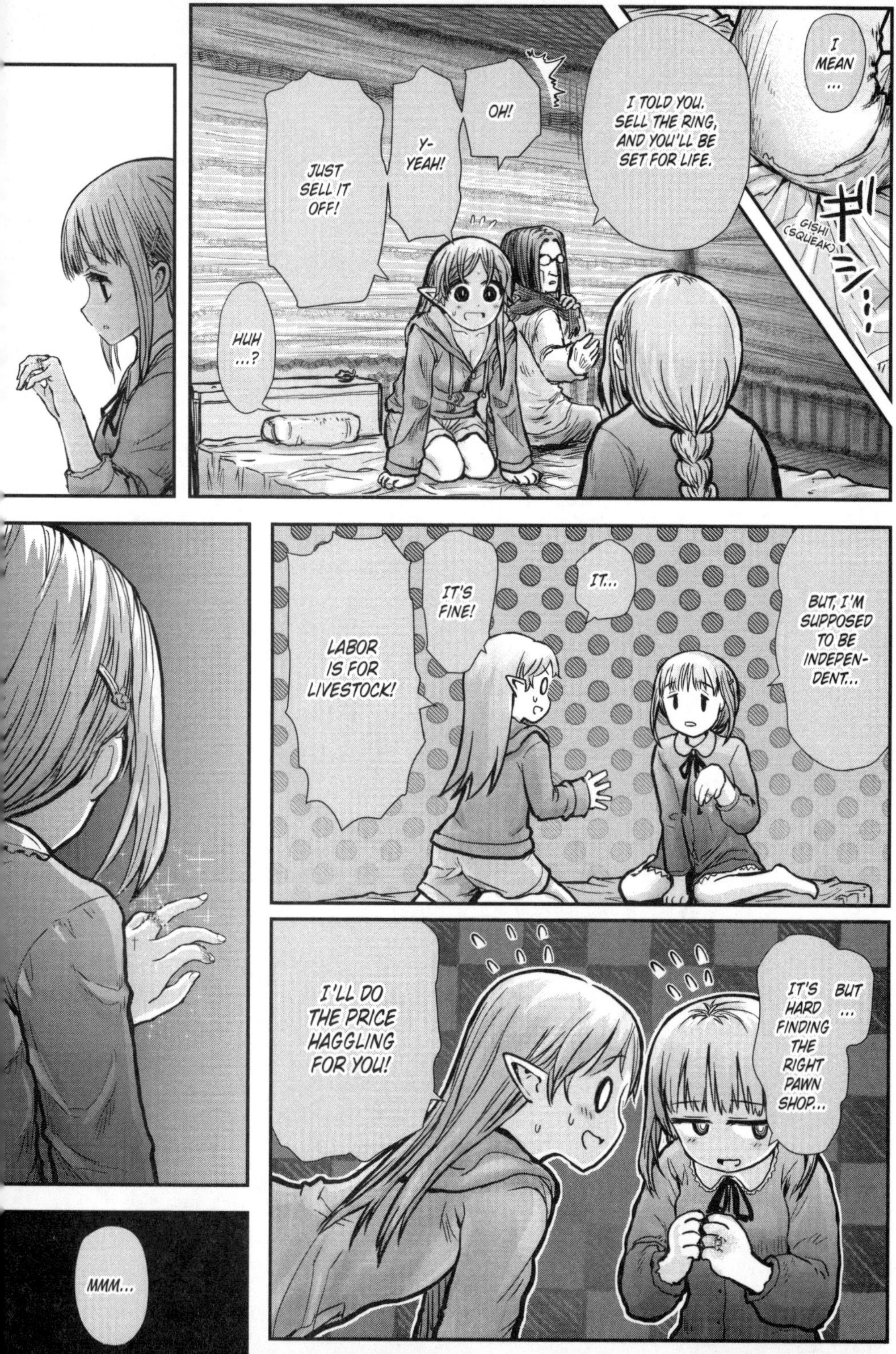

I MEAN...
GISHI (SQUEAK)
I TOLD YOU. SELL THE RING, AND YOU'LL BE SET FOR LIFE.
OH!
Y-YEAH!
JUST SELL IT OFF!
HUH...?
BUT, I'M SUPPOSED TO BE INDEPENDENT...
IT...
IT'S FINE!
LABOR IS FOR LIVESTOCK!
BUT...
IT'S HARD FINDING THE RIGHT PAWN SHOP...
I'LL DO THE PRICE HAGGLING FOR YOU!
MMM...

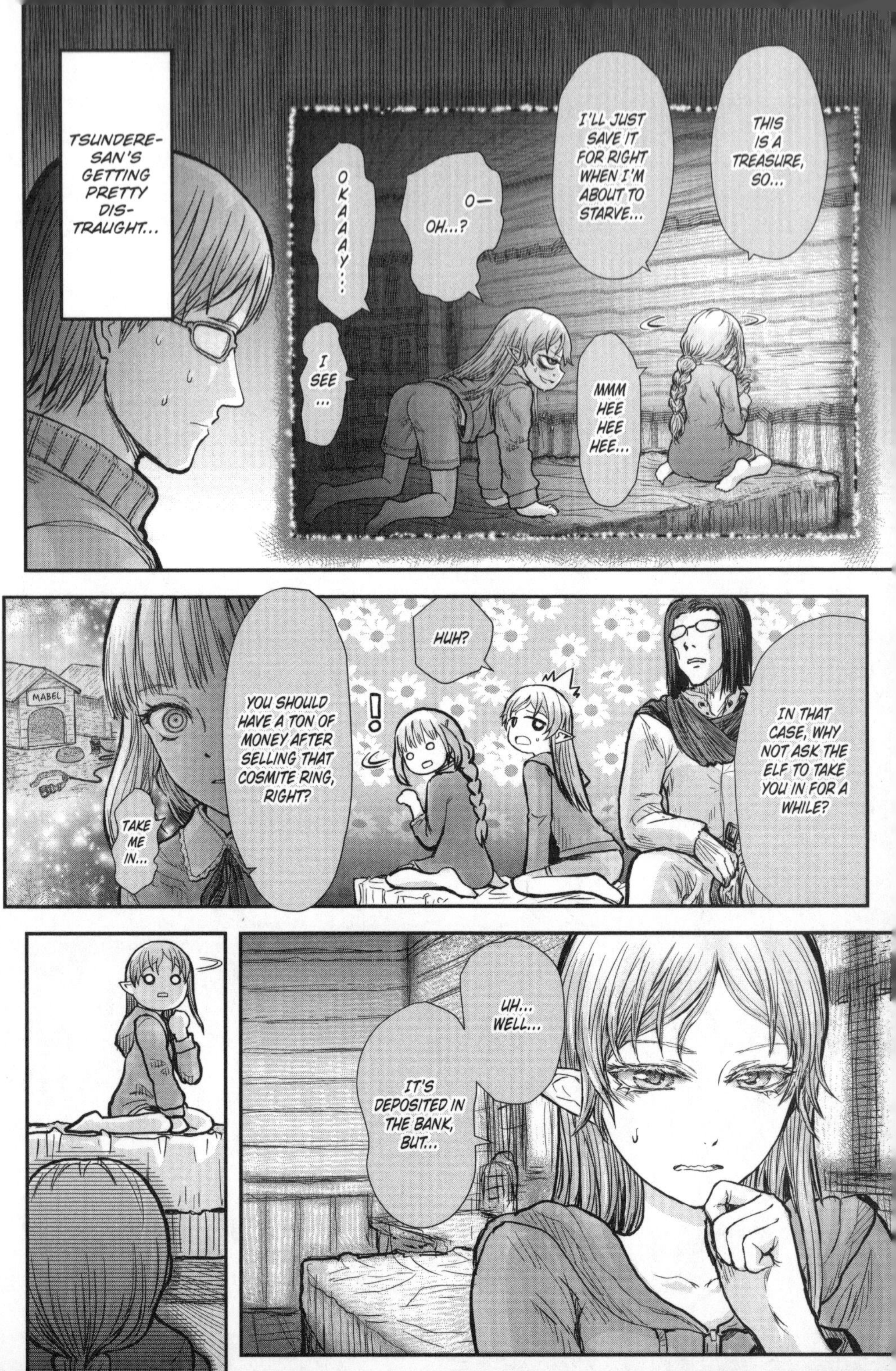
THIS IS A TREASURE, SO...
I'LL JUST SAVE IT FOR RIGHT WHEN I'M ABOUT TO STARVE...
MMM HEE HEE HEE...
O— OH...?
OKAAAAY...
I SEE...
TSUNDERE-SAN'S GETTING PRETTY DIS-TRAUGHT...
IN THAT CASE, WHY NOT ASK THE ELF TO TAKE YOU IN FOR A WHILE?
HUH?
!
YOU SHOULD HAVE A TON OF MONEY AFTER SELLING THAT COSMITE RING, RIGHT?
MABEL
TAKE ME IN...
UH... WELL...
IT'S DEPOSITED IN THE BANK, BUT...

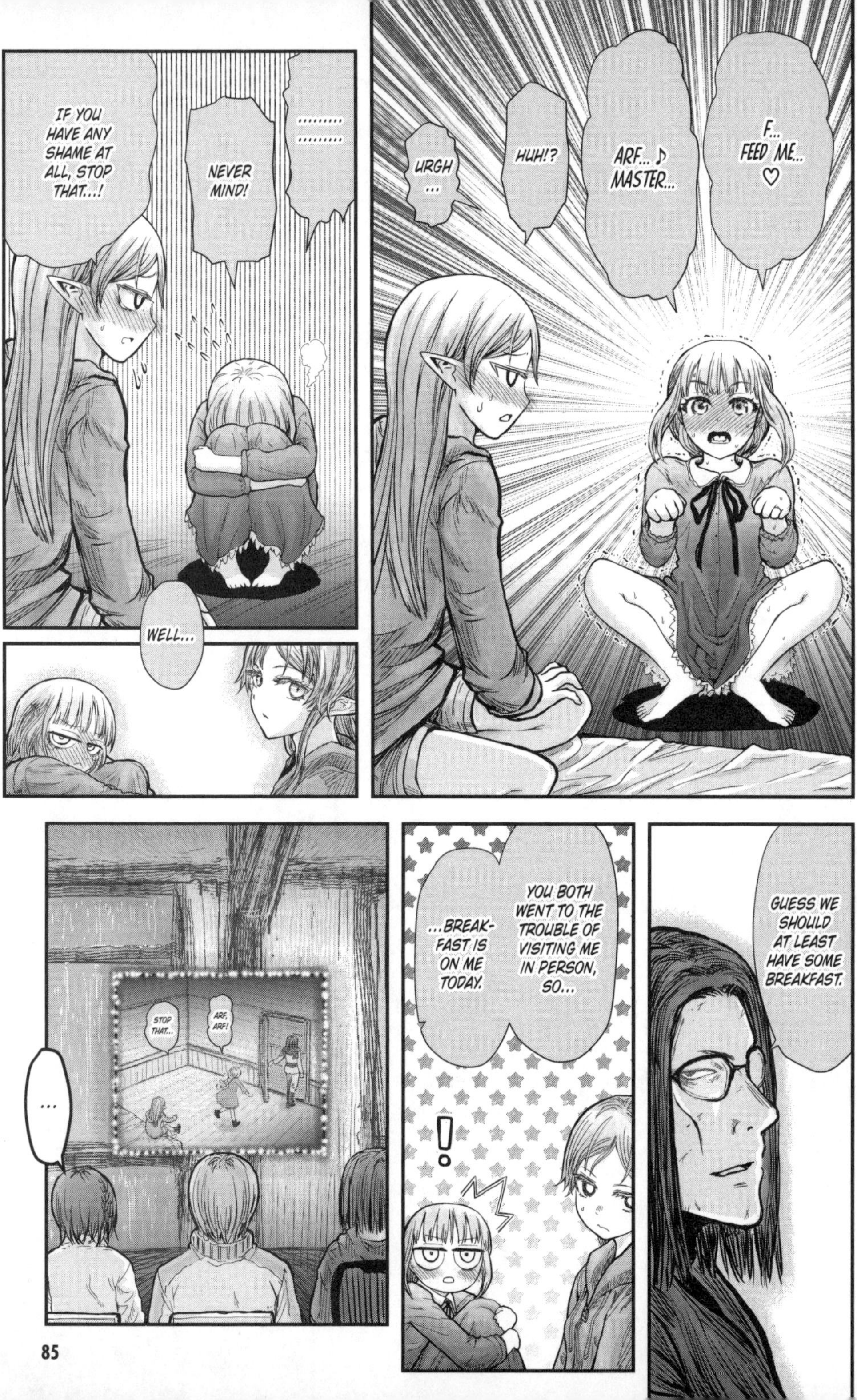
F... FEED ME... ♡
ARF... ♪ MASTER...
HUH!?
URGH...
....
....
NEVER MIND!
IF YOU HAVE ANY SHAME AT ALL, STOP THAT...!
WELL...
GUESS WE SHOULD AT LEAST HAVE SOME BREAKFAST.
YOU BOTH WENT TO THE TROUBLE OF VISITING ME IN PERSON, SO...
...BREAK-FAST IS ON ME TODAY.
!
ARF, ARF!
STOP THAT...
...

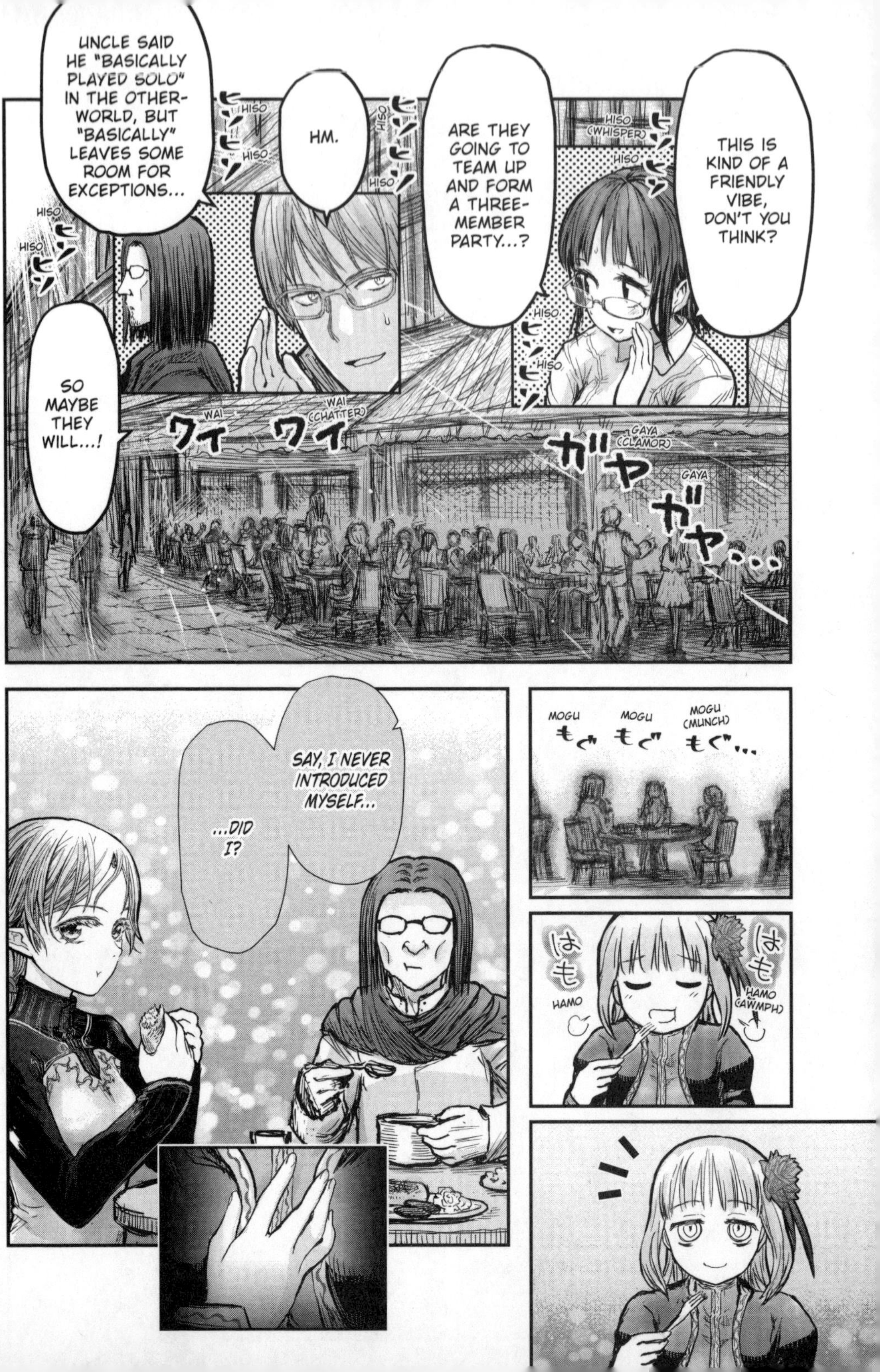
HISO (WHISPER)
HISO
THIS IS KIND OF A FRIENDLY VIBE, DON'T YOU THINK?
HISO
HISO
ARE THEY GOING TO TEAM UP AND FORM A THREE-MEMBER PARTY...?
HISO
HISO
HM.
HISO
HISO
UNCLE SAID HE "BASICALLY PLAYED SOLO" IN THE OTHER-WORLD, BUT "BASICALLY" LEAVES SOME ROOM FOR EXCEPTIONS...
SO MAYBE THEY WILL...!
GAYA (CLAMOR)
ガヤ
GAYA
ガヤ...
WAI (CHATTER)
ワイ
WAI
ワィ
MOGU
MOGU
MOGU (MUNCH)
もぐ もぐ もぐ...
HAMO (AWMPH)
はも
HAMO
はも
SAY, I NEVER INTRODUCED MYSELF...
...DID I?

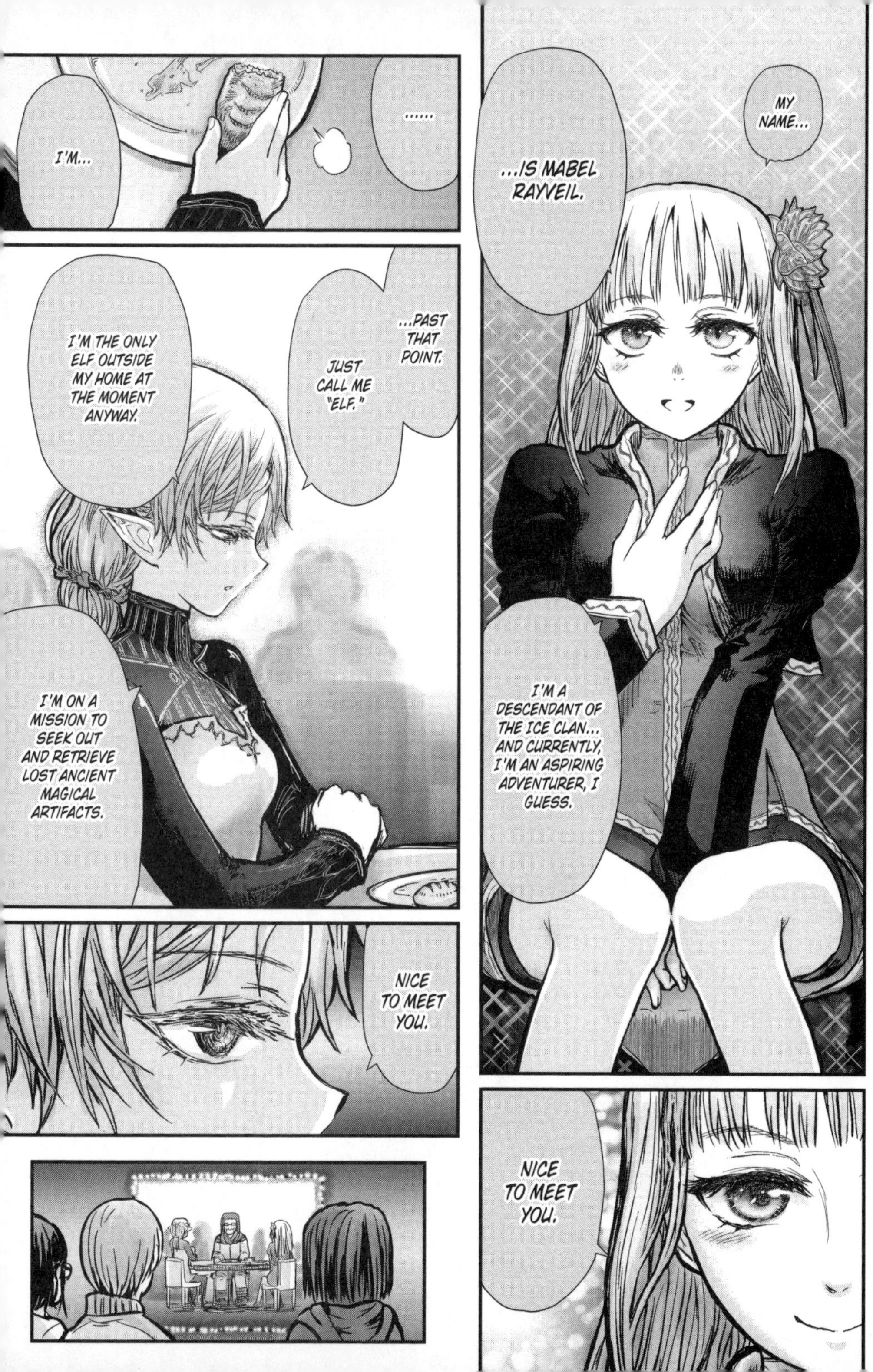
MY NAME...
...IS MABEL RAYVEIL.
I'M A DESCENDANT OF THE ICE CLAN... AND CURRENTLY, I'M AN ASPIRING ADVENTURER, I GUESS.
NICE TO MEET YOU.
......
I'M...
...PAST THAT POINT.
JUST CALL ME "ELF."
I'M THE ONLY ELF OUTSIDE MY HOME AT THE MOMENT ANYWAY.
I'M ON A MISSION TO SEEK OUT AND RETRIEVE LOST ANCIENT MAGICAL ARTIFACTS.
NICE TO MEET YOU.

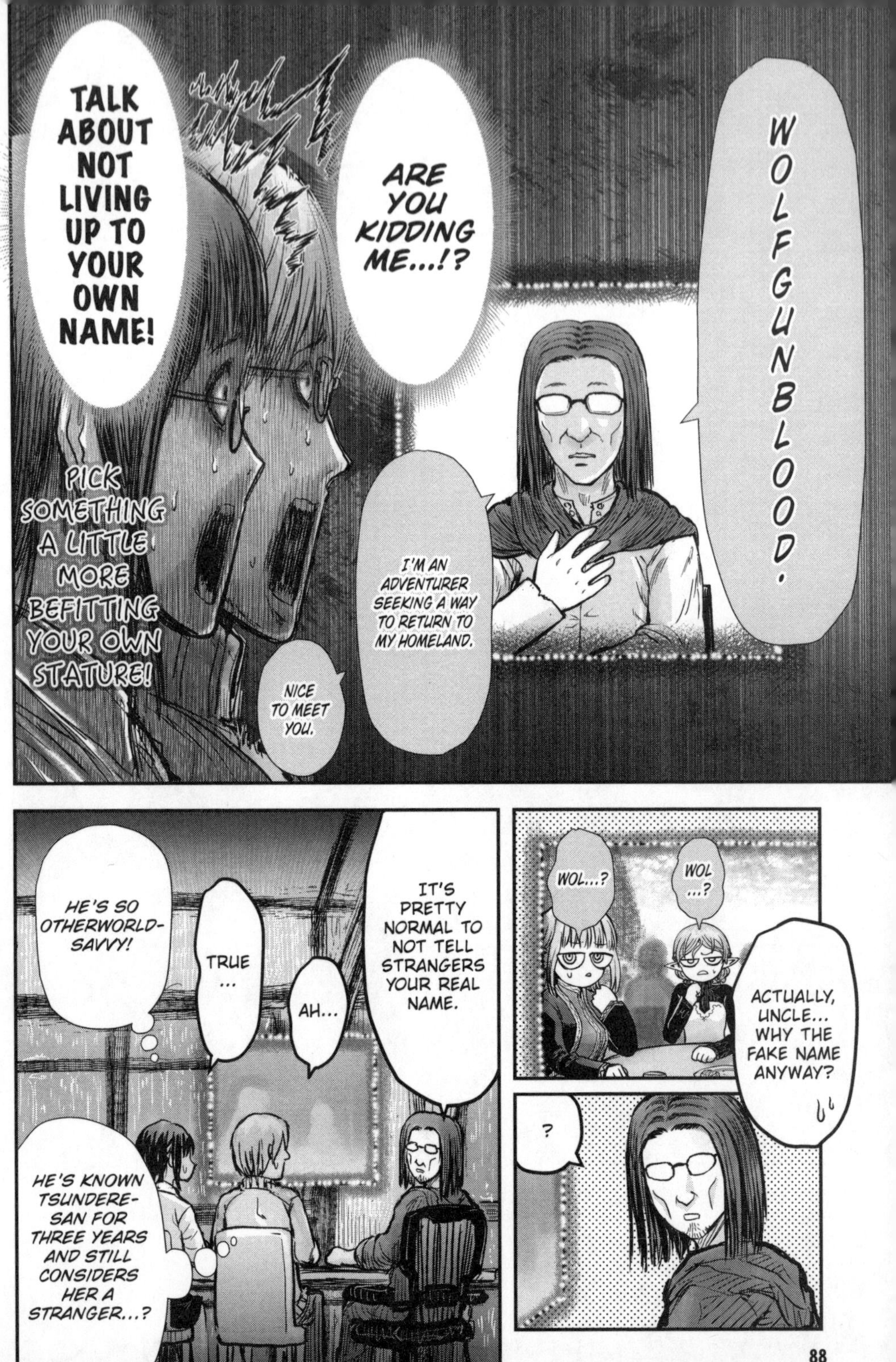
WOLFGUNBLOOD.
I'M AN ADVENTURER SEEKING A WAY TO RETURN TO MY HOMELAND.
NICE TO MEET YOU.
ARE YOU KIDDING ME...!?
TALK ABOUT NOT LIVING UP TO YOUR OWN NAME!
PICK SOMETHING A LITTLE MORE BEFITTING YOUR OWN STATURE!
WOL ...?
WOL...?
ACTUALLY, UNCLE... WHY THE FAKE NAME ANYWAY?
?
IT'S PRETTY NORMAL TO NOT TELL STRANGERS YOUR REAL NAME.
AH...
TRUE ...
HE'S SO OTHERWORLD-SAVVY!
HE'S KNOWN TSUNDERE-SAN FOR THREE YEARS AND STILL CONSIDERS HER A STRANGER...?

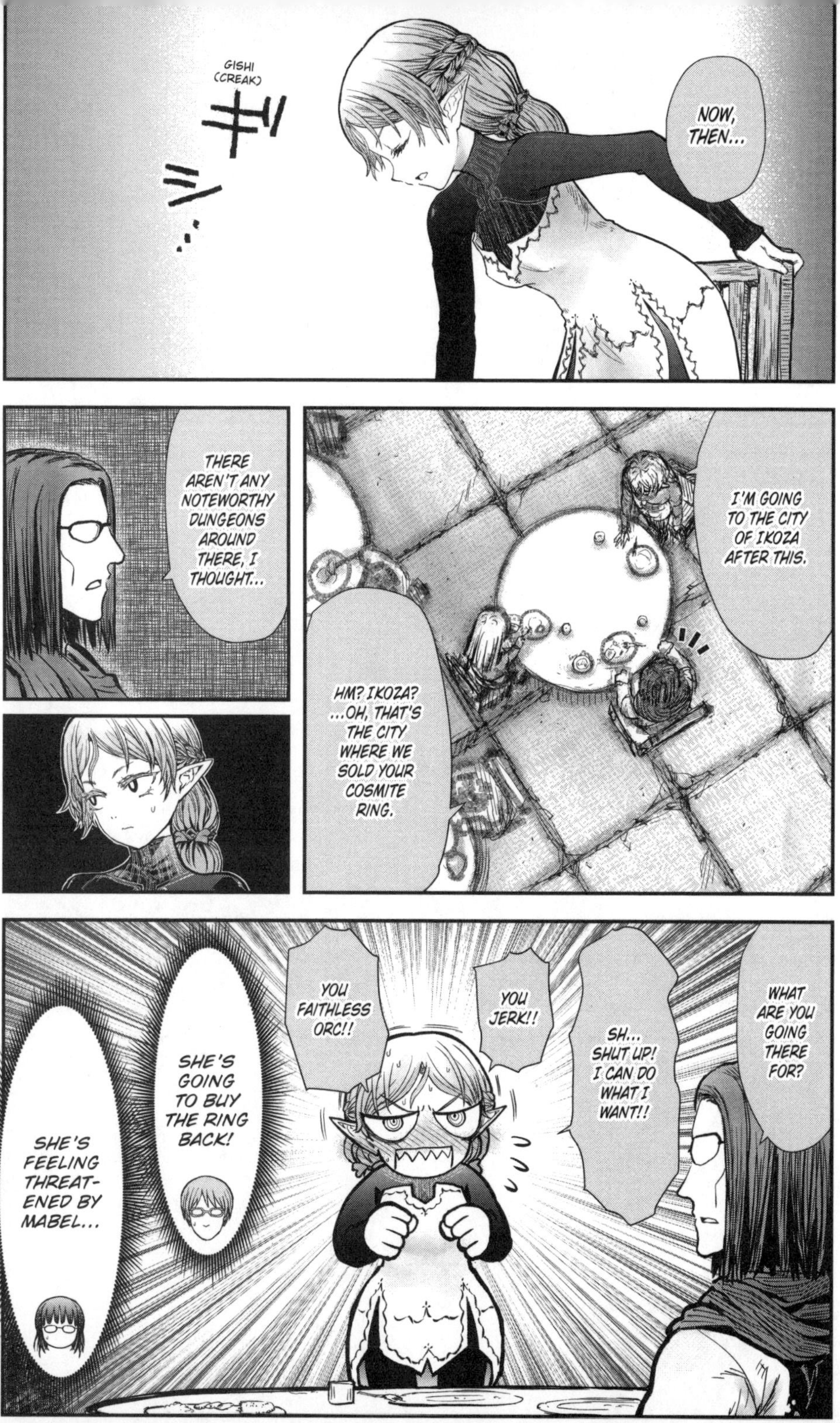
NOW, THEN...
GISHI (CREAK)
I'M GOING TO THE CITY OF IKOZA AFTER THIS.
HM? IKOZA? ...OH, THAT'S THE CITY WHERE WE SOLD YOUR COSMITE RING.
THERE AREN'T ANY NOTEWORTHY DUNGEONS AROUND THERE, I THOUGHT...
WHAT ARE YOU GOING THERE FOR?
SH... SHUT UP! I CAN DO WHAT I WANT!!
YOU JERK!!
YOU FAITHLESS ORC!!
SHE'S GOING TO BUY THE RING BACK!
SHE'S FEELING THREAT-ENED BY MABEL...

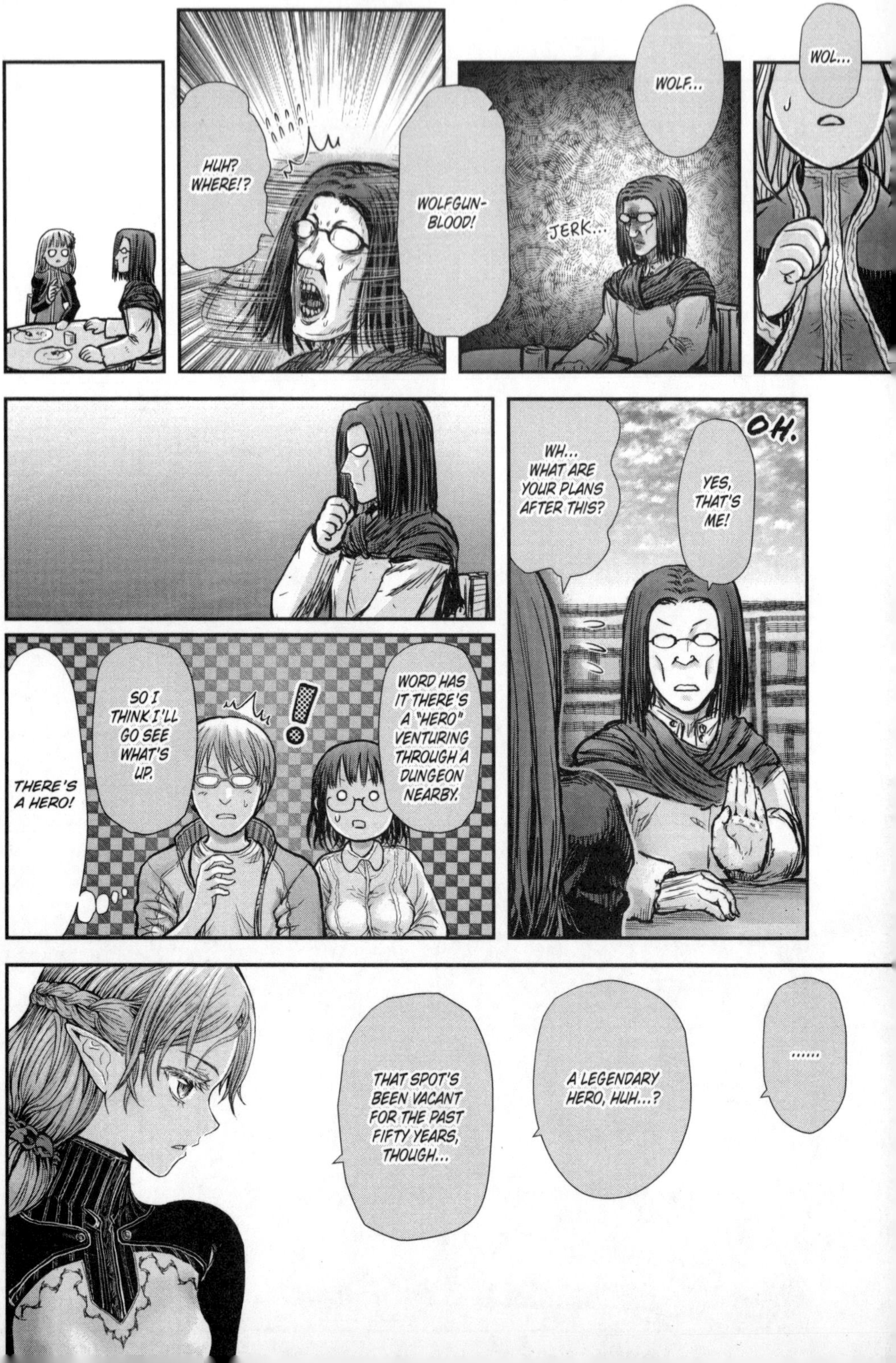
WOL...
WOLF...
JERK...
WOLFGUN-BLOOD!
HUH? WHERE!?
OH.
YES, THAT'S ME!
WH... WHAT ARE YOUR PLANS AFTER THIS?
WORD HAS IT THERE'S A "HERO" VENTURING THROUGH A DUNGEON NEARBY.
SO I THINK I'LL GO SEE WHAT'S UP.
THERE'S A HERO!
......
A LEGENDARY HERO, HUH...?
THAT SPOT'S BEEN VACANT FOR THE PAST FIFTY YEARS, THOUGH...

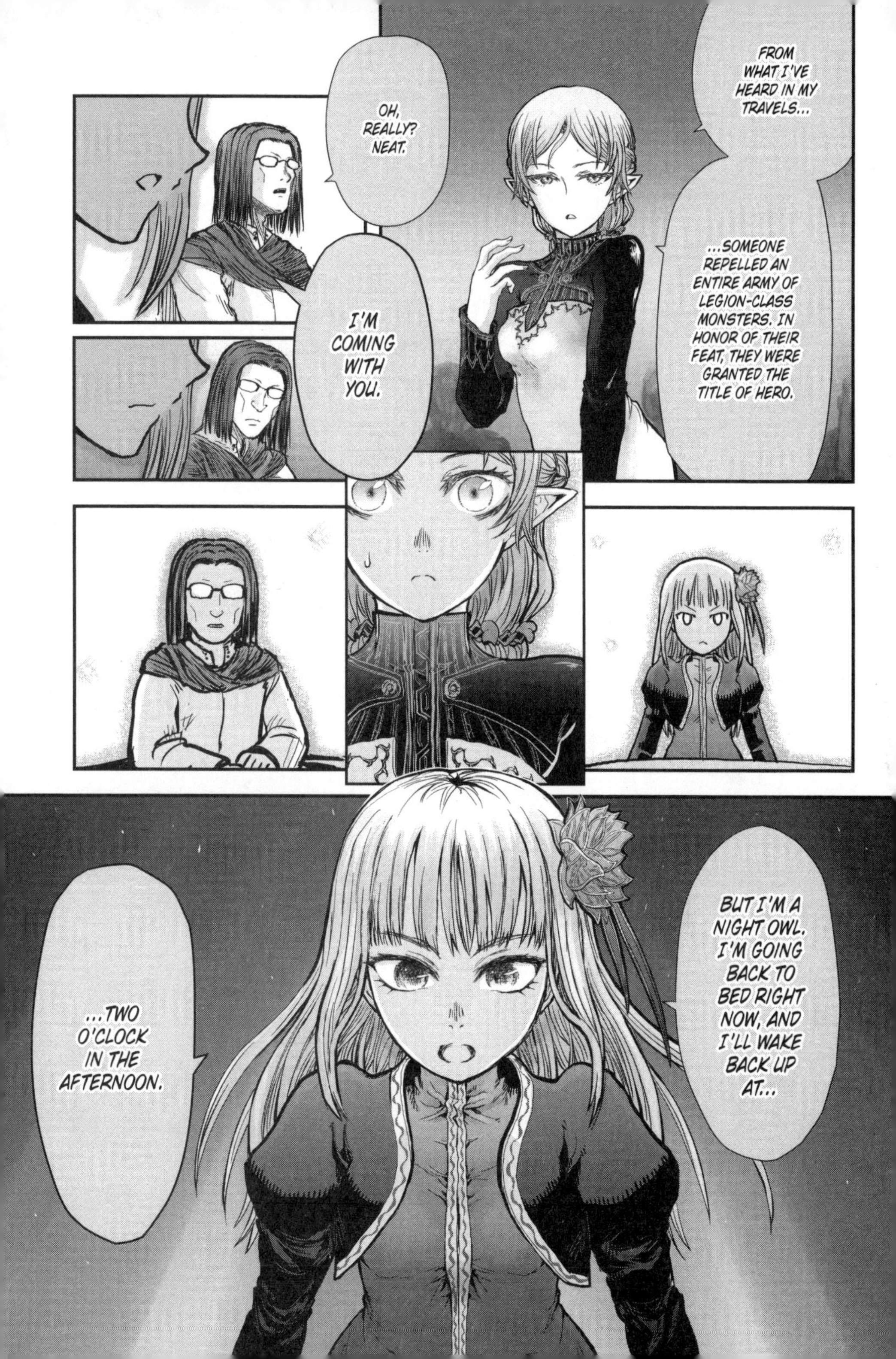
FROM WHAT I'VE HEARD IN MY TRAVELS...
...SOMEONE REPELLED AN ENTIRE ARMY OF LEGION-CLASS MONSTERS. IN HONOR OF THEIR FEAT, THEY WERE GRANTED THE TITLE OF HERO.
OH, REALLY? NEAT.
I'M COMING WITH YOU.
BUT I'M A NIGHT OWL. I'M GOING BACK TO BED RIGHT NOW, AND I'LL WAKE BACK UP AT...
...TWO O'CLOCK IN THE AFTERNOON.

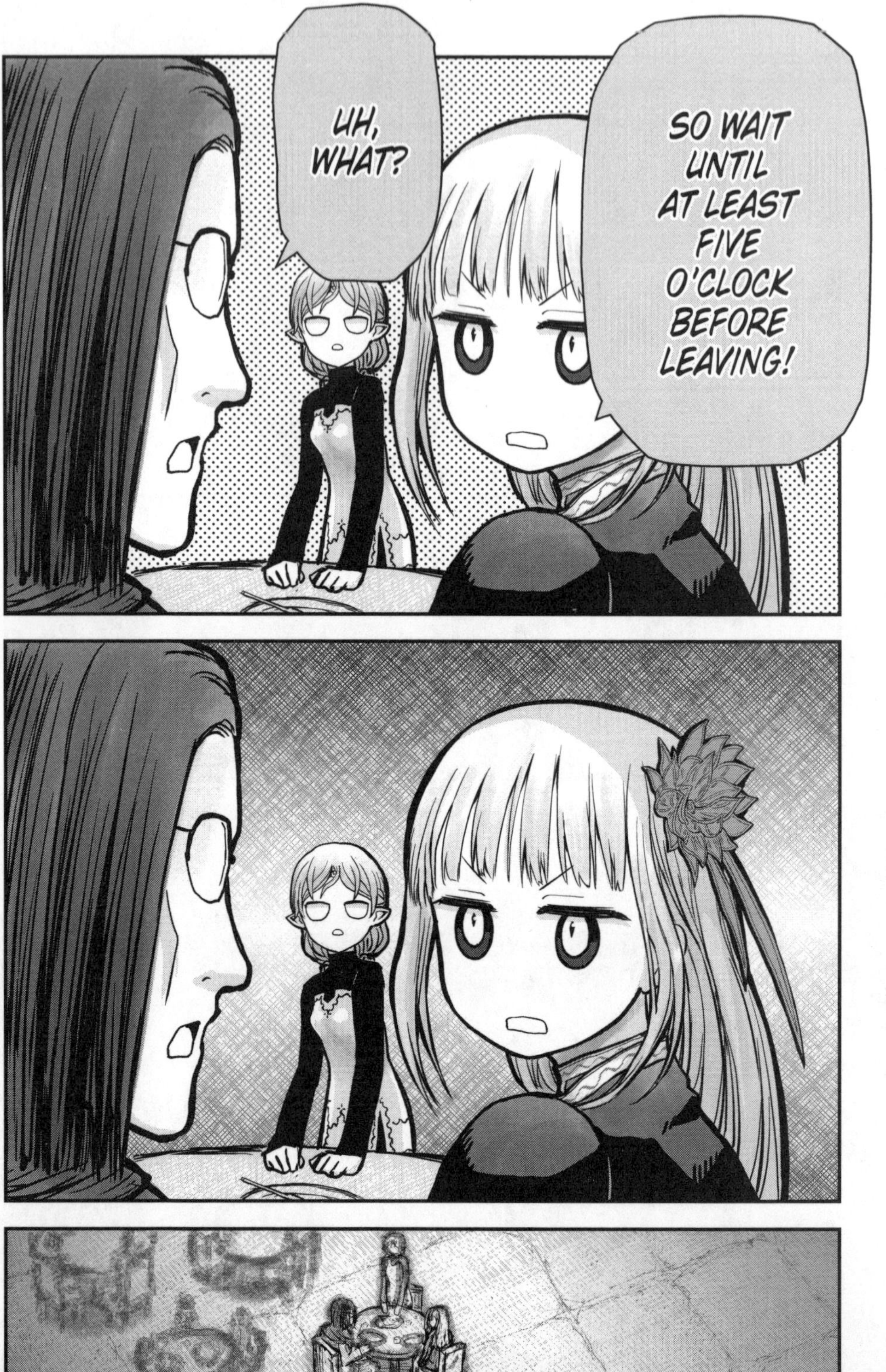
SO WAIT UNTIL AT LEAST FIVE O'CLOCK BEFORE LEAVING!
UH, WHAT?

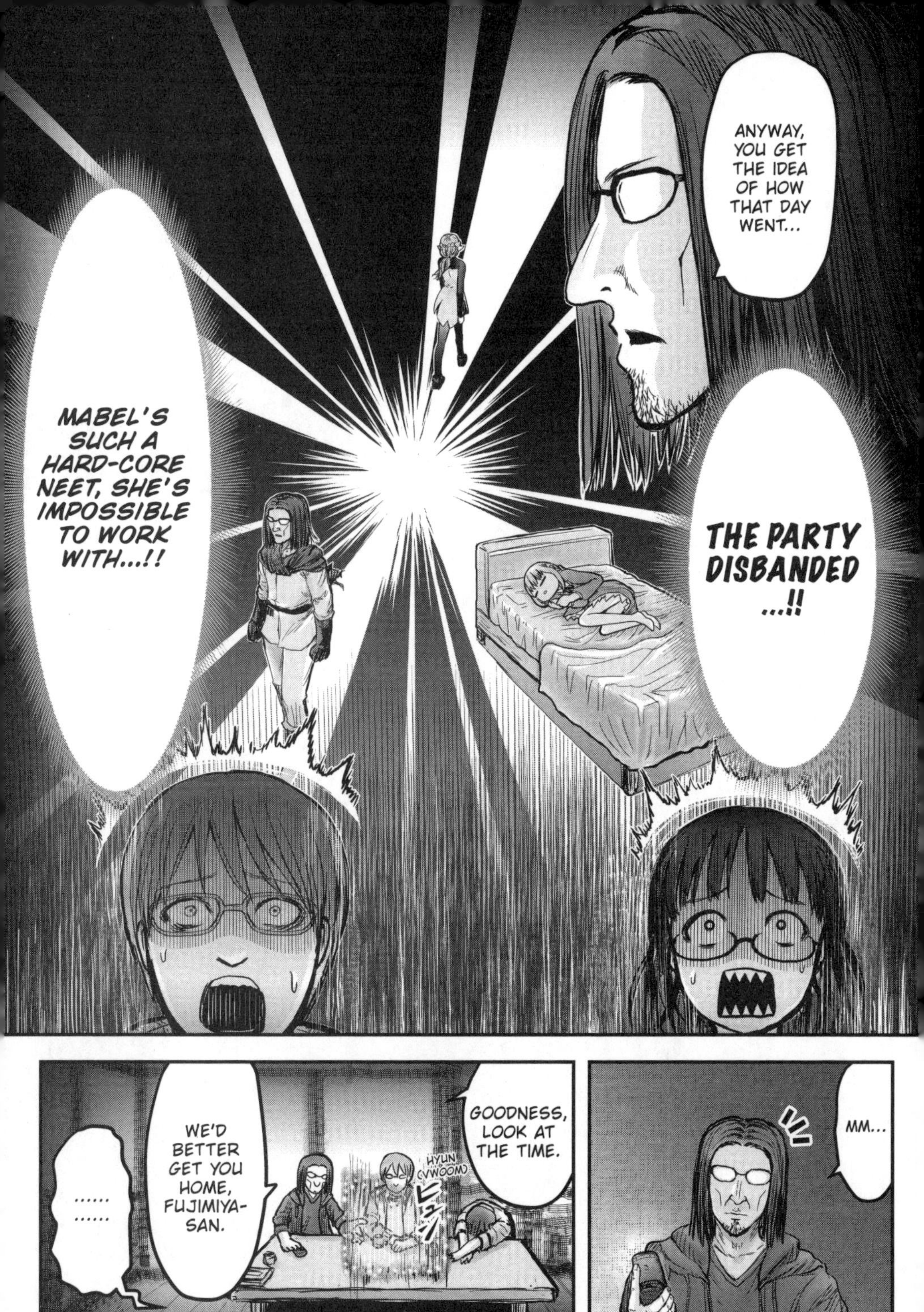
ANYWAY, YOU GET THE IDEA OF HOW THAT DAY WENT...
THE PARTY DISBANDED ...!!
MABEL'S SUCH A HARD-CORE NEET, SHE'S IMPOSSIBLE TO WORK WITH...!!
!!
MM...
GOODNESS, LOOK AT THE TIME.
HYUN (VWOOM)
WE'D BETTER GET YOU HOME, FUJIMIYA-SAN.
....

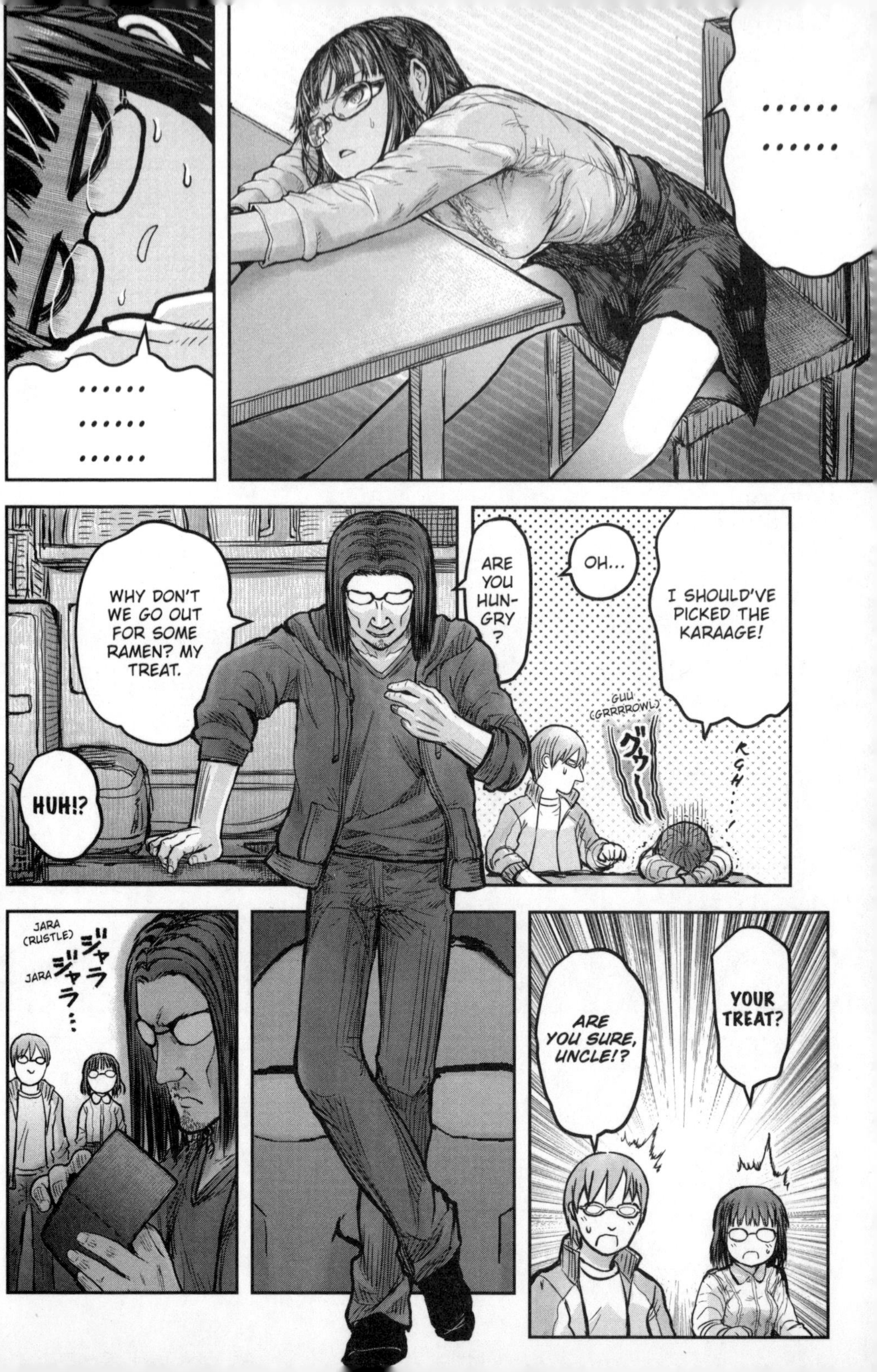
……
……
……
……
……
I SHOULD'VE PICKED THE KARAAGE!
OH...
ARE YOU HUN-GRY?
GUU (GRRRROWL)
グウー
KGH…!
WHY DON'T WE GO OUT FOR SOME RAMEN? MY TREAT.
HUH!?
YOUR TREAT?
ARE YOU SURE, UNCLE!?
JARA (RUSTLE) JARA
ジャラ
ジャラ…

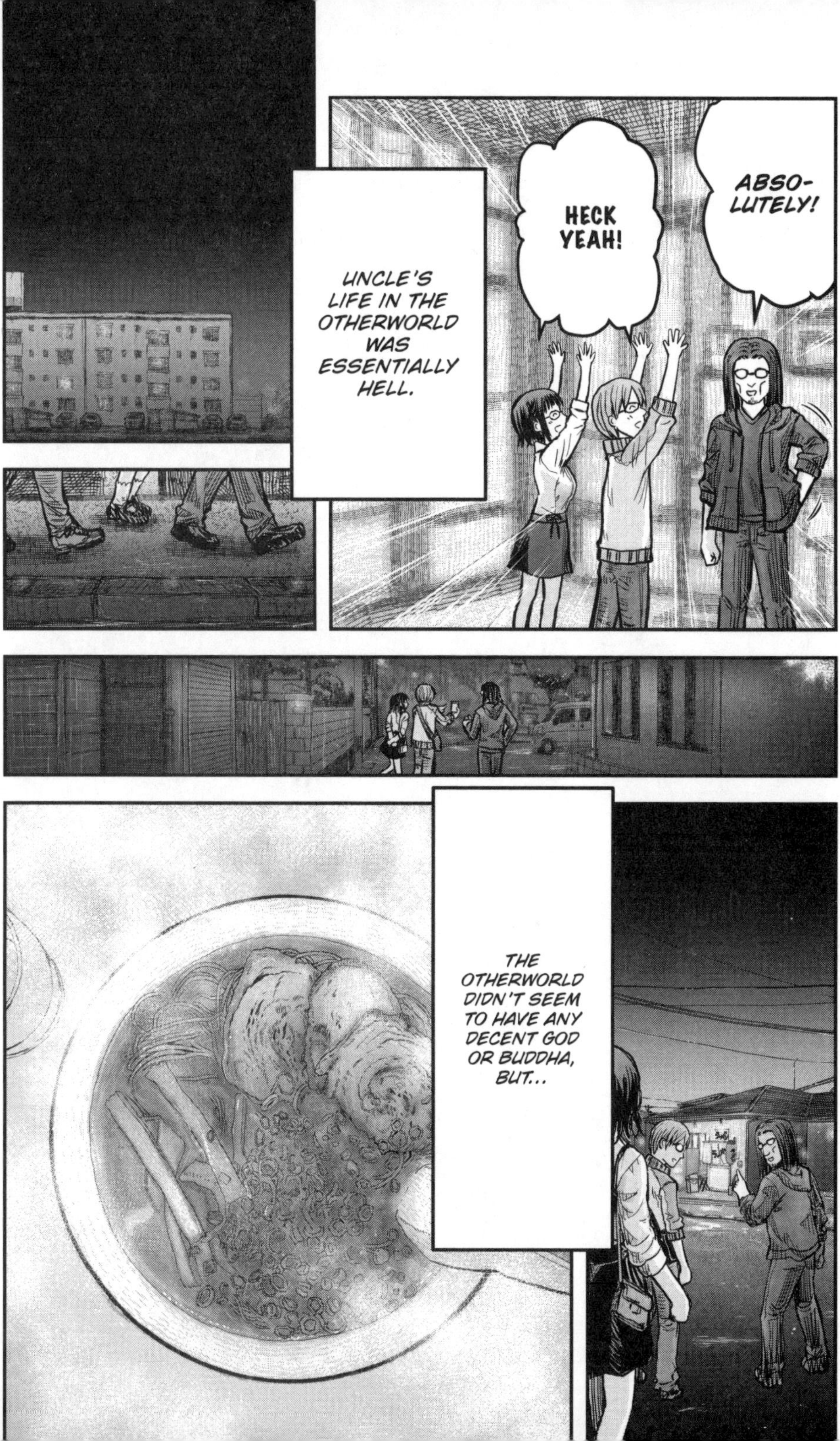
ABSO-LUTELY!
HECK YEAH!
UNCLE'S LIFE IN THE OTHERWORLD WAS ESSENTIALLY HELL.
THE OTHERWORLD DIDN'T SEEM TO HAVE ANY DECENT GOD OR BUDDHA, BUT...

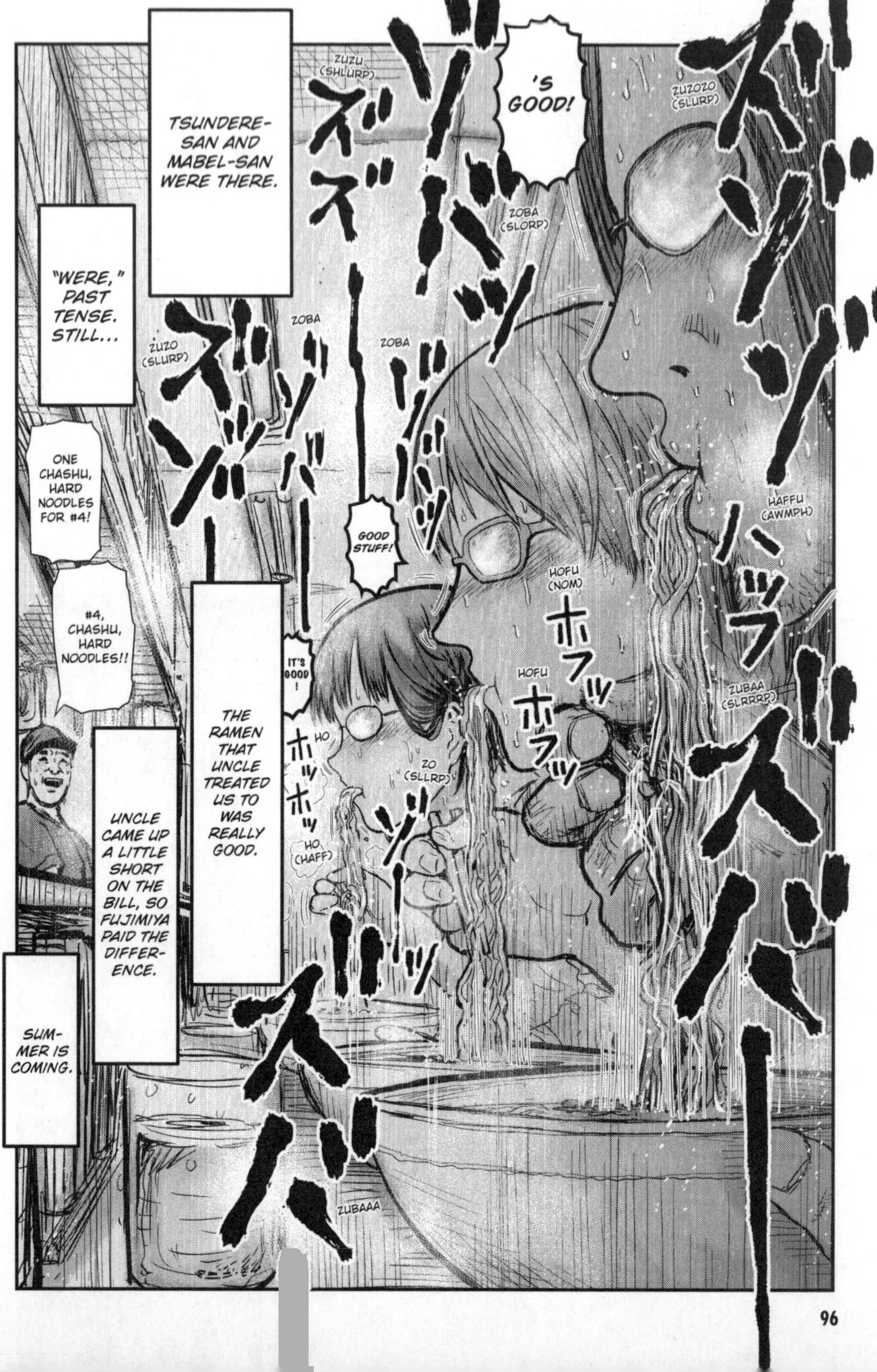

ZUZOZO (SLURP)
'S GOOD!
ZUZU (SHLURP)
TSUNDERE-SAN AND MABEL-SAN WERE THERE.
ZOBA (SLORP)
"WERE," PAST TENSE. STILL...
ZOBA
ZOBA
ZUZO (SLURP)
HAFFU (AWMPH)
HOFU (NOM)
GOOD STUFF!
ONE CHASHU, HARD NOODLES FOR #4!
#4, CHASHU, HARD NOODLES!!
HOFU
ZUBAA (SLRRRP)
IT'S GOOD!
ZO (SLLRP)
HO
HO (CHAFF)
THE RAMEN THAT UNCLE TREATED US TO WAS REALLY GOOD.
UNCLE CAME UP A LITTLE SHORT ON THE BILL, SO FUJIMIYA PAID THE DIFFERENCE.
SUMMER IS COMING.
ZUBAAA

Karaage

A type of cuisine made by coating ingredients (primarily chicken thigh meat) in a light layer of wheat flour or potato starch and deep-frying them in hot oil.
It is difficult to say whether or not it's more enjoyable to eat than ramen.

UNCLE from ANOTHER WORLD

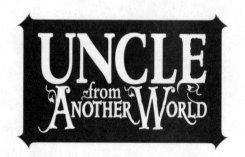

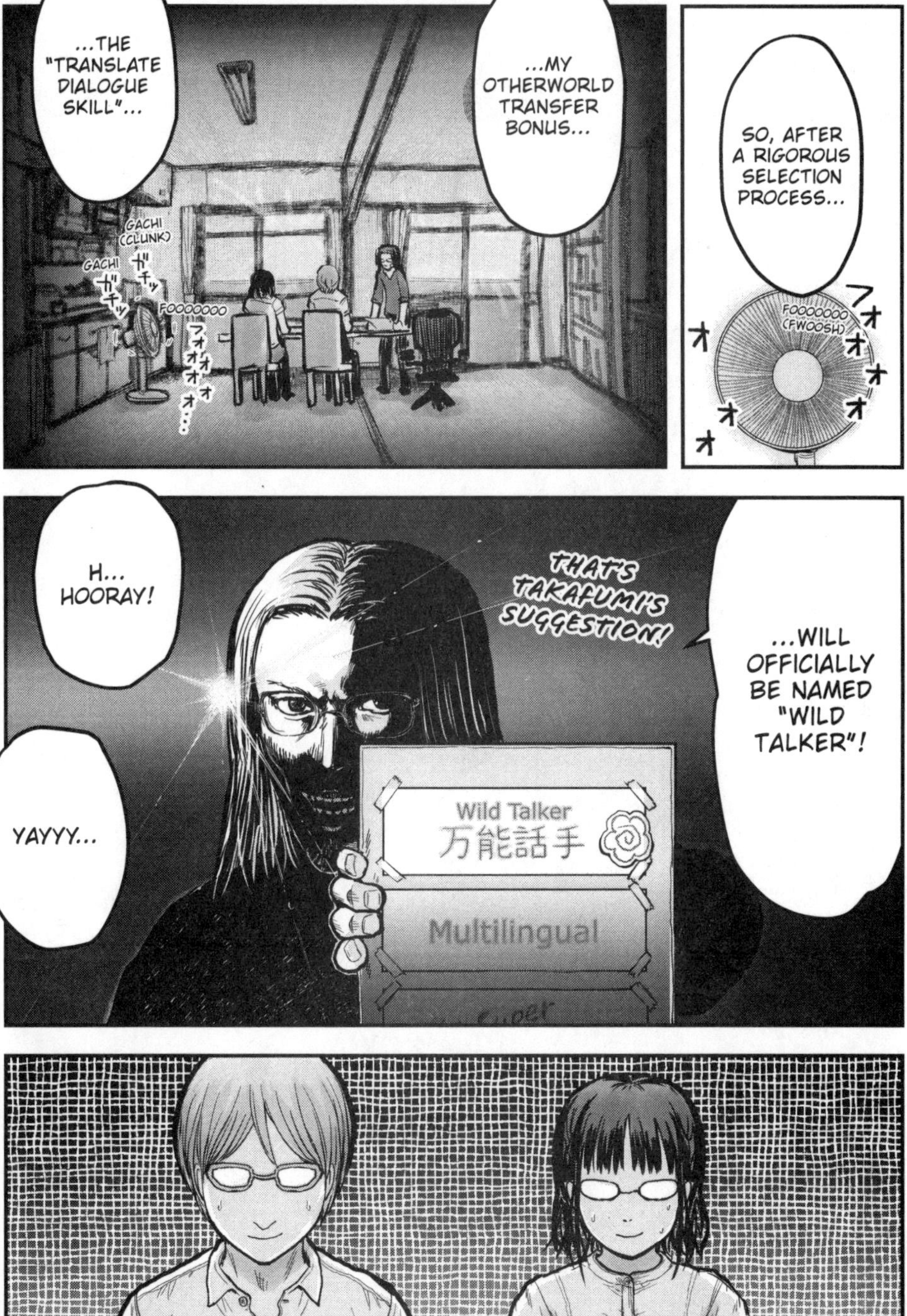
SO, AFTER A RIGOROUS SELECTION PROCESS...
FOOOOOOO (FWOOSH)
フォォォォォォ
...MY OTHERWORLD TRANSFER BONUS...
...THE "TRANSLATE DIALOGUE SKILL"...
GACHI (CLUNK)
ガチッ
GACHI
ガチッ
FOOOOOOO
フォォォォォ...
...WILL OFFICIALLY BE NAMED "WILD TALKER"!
THAT'S TAKAFUMI'S SUGGESTION!
Wild Talker
万能話手
Multilingual
H... HOORAY!
YAYYY...

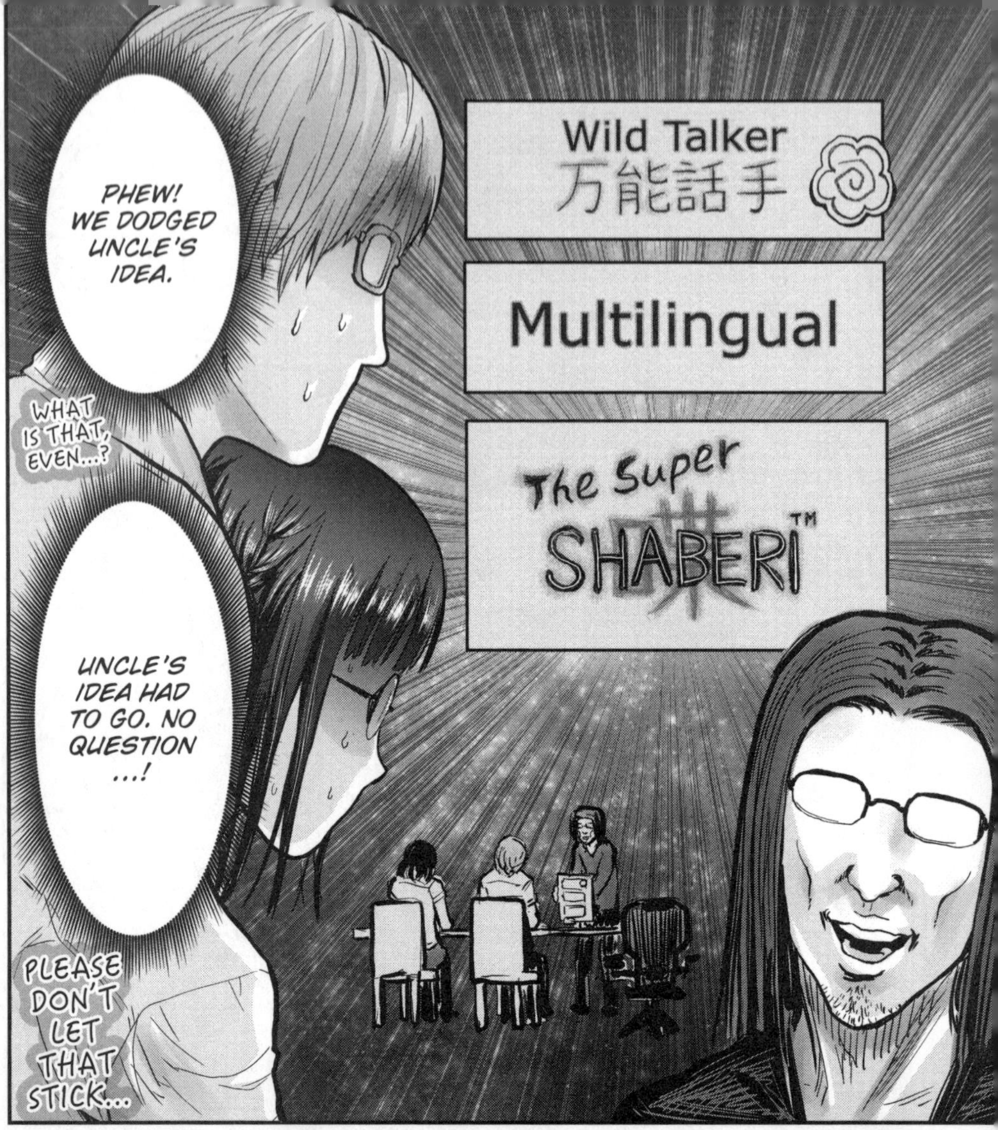
Wild Talker
万能話手
Multilingual
The Super SHABERI™
PHEW! WE DODGED UNCLE'S IDEA.
WHAT IS THAT, EVEN...?
UNCLE'S IDEA HAD TO GO. NO QUESTION ...!
PLEASE DON'T LET THAT STICK...

JULY 2018

CHAPTER 17

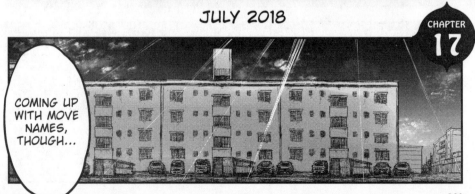

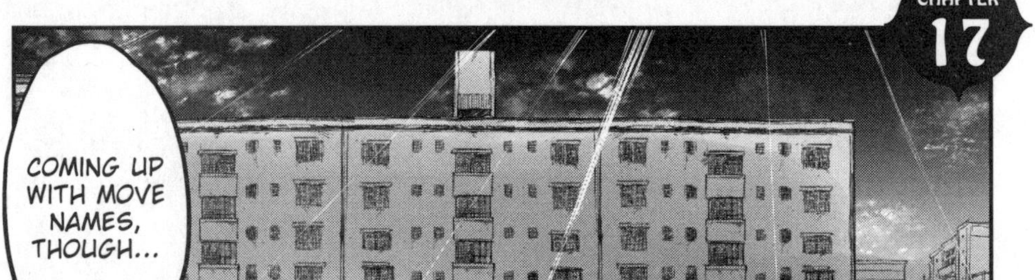
COMING UP WITH MOVE NAMES, THOUGH...

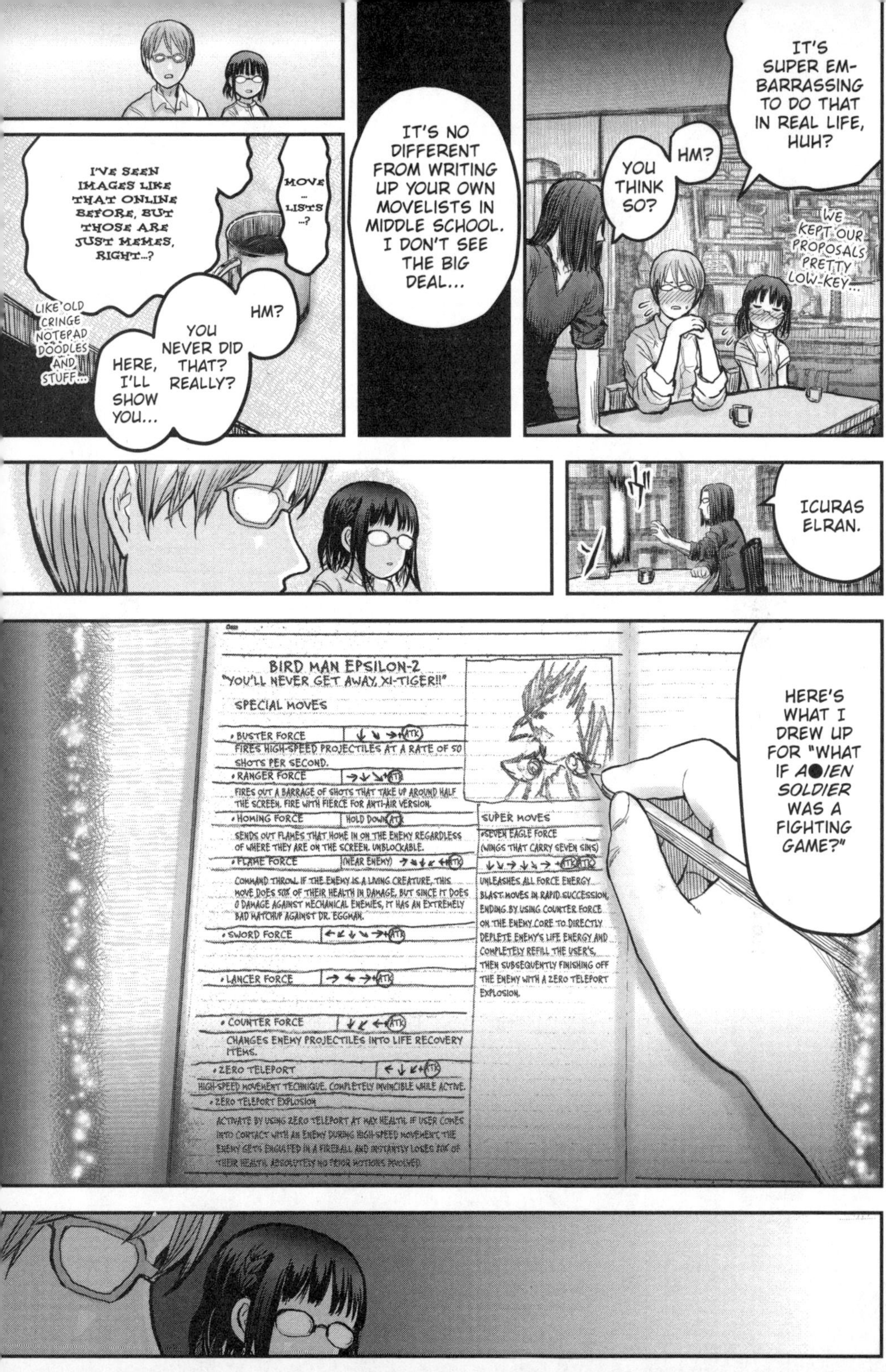
IT'S SUPER EM-BARRASSING TO DO THAT IN REAL LIFE, HUH?
WE KEPT OUR PROPOSALS PRETTY LOW-KEY...
HM?
YOU THINK SO?
IT'S NO DIFFERENT FROM WRITING UP YOUR OWN MOVELISTS IN MIDDLE SCHOOL. I DON'T SEE THE BIG DEAL...
MOVE... LISTS...?
I'VE SEEN IMAGES LIKE THAT ONLINE BEFORE, BUT THOSE ARE JUST MEMES, RIGHT...?
HM?
YOU NEVER DID THAT? REALLY?
HERE, I'LL SHOW YOU...
LIKE OLD CRINGE NOTEPAD DOODLES AND STUFF...
ICURAS ELRAN.
HERE'S WHAT I DREW UP FOR "WHAT IF A●IEN SOLDIER WAS A FIGHTING GAME?"
BIRD MAN EPSILON-2
"YOU'LL NEVER GET AWAY, XI-TIGER!!"
SPECIAL MOVES
• BUSTER FORCE ↓↘→+ATK
FIRES HIGH-SPEED PROJECTILES AT A RATE OF 50 SHOTS PER SECOND.
• RANGER FORCE →↓↘+ATK
FIRES OUT A BARRAGE OF SHOTS THAT TAKE UP AROUND HALF THE SCREEN. FIRE WITH FIERCE FOR ANTI-AIR VERSION.
• HOMING FORCE HOLD DOWN ATK
SENDS OUT FLAMES THAT HOME IN ON THE ENEMY REGARDLESS OF WHERE THEY ARE ON THE SCREEN. UNBLOCKABLE.
• FLAME FORCE (NEAR ENEMY) →↘↓↙←+ATK
COMMAND THROW. IF THE ENEMY IS A LIVING CREATURE, THIS MOVE DOES 50% OF THEIR HEALTH IN DAMAGE, BUT SINCE IT DOES 0 DAMAGE AGAINST MECHANICAL ENEMIES, IT HAS AN EXTREMELY BAD MATCHUP AGAINST DR. EGGMAN.
• SWORD FORCE ←↙↓↘→+ATK
• LANCER FORCE →←→+ATK
• COUNTER FORCE ↓↙←+ATK
CHANGES ENEMY PROJECTILES INTO LIFE RECOVERY ITEMS.
• ZERO TELEPORT ←↓↙+ATK
HIGH-SPEED MOVEMENT TECHNIQUE. COMPLETELY INVINCIBLE WHILE ACTIVE.
• ZERO TELEPORT EXPLOSION
ACTIVATE BY USING ZERO TELEPORT AT MAX HEALTH. IF USER COMES INTO CONTACT WITH AN ENEMY DURING HIGH-SPEED MOVEMENT, THE ENEMY GETS ENGULFED IN A FIREBALL AND INSTANTLY LOSES 50% OF THEIR HEALTH. ABSOLUTELY NO PRIOR MOTIONS INVOLVED.
SUPER MOVES
• SEVEN EAGLE FORCE (WINGS THAT CARRY SEVEN SINS)
↓↘→↓↘→+ATK ATK
UNLEASHES ALL FORCE ENERGY BLAST MOVES IN RAPID SUCCESSION, ENDING BY USING COUNTER FORCE ON THE ENEMY CORE TO DIRECTLY DEPLETE ENEMY'S LIFE ENERGY AND COMPLETELY REFILL THE USER'S, THEN SUBSEQUENTLY FINISHING OFF THE ENEMY WITH A ZERO TELEPORT EXPLOSION.

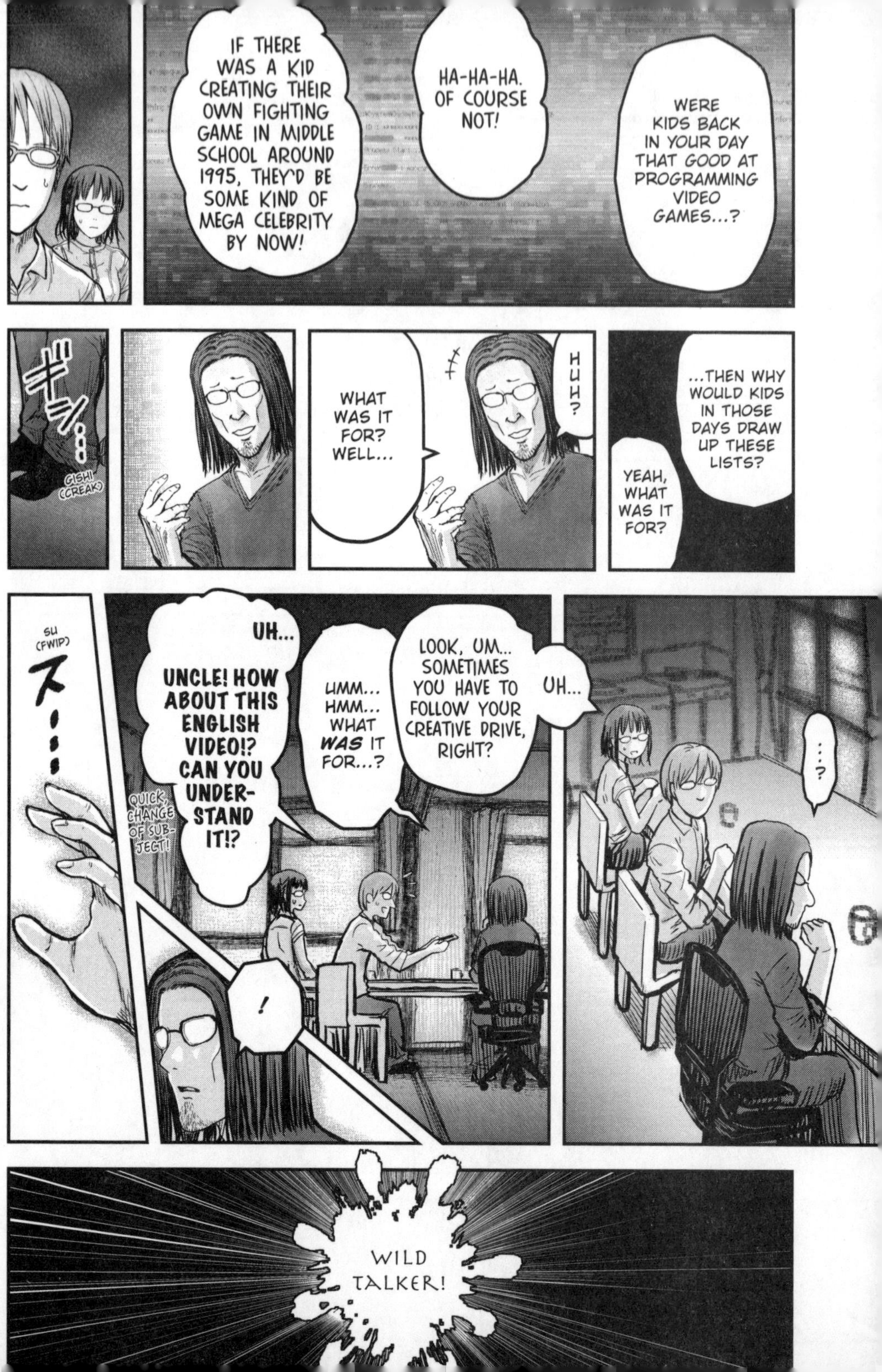
WERE KIDS BACK IN YOUR DAY THAT GOOD AT PROGRAMMING VIDEO GAMES...?
HA-HA-HA. OF COURSE NOT!
IF THERE WAS A KID CREATING THEIR OWN FIGHTING GAME IN MIDDLE SCHOOL AROUND 1995, THEY'D BE SOME KIND OF MEGA CELEBRITY BY NOW!
...THEN WHY WOULD KIDS IN THOSE DAYS DRAW UP THESE LISTS?
YEAH, WHAT WAS IT FOR?
HUH?
WHAT WAS IT FOR? WELL...
GISHI (CREAK)
UH...
...?
LOOK, UM... SOMETIMES YOU HAVE TO FOLLOW YOUR CREATIVE DRIVE, RIGHT?
UMM... HMM... WHAT *WAS* IT FOR...?
UH...
UNCLE! HOW ABOUT THIS ENGLISH VIDEO!? CAN YOU UNDERSTAND IT!?
QUICK, CHANGE OF SUBJECT!
!
SU (FWIP)
WILD TALKER!

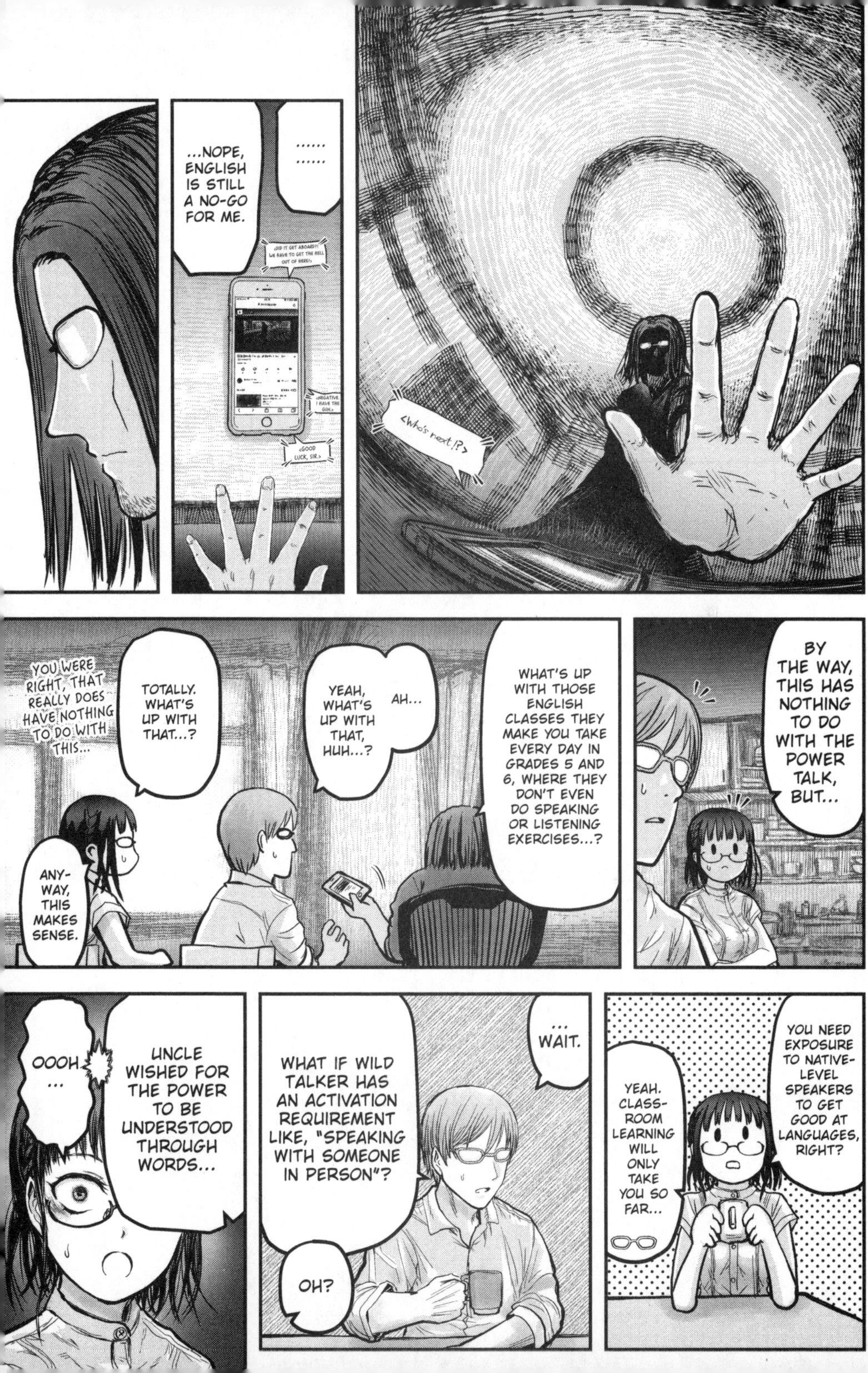
<Who's next!?>
......
......
...NOPE, ENGLISH IS STILL A NO-GO FOR ME.
<DID IT GET ABOARD?! WE HAVE TO GET THE HELL OUT OF HERE!>
<NEGATIVE. I HAVE THE GUN.>
<GOOD LUCK, SIR.>
BY THE WAY, THIS HAS NOTHING TO DO WITH THE POWER TALK, BUT...
WHAT'S UP WITH THOSE ENGLISH CLASSES THEY MAKE YOU TAKE EVERY DAY IN GRADES 5 AND 6, WHERE THEY DON'T EVEN DO SPEAKING OR LISTENING EXERCISES...?
AH...
YEAH, WHAT'S UP WITH THAT, HUH...?
TOTALLY. WHAT'S UP WITH THAT...?
YOU WERE RIGHT, THAT REALLY DOES HAVE NOTHING TO DO WITH THIS...
ANY-WAY, THIS MAKES SENSE.
YOU NEED EXPOSURE TO NATIVE-LEVEL SPEAKERS TO GET GOOD AT LANGUAGES, RIGHT?
YEAH. CLASS-ROOM LEARNING WILL ONLY TAKE YOU SO FAR...
...WAIT.
WHAT IF WILD TALKER HAS AN ACTIVATION REQUIREMENT LIKE, "SPEAKING WITH SOMEONE IN PERSON"?
OH?
UNCLE WISHED FOR THE POWER TO BE UNDERSTOOD THROUGH WORDS...
OOOH...

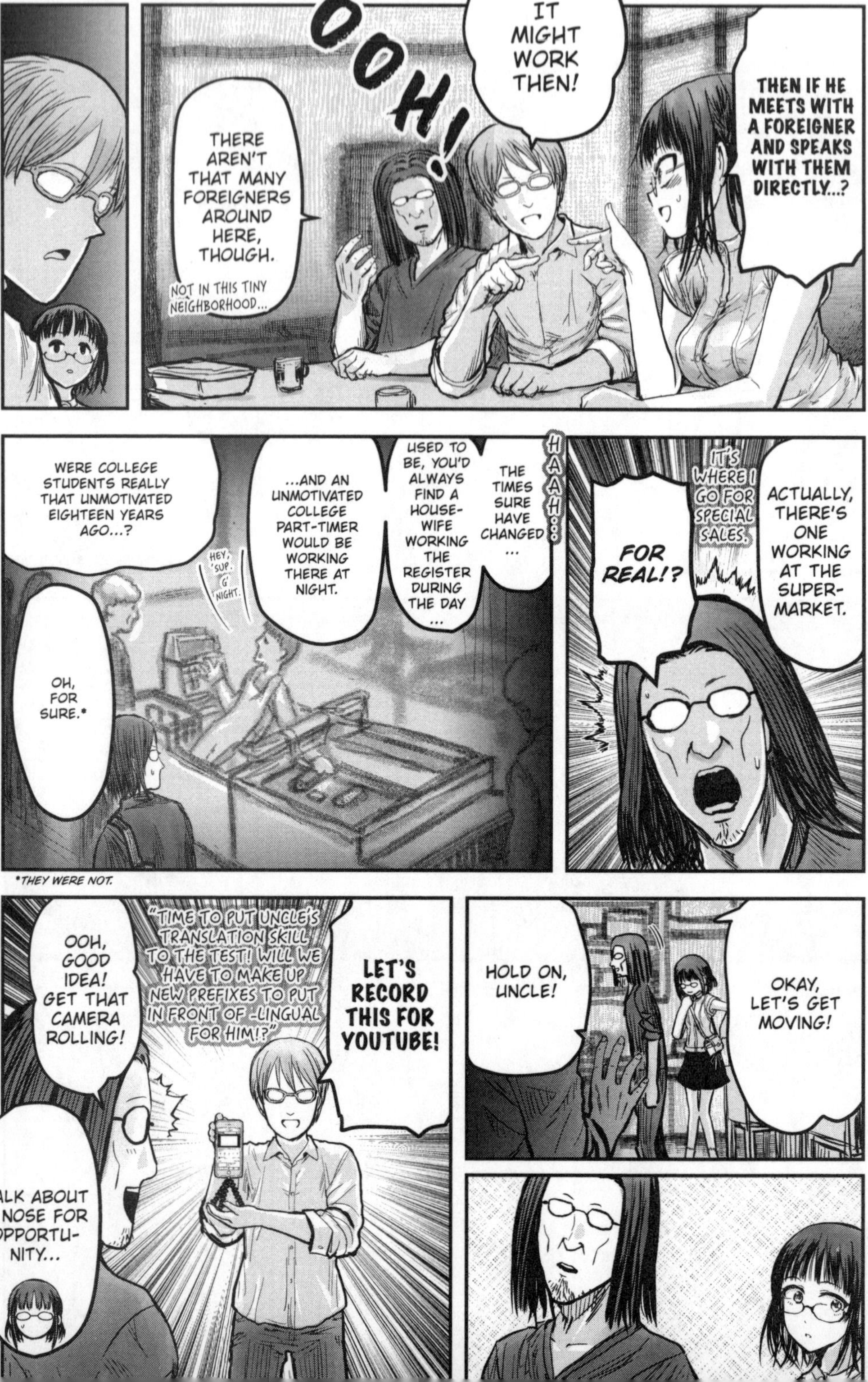
THEN IF HE MEETS WITH A FOREIGNER AND SPEAKS WITH THEM DIRECTLY...?
IT MIGHT WORK THEN!
OOH!
THERE AREN'T THAT MANY FOREIGNERS AROUND HERE, THOUGH.
NOT IN THIS TINY NEIGHBORHOOD...
ACTUALLY, THERE'S ONE WORKING AT THE SUPER-MARKET.
IT'S WHERE I GO FOR SPECIAL SALES.
FOR REAL!?
HAAAH...
THE TIMES SURE HAVE CHANGED...
USED TO BE, YOU'D ALWAYS FIND A HOUSE-WIFE WORKING THE REGISTER DURING THE DAY...
...AND AN UNMOTIVATED COLLEGE PART-TIMER WOULD BE WORKING THERE AT NIGHT.
WERE COLLEGE STUDENTS REALLY THAT UNMOTIVATED EIGHTEEN YEARS AGO...?
HEY, 'SUP.
G' NIGHT.
OH, FOR SURE.*
OKAY, LET'S GET MOVING!
HOLD ON, UNCLE!
LET'S RECORD THIS FOR YOUTUBE!
"TIME TO PUT UNCLE'S TRANSLATION SKILL TO THE TEST! WILL WE HAVE TO MAKE UP NEW PREFIXES TO PUT IN FRONT OF -LINGUAL FOR HIM!?"
OOH, GOOD IDEA! GET THAT CAMERA ROLLING!
TALK ABOUT A NOSE FOR OPPORTU-NITY...

*THEY WERE NOT.

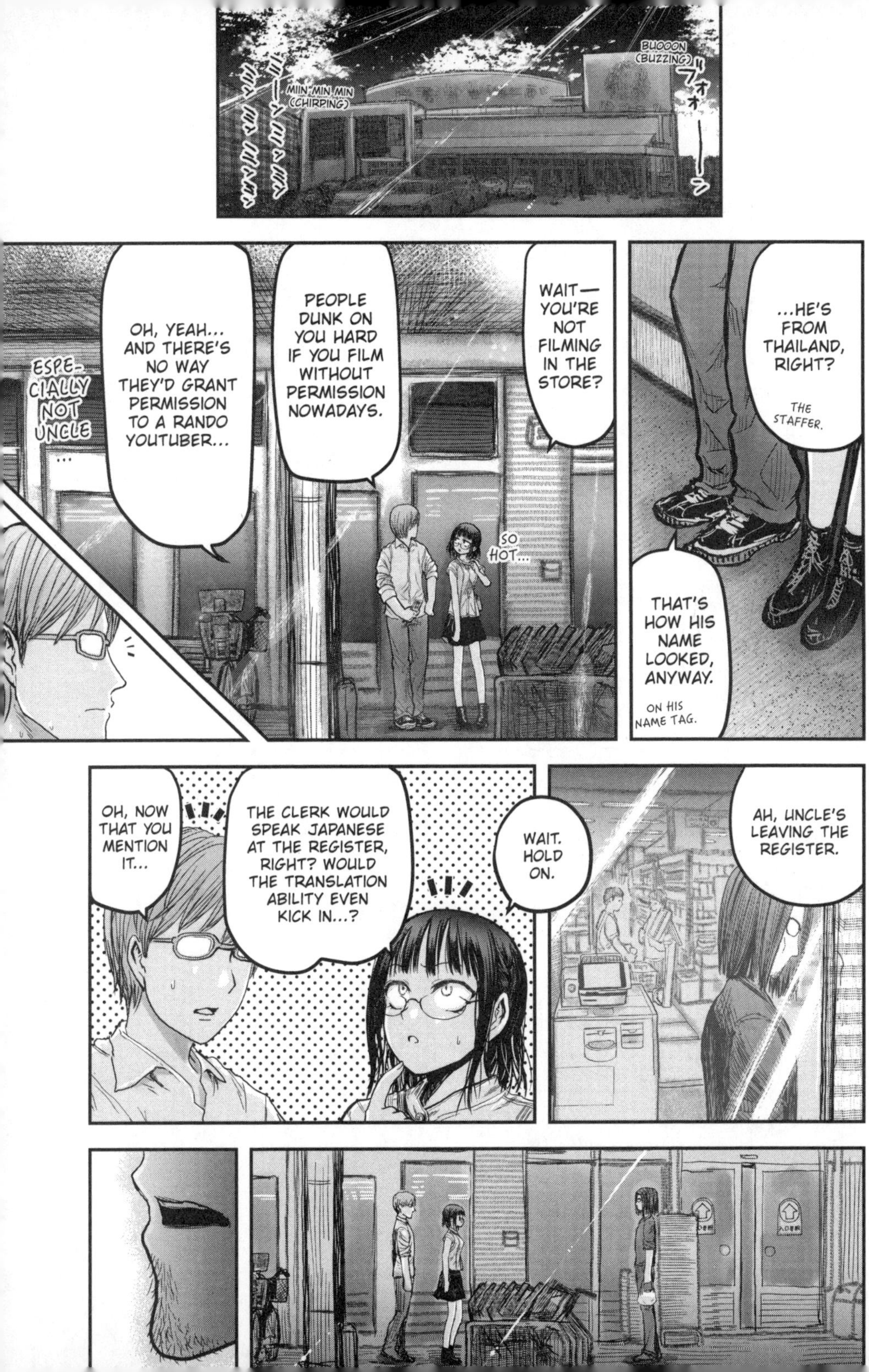
BUOOON (BUZZING)
MIIN MIN MIN (CHIRPING)
...HE'S FROM THAILAND, RIGHT?
THE STAFFER.
THAT'S HOW HIS NAME LOOKED, ANYWAY.
ON HIS NAME TAG.
WAIT—YOU'RE NOT FILMING IN THE STORE?
PEOPLE DUNK ON YOU HARD IF YOU FILM WITHOUT PERMISSION NOWADAYS.
SO HOT...
OH, YEAH... AND THERE'S NO WAY THEY'D GRANT PERMISSION TO A RANDO YOUTUBER...
ESPE-CIALLY NOT UNCLE
...
AH, UNCLE'S LEAVING THE REGISTER.
WAIT. HOLD ON.
THE CLERK WOULD SPEAK JAPANESE AT THE REGISTER, RIGHT? WOULD THE TRANSLATION ABILITY EVEN KICK IN...?
OH, NOW THAT YOU MENTION IT...

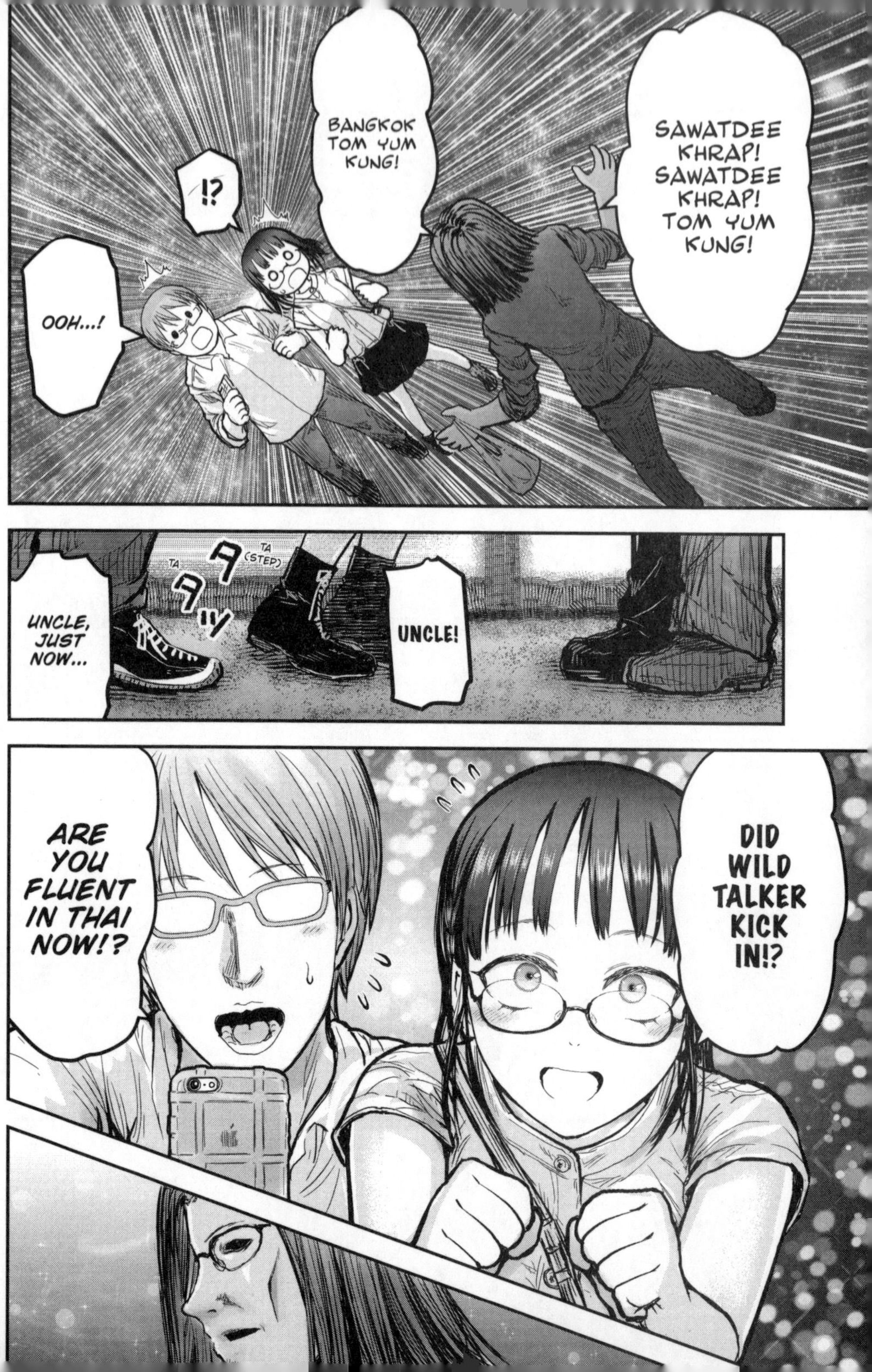
SAWATDEE KHRAP! SAWATDEE KHRAP! TOM YUM KUNG!
BANGKOK TOM YUM KUNG!
!?
OOH...!
UNCLE!
TA (STEP)
TA
UNCLE, JUST NOW...
DID WILD TALKER KICK IN!?
ARE YOU FLUENT IN THAI NOW!?

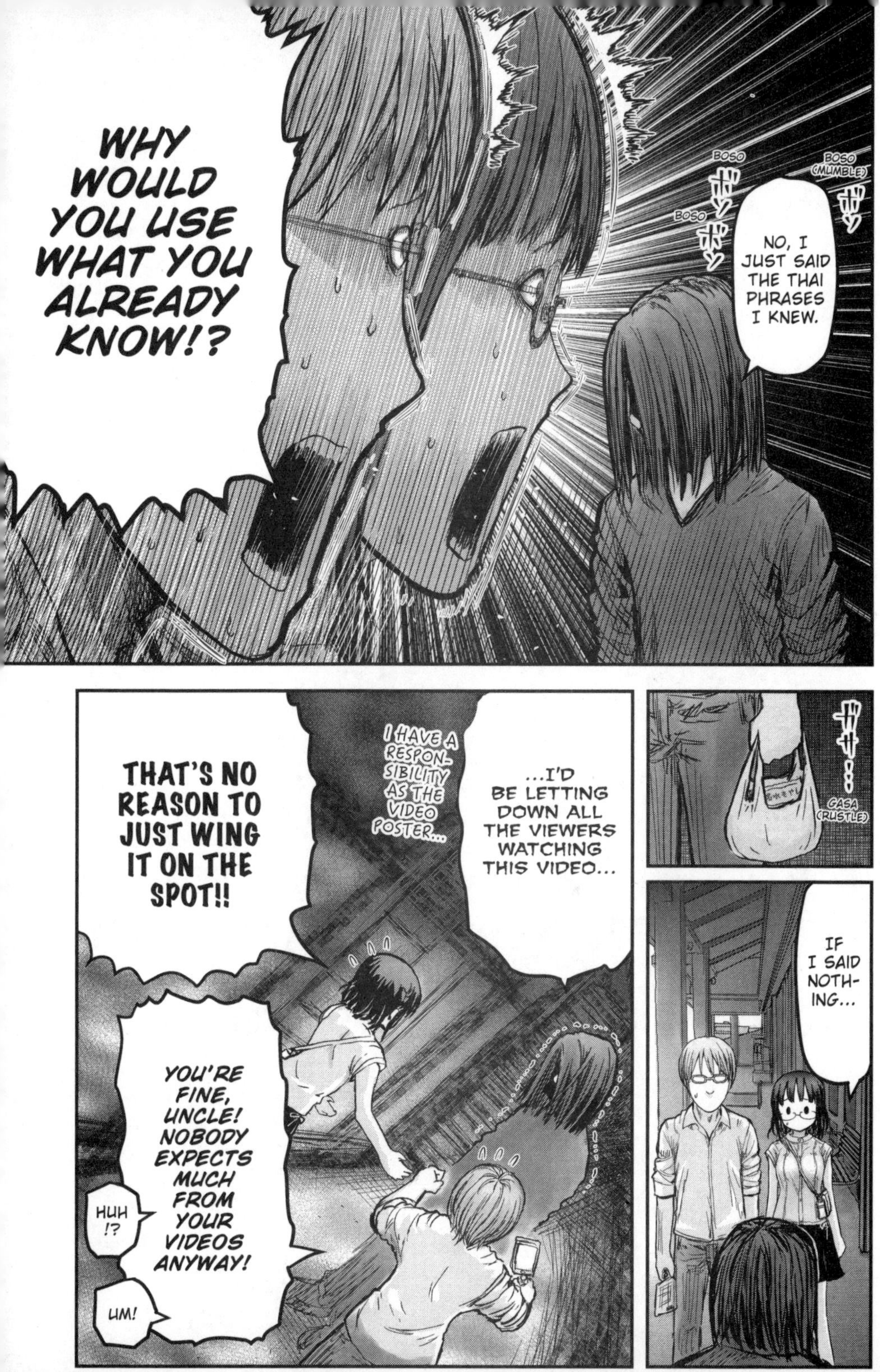
BOSO (MUMBLE)
BOSO
BOSO
NO, I JUST SAID THE THAI PHRASES I KNEW.
WHY WOULD YOU USE WHAT YOU ALREADY KNOW!?
GASA (RUSTLE)
IF I SAID NOTHING...
...I'D BE LETTING DOWN ALL THE VIEWERS WATCHING THIS VIDEO...
I HAVE A RESPONSIBILITY AS THE VIDEO POSTER...
THAT'S NO REASON TO JUST WING IT ON THE SPOT!!
YOU'RE FINE, UNCLE! NOBODY EXPECTS MUCH FROM YOUR VIDEOS ANYWAY!
HUH!?
UM!

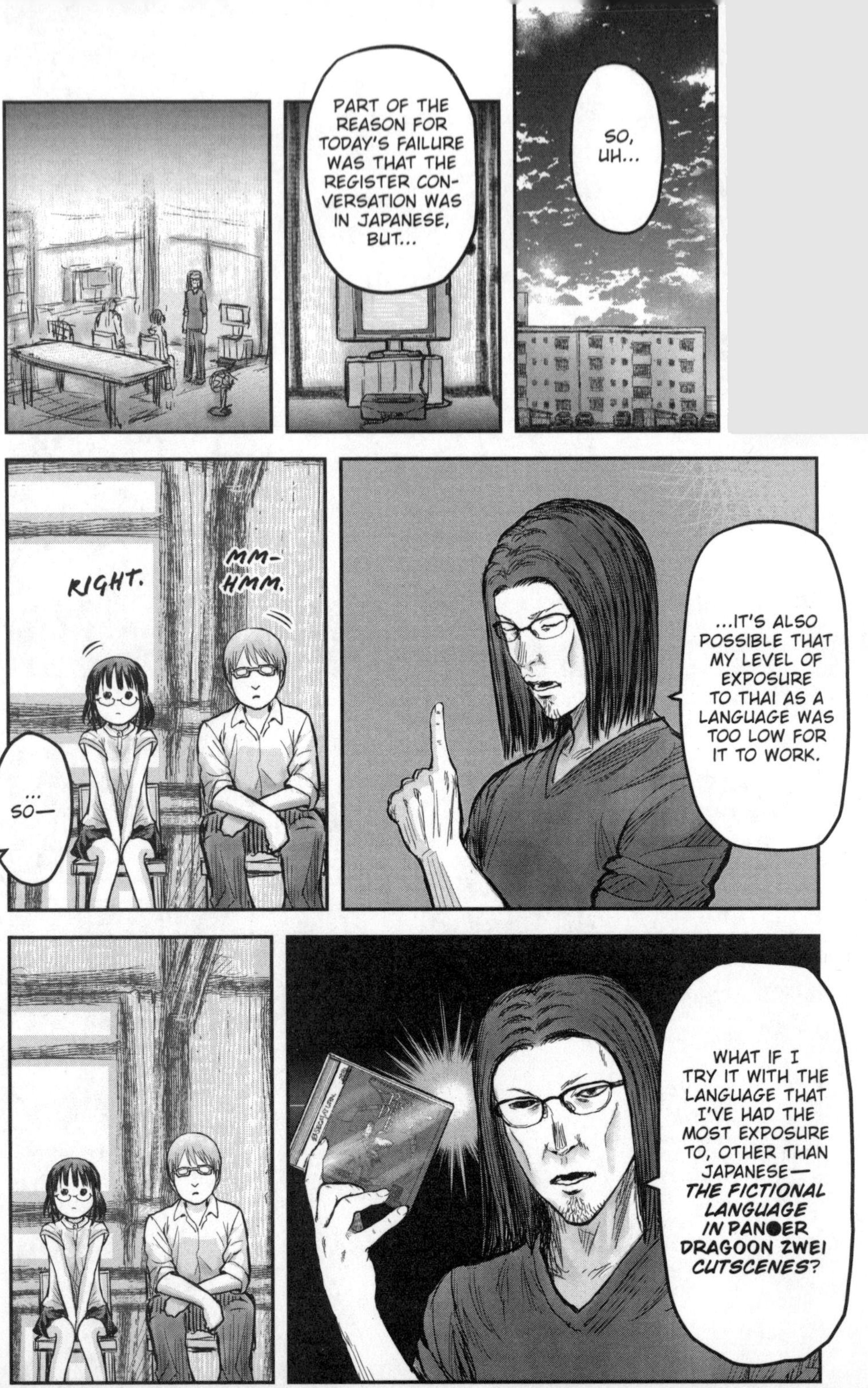
SO, UH...
PART OF THE REASON FOR TODAY'S FAILURE WAS THAT THE REGISTER CONVERSATION WAS IN JAPANESE, BUT...
...IT'S ALSO POSSIBLE THAT MY LEVEL OF EXPOSURE TO THAI AS A LANGUAGE WAS TOO LOW FOR IT TO WORK.
MM-HMM.
RIGHT.
...SO—
WHAT IF I TRY IT WITH THE LANGUAGE THAT I'VE HAD THE MOST EXPOSURE TO, OTHER THAN JAPANESE—***THE FICTIONAL LANGUAGE IN PAN●ER DRAGOON ZWEI CUTSCENES***?

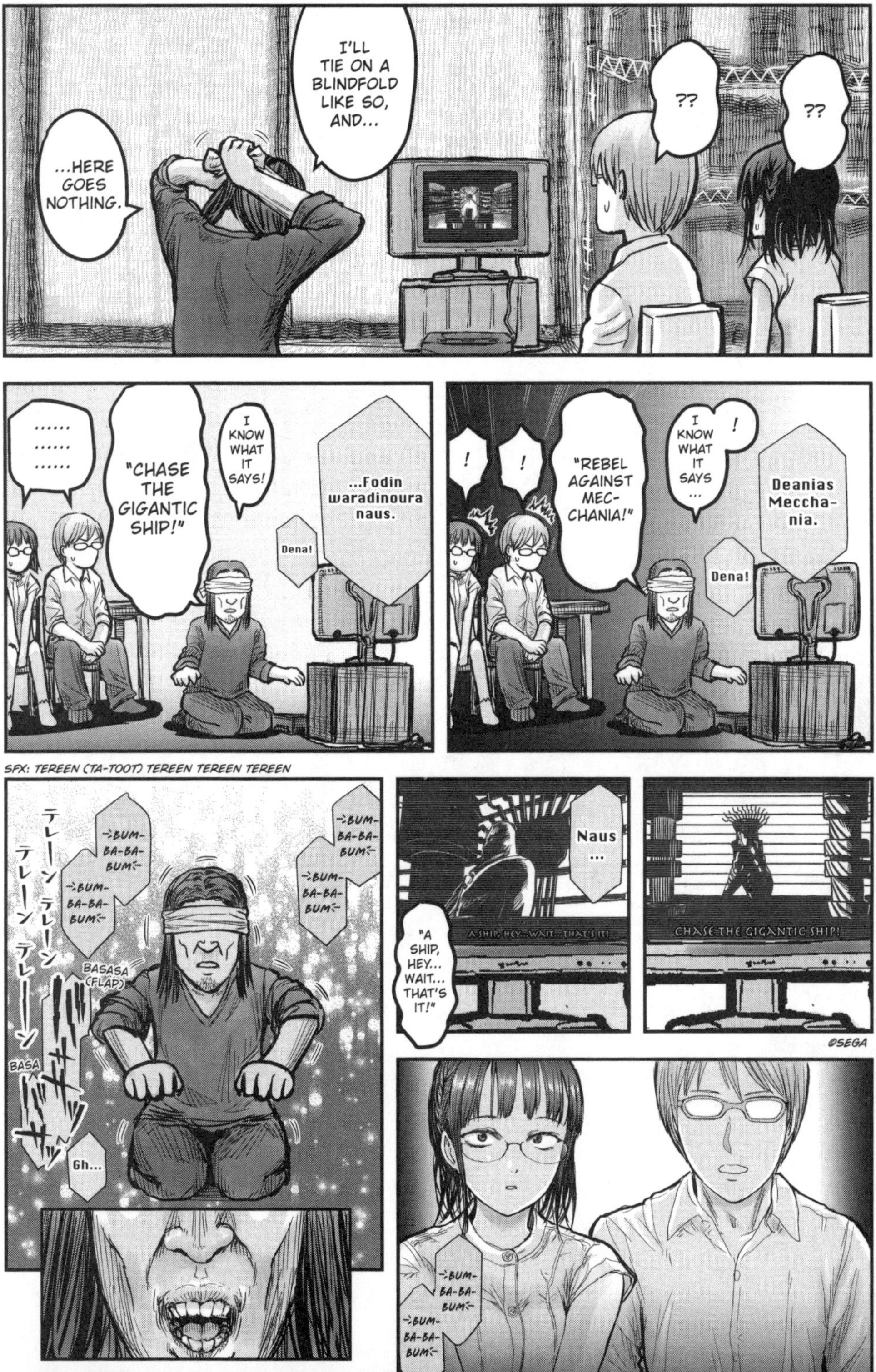
??
??
I'LL TIE ON A BLINDFOLD LIKE SO, AND...
...HERE GOES NOTHING.
Deanias Mecchania.
!
I KNOW WHAT IT SAYS...
Dena!
"REBEL AGAINST MEC-CHANIA!"
!
!
...Fodin waradinoura naus.
I KNOW WHAT IT SAYS!
Dena!
"CHASE THE GIGANTIC SHIP!"
....
SFX: TEREEN (TA-TOOT) TEREEN TEREEN TEREEN
CHASE THE GIGANTIC SHIP!
Naus...
A SHIP, HEY...WAIT...THAT'S IT!
"A SHIP, HEY... WAIT... THAT'S IT!"
©SEGA
~BUM-BA-BA-BUM~
~BUM-BA-BA-BUM~
~BUM-BA-BA-BUM~
~BUM-BA-BA-BUM~
テレーン テレーン テレーン テレーン
~BUM-BA-BA-BUM~
~BUM-BA-BA-BUM~
BASASA (FLAP)
BASA
Gh...

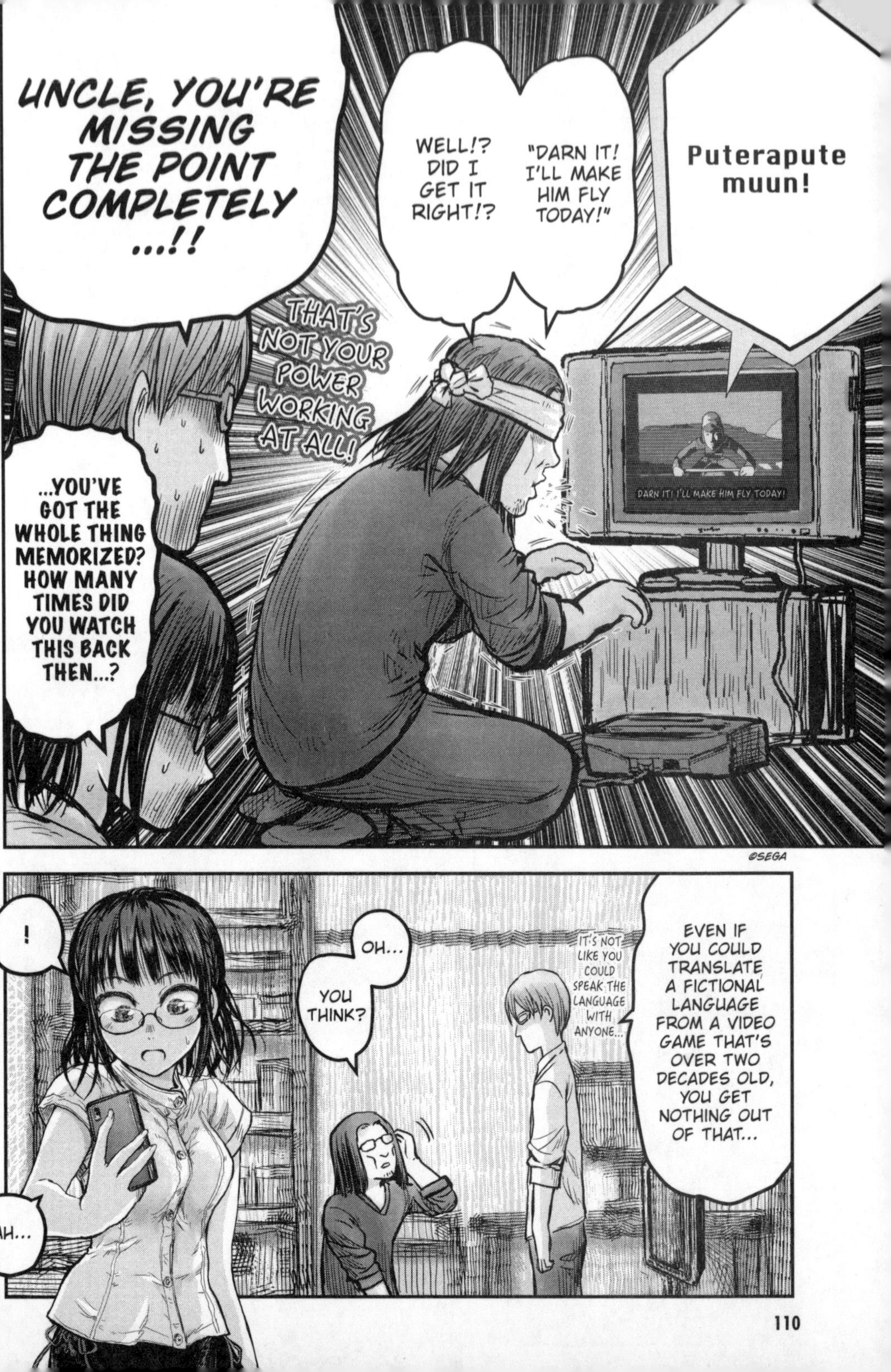

Puterapute muun!
"DARN IT! I'LL MAKE HIM FLY TODAY!"
DARN IT! I'LL MAKE HIM FLY TODAY!
WELL!? DID I GET IT RIGHT!?
THAT'S NOT YOUR POWER WORKING AT ALL!
UNCLE, YOU'RE MISSING THE POINT COMPLETELY ...!!
...YOU'VE GOT THE WHOLE THING MEMORIZED? HOW MANY TIMES DID YOU WATCH THIS BACK THEN...?
©SEGA
EVEN IF YOU COULD TRANSLATE A FICTIONAL LANGUAGE FROM A VIDEO GAME THAT'S OVER TWO DECADES OLD, YOU GET NOTHING OUT OF THAT...
IT'S NOT LIKE YOU COULD SPEAK THE LANGUAGE WITH ANYONE...
OH...
YOU THINK?
!
AH...

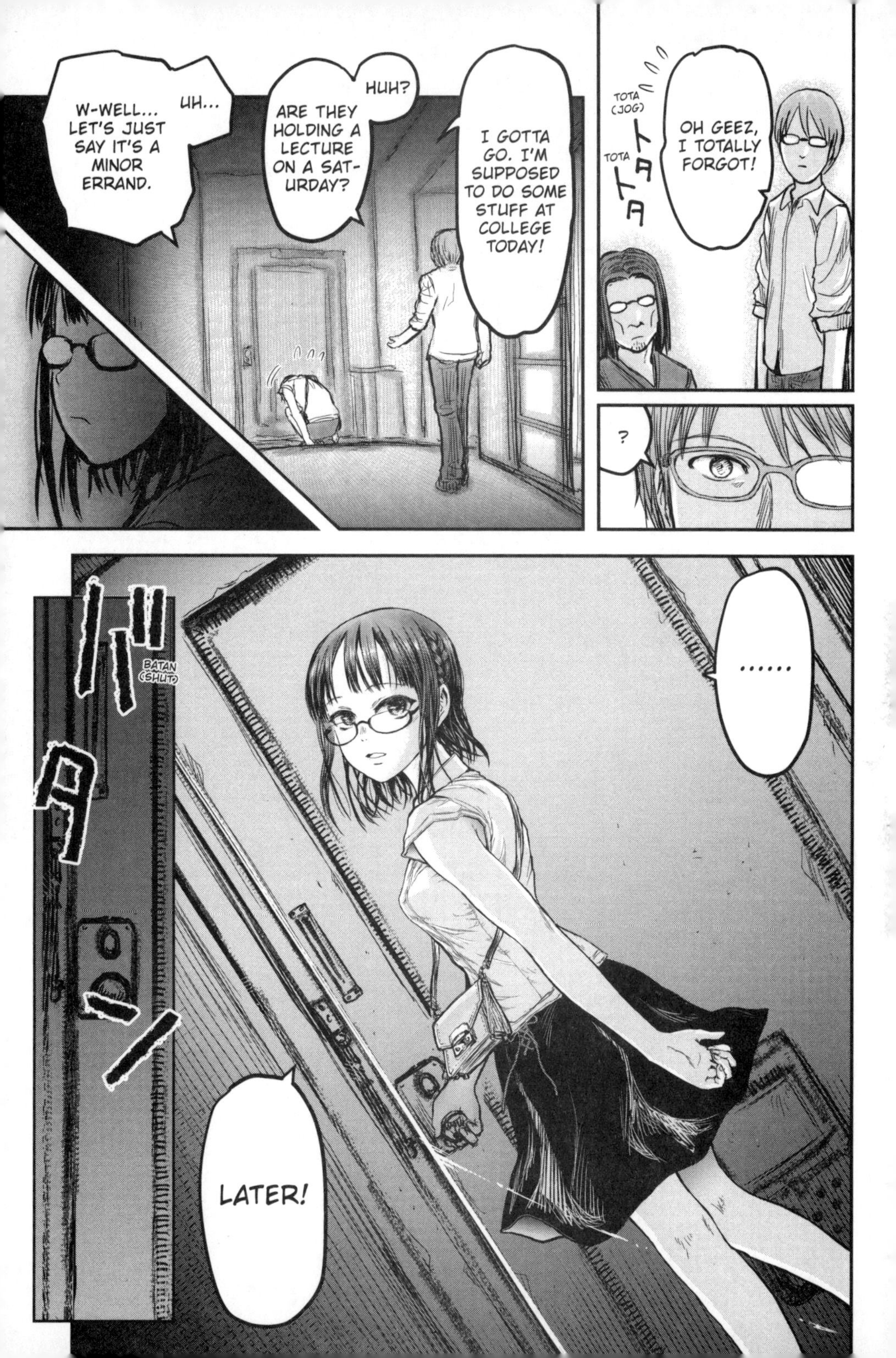
OH GEEZ, I TOTALLY FORGOT!
TOTA (JOG)
TOTA
?
I GOTTA GO. I'M SUPPOSED TO DO SOME STUFF AT COLLEGE TODAY!
HUH?
ARE THEY HOLDING A LECTURE ON A SAT-URDAY?
UH...
W-WELL... LET'S JUST SAY IT'S A MINOR ERRAND.
......
BATAN (SHUT)
LATER!

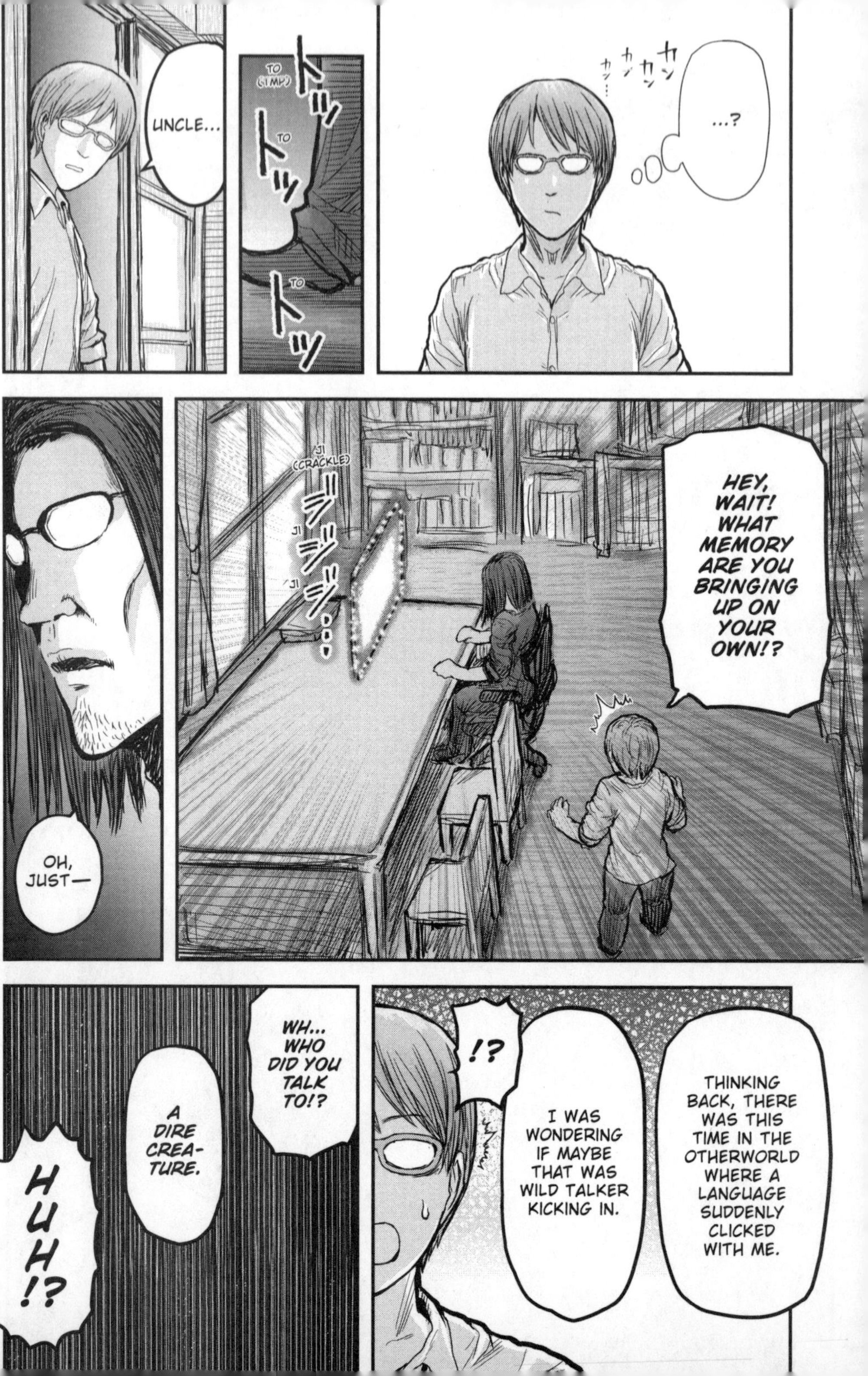

カン
カン
カツ
カツ…
...?
TO (TMP)
トッ
TO
トッ
TO
トッ
UNCLE...
JI (CRACKLE)
ジ
JI
ジ
JI
ジ...
HEY, WAIT! WHAT MEMORY ARE YOU BRINGING UP ON YOUR OWN!?
OH, JUST—
THINKING BACK, THERE WAS THIS TIME IN THE OTHERWORLD WHERE A LANGUAGE SUDDENLY CLICKED WITH ME.
I WAS WONDERING IF MAYBE THAT WAS WILD TALKER KICKING IN.
!?
WH... WHO DID YOU TALK TO!?
A DIRE CREA-TURE.
HUH!?

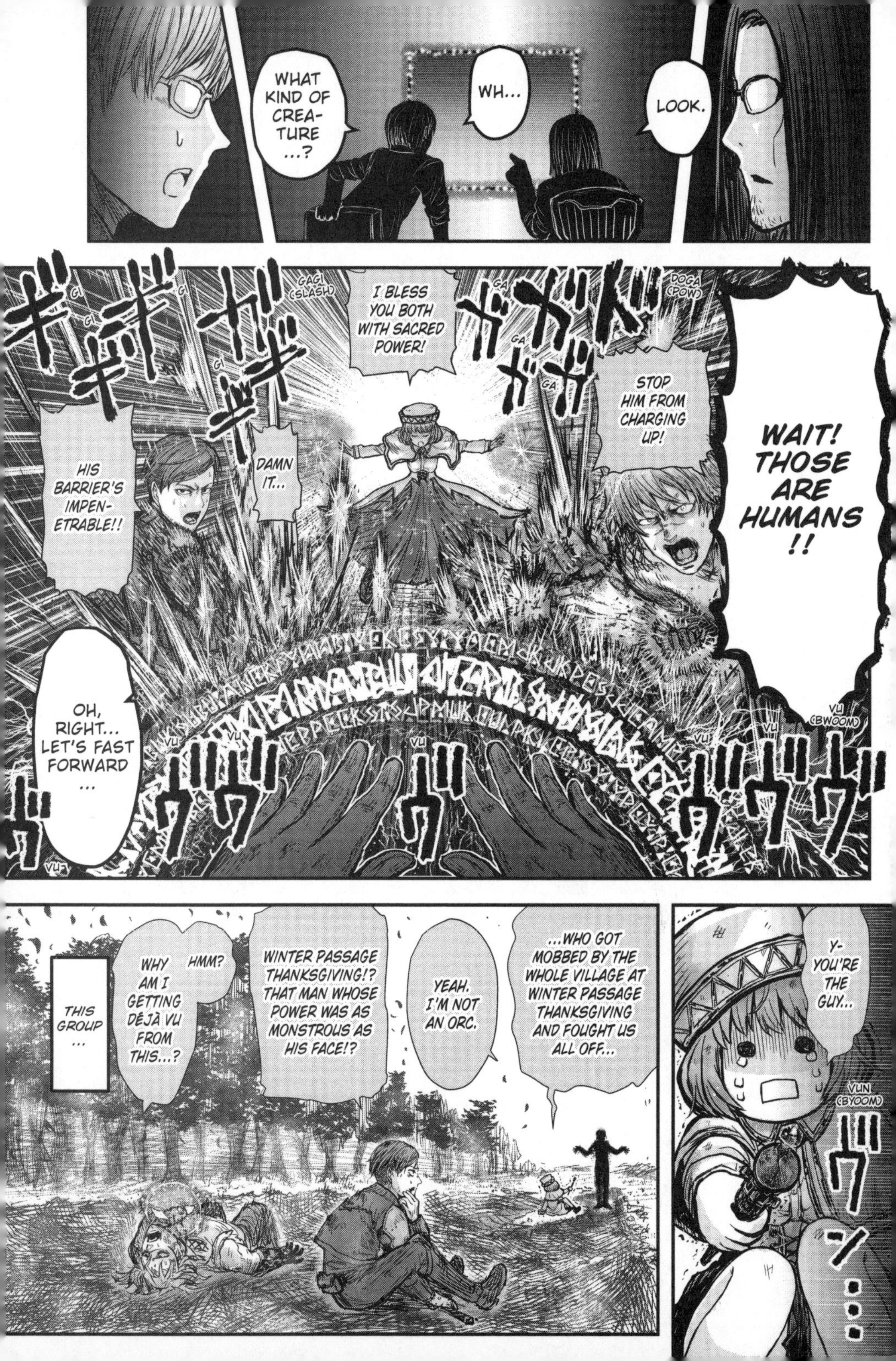
LOOK.
WH...
WHAT KIND OF CREA-TURE ...?
WAIT! THOSE ARE HUMANS!!
DOGA (POW)
STOP HIM FROM CHARGING UP!
I BLESS YOU BOTH WITH SACRED POWER!
GAGI (SLASH)
DAMN IT...
HIS BARRIER'S IMPEN-ETRABLE!!
VU (BWOOM)
OH, RIGHT... LET'S FAST FORWARD ...
Y-YOU'RE THE GUY...
VUN (BYOOM)
...WHO GOT MOBBED BY THE WHOLE VILLAGE AT WINTER PASSAGE THANKSGIVING AND FOUGHT US ALL OFF...
YEAH. I'M NOT AN ORC.
WINTER PASSAGE THANKSGIVING!? THAT MAN WHOSE POWER WAS AS MONSTROUS AS HIS FACE!?
HMM?
WHY AM I GETTING DÉJÀ VU FROM THIS...?
THIS GROUP ...

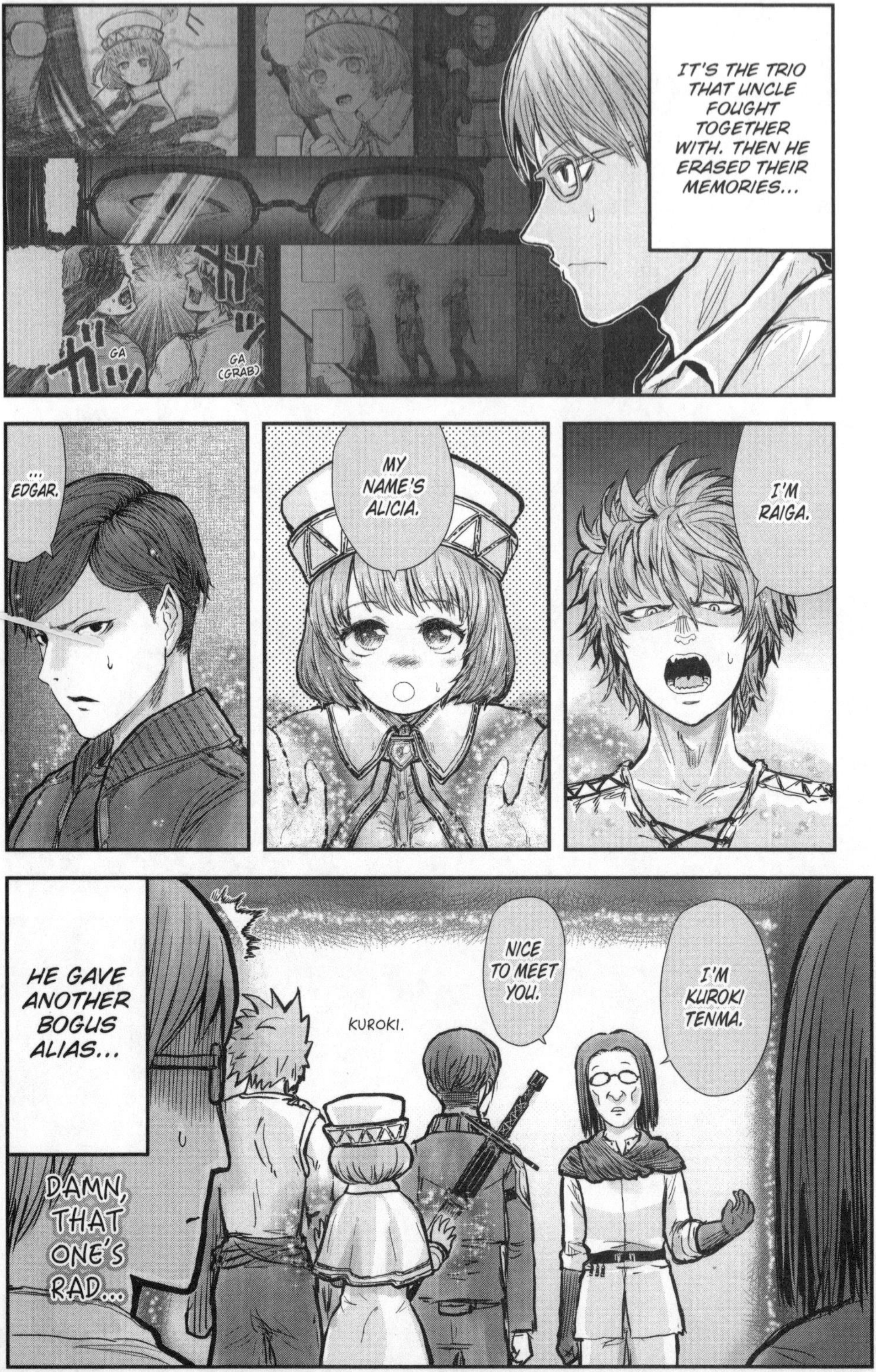
IT'S THE TRIO THAT UNCLE FOUGHT TOGETHER WITH. THEN HE ERASED THEIR MEMORIES...
GA GA (GRAB)
I'M RAIGA.
MY NAME'S ALICIA.
... EDGAR.
I'M KUROKI TENMA.
NICE TO MEET YOU.
KUROKI.
HE GAVE ANOTHER BOGUS ALIAS...
DAMN, THAT ONE'S RAD...

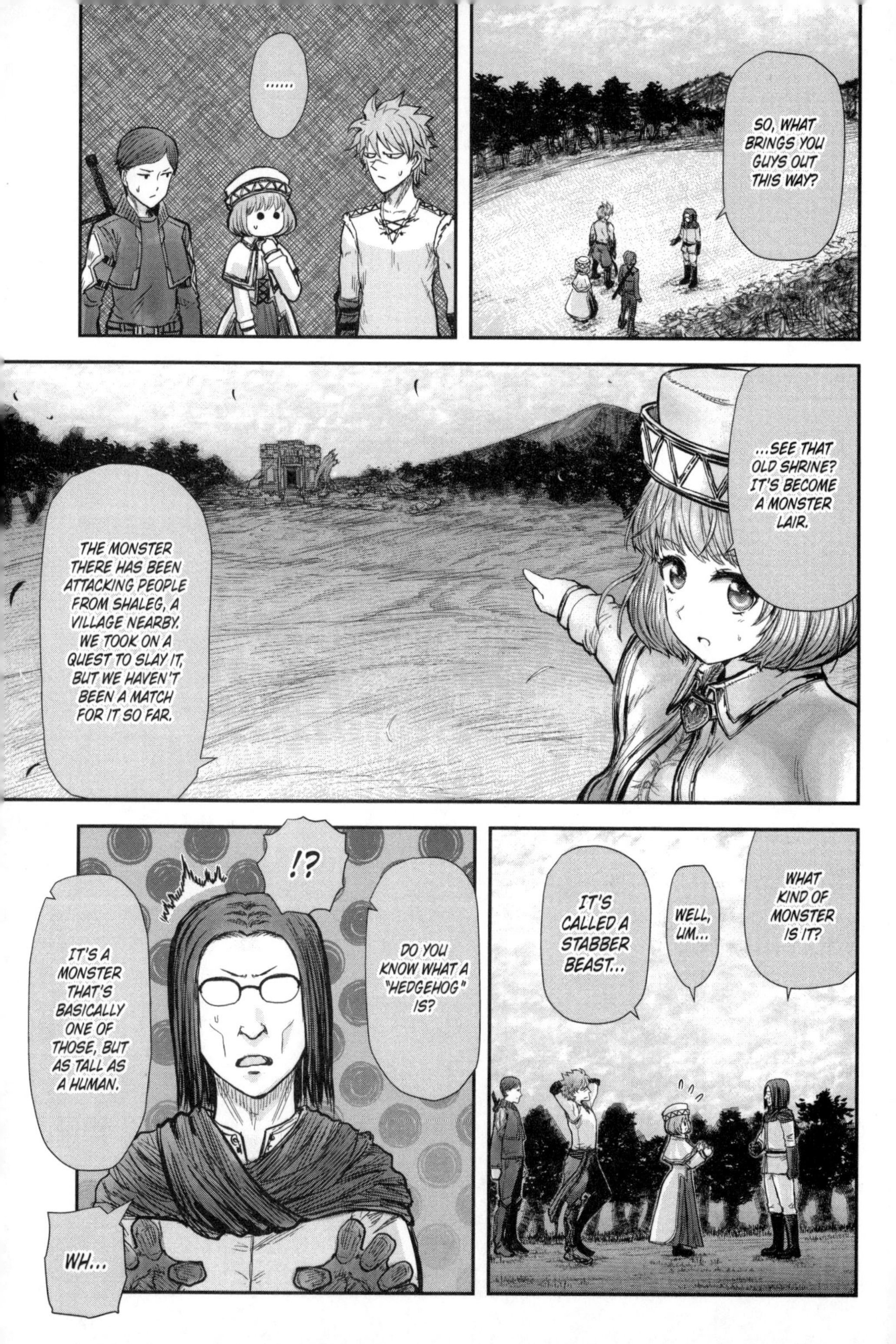
SO, WHAT BRINGS YOU GUYS OUT THIS WAY?
......
...SEE THAT OLD SHRINE? IT'S BECOME A MONSTER LAIR.
THE MONSTER THERE HAS BEEN ATTACKING PEOPLE FROM SHALEG, A VILLAGE NEARBY. WE TOOK ON A QUEST TO SLAY IT, BUT WE HAVEN'T BEEN A MATCH FOR IT SO FAR.
WHAT KIND OF MONSTER IS IT?
WELL, UM...
IT'S CALLED A STABBER BEAST...
!?
DO YOU KNOW WHAT A "HEDGEHOG" IS?
IT'S A MONSTER THAT'S BASICALLY ONE OF THOSE, BUT AS TALL AS A HUMAN.
WH...

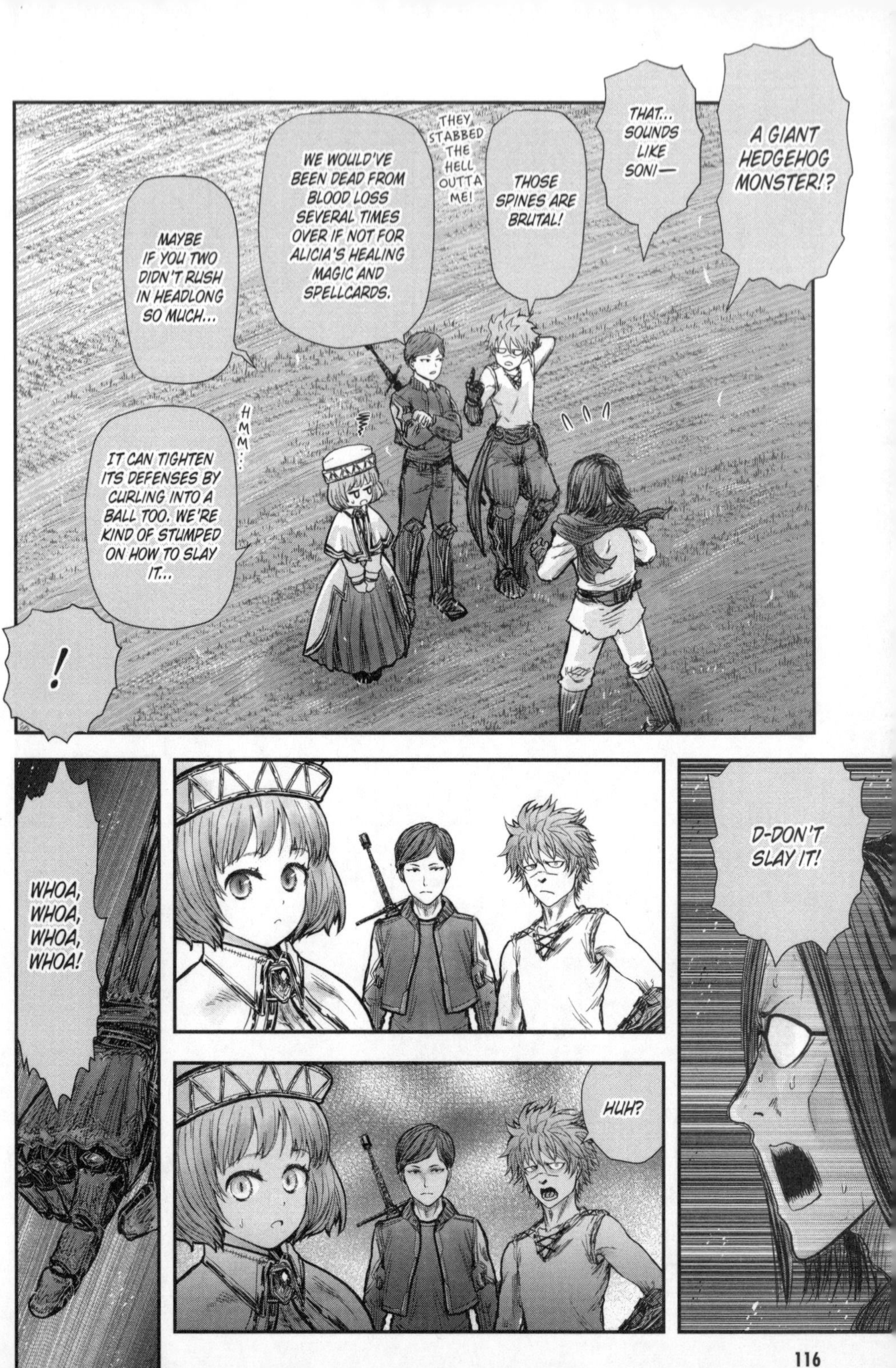
A GIANT HEDGEHOG MONSTER!?
THAT... SOUNDS LIKE SONI—
THOSE SPINES ARE BRUTAL!
THEY STABBED THE HELL OUTTA ME!
WE WOULD'VE BEEN DEAD FROM BLOOD LOSS SEVERAL TIMES OVER IF NOT FOR ALICIA'S HEALING MAGIC AND SPELLCARDS.
MAYBE IF YOU TWO DIDN'T RUSH IN HEADLONG SO MUCH...
HMM...
IT CAN TIGHTEN ITS DEFENSES BY CURLING INTO A BALL TOO. WE'RE KIND OF STUMPED ON HOW TO SLAY IT...
!
D-DON'T SLAY IT!
HUH?
WHOA, WHOA, WHOA, WHOA!

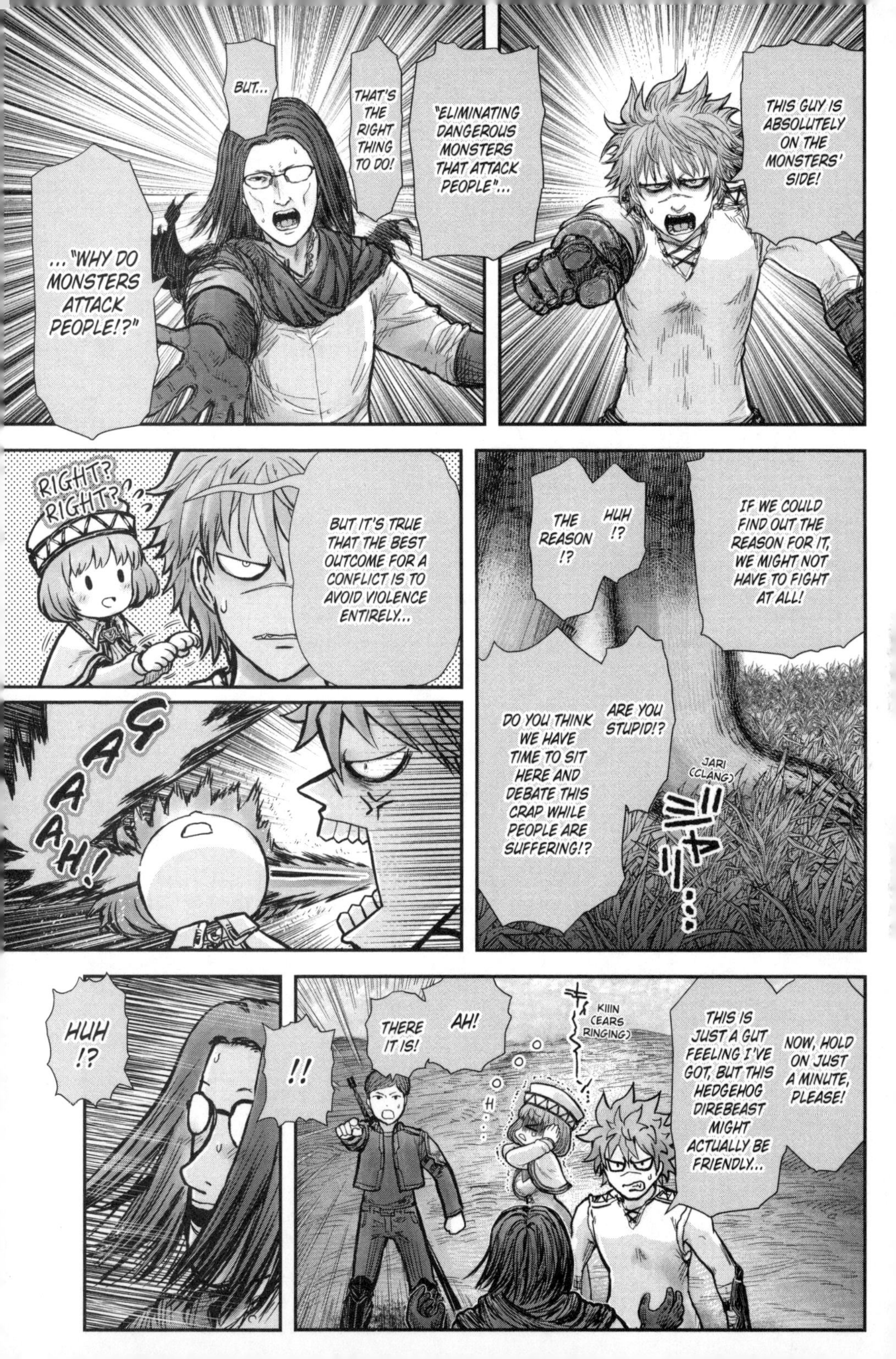
THIS GUY IS ABSOLUTELY ON THE MONSTERS' SIDE!
"ELIMINATING DANGEROUS MONSTERS THAT ATTACK PEOPLE"...
THAT'S THE RIGHT THING TO DO!
BUT...
..."WHY DO MONSTERS ATTACK PEOPLE!?"
IF WE COULD FIND OUT THE REASON FOR IT, WE MIGHT NOT HAVE TO FIGHT AT ALL!
HUH !?
THE REASON !?
ARE YOU STUPID!?
DO YOU THINK WE HAVE TIME TO SIT HERE AND DEBATE THIS CRAP WHILE PEOPLE ARE SUFFERING!?
JARI (CLANG)
BUT IT'S TRUE THAT THE BEST OUTCOME FOR A CONFLICT IS TO AVOID VIOLENCE ENTIRELY...
RIGHT? RIGHT?
GAAAAH!
NOW, HOLD ON JUST A MINUTE, PLEASE!
THIS IS JUST A GUT FEELING I'VE GOT, BUT THIS HEDGEHOG DIREBEAST MIGHT ACTUALLY BE FRIENDLY...
KIIIN (EARS RINGING)
AH!
THERE IT IS!
OOOH...
!!
HUH !?

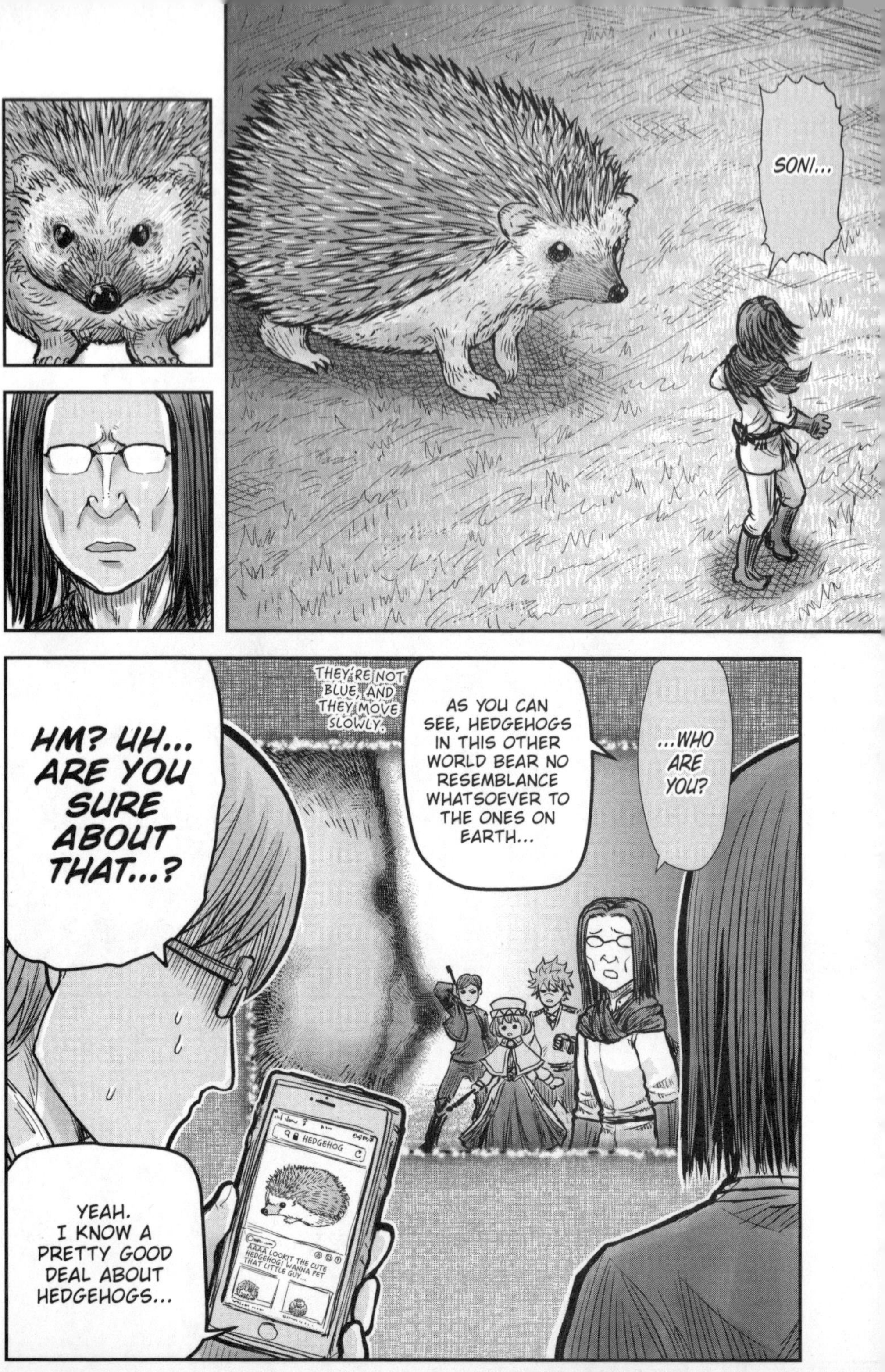
SONI...
...WHO ARE YOU?
AS YOU CAN SEE, HEDGEHOGS IN THIS OTHER WORLD BEAR NO RESEMBLANCE WHATSOEVER TO THE ONES ON EARTH...
THEY'RE NOT BLUE, AND THEY MOVE SLOWLY.
HM? UH... ARE YOU SURE ABOUT THAT...?
HEDGEHOG
AAAA LOOKIT THE CUTE HEDGEHOG! WANNA PET THAT LITTLE GUY...
YEAH. I KNOW A PRETTY GOOD DEAL ABOUT HEDGEHOGS...

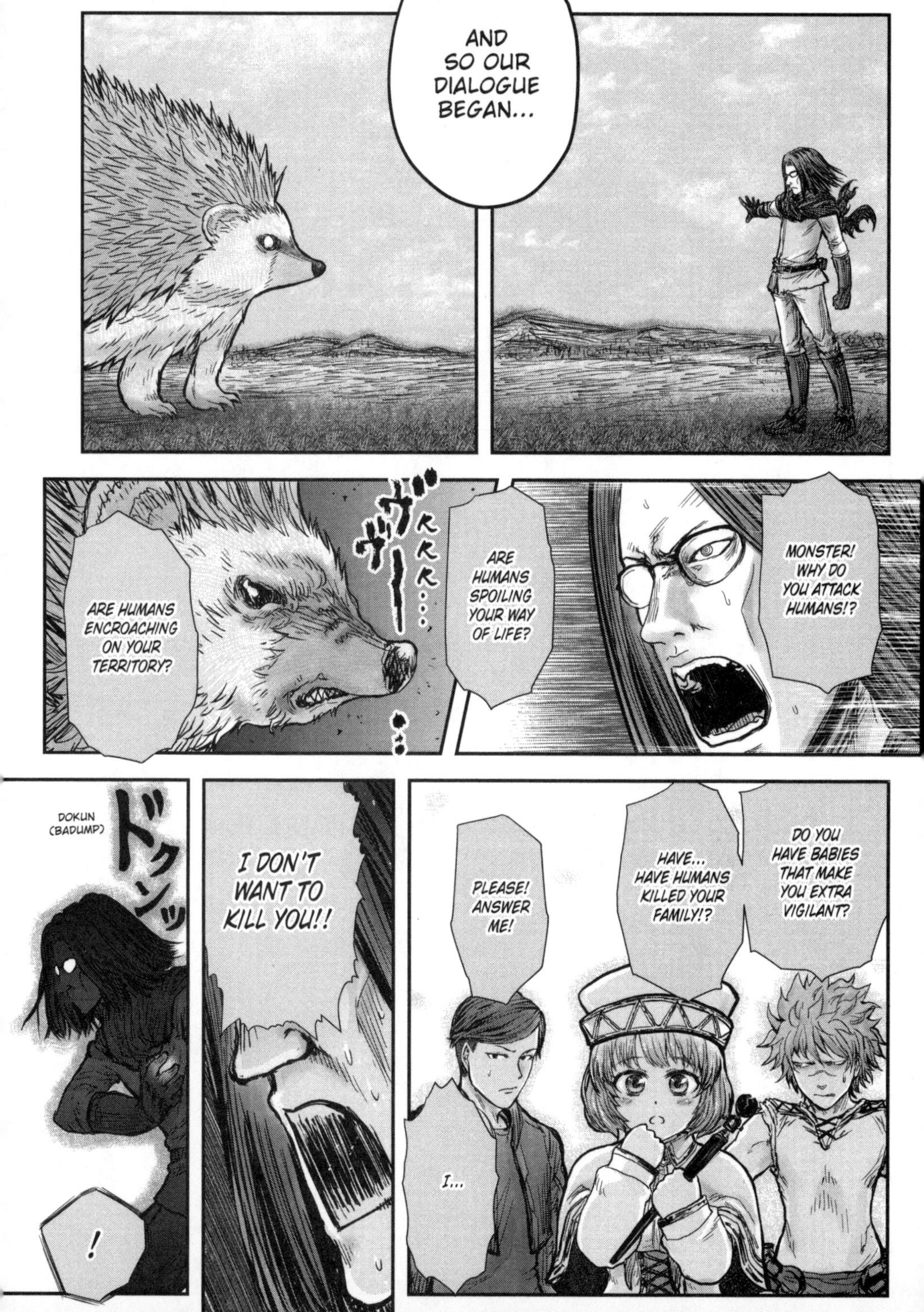
AND SO OUR DIALOGUE BEGAN...
MONSTER! WHY DO YOU ATTACK HUMANS!?
ARE HUMANS SPOILING YOUR WAY OF LIFE?
RRR...
ARE HUMANS ENCROACHING ON YOUR TERRITORY?
DO YOU HAVE BABIES THAT MAKE YOU EXTRA VIGILANT?
HAVE... HAVE HUMANS KILLED YOUR FAMILY!?
PLEASE! ANSWER ME!
I...
I DON'T WANT TO KILL YOU!!
ドクンッ
DOKUN (BADUMP)
!

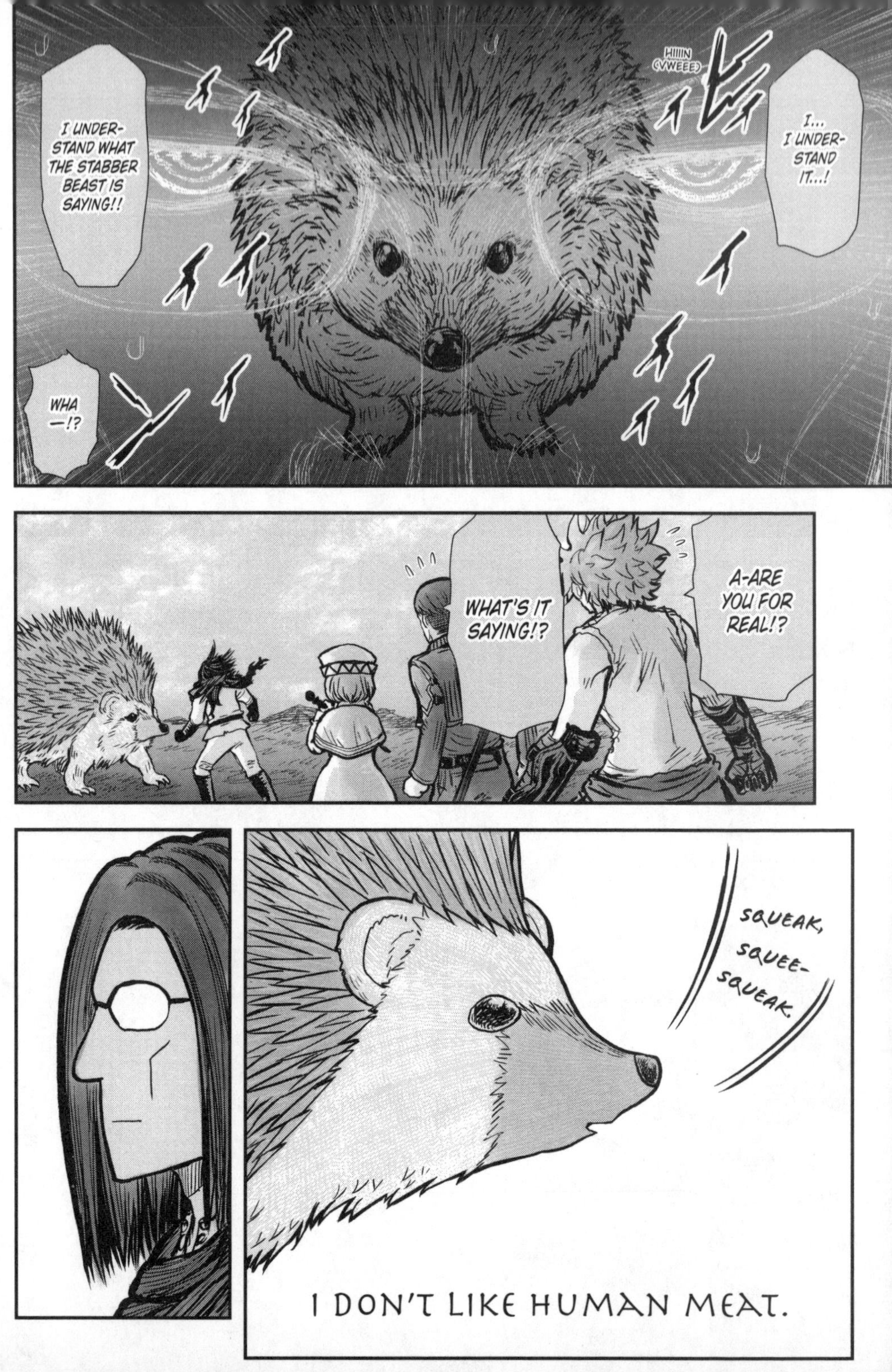
HIIIN (VWEEE)
I... I UNDER-STAND IT...!
I UNDER-STAND WHAT THE STABBER BEAST IS SAYING!!
WHA—!?
A-ARE YOU FOR REAL!?
WHAT'S IT SAYING!?
SQUEAK, SQUEE-SQUEAK.
I DON'T LIKE HUMAN MEAT.

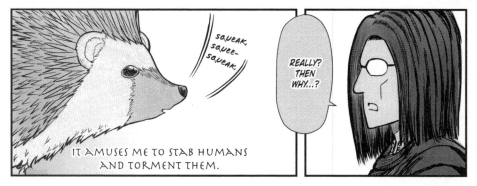

SQUEAK, SQUEE- SQUEAK.

REALLY? THEN WHY...?

IT AMUSES ME TO STAB HUMANS AND TORMENT THEM.

SQUEAK, SQUEE- SQUEAK.

UH...

IT PLEASES ME TO HEAR THE SCREAMS OF HUMANS IN THEIR DEATH THROES.

SQUEAK, SQUEE- SQUEAK.

I LIKE TO KILL HUMANS IN THE MOST PAINFUL WAY POSSIBLE—

FIREBIRD ANNIHILATION

BARAIBHUT FOLG BASTOHL.

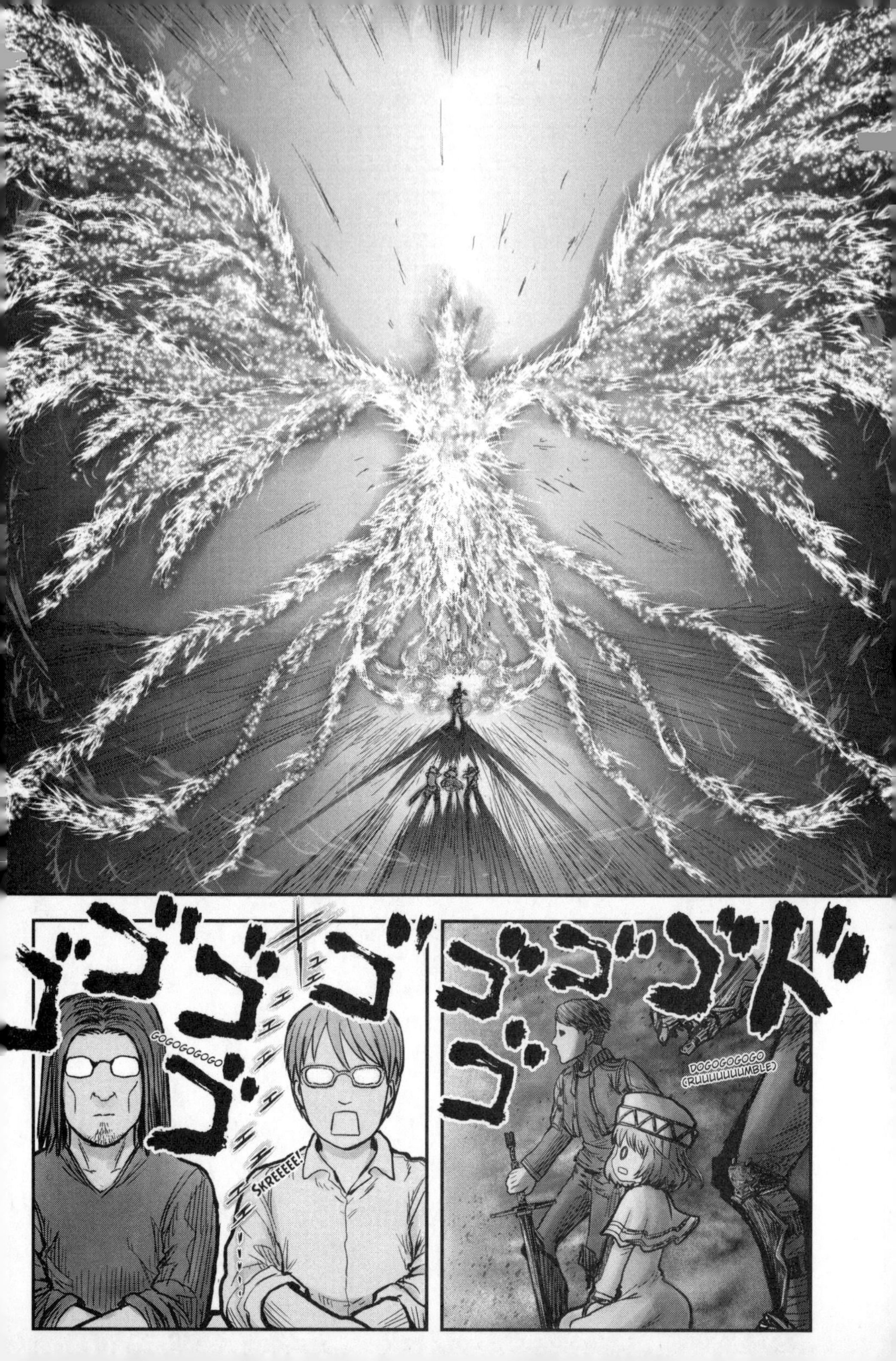
DOGOGOGOGO
(RUUUUUUUUMBLE)
GOGOGOGOGO
SKREEEEEE!

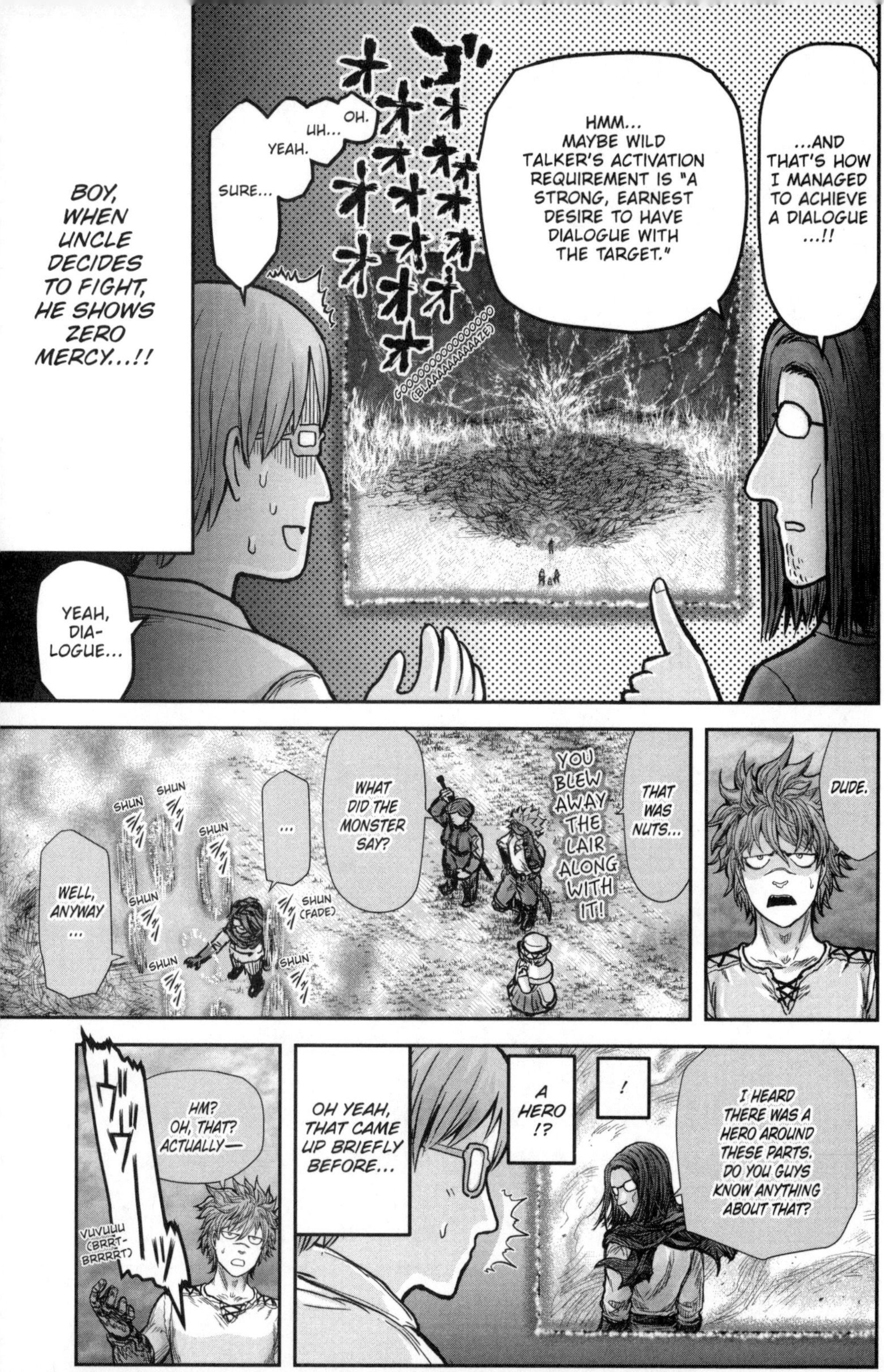
...AND THAT'S HOW I MANAGED TO ACHIEVE A DIALOGUE ...!!
HMM... MAYBE WILD TALKER'S ACTIVATION REQUIREMENT IS "A STRONG, EARNEST DESIRE TO HAVE DIALOGUE WITH THE TARGET."
GOOOOOOOOOOOOOOO (BLAAAAAAAAAAZE)
OH. UH... YEAH. SURE...
BOY, WHEN UNCLE DECIDES TO FIGHT, HE SHOWS ZERO MERCY...!!
YEAH, DIA-LOGUE...
DUDE.
THAT WAS NUTS...
YOU BLEW AWAY THE LAIR ALONG WITH IT!
WHAT DID THE MONSTER SAY?
...
SHUN
SHUN (FADE)
WELL, ANYWAY ...
I HEARD THERE WAS A HERO AROUND THESE PARTS. DO YOU GUYS KNOW ANYTHING ABOUT THAT?
!
A HERO !?
OH YEAH, THAT CAME UP BRIEFLY BEFORE...
HM? OH, THAT? ACTUALLY—
VUVUUU (BRRT-BRRRRT)

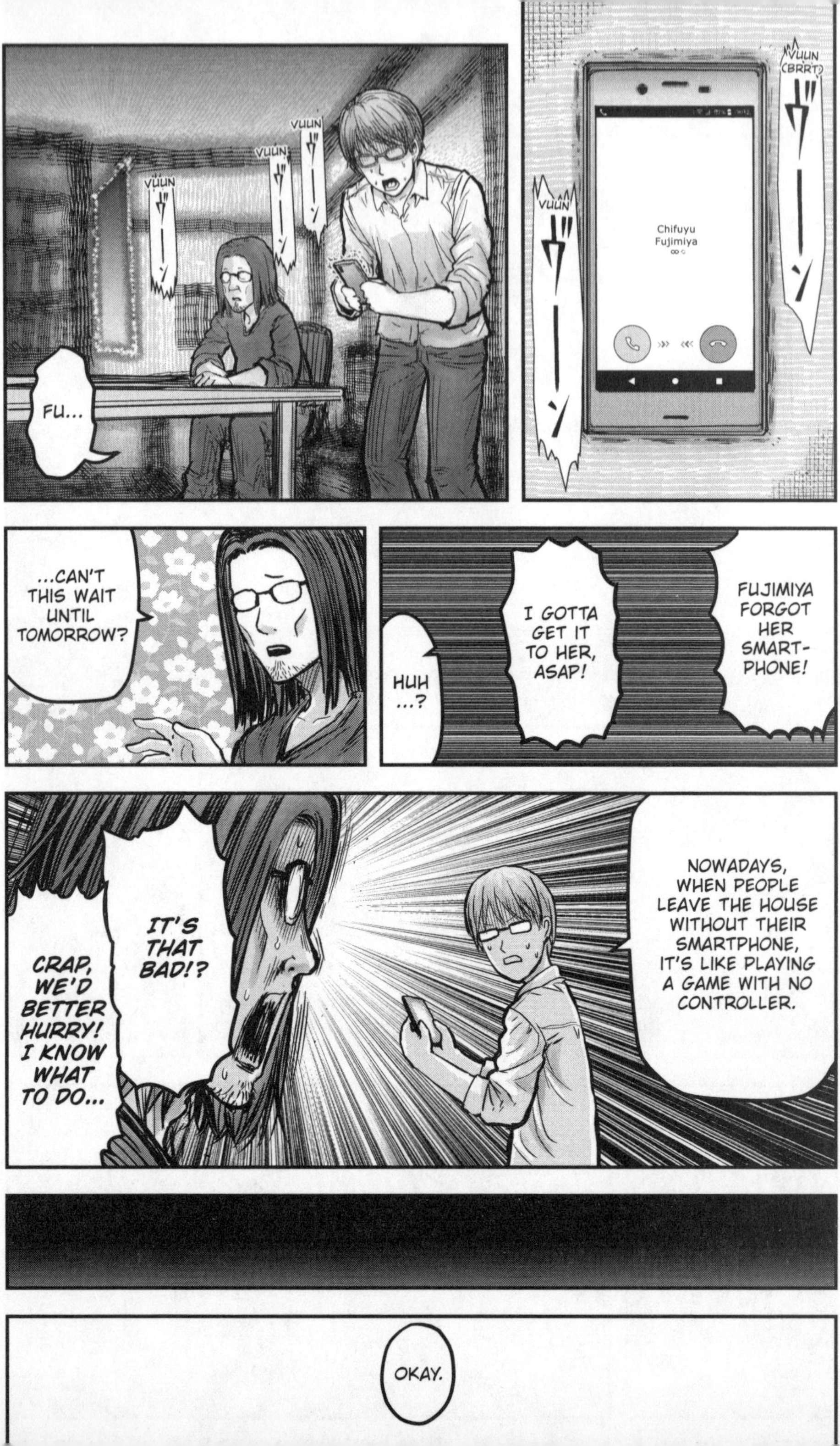
VUUN (BRRT)
VUUN
Chifuyu Fujimiya
VUUN
VUUN
VUUN
FU...
FUJIMIYA FORGOT HER SMARTPHONE!
I GOTTA GET IT TO HER, ASAP!
HUH...?
...CAN'T THIS WAIT UNTIL TOMORROW?
NOWADAYS, WHEN PEOPLE LEAVE THE HOUSE WITHOUT THEIR SMARTPHONE, IT'S LIKE PLAYING A GAME WITH NO CONTROLLER.
IT'S THAT BAD!?
CRAP, WE'D BETTER HURRY! I KNOW WHAT TO DO...
OKAY.

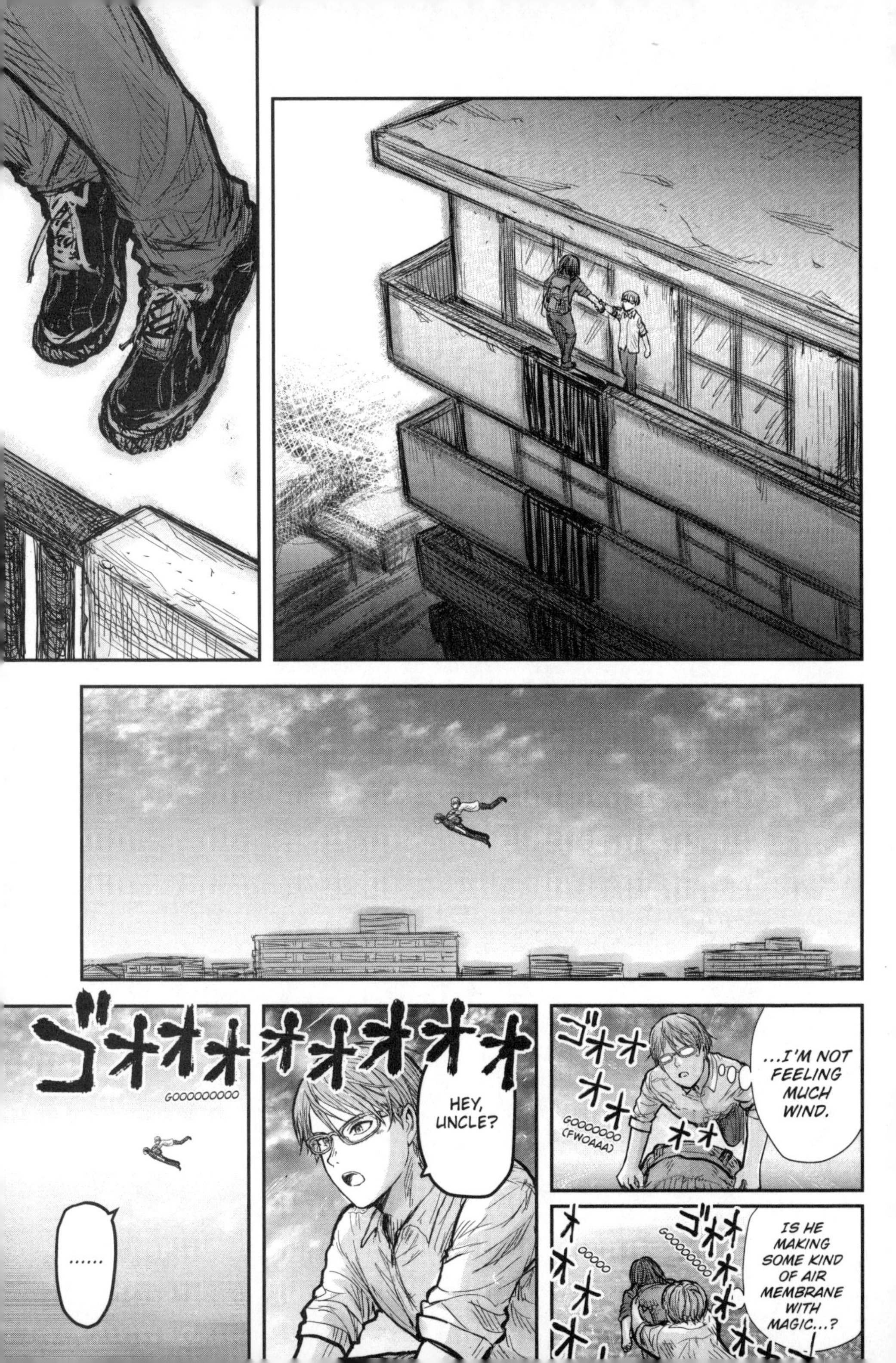
ゴオオ
オオ
オオ
GOOOOOOOO
(FWOAAA)
...I'M NOT FEELING MUCH WIND.
ゴオオオオオ
GOOOOOOOO
オオオ
OOOOO
IS HE MAKING SOME KIND OF AIR MEMBRANE WITH MAGIC...?
ゴオオオオオオオオオ
GOOOOOOOOO
HEY, UNCLE?
......

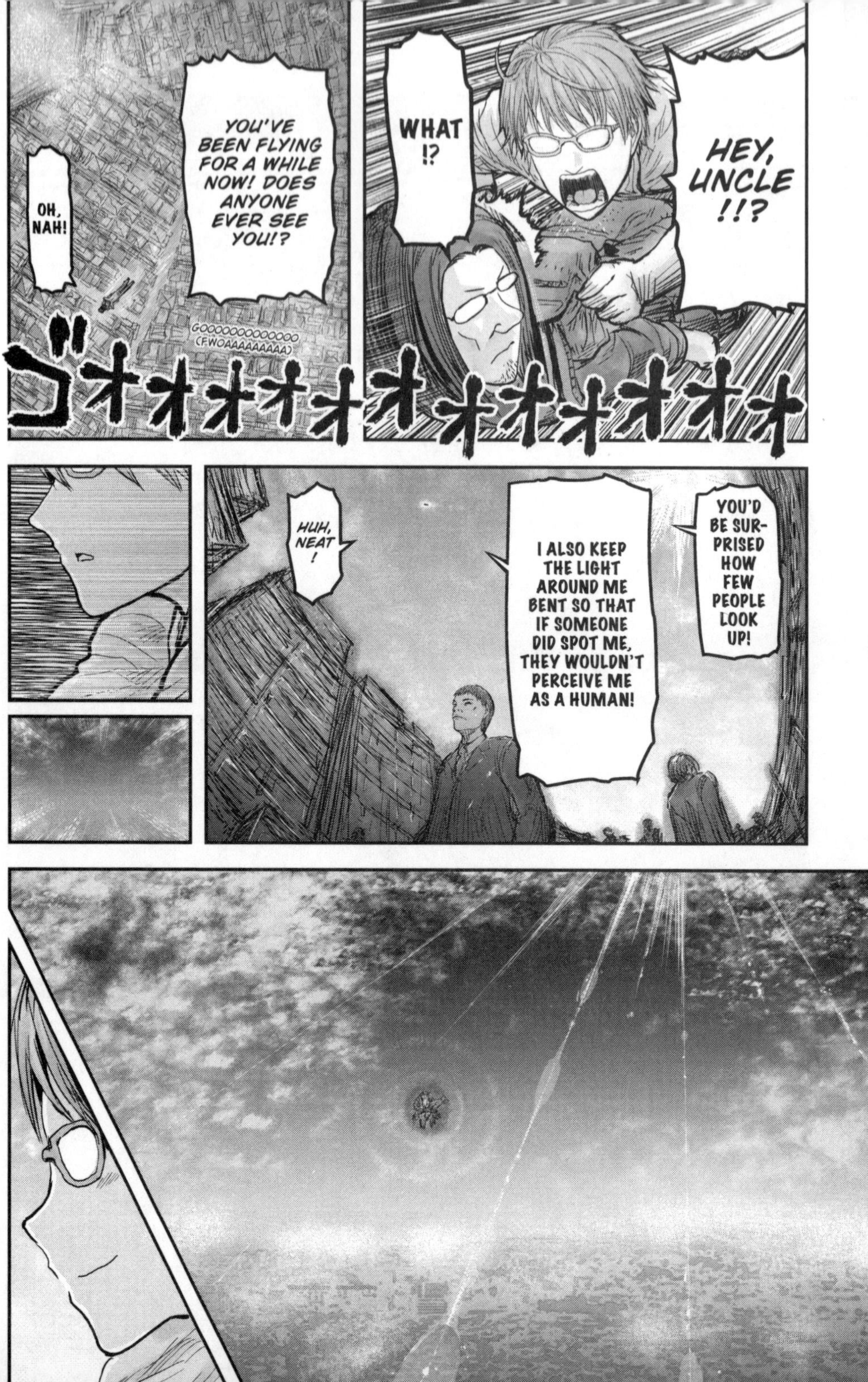
HEY, UNCLE!!?
WHAT!?
YOU'VE BEEN FLYING FOR A WHILE NOW! DOES ANYONE EVER SEE YOU!?
OH, NAH!
GOOOOOOOOOOOOO (FWOAAAAAAAAA)
ゴオオオオオオオオオオオオ
YOU'D BE SUR-PRISED HOW FEW PEOPLE LOOK UP!
I ALSO KEEP THE LIGHT AROUND ME BENT SO THAT IF SOMEONE DID SPOT ME, THEY WOULDN'T PERCEIVE ME AS A HUMAN!
HUH, NEAT!

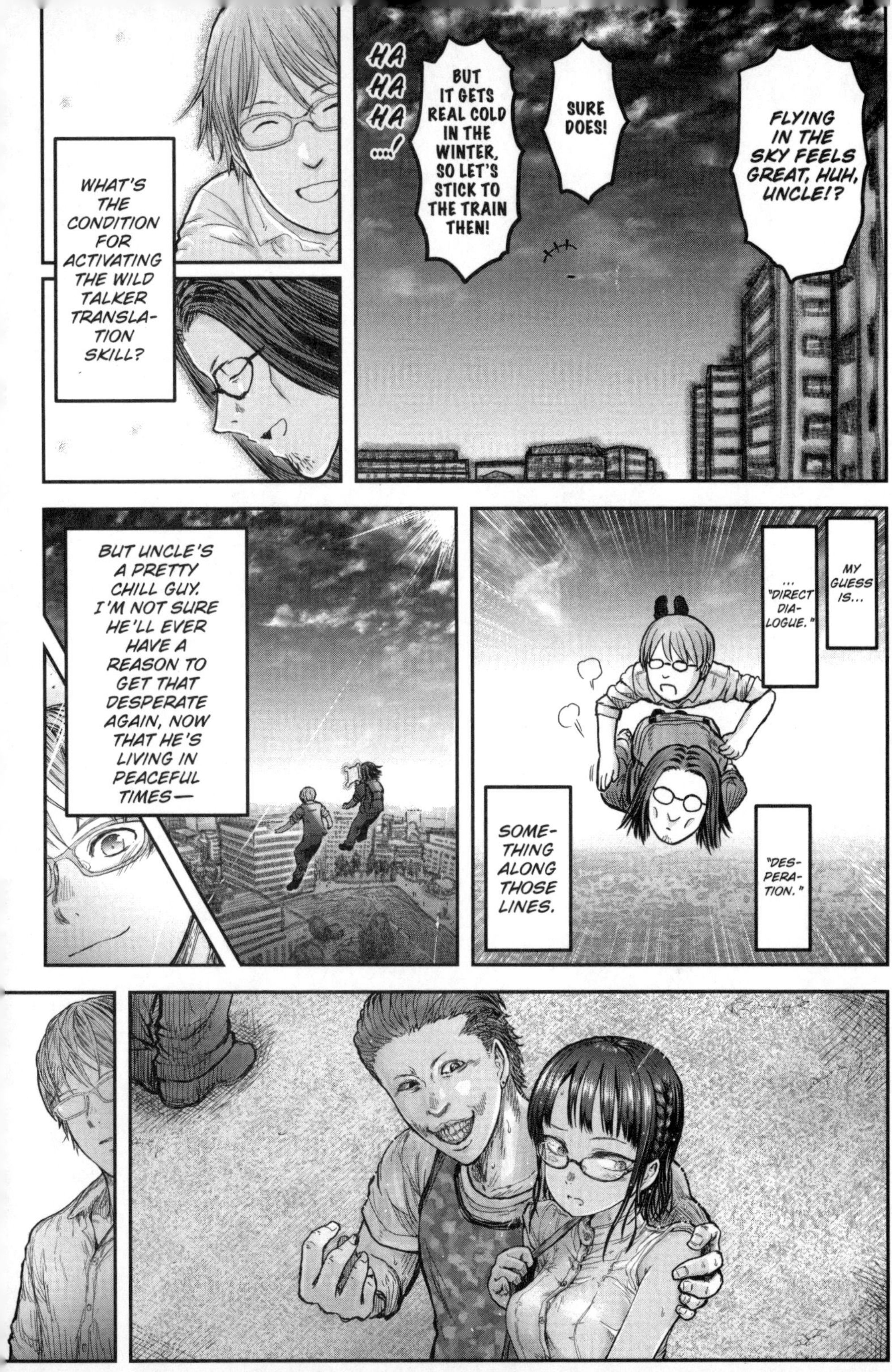
FLYING IN THE SKY FEELS GREAT, HUH, UNCLE!?
SURE DOES!
BUT IT GETS REAL COLD IN THE WINTER, SO LET'S STICK TO THE TRAIN THEN!
HA HA HA HA...!
WHAT'S THE CONDITION FOR ACTIVATING THE WILD TALKER TRANSLA-TION SKILL?
MY GUESS IS...
... "DIRECT DIA-LOGUE."
"DES-PERA-TION."
SOME-THING ALONG THOSE LINES.
BUT UNCLE'S A PRETTY CHILL GUY. I'M NOT SURE HE'LL EVER HAVE A REASON TO GET THAT DESPERATE AGAIN, NOW THAT HE'S LIVING IN PEACEFUL TIMES—

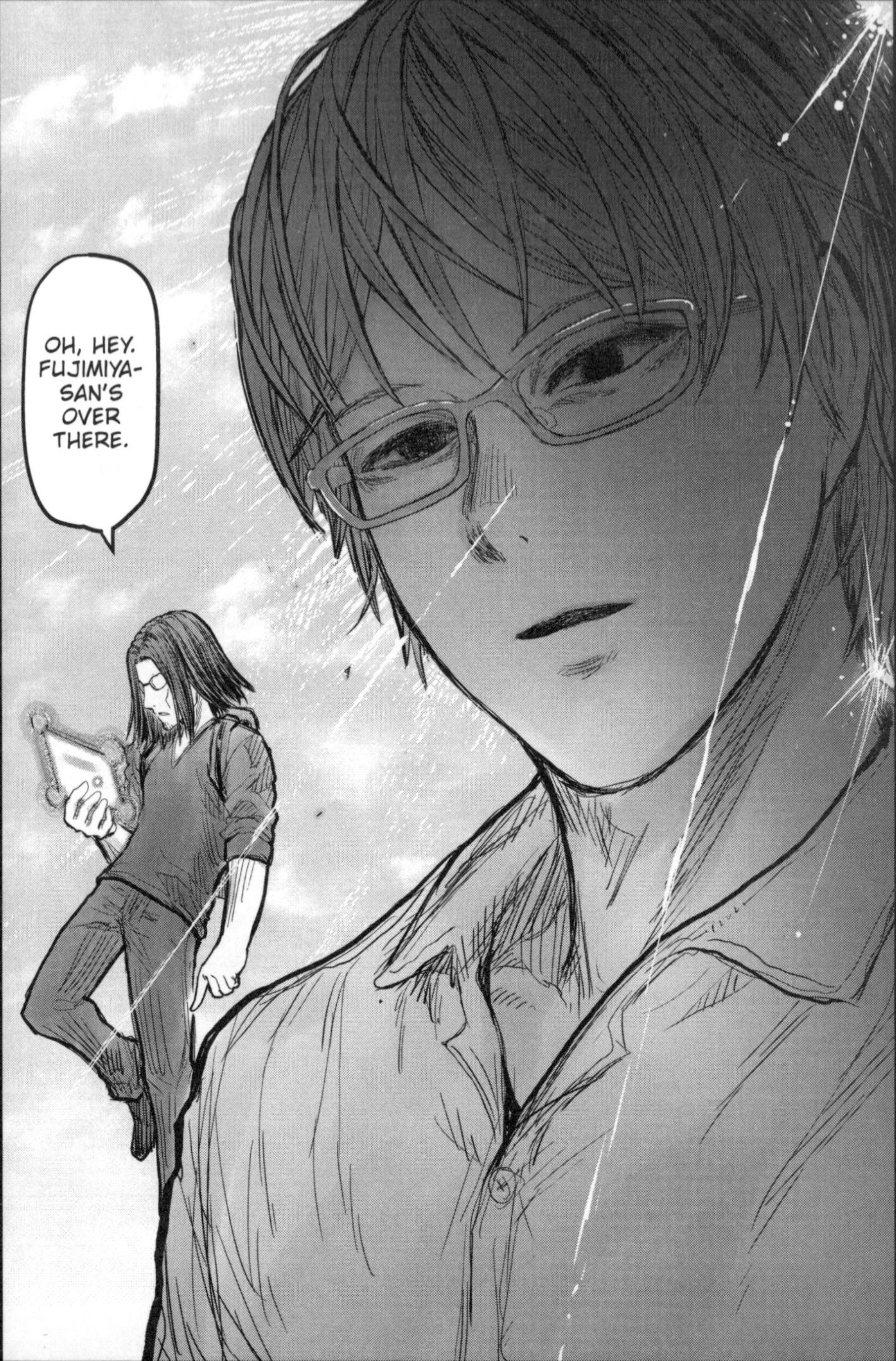
OH, HEY. FUJIMIYA-SAN'S OVER THERE.

Hedgehog

Any of the spiny mammals of the subfamily Erinaceinae, in the eulipotyphlan family Erinaceidae. In Japanese, they are called *harinezumi* ("needle" + "mouse").

TIPS

UNCLE from ANOTHER WORLD

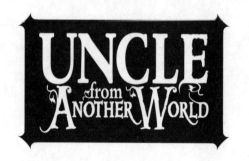

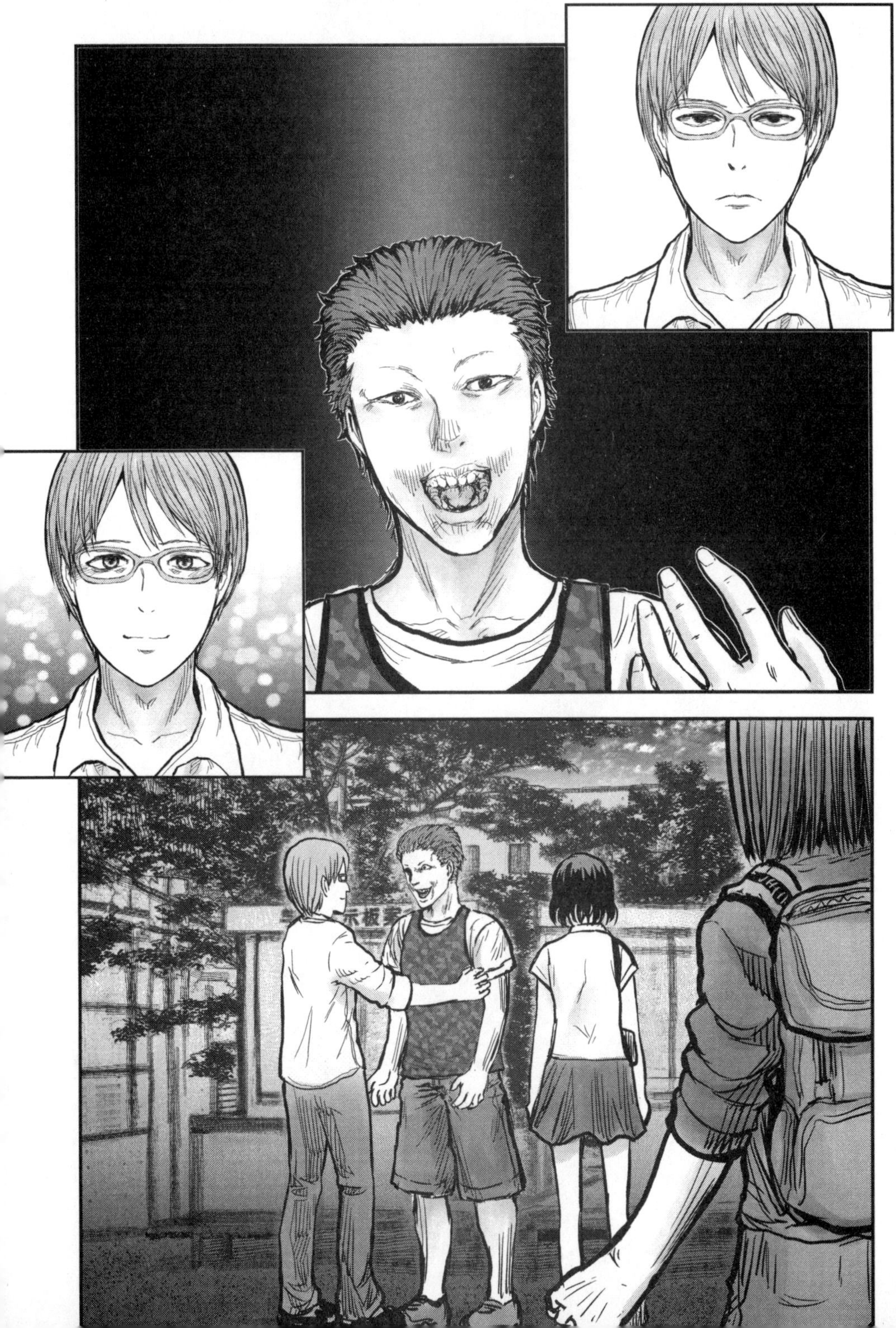

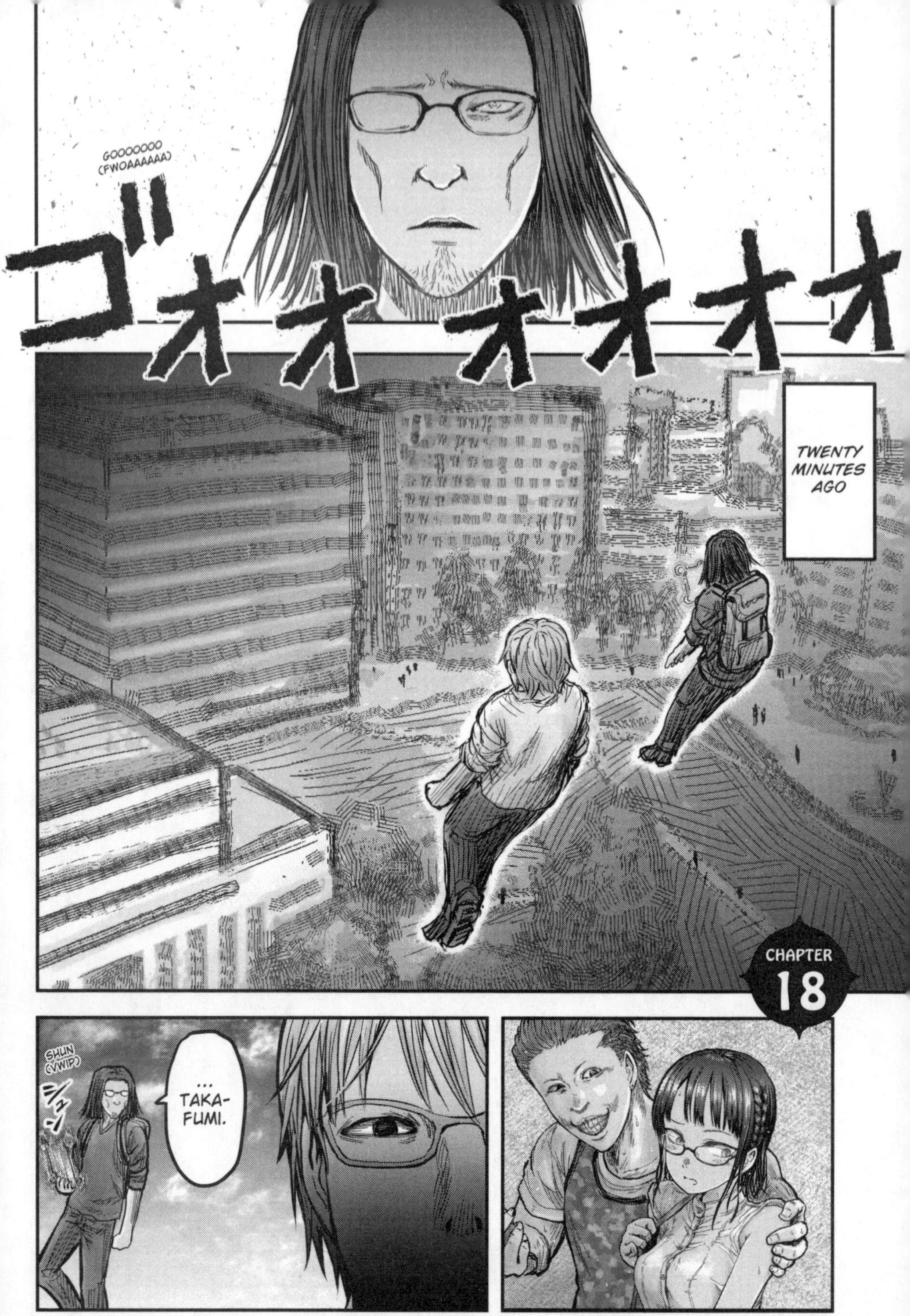

ゴォオオオオ
GOOOOOOO (FWOAAAAAA)
TWENTY MINUTES AGO
CHAPTER 18
... TAKA-FUMI.
シュ
SHUN (VWIP)

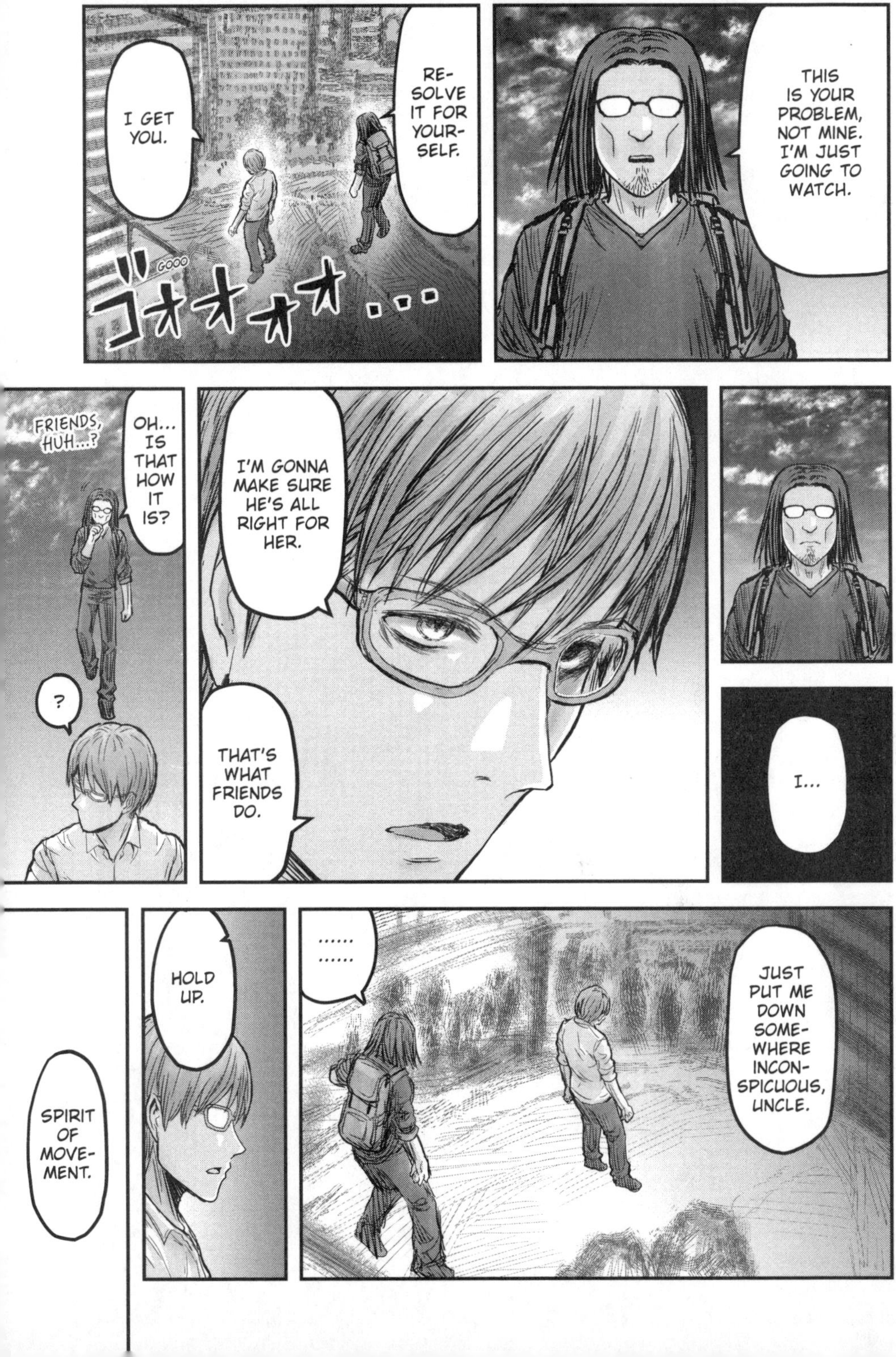
THIS IS YOUR PROBLEM, NOT MINE. I'M JUST GOING TO WATCH.
RE-SOLVE IT FOR YOUR-SELF.
I GET YOU.
GOOO
I...
I'M GONNA MAKE SURE HE'S ALL RIGHT FOR HER.
THAT'S WHAT FRIENDS DO.
OH... IS THAT HOW IT IS?
FRIENDS, HUH...?
?
JUST PUT ME DOWN SOME-WHERE INCON-SPICUOUS, UNCLE.
....
HOLD UP.
SPIRIT OF MOVE-MENT.

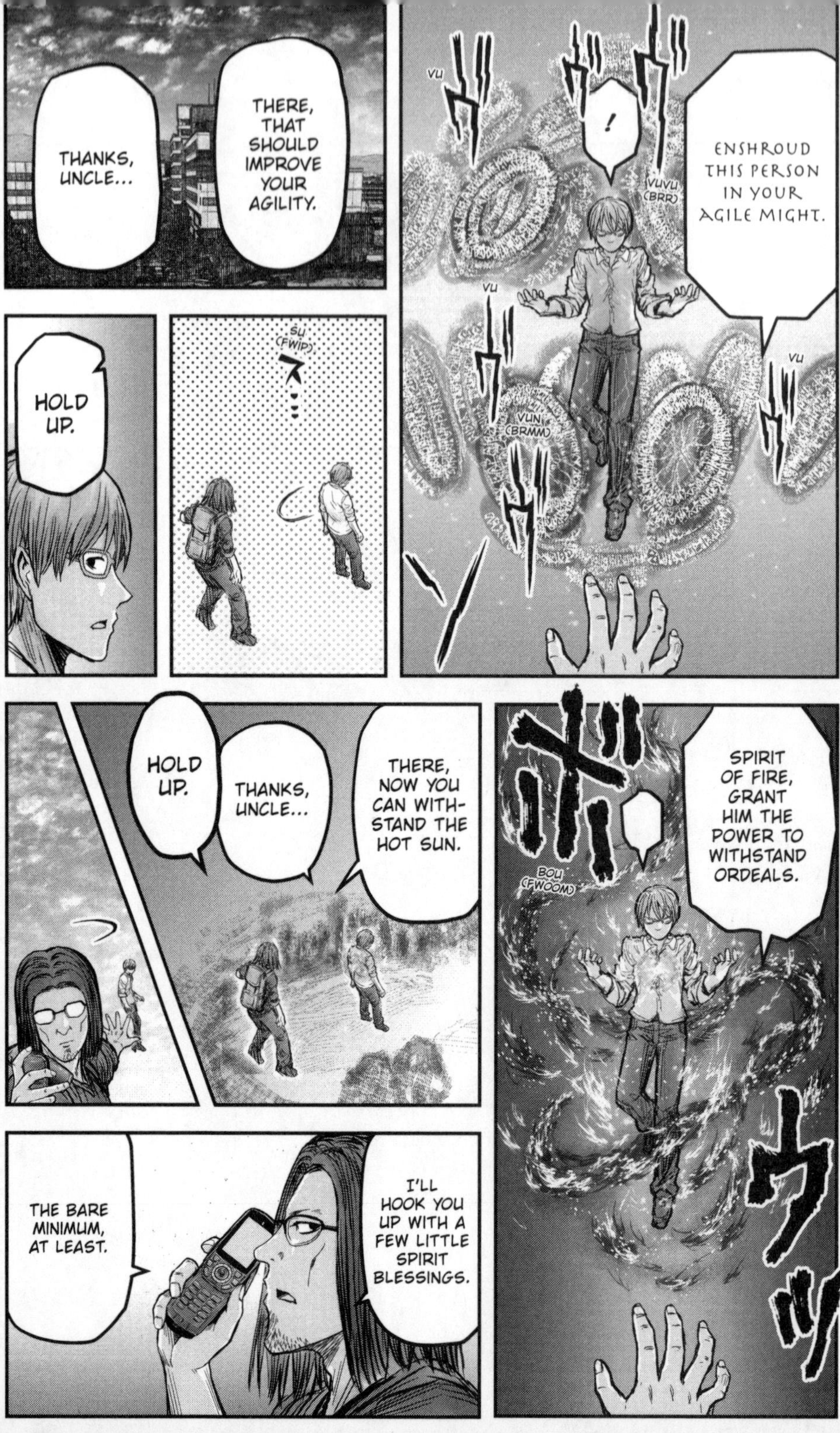
ENSHROUD THIS PERSON IN YOUR AGILE MIGHT.
VU
!
VUVU (BRR)
VU
VU
VUN (BRMM)
THERE, THAT SHOULD IMPROVE YOUR AGILITY.
THANKS, UNCLE...
SU (FWIP)
HOLD UP.
SPIRIT OF FIRE, GRANT HIM THE POWER TO WITHSTAND ORDEALS.
BOU (FWOOM)
THERE, NOW YOU CAN WITH-STAND THE HOT SUN.
THANKS, UNCLE...
HOLD UP.
I'LL HOOK YOU UP WITH A FEW LITTLE SPIRIT BLESSINGS.
THE BARE MINIMUM, AT LEAST.

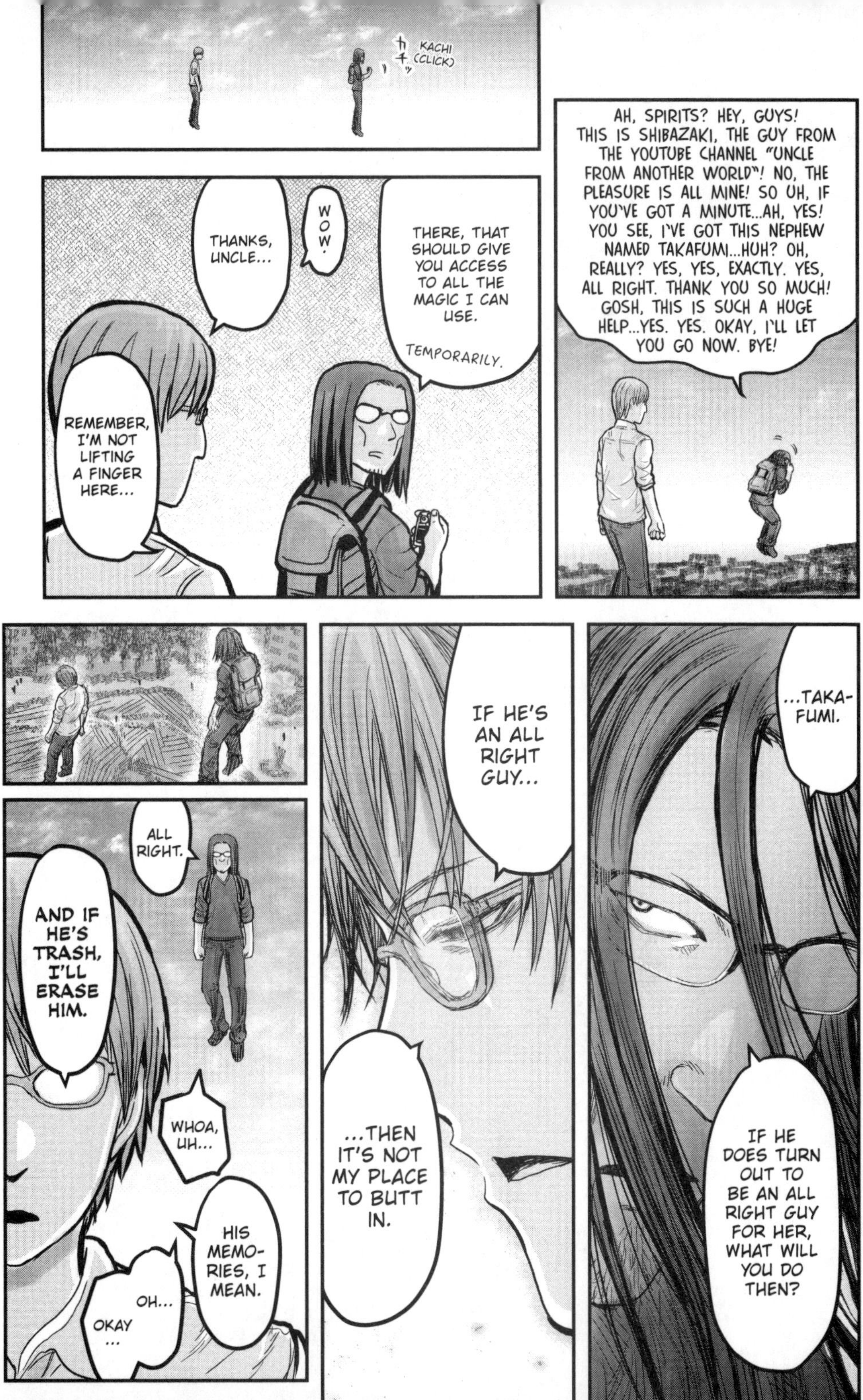
AH, SPIRITS? HEY, GUYS! THIS IS SHIBAZAKI, THE GUY FROM THE YOUTUBE CHANNEL "UNCLE FROM ANOTHER WORLD"! NO, THE PLEASURE IS ALL MINE! SO UH, IF YOU'VE GOT A MINUTE...AH, YES! YOU SEE, I'VE GOT THIS NEPHEW NAMED TAKAFUMI...HUH? OH, REALLY? YES, YES, EXACTLY. YES, ALL RIGHT. THANK YOU SO MUCH! GOSH, THIS IS SUCH A HUGE HELP...YES. YES. OKAY, I'LL LET YOU GO NOW. BYE!
カチッ
KACHI (CLICK)
THERE, THAT SHOULD GIVE YOU ACCESS TO ALL THE MAGIC I CAN USE.
TEMPORARILY.
WOW!
THANKS, UNCLE...
REMEMBER, I'M NOT LIFTING A FINGER HERE...
...TAKA-FUMI.
IF HE DOES TURN OUT TO BE AN ALL RIGHT GUY FOR HER, WHAT WILL YOU DO THEN?
IF HE'S AN ALL RIGHT GUY...
...THEN IT'S NOT MY PLACE TO BUTT IN.
ALL RIGHT.
AND IF HE'S TRASH, I'LL ERASE HIM.
WHOA, UH...
HIS MEMORIES, I MEAN.
OH... OKAY...

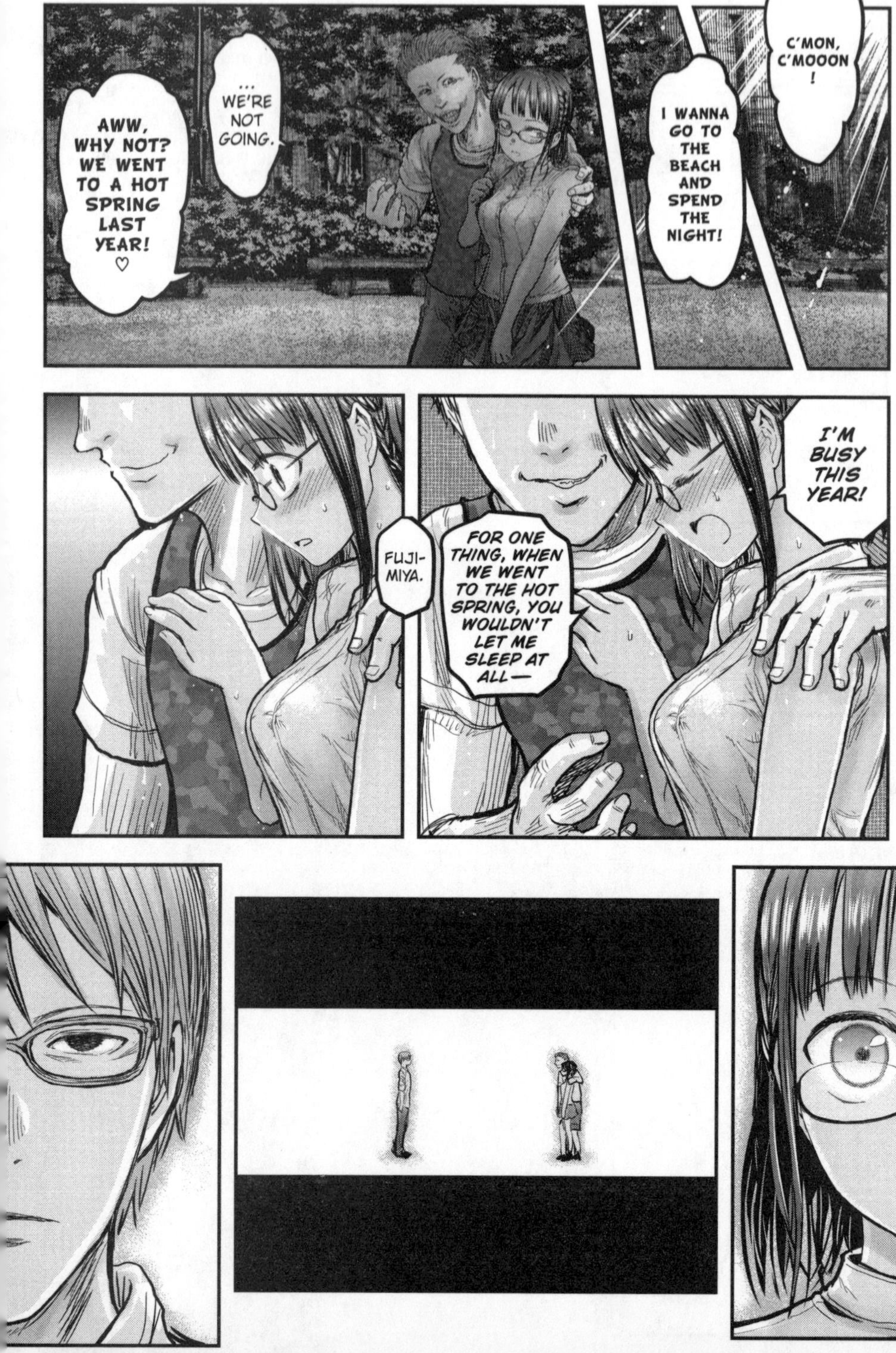
C'MON, C'MOOON!
I WANNA GO TO THE BEACH AND SPEND THE NIGHT!
... WE'RE NOT GOING.
AWW, WHY NOT? WE WENT TO A HOT SPRING LAST YEAR! ♡
I'M BUSY THIS YEAR!
FOR ONE THING, WHEN WE WENT TO THE HOT SPRING, YOU WOULDN'T LET ME SLEEP AT ALL—
FUJI-MIYA.

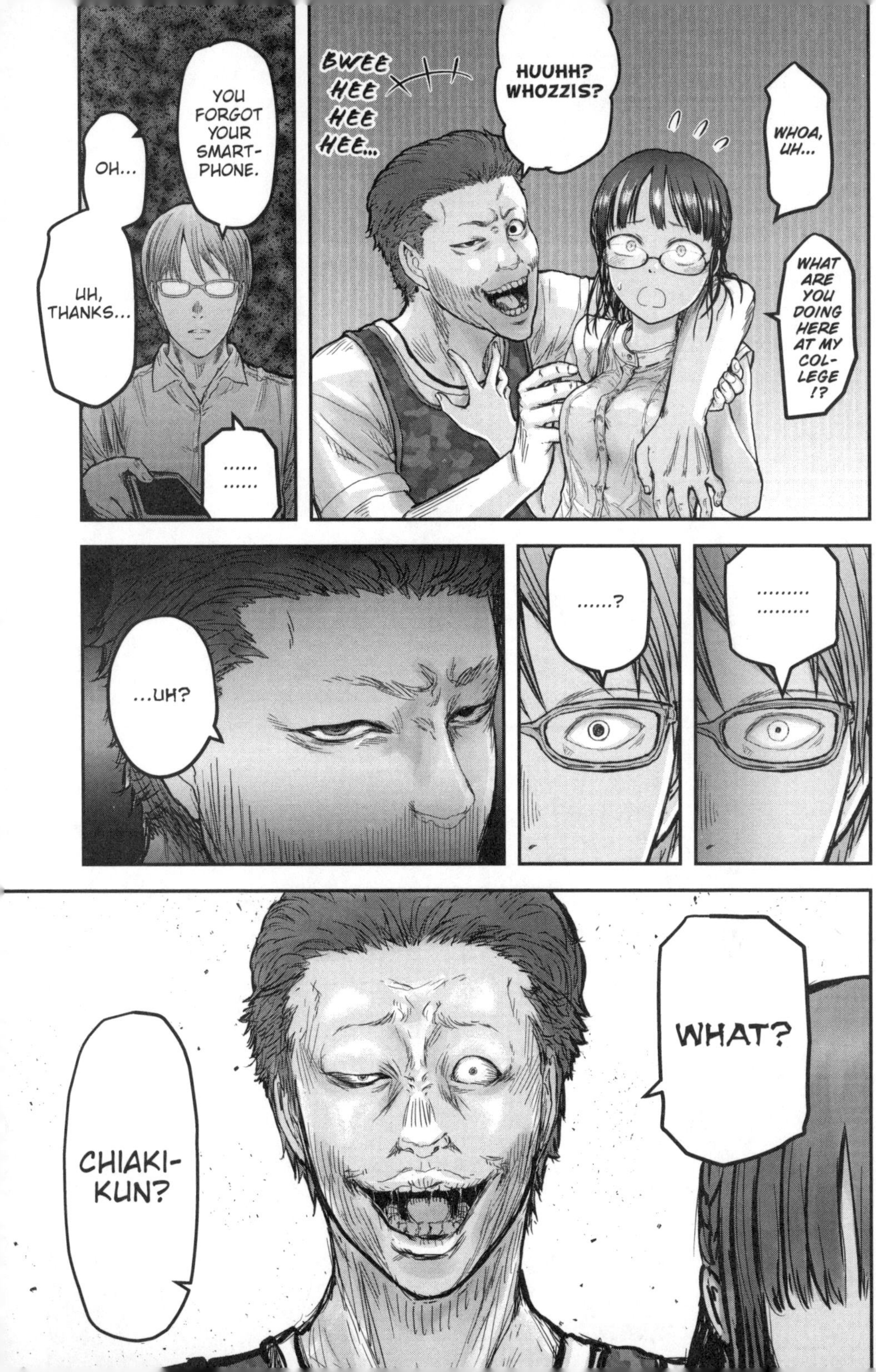
WHOA, UH...
WHAT ARE YOU DOING HERE AT MY COL-LEGE!?
HUUHH? WHOZZIS?
BWEE HEE HEE HEE...
YOU FORGOT YOUR SMART-PHONE.
OH...
UH, THANKS...
....
....
......?
...UH?
WHAT?
CHIAKI-KUN?

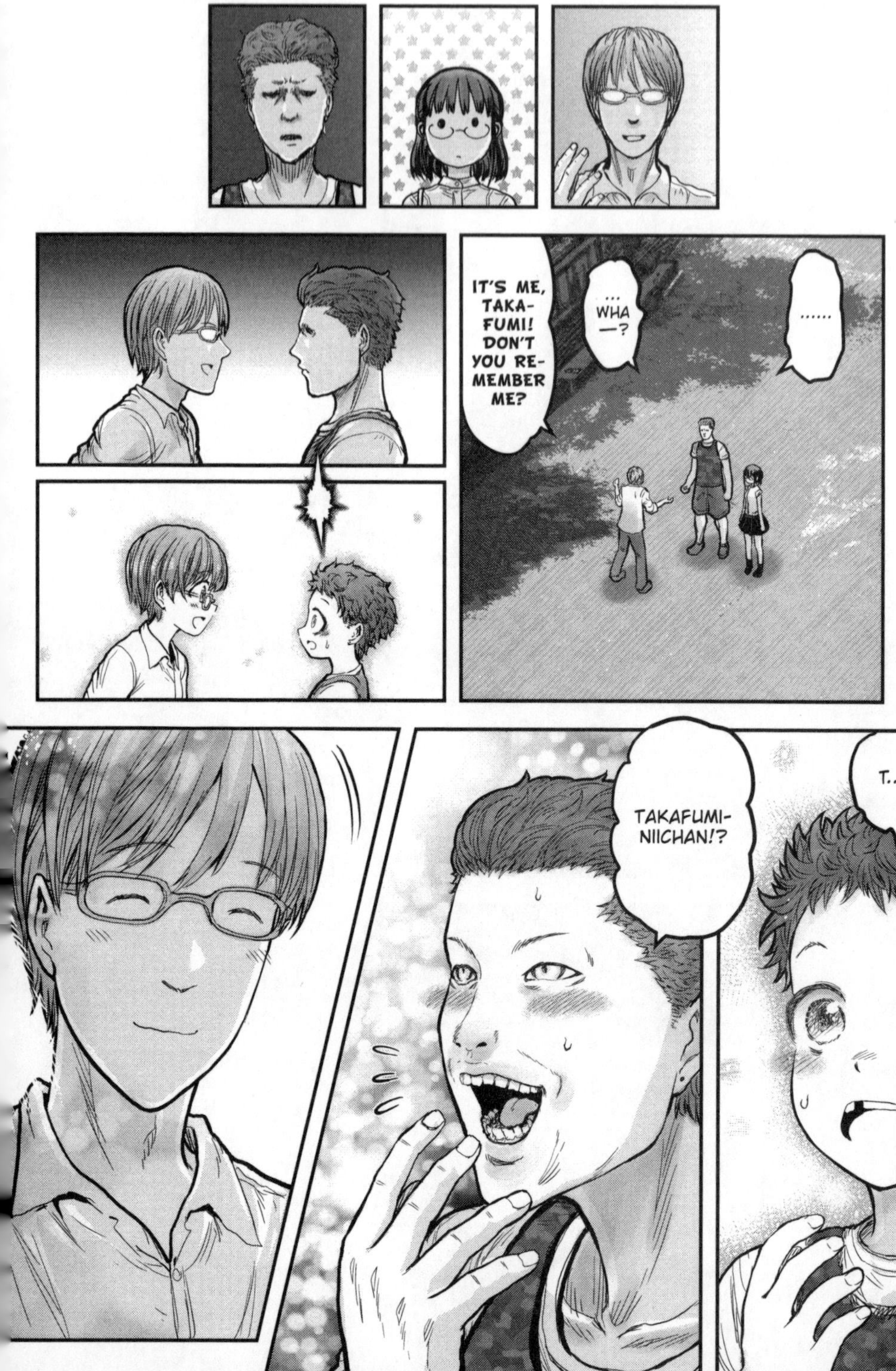
......
...WHA—?
IT'S ME, TAKAFUMI! DON'T YOU REMEMBER ME?
T...
TAKAFUMI-NIICHAN!?

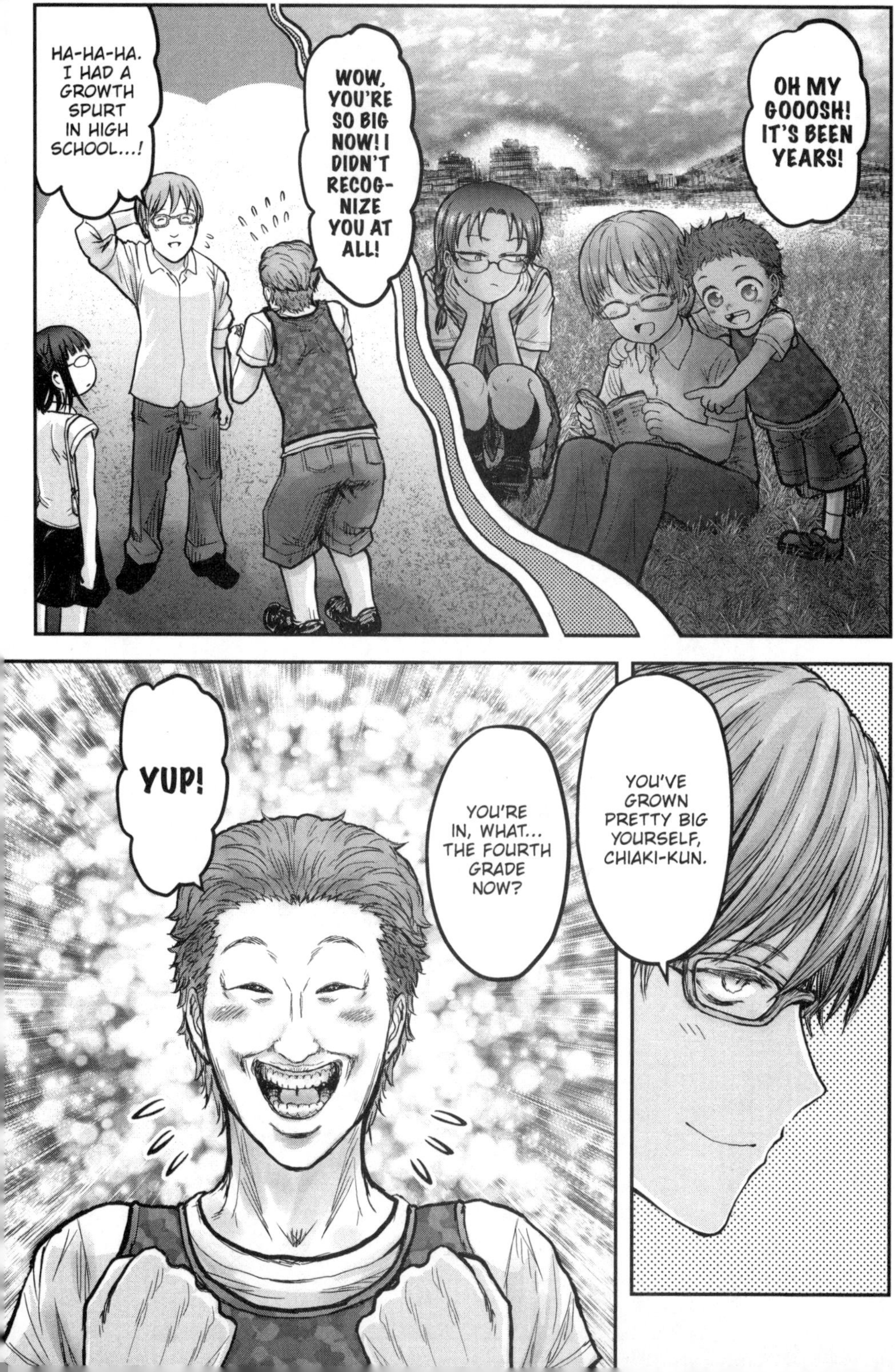
OH MY GOOOSH! IT'S BEEN YEARS!
WOW, YOU'RE SO BIG NOW! I DIDN'T RECOG-NIZE YOU AT ALL!
HA-HA-HA. I HAD A GROWTH SPURT IN HIGH SCHOOL...!
YOU'VE GROWN PRETTY BIG YOURSELF, CHIAKI-KUN.
YOU'RE IN, WHAT... THE FOURTH GRADE NOW?
YUP!

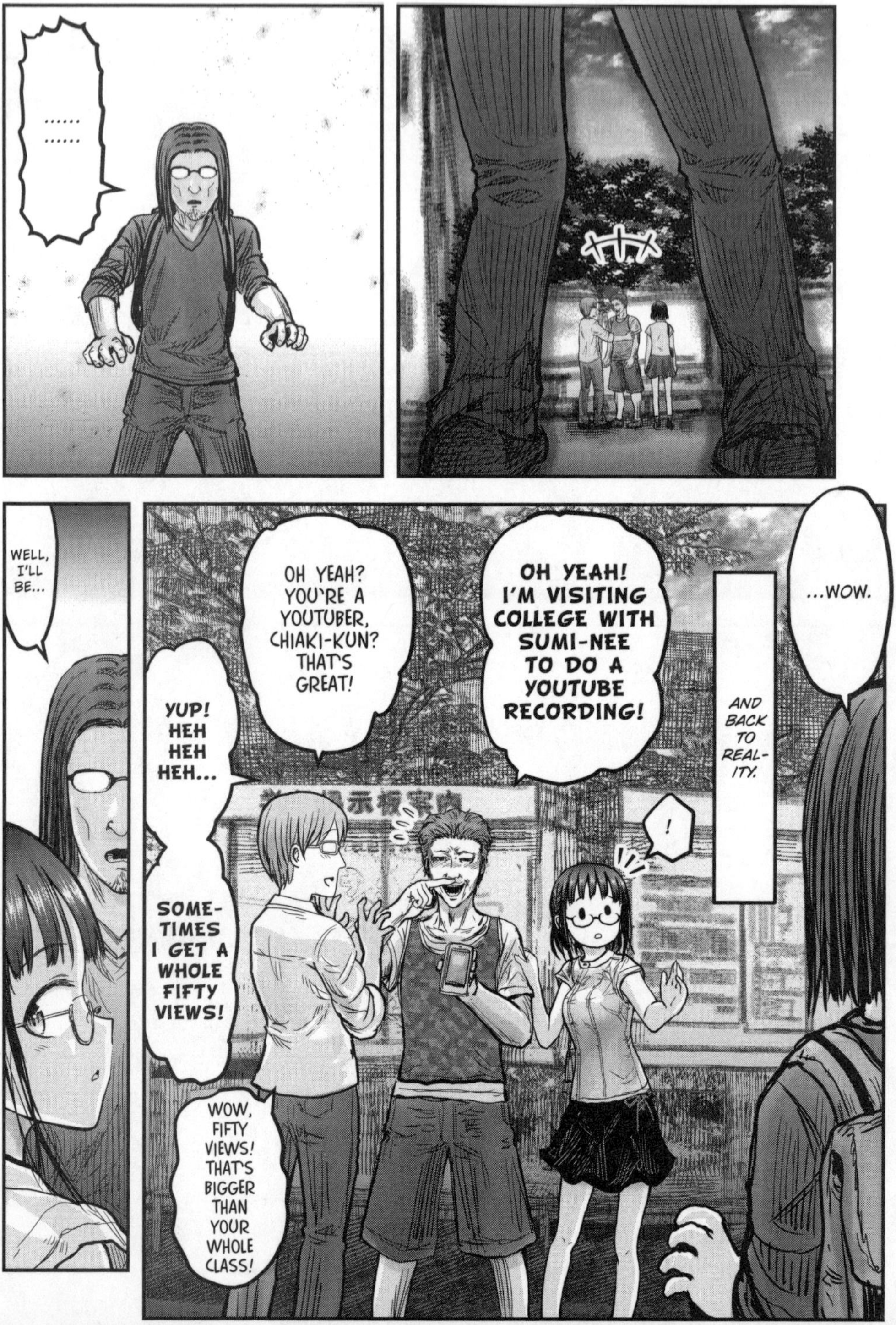
......
......
...WOW.
AND BACK TO REALITY.
!
OH YEAH! I'M VISITING COLLEGE WITH SUMI-NEE TO DO A YOUTUBE RECORDING!
OH YEAH? YOU'RE A YOUTUBER, CHIAKI-KUN? THAT'S GREAT!
YUP! HEH HEH HEH...
SOME-TIMES I GET A WHOLE FIFTY VIEWS!
WOW, FIFTY VIEWS! THAT'S BIGGER THAN YOUR WHOLE CLASS!
WELL, I'LL BE...

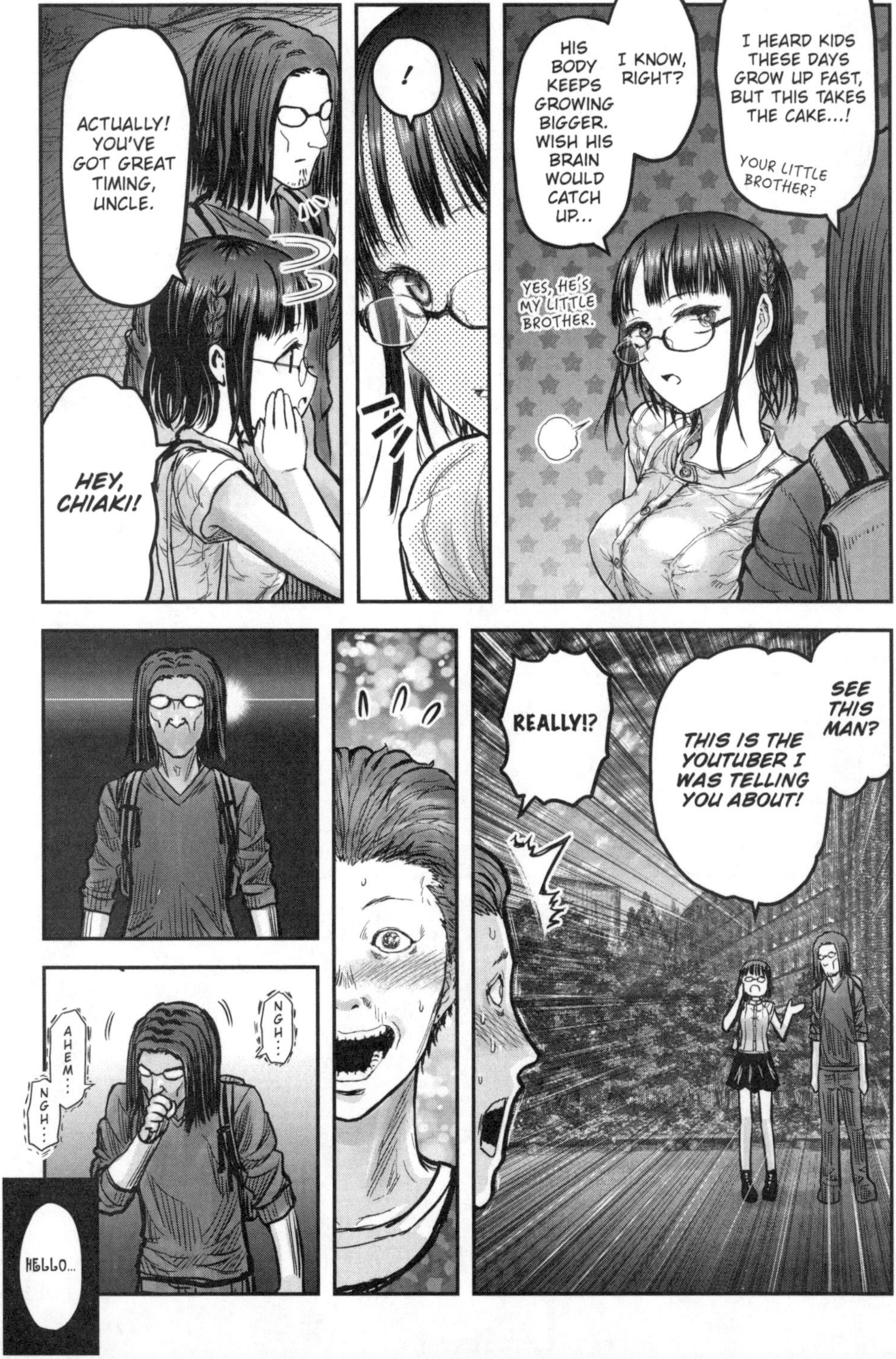
I HEARD KIDS THESE DAYS GROW UP FAST, BUT THIS TAKES THE CAKE...!
YOUR LITTLE BROTHER?
I KNOW, RIGHT?
HIS BODY KEEPS GROWING BIGGER. WISH HIS BRAIN WOULD CATCH UP...
YES, HE'S MY LITTLE BROTHER.
!
ACTUALLY! YOU'VE GOT GREAT TIMING, UNCLE.
HEY, CHIAKI!
SEE THIS MAN?
THIS IS THE YOUTUBER I WAS TELLING YOU ABOUT!
REALLY!?
NGH...
AHEM...
NGH...
HELLO...

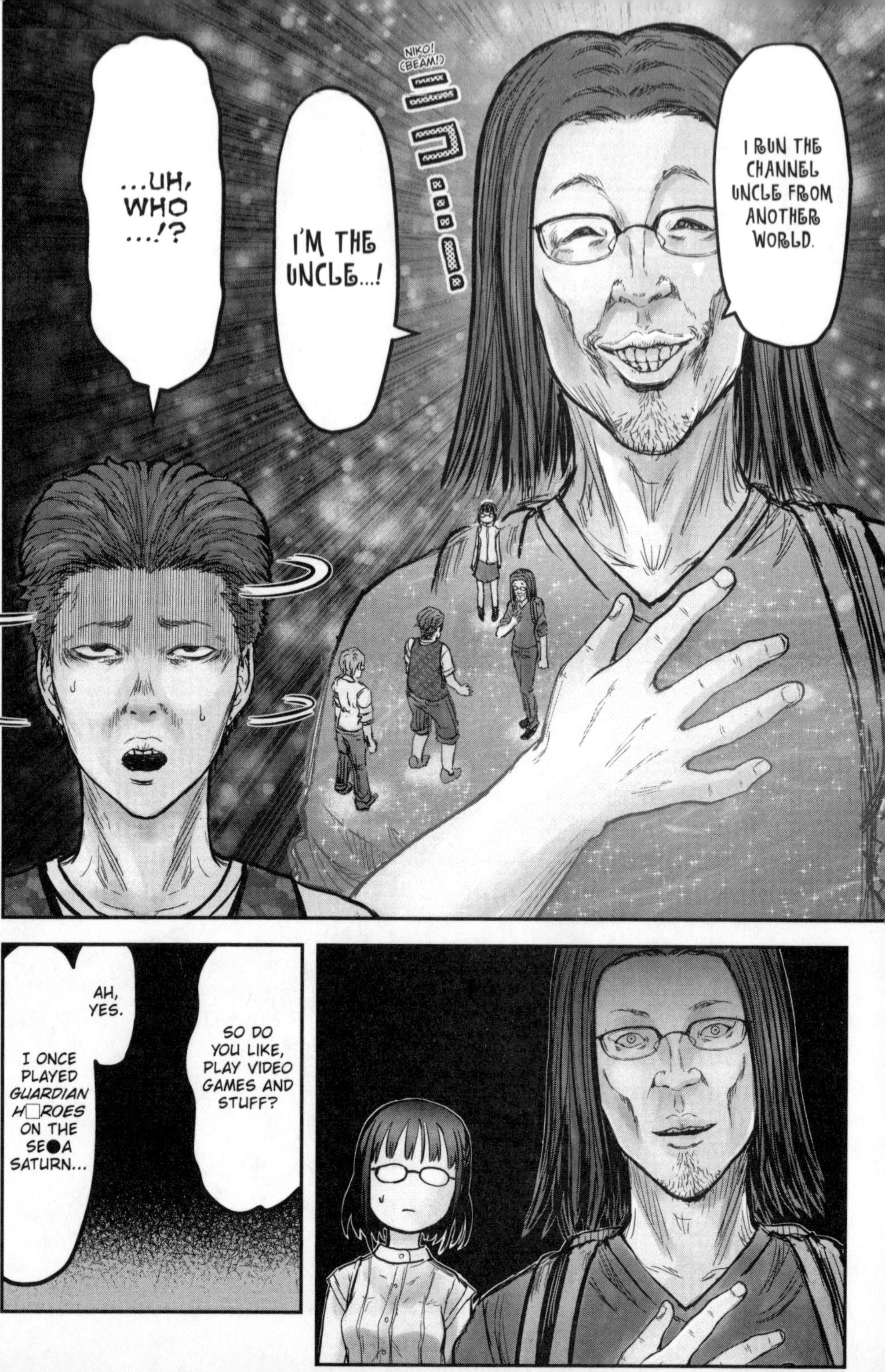
I RUN THE CHANNEL UNCLE FROM ANOTHER WORLD.
NIKO! (BEAM!)
I'M THE UNCLE...!
...UH, WHO ...!?
SO DO YOU LIKE, PLAY VIDEO GAMES AND STUFF?
AH, YES.
I ONCE PLAYED *GUARDIAN H□ROES* ON THE SE●A SATURN...

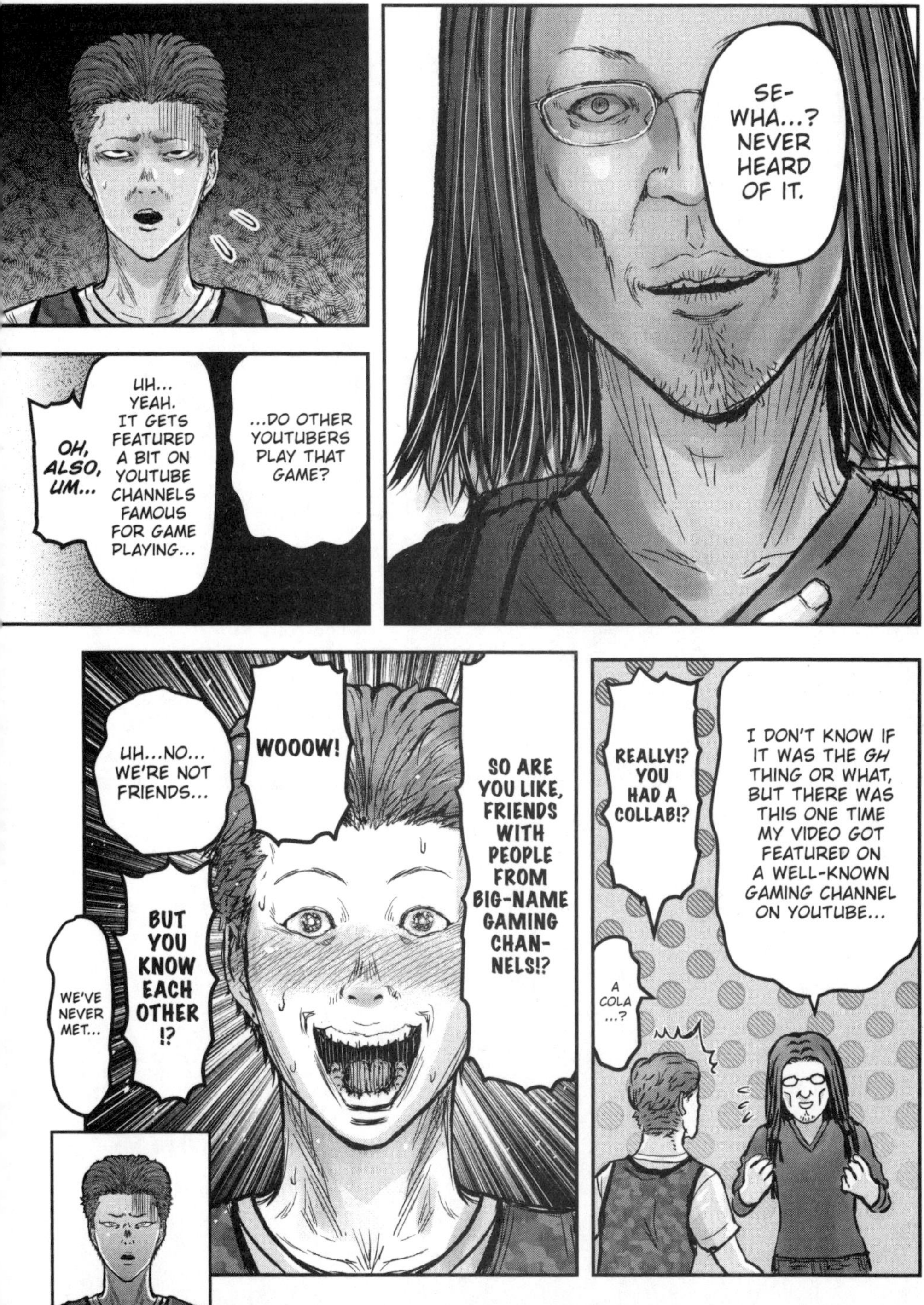
SE-WHA...? NEVER HEARD OF IT.
...DO OTHER YOUTUBERS PLAY THAT GAME?
UH... YEAH. IT GETS FEATURED A BIT ON YOUTUBE CHANNELS FAMOUS FOR GAME PLAYING...
OH, ALSO, UM...
I DON'T KNOW IF IT WAS THE GH THING OR WHAT, BUT THERE WAS THIS ONE TIME MY VIDEO GOT FEATURED ON A WELL-KNOWN GAMING CHANNEL ON YOUTUBE...
REALLY!? YOU HAD A COLLAB!?
A COLA ...?
SO ARE YOU LIKE, FRIENDS WITH PEOPLE FROM BIG-NAME GAMING CHAN-NELS!?
WOOOW!
UH...NO... WE'RE NOT FRIENDS...
BUT YOU KNOW EACH OTHER !?
WE'VE NEVER MET...

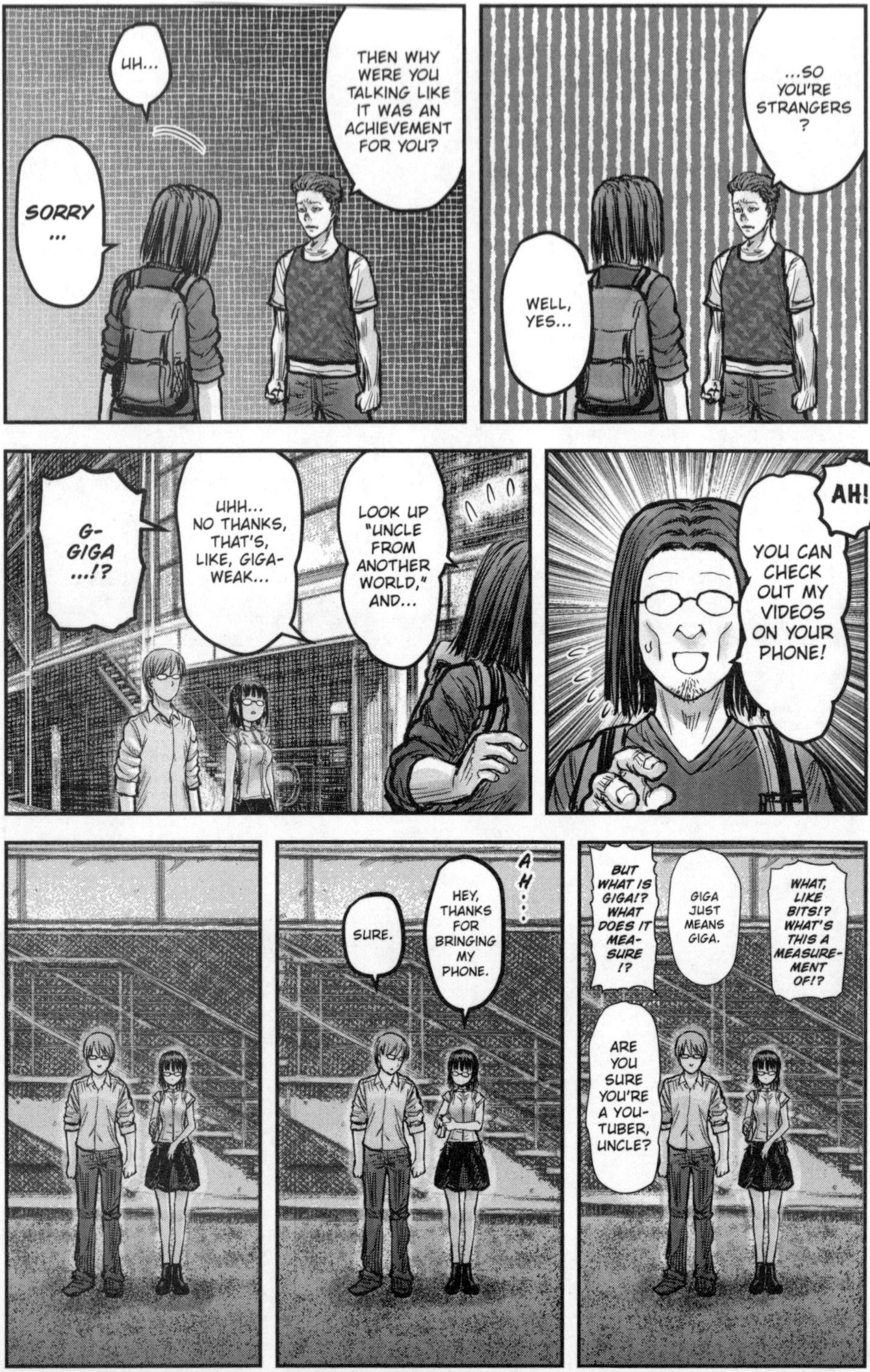
...SO YOU'RE STRANGERS?
WELL, YES...
THEN WHY WERE YOU TALKING LIKE IT WAS AN ACHIEVEMENT FOR YOU?
UH...
SORRY...
AH!
YOU CAN CHECK OUT MY VIDEOS ON YOUR PHONE!
LOOK UP "UNCLE FROM ANOTHER WORLD," AND...
UHH... NO THANKS, THAT'S, LIKE, GIGA-WEAK...
G-GIGA...!?
WHAT, LIKE BITS!? WHAT'S THIS A MEASUREMENT OF!?
GIGA JUST MEANS GIGA.
BUT WHAT IS GIGA!? WHAT DOES IT MEASURE!?
ARE YOU SURE YOU'RE A YOUTUBER, UNCLE?
AH...
HEY, THANKS FOR BRINGING MY PHONE.
SURE.

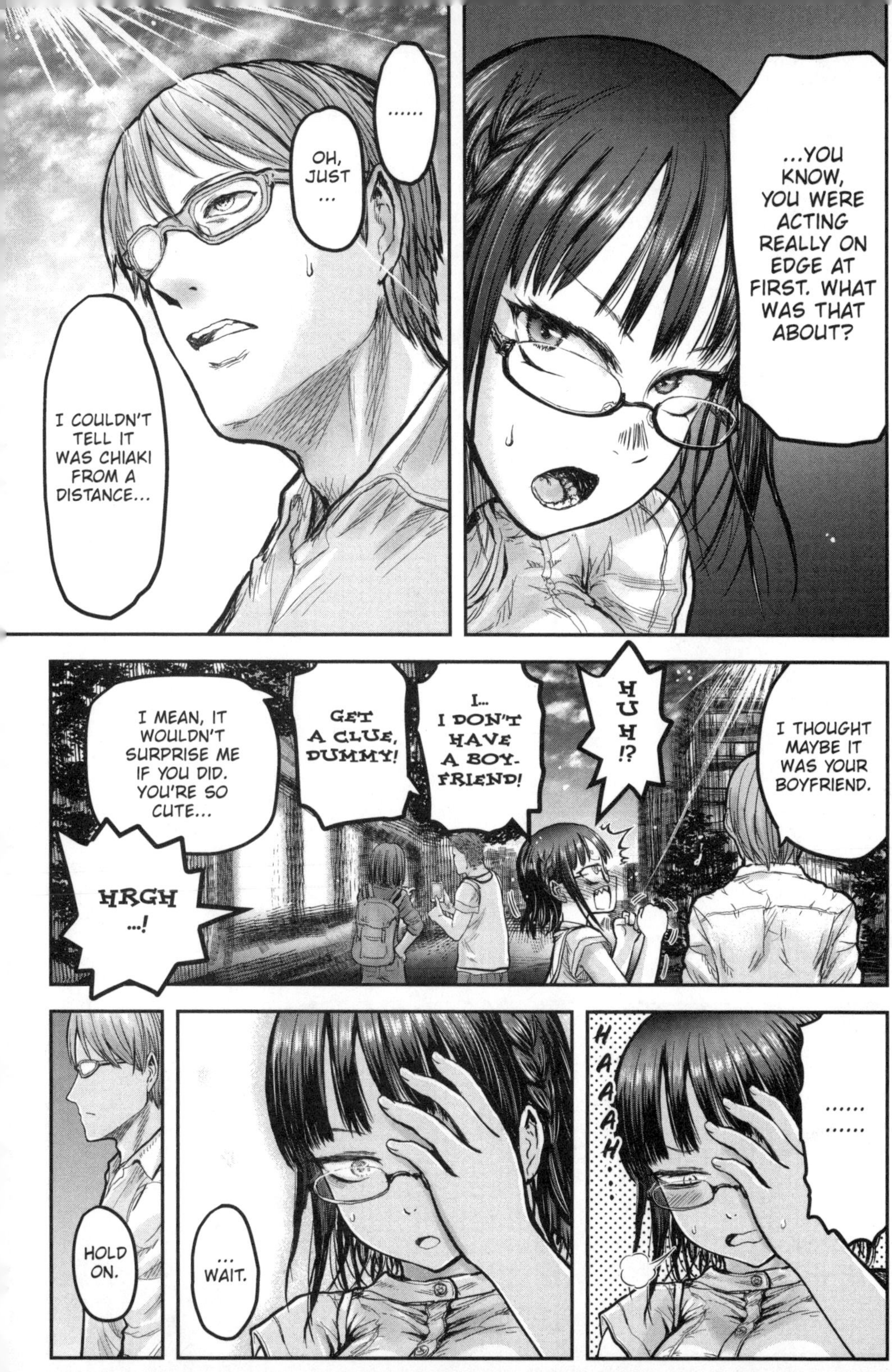
...YOU KNOW, YOU WERE ACTING REALLY ON EDGE AT FIRST. WHAT WAS THAT ABOUT?
......
OH, JUST ...
I COULDN'T TELL IT WAS CHIAKI FROM A DISTANCE...
I THOUGHT MAYBE IT WAS YOUR BOYFRIEND.
HUH!?
I... I DON'T HAVE A BOY-FRIEND!
GET A CLUE, DUMMY!
I MEAN, IT WOULDN'T SURPRISE ME IF YOU DID. YOU'RE SO CUTE...
HRGH ...!
HAAAAH...
....
... WAIT.
HOLD ON.

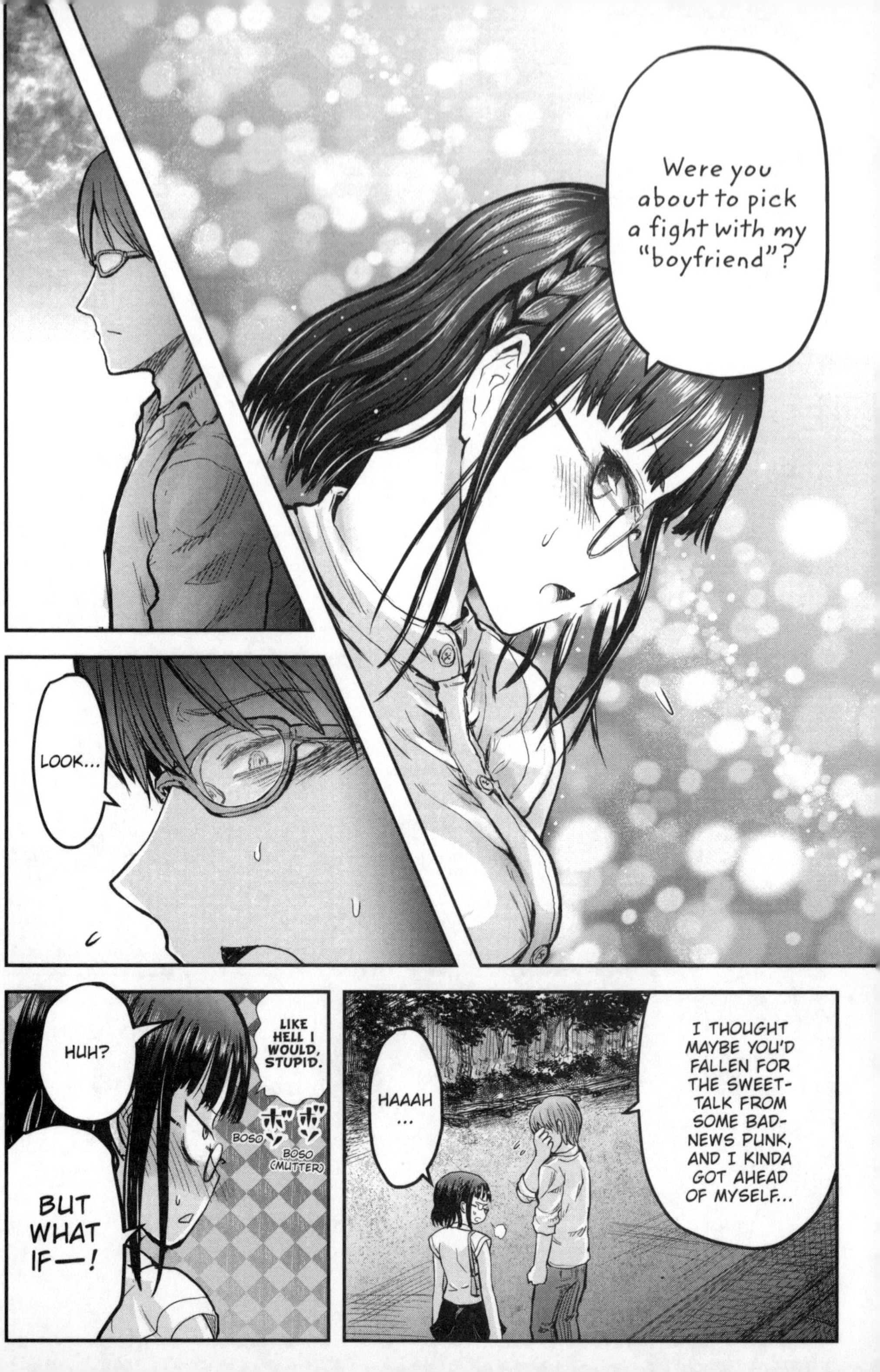
Were you about to pick a fight with my "boyfriend"?
LOOK...
I THOUGHT MAYBE YOU'D FALLEN FOR THE SWEET-TALK FROM SOME BAD-NEWS PUNK, AND I KINDA GOT AHEAD OF MYSELF...
HAAAH...
LIKE HELL I WOULD, STUPID.
HUH?
BOSO BOSO (MUTTER)
BUT WHAT IF—!

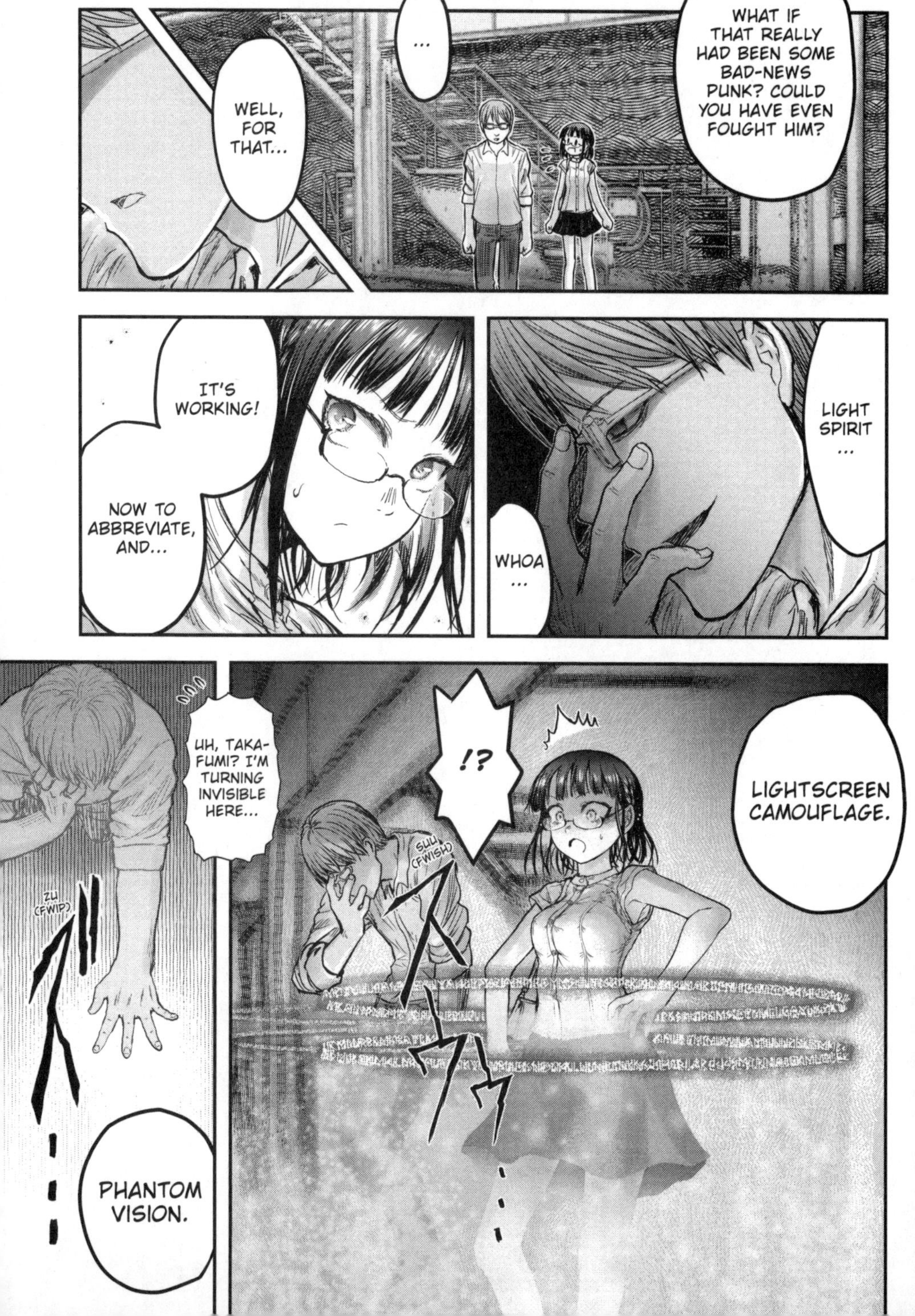
WHAT IF THAT REALLY HAD BEEN SOME BAD-NEWS PUNK? COULD YOU HAVE EVEN FOUGHT HIM?
...
WELL, FOR THAT...
LIGHT SPIRIT...
WHOA...
IT'S WORKING!
NOW TO ABBREVIATE, AND...
LIGHTSCREEN CAMOUFLAGE.
!?
SUU (FWISH)
UH, TAKA-FUMI? I'M TURNING INVISIBLE HERE...
ZU (FWIP)
PHANTOM VISION.

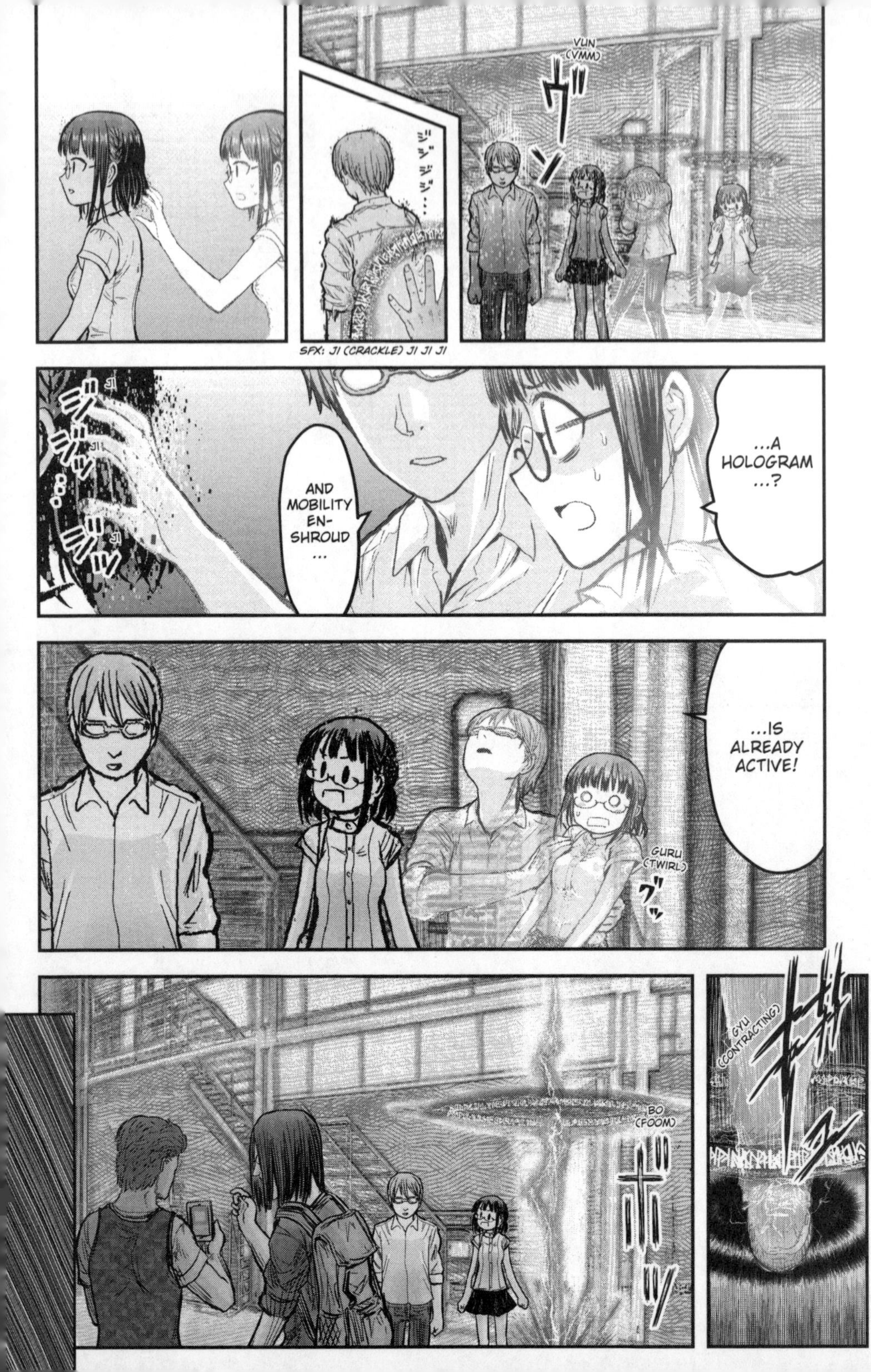
VUN (VMM)
ヴン
ジジジジ…
SFX: JI (CRACKLE) JI JI JI
…A HOLOGRAM …?
AND MOBILITY EN-SHROUD …
JI
JI
JI
…IS ALREADY ACTIVE!
GURU (TWIRL)
GYU (CONTRACTING)
BO (FOOM)

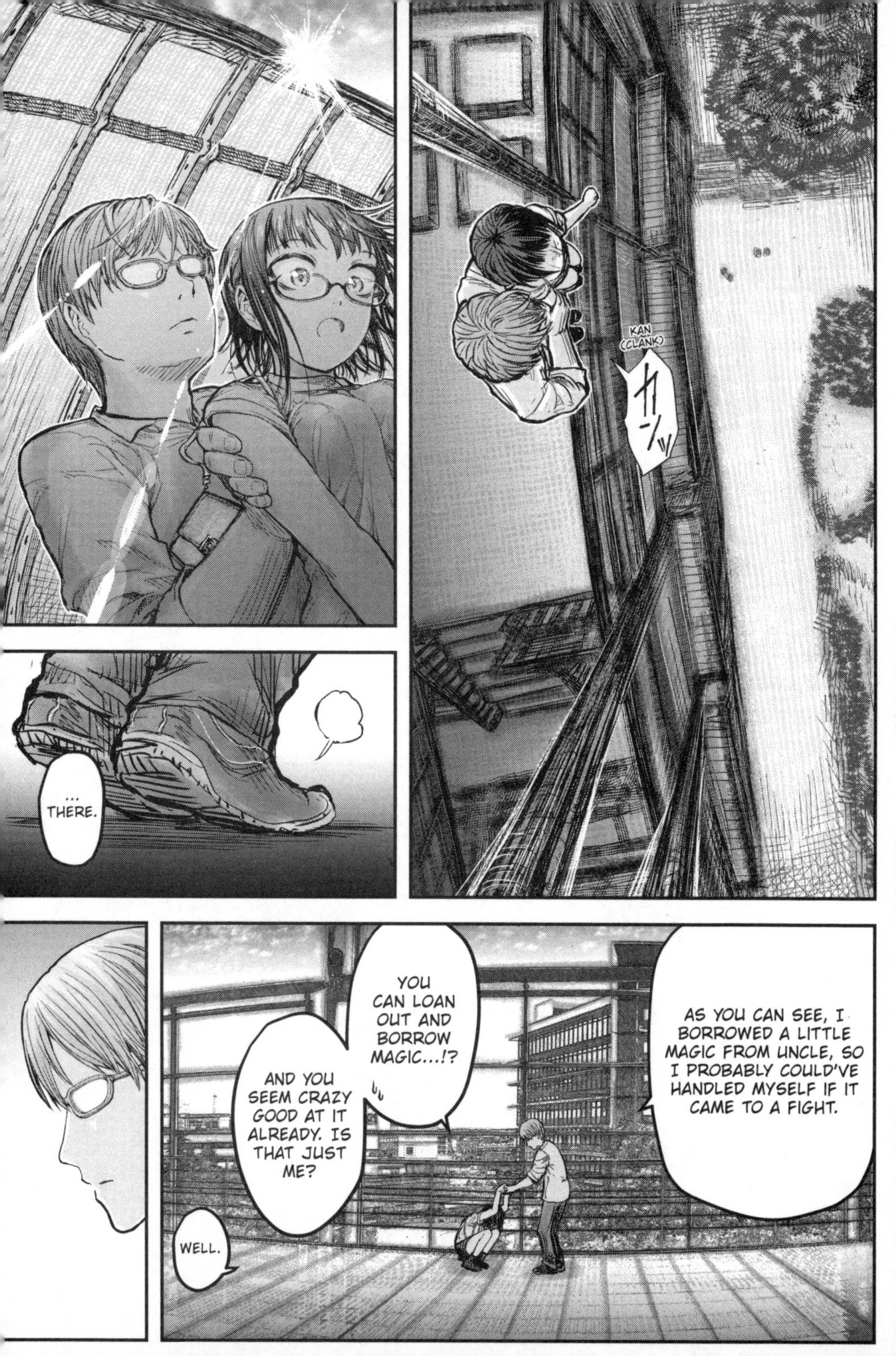
KAN (CLANK)
カーンッ
...THERE.
AS YOU CAN SEE, I BORROWED A LITTLE MAGIC FROM UNCLE, SO I PROBABLY COULD'VE HANDLED MYSELF IF IT CAME TO A FIGHT.
YOU CAN LOAN OUT AND BORROW MAGIC...!?
AND YOU SEEM CRAZY GOOD AT IT ALREADY. IS THAT JUST ME?
WELL.

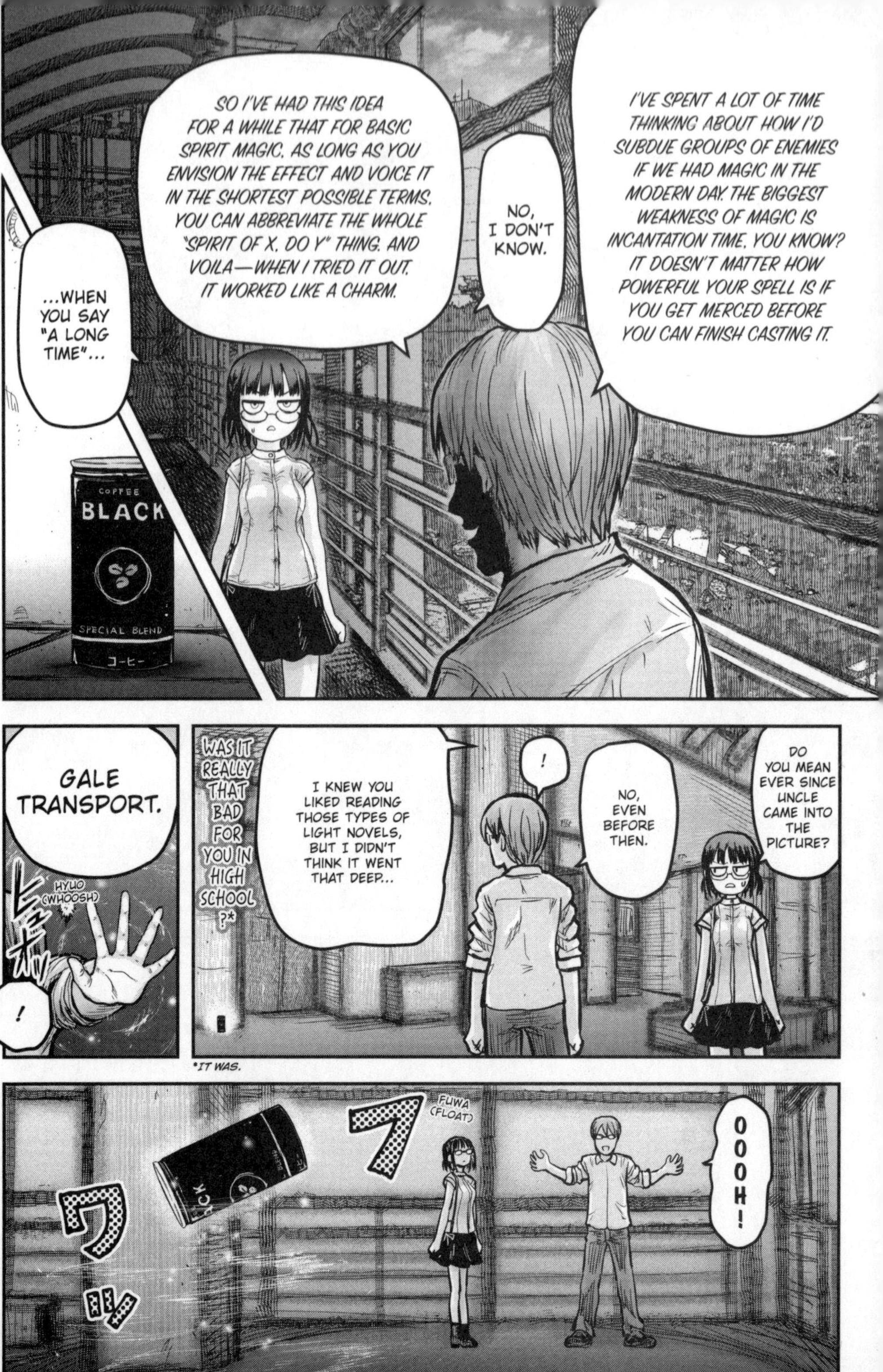
I'VE SPENT A LOT OF TIME THINKING ABOUT HOW I'D SUBDUE GROUPS OF ENEMIES IF WE HAD MAGIC IN THE MODERN DAY. THE BIGGEST WEAKNESS OF MAGIC IS INCANTATION TIME, YOU KNOW? IT DOESN'T MATTER HOW POWERFUL YOUR SPELL IS IF YOU GET MERCED BEFORE YOU CAN FINISH CASTING IT.
NO, I DON'T KNOW.
SO I'VE HAD THIS IDEA FOR A WHILE THAT FOR BASIC SPIRIT MAGIC, AS LONG AS YOU ENVISION THE EFFECT AND VOICE IT IN THE SHORTEST POSSIBLE TERMS, YOU CAN ABBREVIATE THE WHOLE "SPIRIT OF X, DO Y" THING. AND VOILA—WHEN I TRIED IT OUT, IT WORKED LIKE A CHARM.
...WHEN YOU SAY "A LONG TIME"...
COFFEE
BLACK
SPECIAL BLEND
コーヒー
DO YOU MEAN EVER SINCE UNCLE CAME INTO THE PICTURE?
NO, EVEN BEFORE THEN.
!
I KNEW YOU LIKED READING THOSE TYPES OF LIGHT NOVELS, BUT I DIDN'T THINK IT WENT THAT DEEP...
WAS IT REALLY THAT BAD FOR YOU IN HIGH SCHOOL?*
GALE TRANSPORT.
HYUO (WHOOSH)
!
*IT WAS.
OOOH!
FUWA (FLOAT)

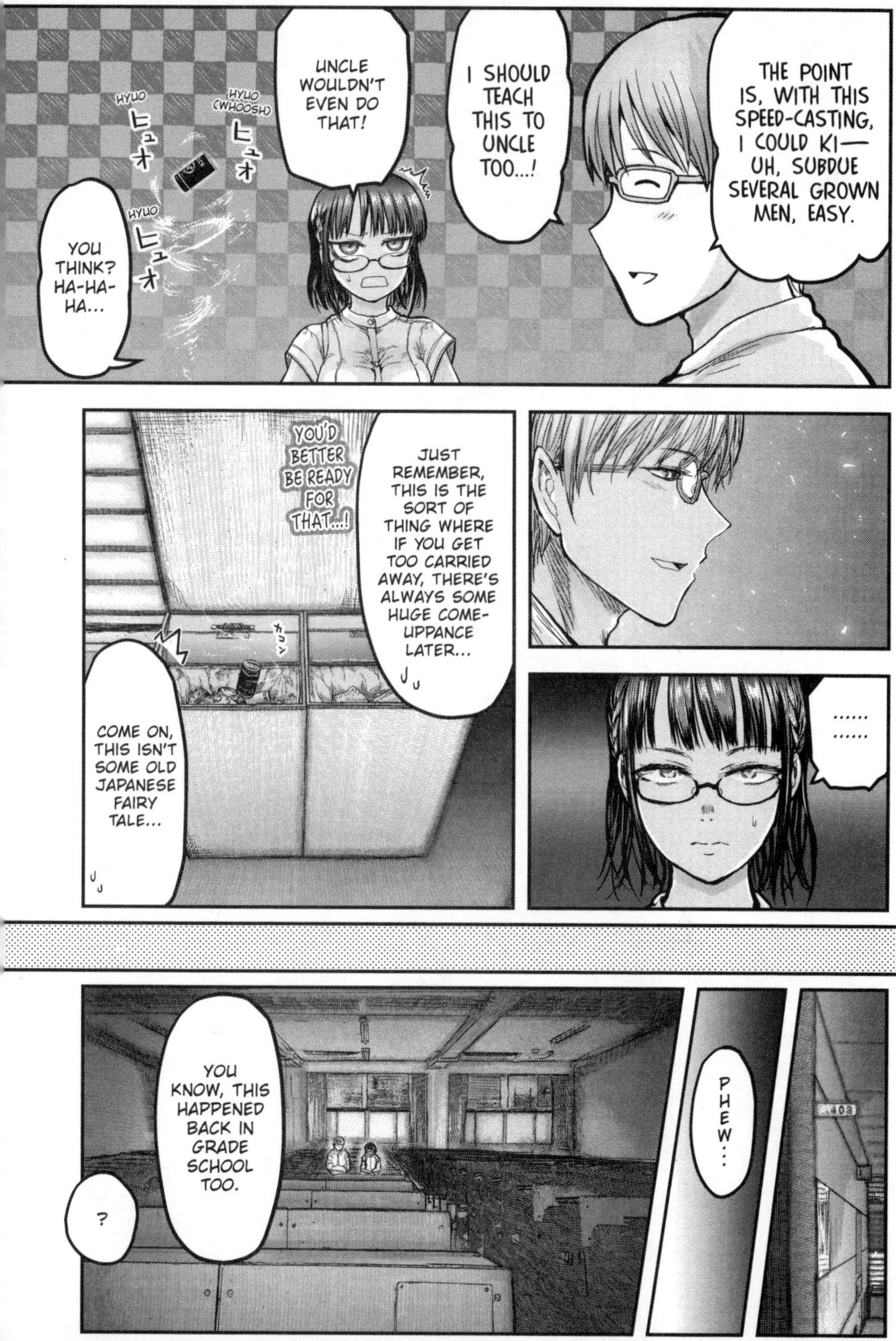
THE POINT IS, WITH THIS SPEED-CASTING, I COULD KI— UH, SUBDUE SEVERAL GROWN MEN, EASY.
I SHOULD TEACH THIS TO UNCLE TOO...!
UNCLE WOULDN'T EVEN DO THAT!
HYUO (WHOOSH) ヒュオ
HYUO ヒュオ
HYUO ヒュオ
YOU THINK? HA-HA-HA...
......
......
JUST REMEMBER, THIS IS THE SORT OF THING WHERE IF YOU GET TOO CARRIED AWAY, THERE'S ALWAYS SOME HUGE COME-UPPANCE LATER...
YOU'D BETTER BE READY FOR THAT...!
カコン
COME ON, THIS ISN'T SOME OLD JAPANESE FAIRY TALE...
403
PHEW...
YOU KNOW, THIS HAPPENED BACK IN GRADE SCHOOL TOO.
?

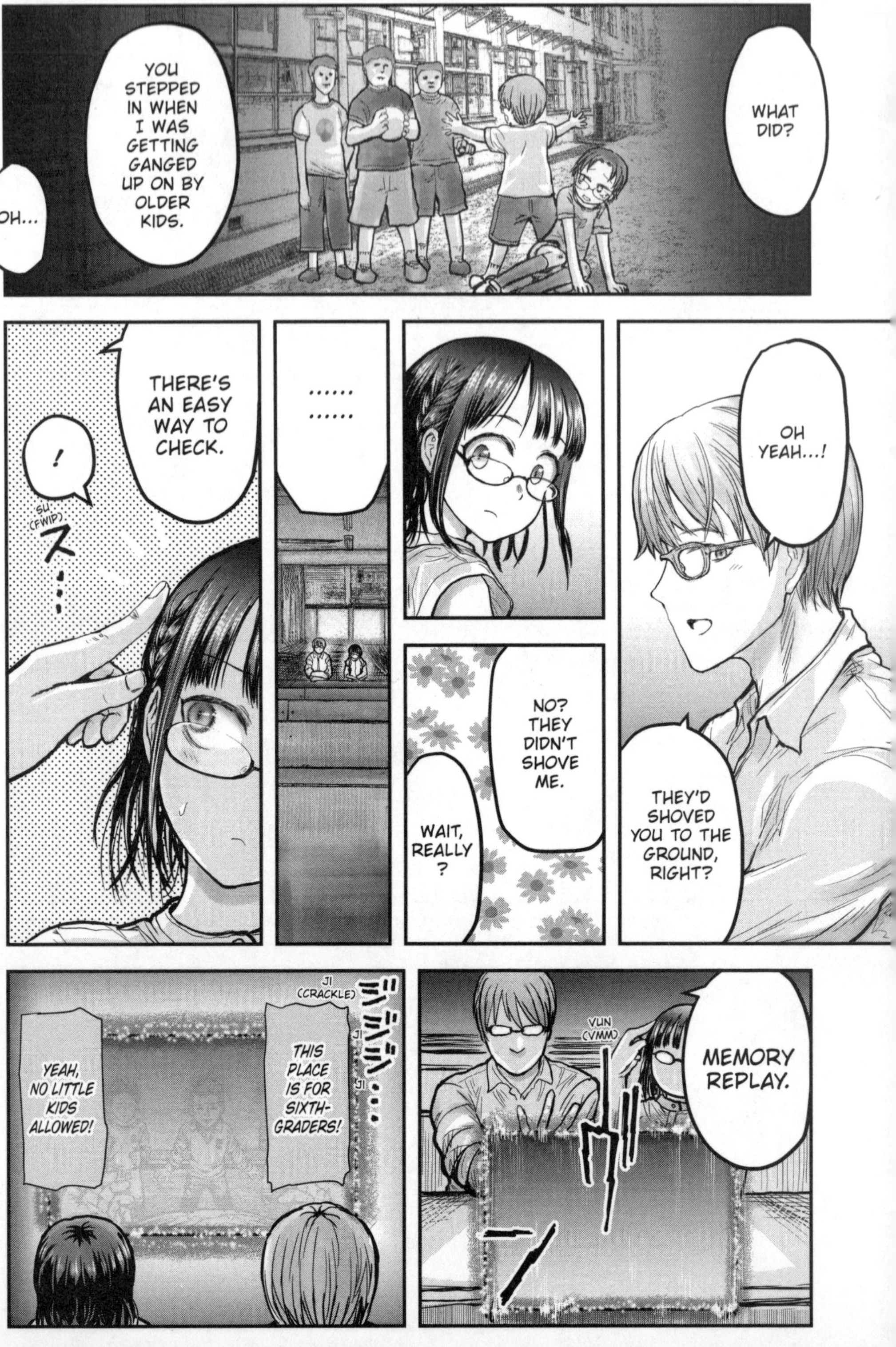
WHAT DID?
YOU STEPPED IN WHEN I WAS GETTING GANGED UP ON BY OLDER KIDS.
OH...
OH YEAH...!
THEY'D SHOVED YOU TO THE GROUND, RIGHT?
NO? THEY DIDN'T SHOVE ME.
WAIT, REALLY?
......
......
THERE'S AN EASY WAY TO CHECK.
!
SU (FWIP)
MEMORY REPLAY.
VUN (VMM)
JI (CRACKLE)
THIS PLACE IS FOR SIXTH-GRADERS!
YEAH, NO LITTLE KIDS ALLOWED!

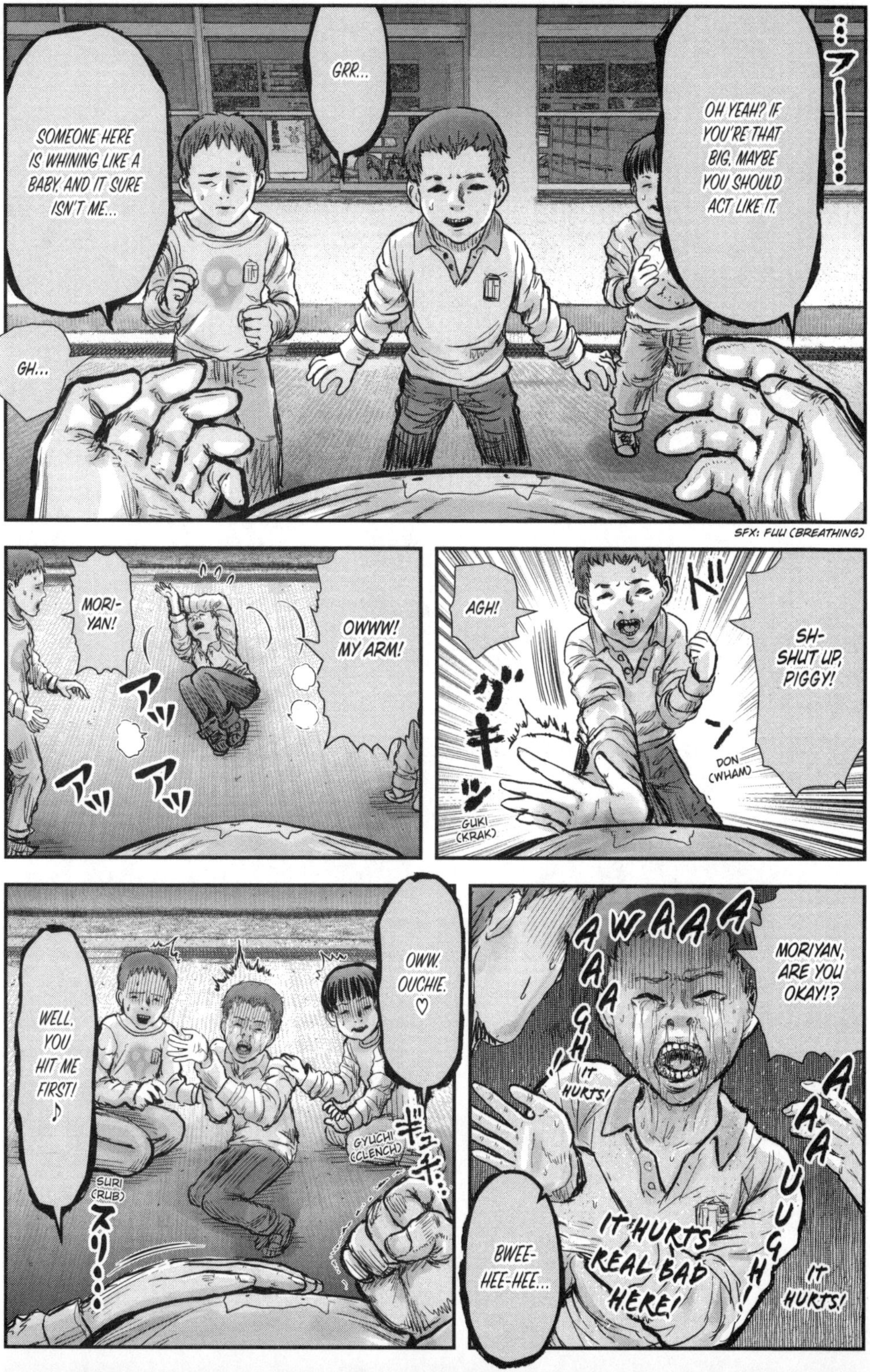
…フー…
OH YEAH? IF YOU'RE THAT BIG, MAYBE YOU SHOULD ACT LIKE IT.
GRR...
SOMEONE HERE IS WHINING LIKE A BABY, AND IT SURE ISN'T ME...
GH...
SFX: FUU (BREATHING)
SH- SHUT UP, PIGGY!
ドン
DON (WHAM)
AGH!
グキッ
GUKI (KRAK)
OWWW! MY ARM!
MORI-YAN!
アッ
アッ
アッ
MORIYAN, ARE YOU OKAY!?
AAAUUGH!
IT HURTS!
AWAAAAAAAGH!
IT HURTS!
IT HURTS REAL BAD HERE!
BWEE-HEE-HEE...
OWW. OUCHIE. ♡
ギュチ…
GYUCHI (CLENCH)
WELL, YOU HIT ME FIRST! ♪
SURI (RUB)
スリ…

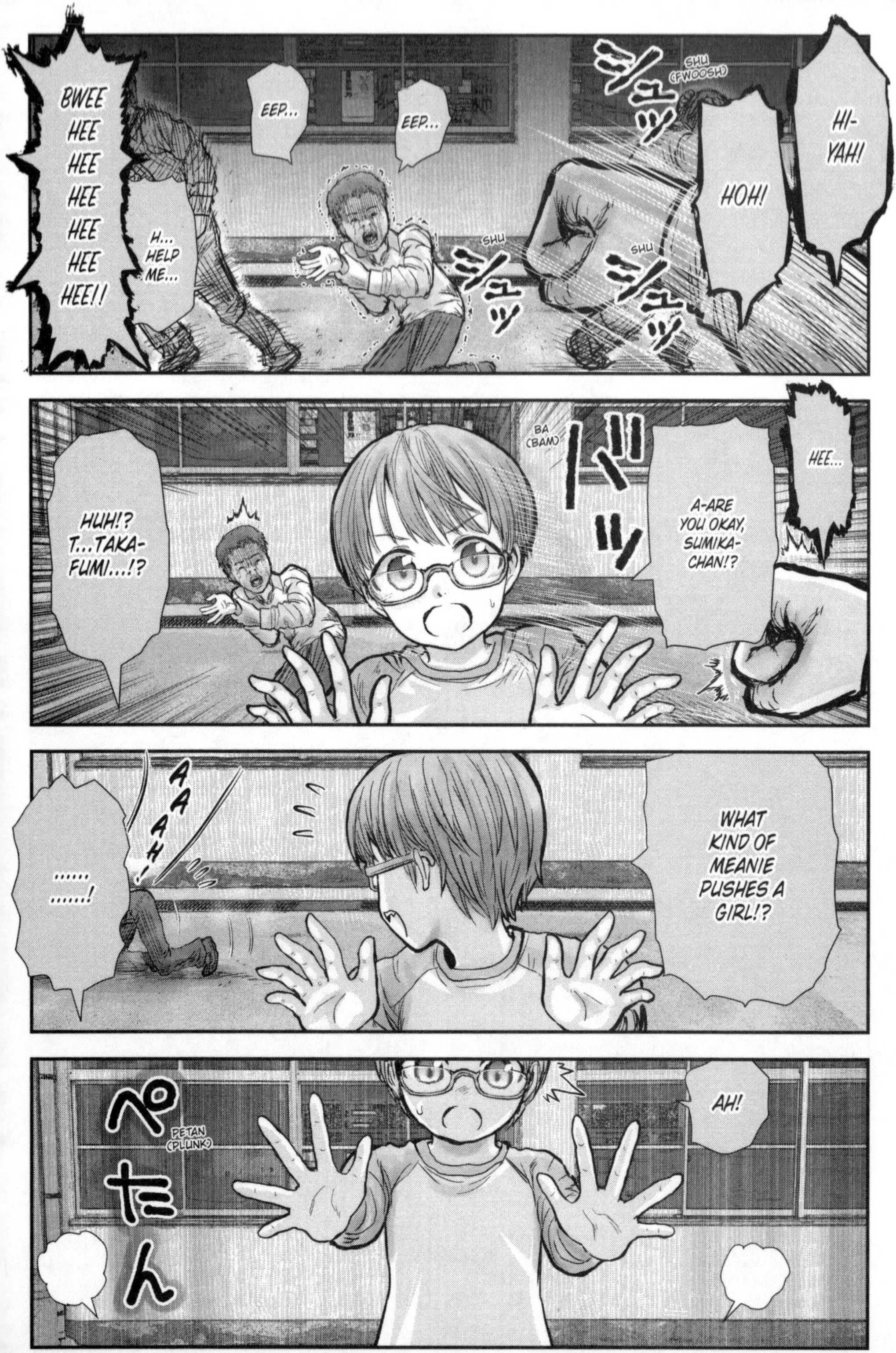

HI-YAH!
HOH!
SHU (FWOOSH)
SHU
SHU
EEP...
EEP...
H... HELP ME...
BWEE HEE HEE HEE HEE HEE HEE!!
HEE...
BA (BAM)
A-ARE YOU OKAY, SUMIKA-CHAN!?
HUH!? T...TAKA-FUMI...!?
WHAT KIND OF MEANIE PUSHES A GIRL!?
AAAAH!
....!
AH!
PETAN (PLUNK)

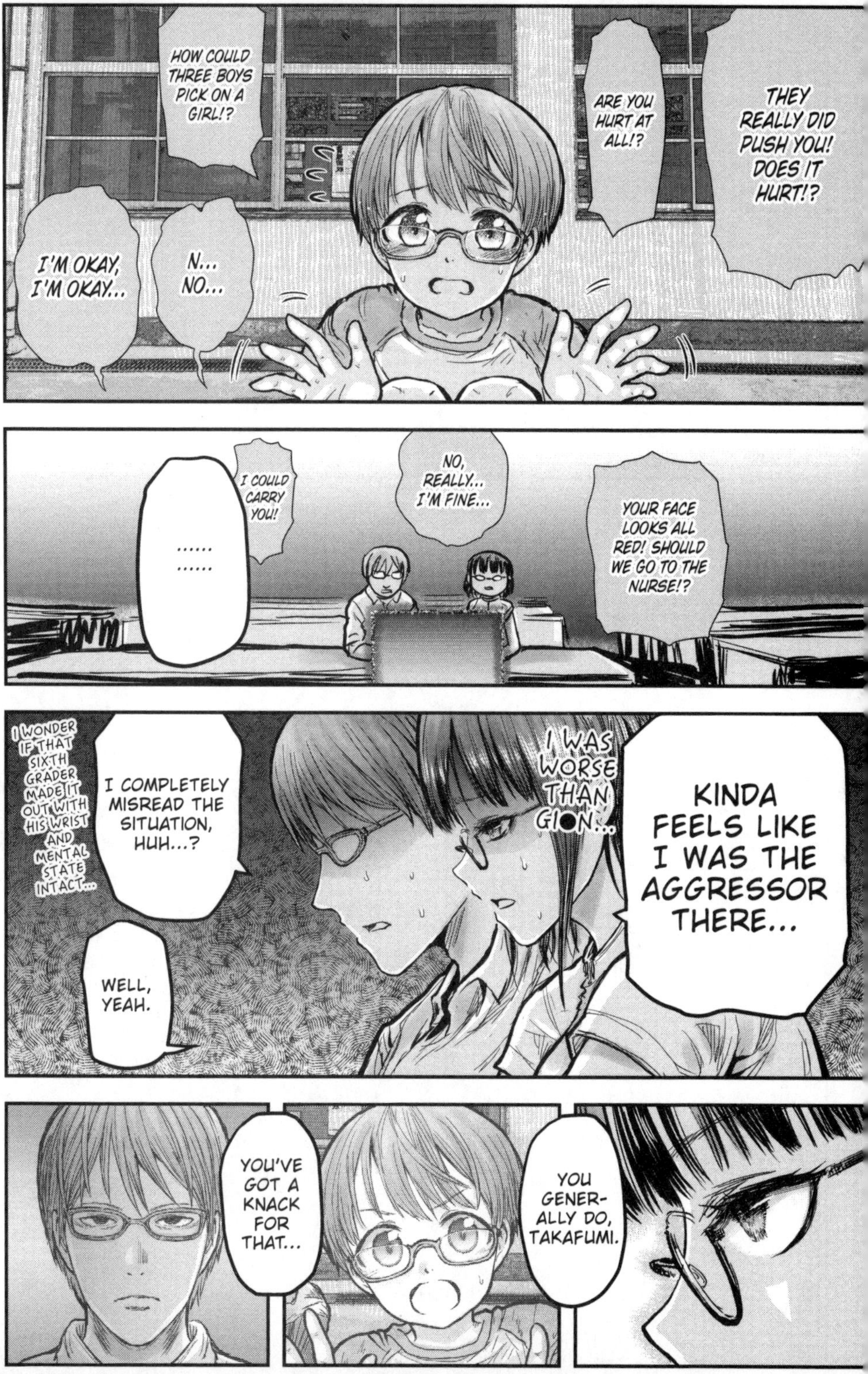
THEY REALLY DID PUSH YOU! DOES IT HURT!?
ARE YOU HURT AT ALL!?
HOW COULD THREE BOYS PICK ON A GIRL!?
N... NO...
I'M OKAY, I'M OKAY...
YOUR FACE LOOKS ALL RED! SHOULD WE GO TO THE NURSE!?
NO, REALLY... I'M FINE...
I COULD CARRY YOU!
....
KINDA FEELS LIKE I WAS THE AGGRESSOR THERE...
I WAS WORSE THAN GION...
I COMPLETELY MISREAD THE SITUATION, HUH...?
I WONDER IF THAT SIXTH GRADER MADE IT OUT WITH HIS WRIST AND MENTAL STATE INTACT...
WELL, YEAH.
YOU GENER-ALLY DO, TAKAFUMI.
YOU'VE GOT A KNACK FOR THAT...

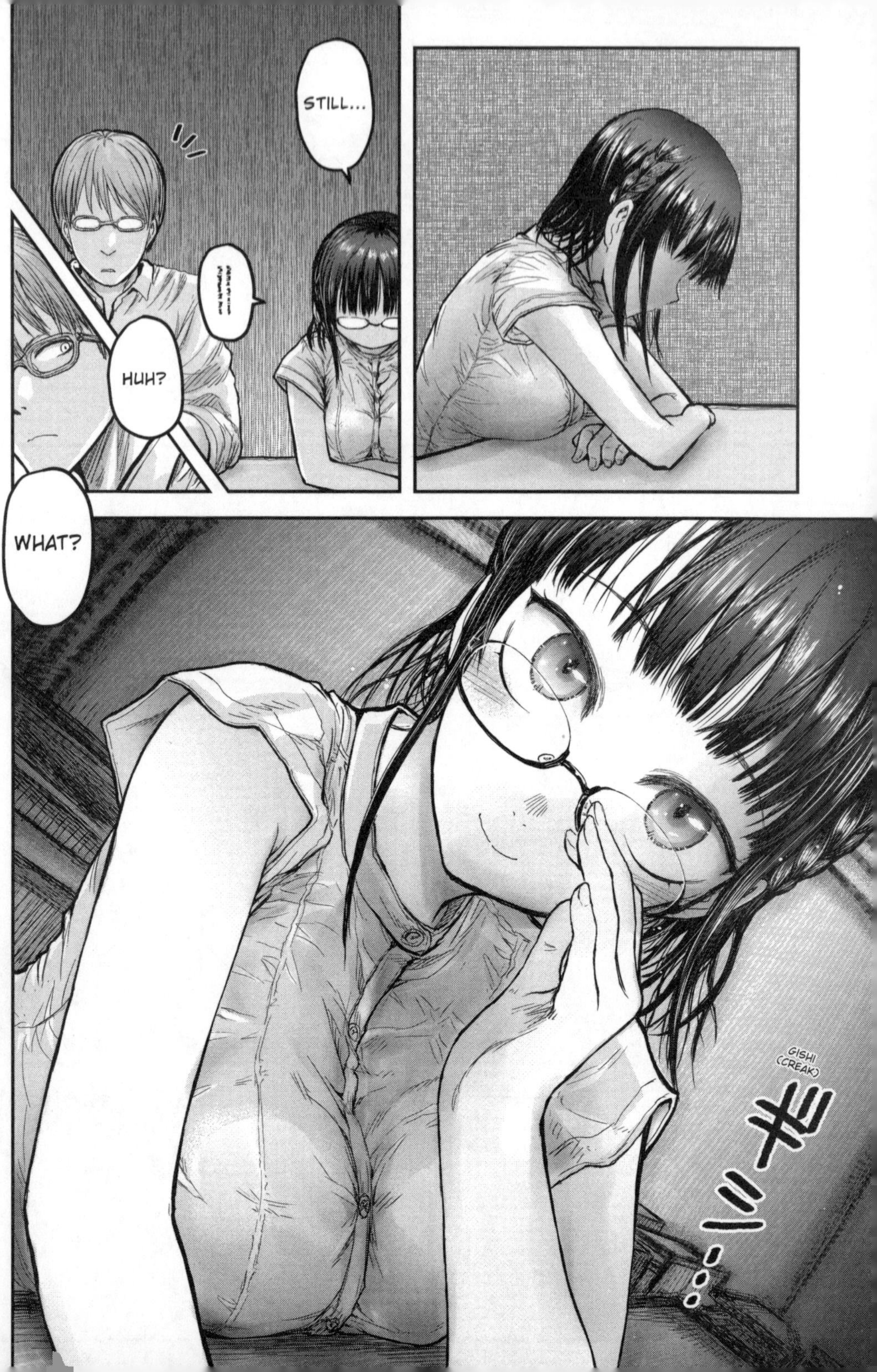
STILL...
HUH?
WHAT?
GISHI (CREAK)

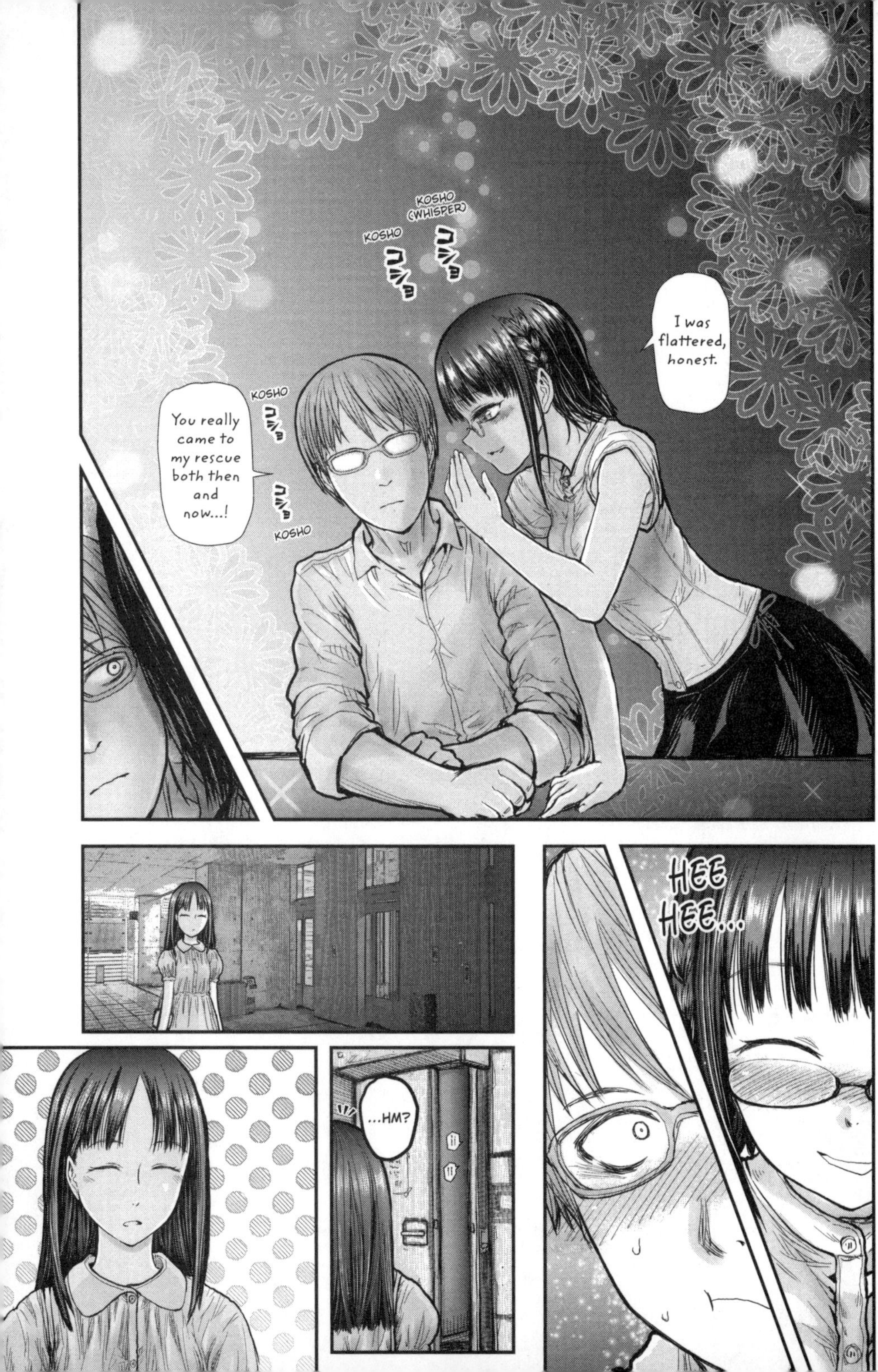
KOSHO (WHISPER)
KOSHO
I was flattered, honest.
KOSHO
You really came to my rescue both then and now...!
KOSHO
HEE HEE...
...HM?

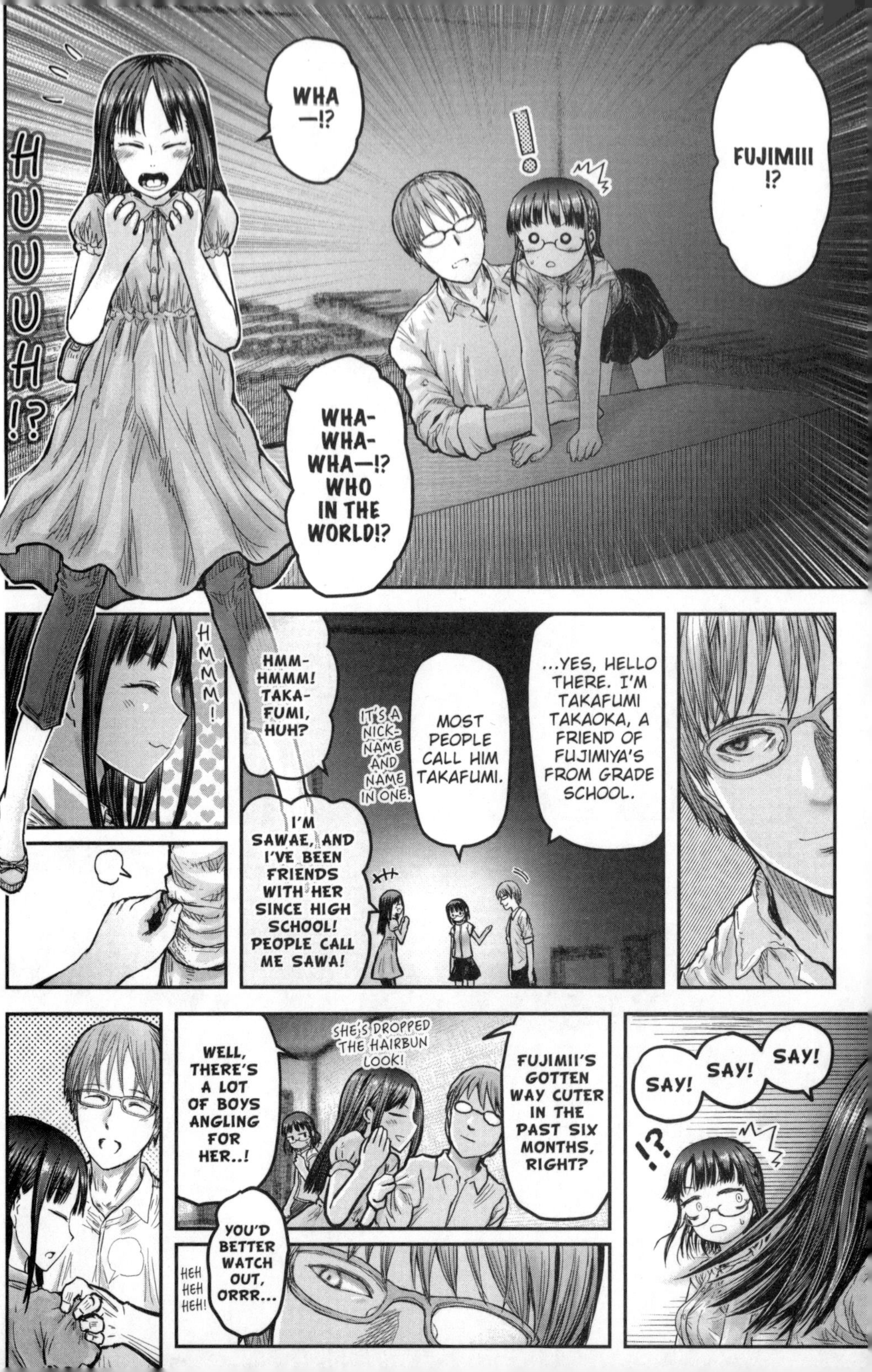
FUJIMIII!?
!
WHA—!?
HUUUUH!?
WHA-WHA-WHA—!? WHO IN THE WORLD!?
...YES, HELLO THERE. I'M TAKAFUMI TAKAOKA, A FRIEND OF FUJIMIYA'S FROM GRADE SCHOOL.
MOST PEOPLE CALL HIM TAKAFUMI.
IT'S A NICKNAME AND NAME IN ONE.
I'M SAWAE, AND I'VE BEEN FRIENDS WITH HER SINCE HIGH SCHOOL! PEOPLE CALL ME SAWA!
HMM-HMMM! TAKA-FUMI, HUH?
HMMMM!
SAY! SAY! SAY!
!?
FUJIMII'S GOTTEN WAY CUTER IN THE PAST SIX MONTHS, RIGHT?
SHE'S DROPPED THE HAIRBUN LOOK!
WELL, THERE'S A LOT OF BOYS ANGLING FOR HER..!
YOU'D BETTER WATCH OUT, ORRR...
HEH HEH HEH!

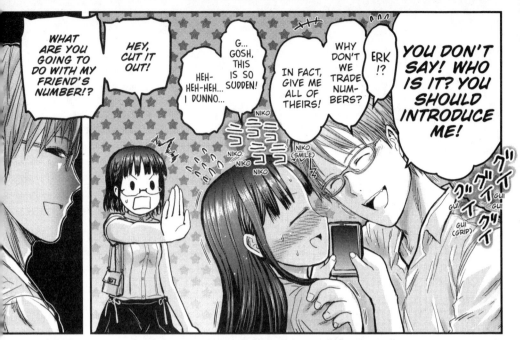

YOU DON'T SAY! WHO IS IT? YOU SHOULD INTRODUCE ME!
ERK!?
WHY DON'T WE TRADE NUM-BERS?
IN FACT, GIVE ME ALL OF THEIRS!
GUI GUI GUI GUI (GRIP)
NIKO NIKO NIKO NIKO NIKO (SMILE)
G... GOSH, THIS IS SO SUDDEN!
HEH-HEH-HEH... I DUNNO...
HEY, CUT IT OUT!
WHAT ARE YOU GOING TO DO WITH MY FRIEND'S NUMBER!?
OH, NOTHING.
NOT GETTING THE NUM-BER AND NOT DOING ANYTHING WITH IT ARE BASICALLY THE SAME...
BOSO (MUTTER) BOSO
YOU'RE CLEARLY THE TYPE THAT CAN'T BE TRUSTED WITH ANY AMOUNT OF POWER...!
FOR ONCE, YOU COULD STAND TO TAKE A CUE FROM UNCLE...!
...LOOK. ALL I'M SAYING IS, COLLEGE GUYS ARE INHUMAN.
THEY'RE BUGS...
GRR... YOU HAVE TO SWAT THEM DOWN...
...OR ELSE THEY'LL USE HYPNOSIS ON YOU AT A PARTY AND GASLIGHT YOU INTO COMING HOME WITH THEM...!
STOP TREATING LUDICROUSLY LOPSIDED INTERNET CLAIMS AS THE GOSPEL TRUTH!
MOST COLLEGE STUDENTS ARE DILI-GENT AND SHOW UP FOR CLASS!*

*NOT NECESSARILY TRUE FOR ALL STUDENTS.

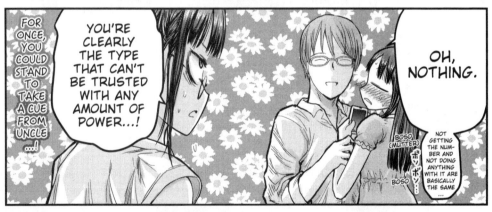

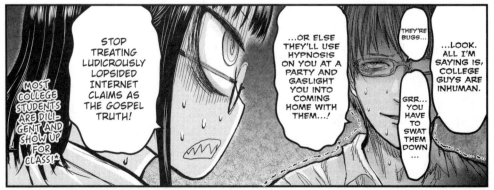

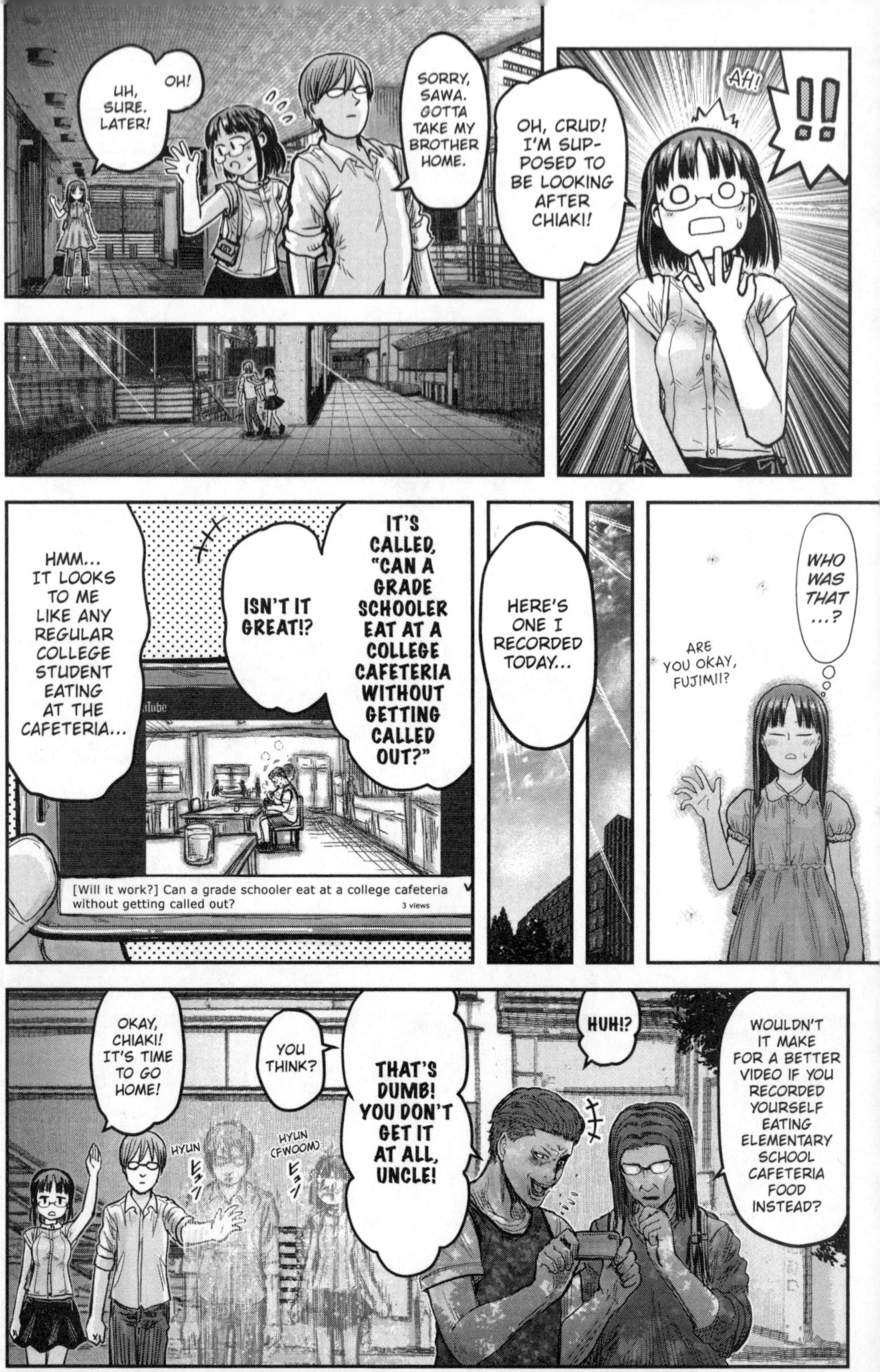
AH!
!!
OH, CRUD! I'M SUP-POSED TO BE LOOKING AFTER CHIAKI!
SORRY, SAWA. GOTTA TAKE MY BROTHER HOME.
OH!
UH, SURE. LATER!
WHO WAS THAT ...?
ARE YOU OKAY, FUJIMI!?
HERE'S ONE I RECORDED TODAY...
IT'S CALLED, "CAN A GRADE SCHOOLER EAT AT A COLLEGE CAFETERIA WITHOUT GETTING CALLED OUT?"
ISN'T IT GREAT!?
HMM... IT LOOKS TO ME LIKE ANY REGULAR COLLEGE STUDENT EATING AT THE CAFETERIA...
[Will it work?] Can a grade schooler eat at a college cafeteria without getting called out?
3 views
WOULDN'T IT MAKE FOR A BETTER VIDEO IF YOU RECORDED YOURSELF EATING ELEMENTARY SCHOOL CAFETERIA FOOD INSTEAD?
HUH!?
THAT'S DUMB! YOU DON'T GET IT AT ALL, UNCLE!
YOU THINK?
OKAY, CHIAKI! IT'S TIME TO GO HOME!
HYUN
HYUN (FWOOM)

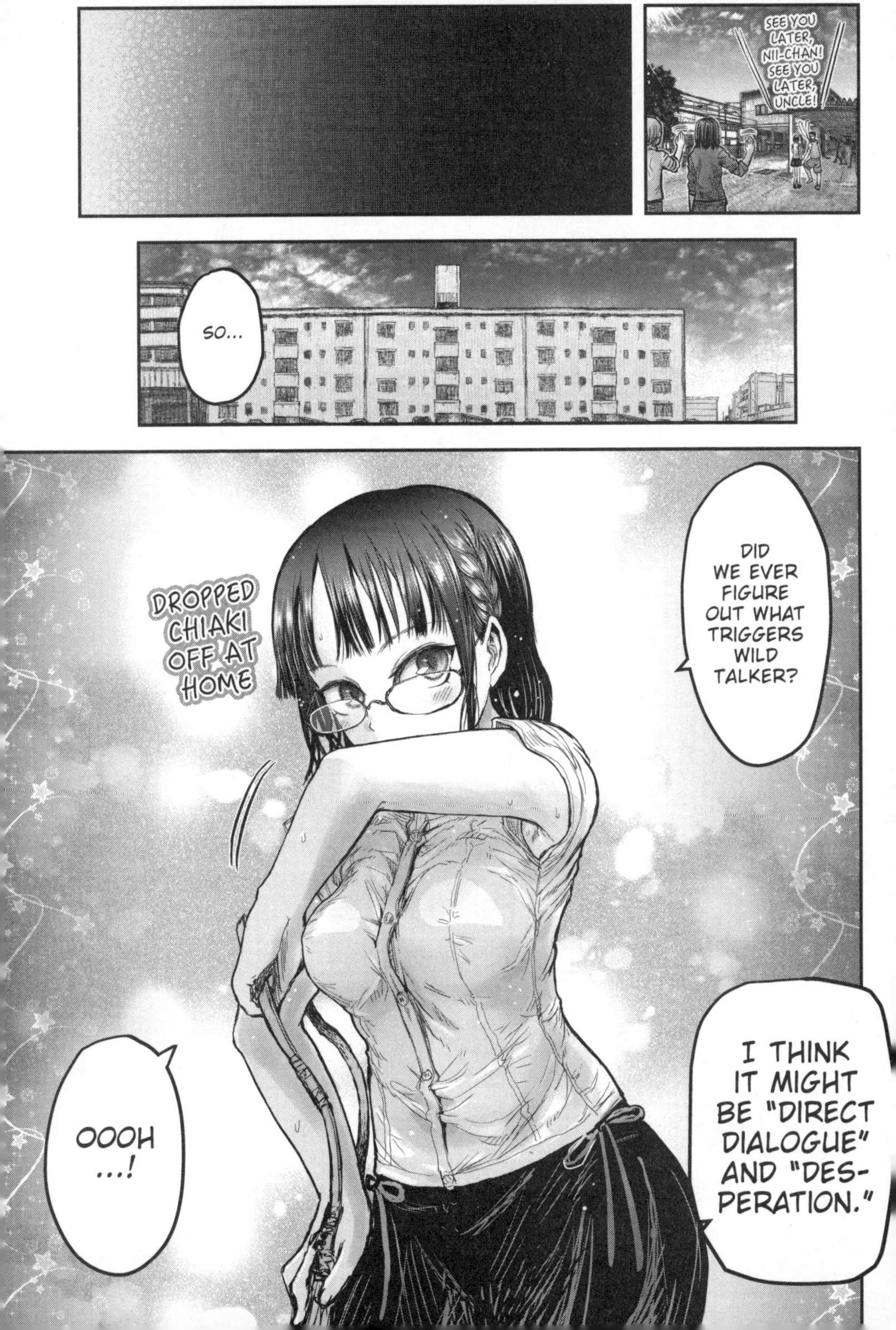
SEE YOU LATER, NII-CHAN! SEE YOU LATER, UNCLE!
SO...
DID WE EVER FIGURE OUT WHAT TRIGGERS WILD TALKER?
DROPPED CHIAKI OFF AT HOME
I THINK IT MIGHT BE "DIRECT DIALOGUE" AND "DES-PERATION."
OOOH ...!

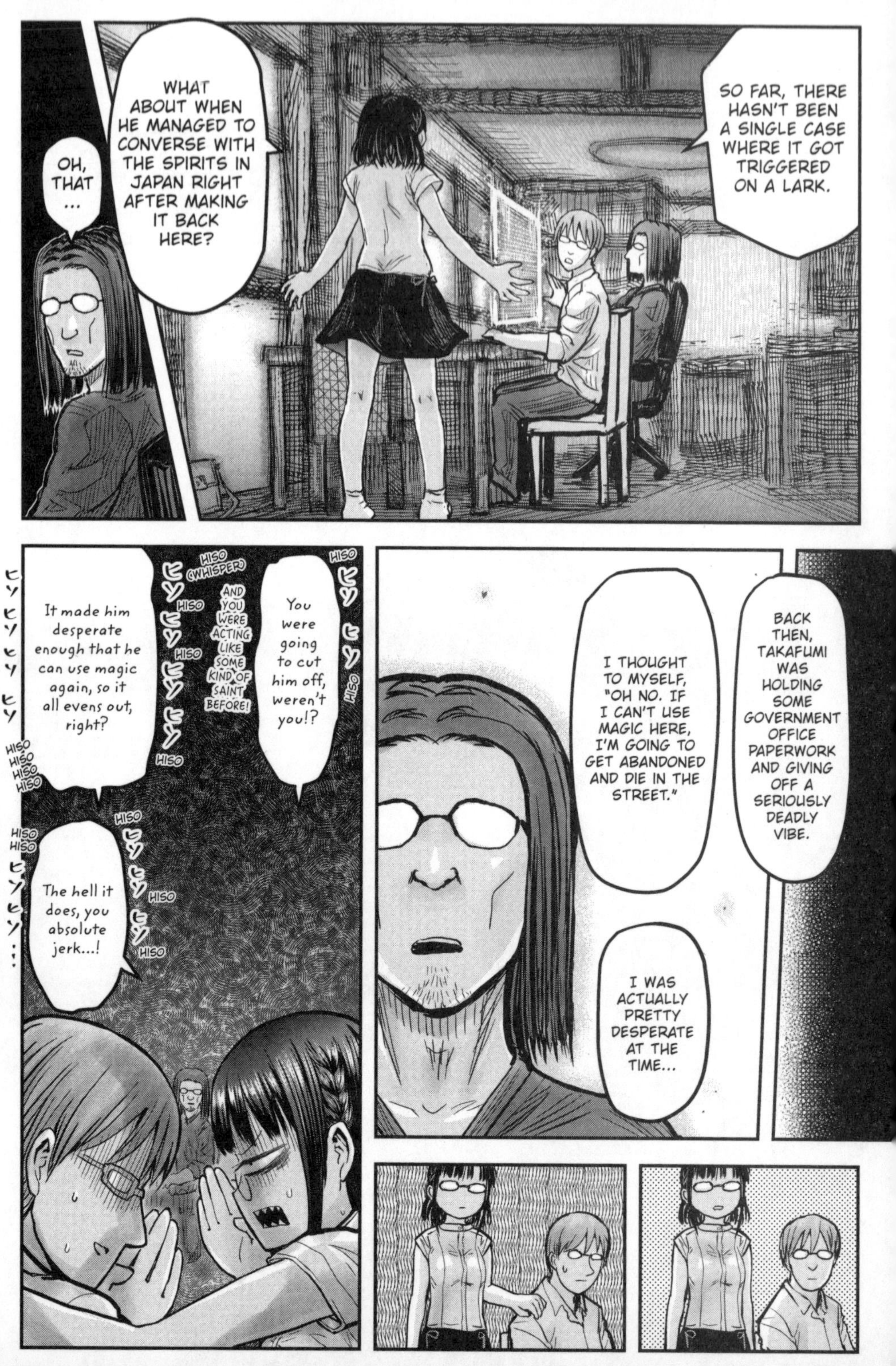
SO FAR, THERE HASN'T BEEN A SINGLE CASE WHERE IT GOT TRIGGERED ON A LARK.
WHAT ABOUT WHEN HE MANAGED TO CONVERSE WITH THE SPIRITS IN JAPAN RIGHT AFTER MAKING IT BACK HERE?
OH, THAT ...
BACK THEN, TAKAFUMI WAS HOLDING SOME GOVERNMENT OFFICE PAPERWORK AND GIVING OFF A SERIOUSLY DEADLY VIBE.
I THOUGHT TO MYSELF, "OH NO. IF I CAN'T USE MAGIC HERE, I'M GOING TO GET ABANDONED AND DIE IN THE STREET."
I WAS ACTUALLY PRETTY DESPERATE AT THE TIME...
HISO ヒソ HISO ヒソ HISO
You were going to cut him off, weren't you!?
HISO (WHISPER) ヒソ HISO ヒソ HISO ヒソ ヒソ HISO
AND YOU WERE ACTING LIKE SOME KIND OF SAINT BEFORE!
It made him desperate enough that he can use magic again, so it all evens out, right?
ヒソヒソヒソヒソ
HISO HISO HISO HISO
HISO ヒソ ヒソ HISO ヒソ HISO
HISO HISO ヒソヒソ…
The hell it does, you absolute jerk...!

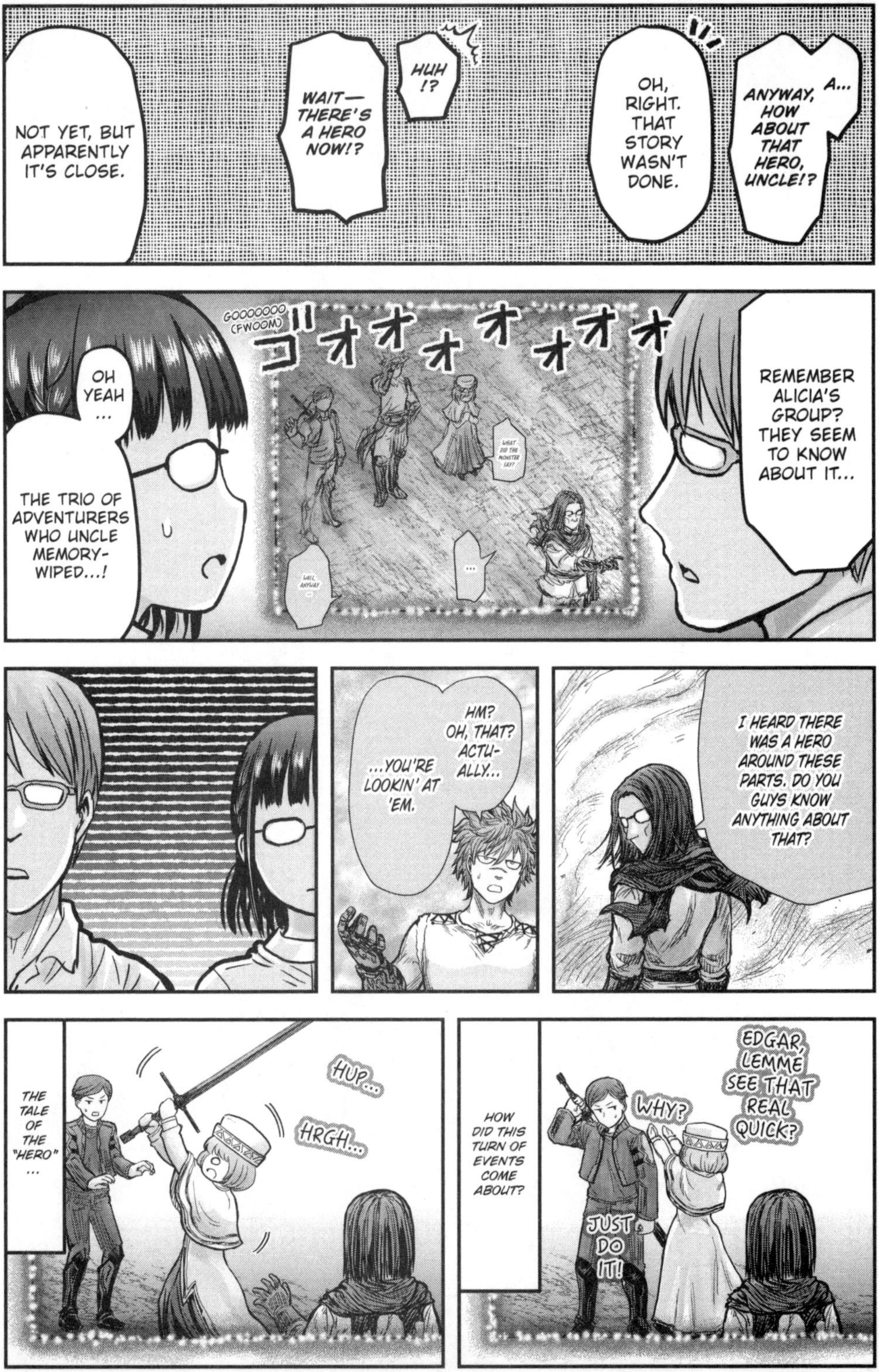
A...
ANYWAY, HOW ABOUT THAT HERO, UNCLE!?
OH, RIGHT. THAT STORY WASN'T DONE.
HUH!?
WAIT— THERE'S A HERO NOW!?
NOT YET, BUT APPARENTLY IT'S CLOSE.
GOOOOOOO (FWOOM)
ゴオオオオオオオ
REMEMBER ALICIA'S GROUP? THEY SEEM TO KNOW ABOUT IT...
WHAT DID THE MONSTER SAY?
...
WELL, ANYWAY...
OH YEAH...
THE TRIO OF ADVENTURERS WHO UNCLE MEMORY-WIPED...!
I HEARD THERE WAS A HERO AROUND THESE PARTS. DO YOU GUYS KNOW ANYTHING ABOUT THAT?
HM? OH, THAT? ACTU-ALLY...
...YOU'RE LOOKIN' AT 'EM.
EDGAR, LEMME SEE THAT REAL QUICK?
WHY?
JUST DO IT!
HOW DID THIS TURN OF EVENTS COME ABOUT?
HUP...
HRGH...
THE TALE OF THE "HERO"...

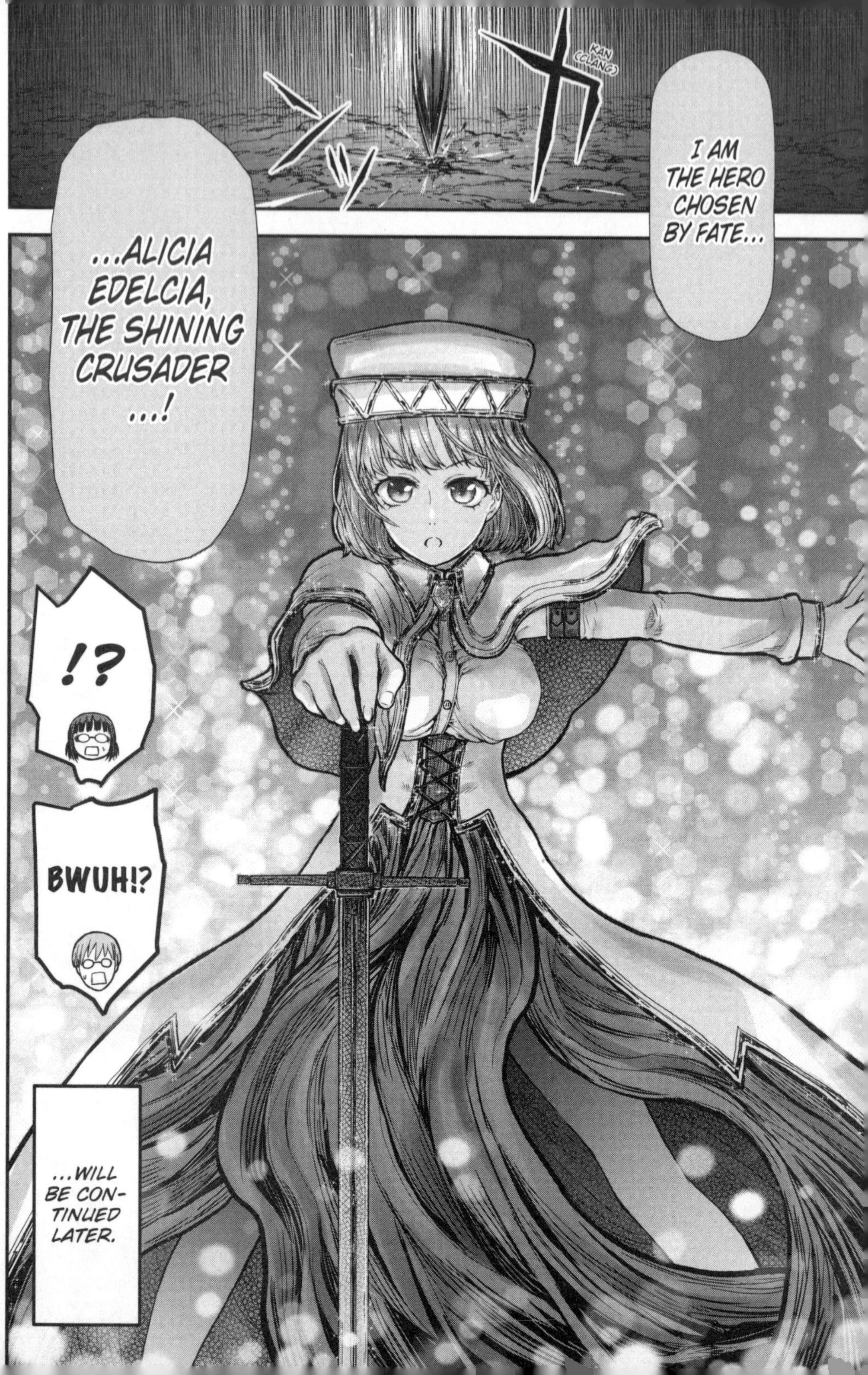
KAN (CLANG)
I AM THE HERO CHOSEN BY FATE...
...ALICIA EDELCIA, THE SHINING CRUSADER ...!
!?
BWUH!?
...WILL BE CON-TINUED LATER.

UNCLE from ANOTHER WORLD

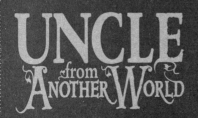

UNCLE from ANOTHER WORLD

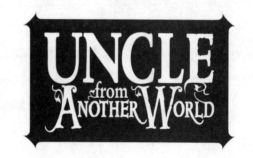

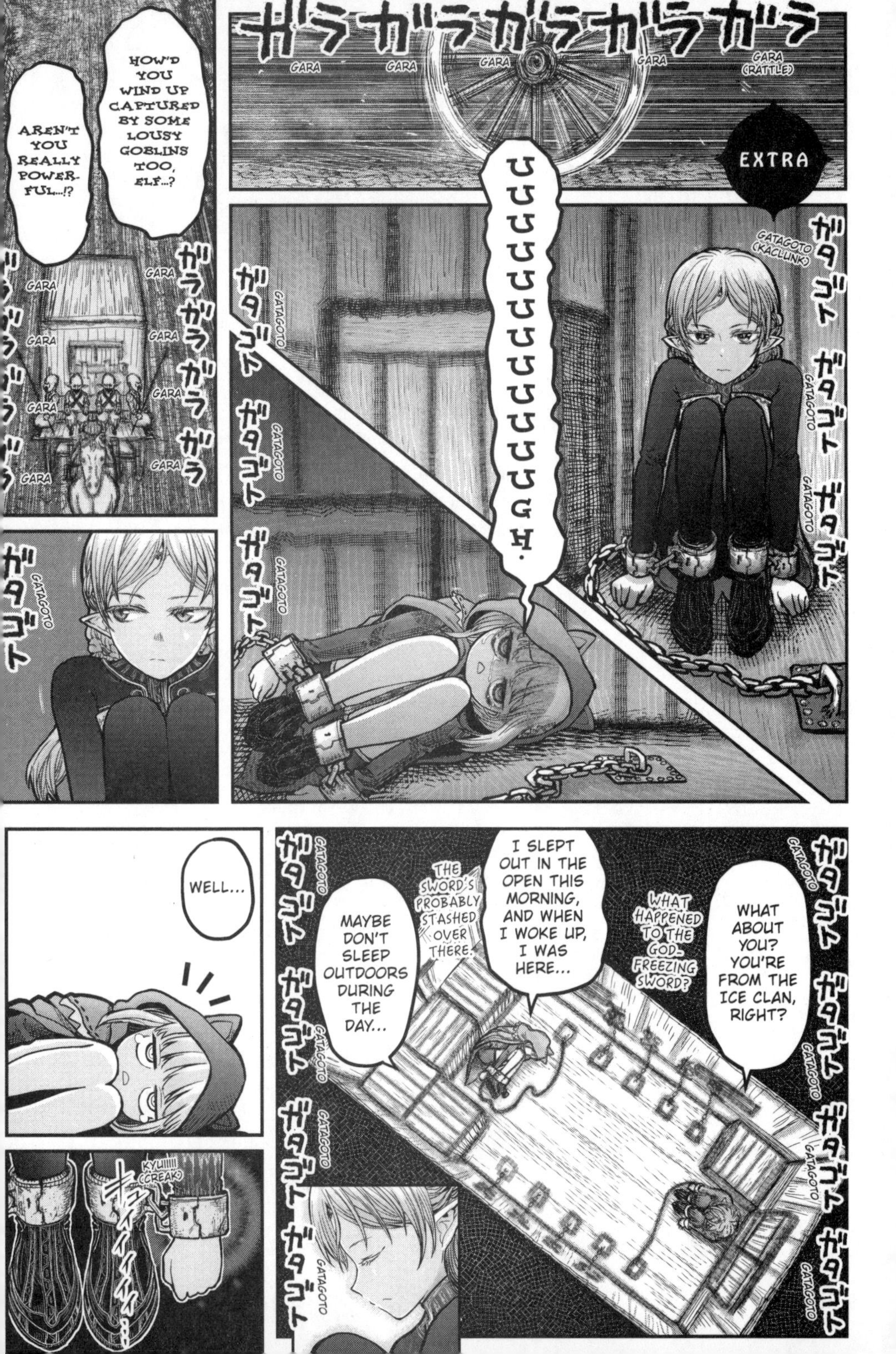

ガラガラガラガラガラ
GARA GARA GARA GARA GARA (RATTLE)
EXTRA
GATAGOTO (KACLUNK)
ガタゴト ガタゴト ガタゴト
GATAGOTO GATAGOTO
ガタゴト ガタゴト
GATAGOTO GATAGOTO
UUUUUUUUUUUUUUUUGH.
HOW'D YOU WIND UP CAPTURED BY SOME LOUSY GOBLINS TOO, ELF...?
AREN'T YOU REALLY POWERFUL...!?
ガラガラガラガラ
GARA GARA GARA GARA
GARA GARA GARA GARA
ガタゴト
GATAGOTO
ガタゴト ガタゴト ガタゴト ガタゴト
GATAGOTO GATAGOTO GATAGOTO GATAGOTO
WHAT ABOUT YOU? YOU'RE FROM THE ICE CLAN, RIGHT?
WHAT HAPPENED TO THE GOD-FREEZING SWORD?
I SLEPT OUT IN THE OPEN THIS MORNING, AND WHEN I WOKE UP, I WAS HERE...
THE SWORD'S PROBABLY STASHED OVER THERE.
MAYBE DON'T SLEEP OUTDOORS DURING THE DAY...
ガタゴト ガタゴト ガタゴト ガタゴト
GATAGOTO GATAGOTO GATAGOTO GATAGOTO
WELL...
KYUIIIII (CREAK)

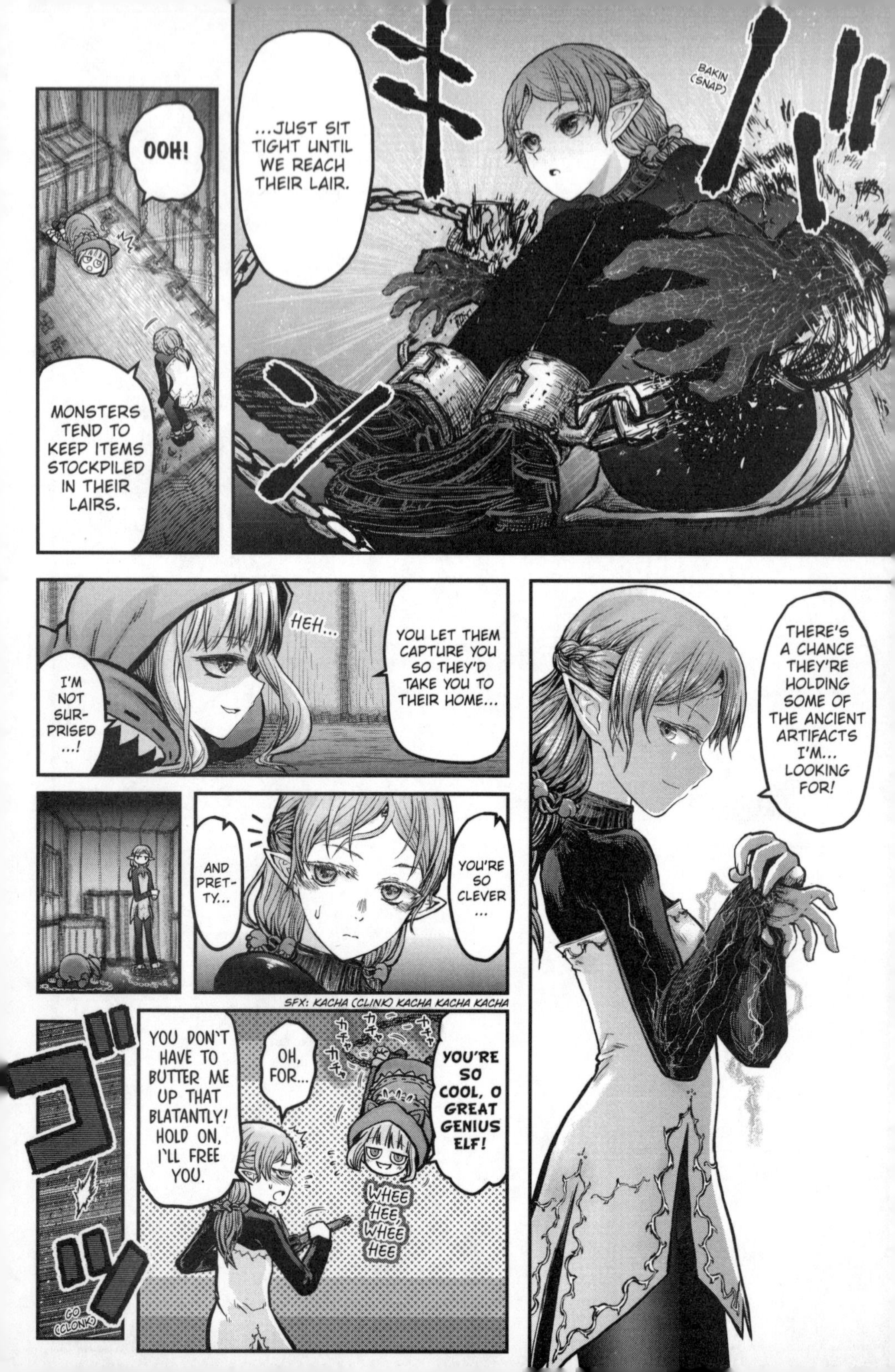
BAKIN (SNAP)
...JUST SIT TIGHT UNTIL WE REACH THEIR LAIR.
OOH!
MONSTERS TEND TO KEEP ITEMS STOCKPILED IN THEIR LAIRS.
THERE'S A CHANCE THEY'RE HOLDING SOME OF THE ANCIENT ARTIFACTS I'M... LOOKING FOR!
YOU LET THEM CAPTURE YOU SO THEY'D TAKE YOU TO THEIR HOME...
HEH...
I'M NOT SUR-PRISED ...!
YOU'RE SO CLEVER ...
AND PRET-TY...
SFX: KACHA (CLINK) KACHA KACHA KACHA
YOU'RE SO COOL, O GREAT GENIUS ELF!
OH, FOR...
YOU DON'T HAVE TO BUTTER ME UP THAT BLATANTLY! HOLD ON, I'LL FREE YOU.
WHEE HEE, WHEE HEE
GO (CLONK)

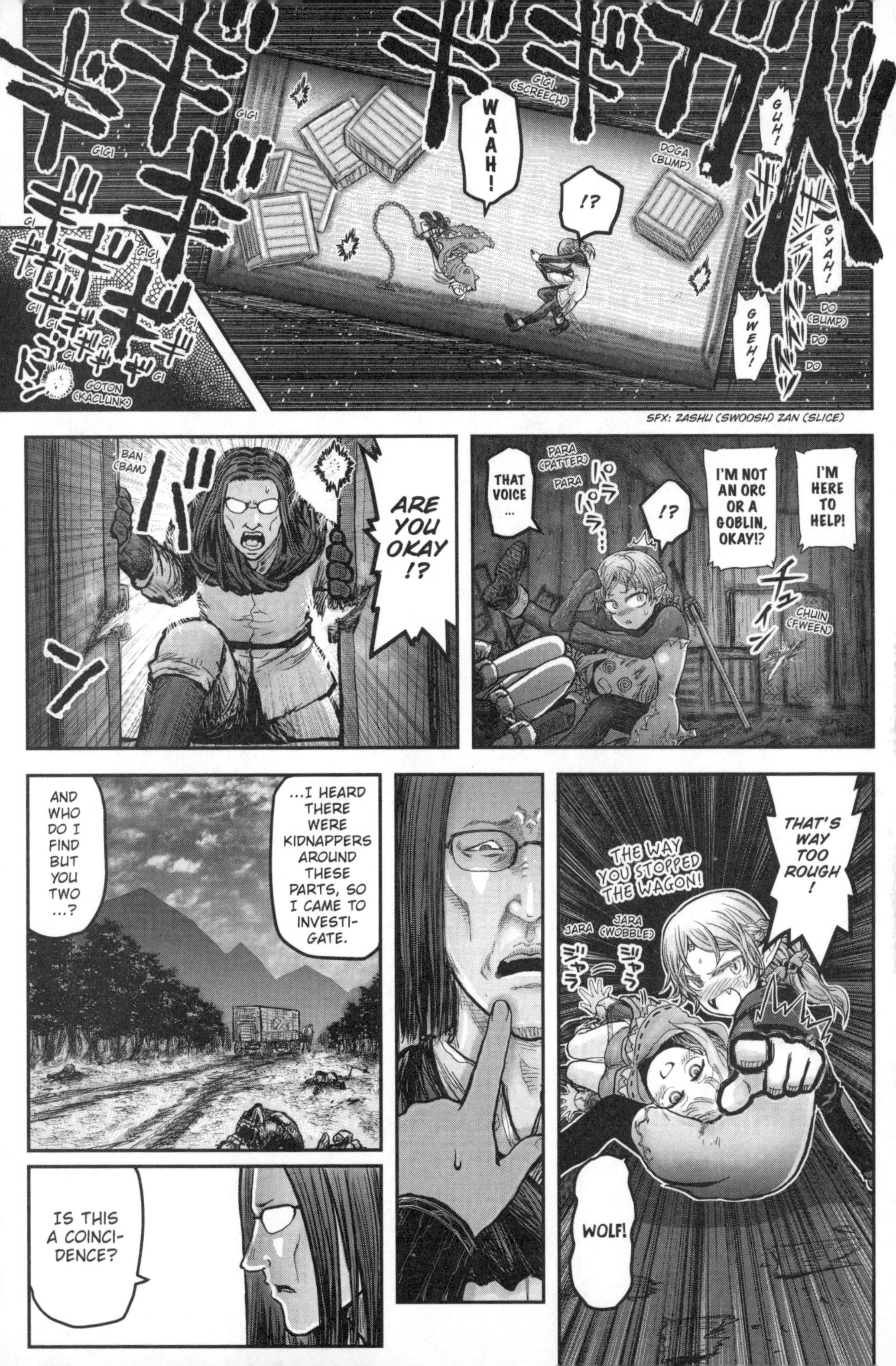
GUH!
GYAH!
DO (BUMP) DO DO
GWEH!
DOGA (BUMP)
!?
GIGI (SCREECH)
WAAH!
GIGI
GIGI
GI GIGI GI GI GI GI GI GI
GOTON (KACLUNK)
SFX: ZASHU (SWOOSH) ZAN (SLICE)
I'M HERE TO HELP!
I'M NOT AN ORC OR A GOBLIN, OKAY!?
!?
PARA (PATTER) PARA
THAT VOICE...
CHUIN (FWEEN)
ARE YOU OKAY!?
BAN (BAM)
THAT'S WAY TOO ROUGH!
THE WAY YOU STOPPED THE WAGON!
JARA (WOBBLE) JARA
WOLF!
...I HEARD THERE WERE KIDNAPPERS AROUND THESE PARTS, SO I CAME TO INVESTIGATE.
AND WHO DO I FIND BUT YOU TWO...?
IS THIS A COINCIDENCE?

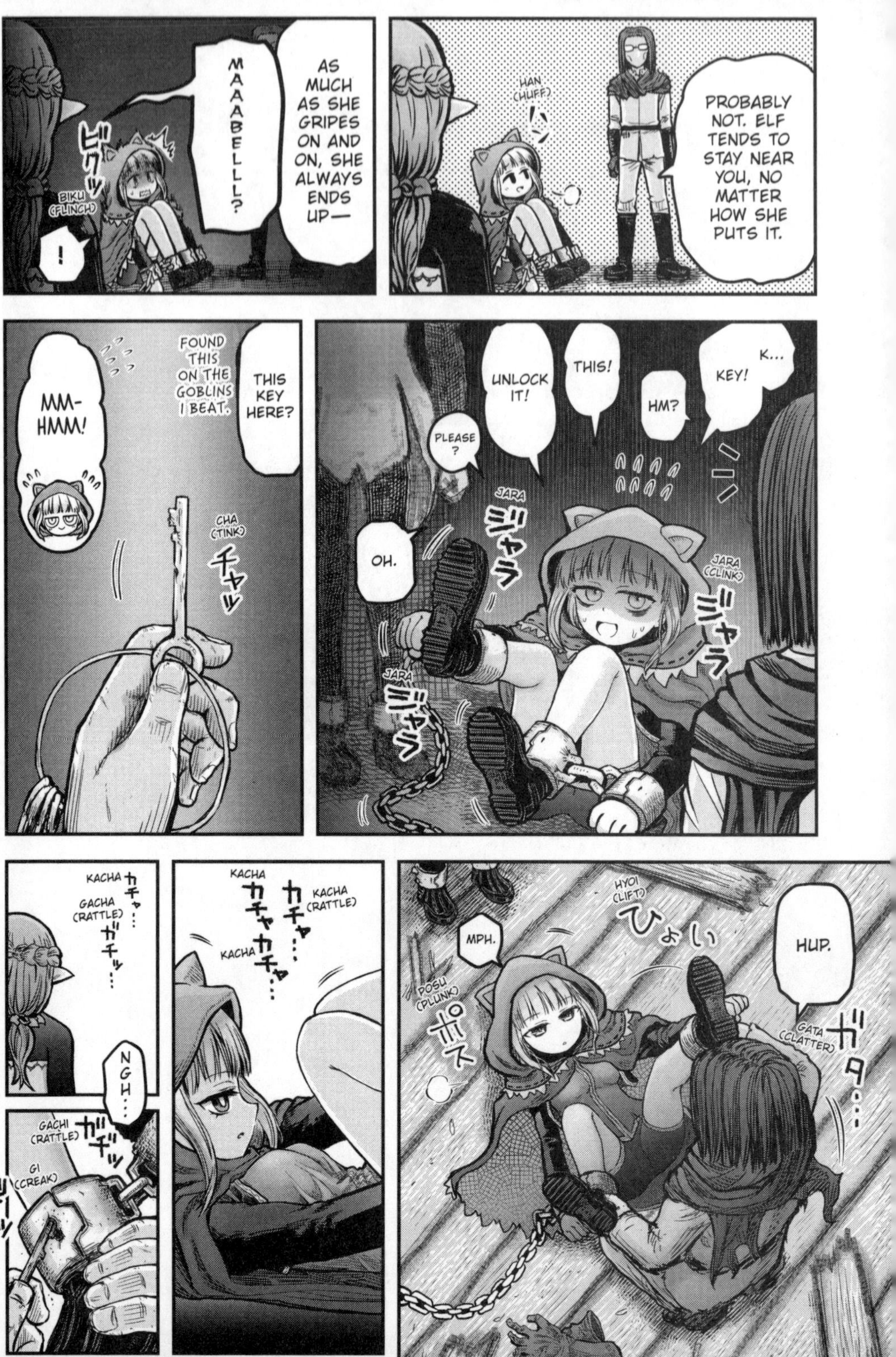
PROBABLY NOT. ELF TENDS TO STAY NEAR YOU, NO MATTER HOW SHE PUTS IT.
HAN (HUFF)
AS MUCH AS SHE GRIPES ON AND ON, SHE ALWAYS ENDS UP—
MAAABELLL?
BIKU (FLINCH)
!
K... KEY!
HM?
THIS!
UNLOCK IT!
PLEASE?
JARA (CLINK)
JARA
OH.
JARA
THIS KEY HERE?
FOUND THIS ON THE GOBLINS I BEAT.
MM-HMM!
CHA (TINK)
HUP.
GATA (CLATTER)
HYOI (LIFT)
MPH.
POSU (PLUNK)
KACHA (RATTLE)
KACHA
KACHA
NGH...
KACHA
GACHA (RATTLE)
GACHI (RATTLE)
GI (CREAK)

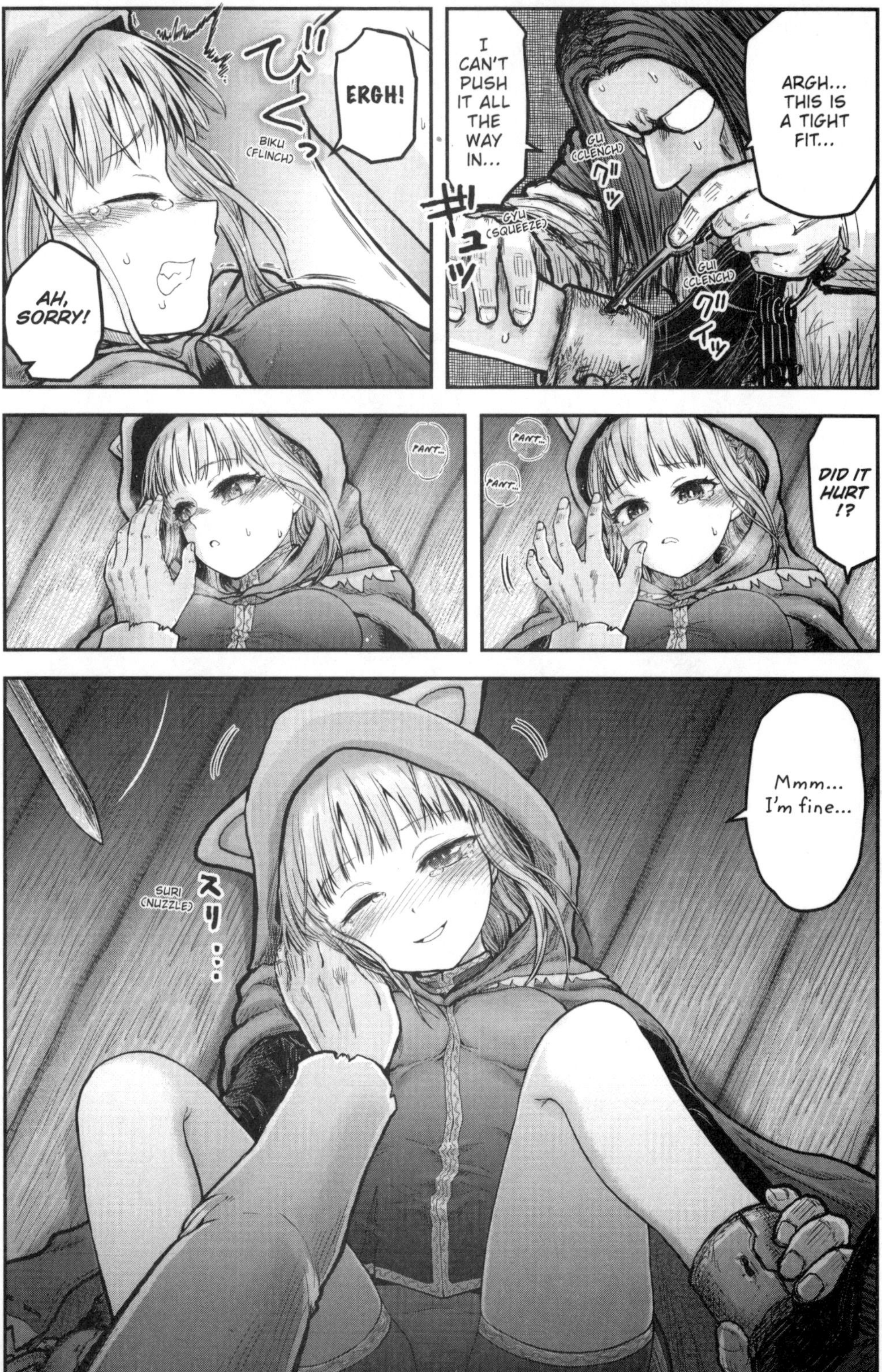
ARGH... THIS IS A TIGHT FIT...
I CAN'T PUSH IT ALL THE WAY IN...
GU (CLENCH)
グッ
GYU (SQUEEZE)
ギュッ
GUI (CLENCH)
グイッ
ERGH!
びくっ
BIKU (FLINCH)
AH, SORRY!
DID IT HURT!?
PANT...
PANT...
PANT...
Mmm... I'm fine...
SURI (NUZZLE)
スリ...

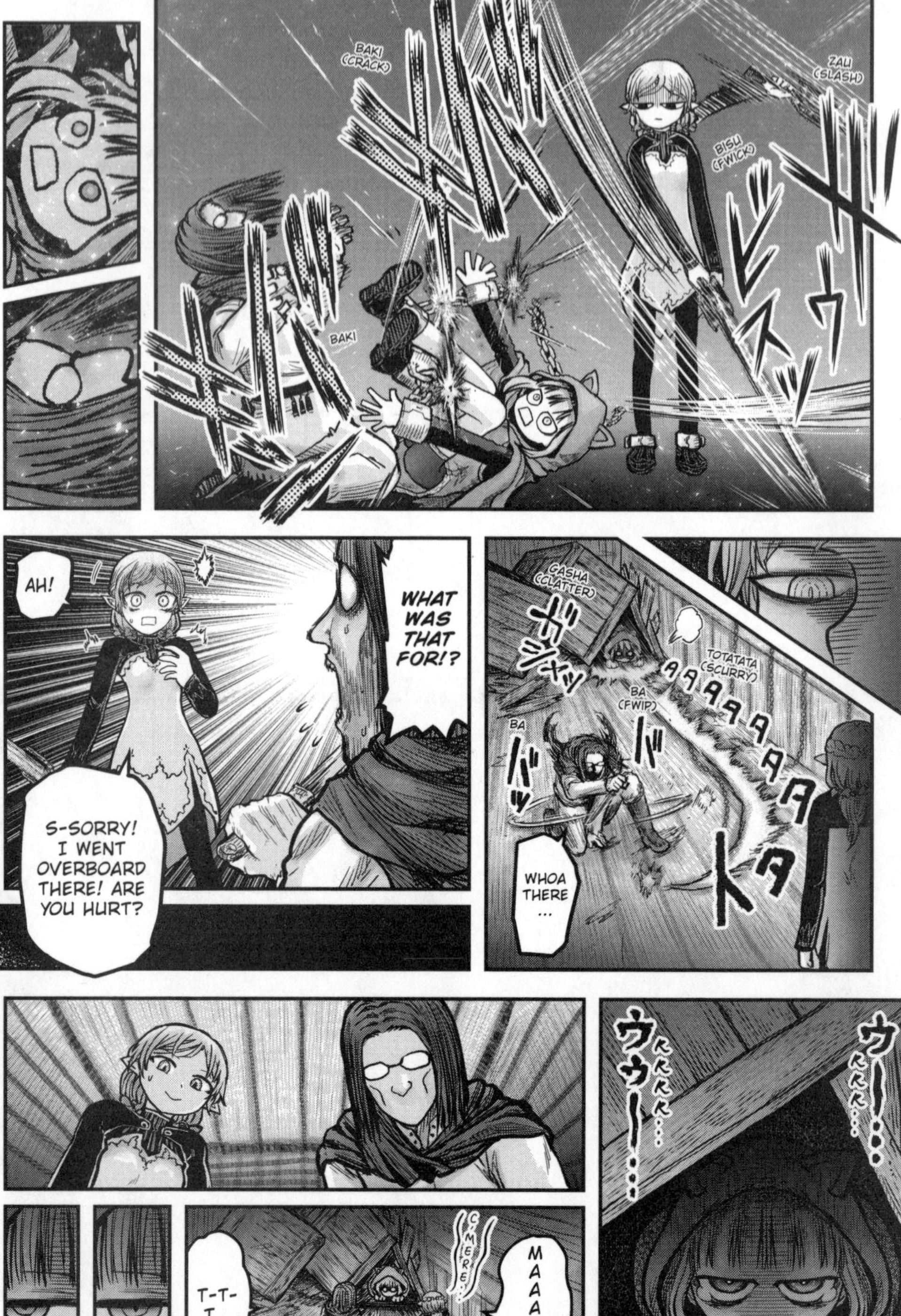
ZAU (SLASH)
BISU (FWICK)
BAKI (CRACK)
BAKI
GASHA (CLATTER)
TOTATATA (SCURRY)
BA (FWIP)
BA
WHOA THERE ...
WHAT WAS THAT FOR!?
AH!
S-SORRY! I WENT OVERBOARD THERE! ARE YOU HURT?
RRRR...
RRRR...
MAAABEL...
C'MERE!
T-T-T...

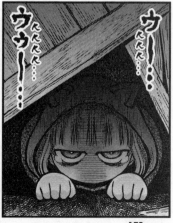

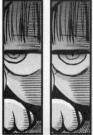

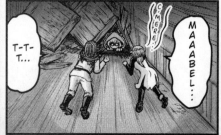

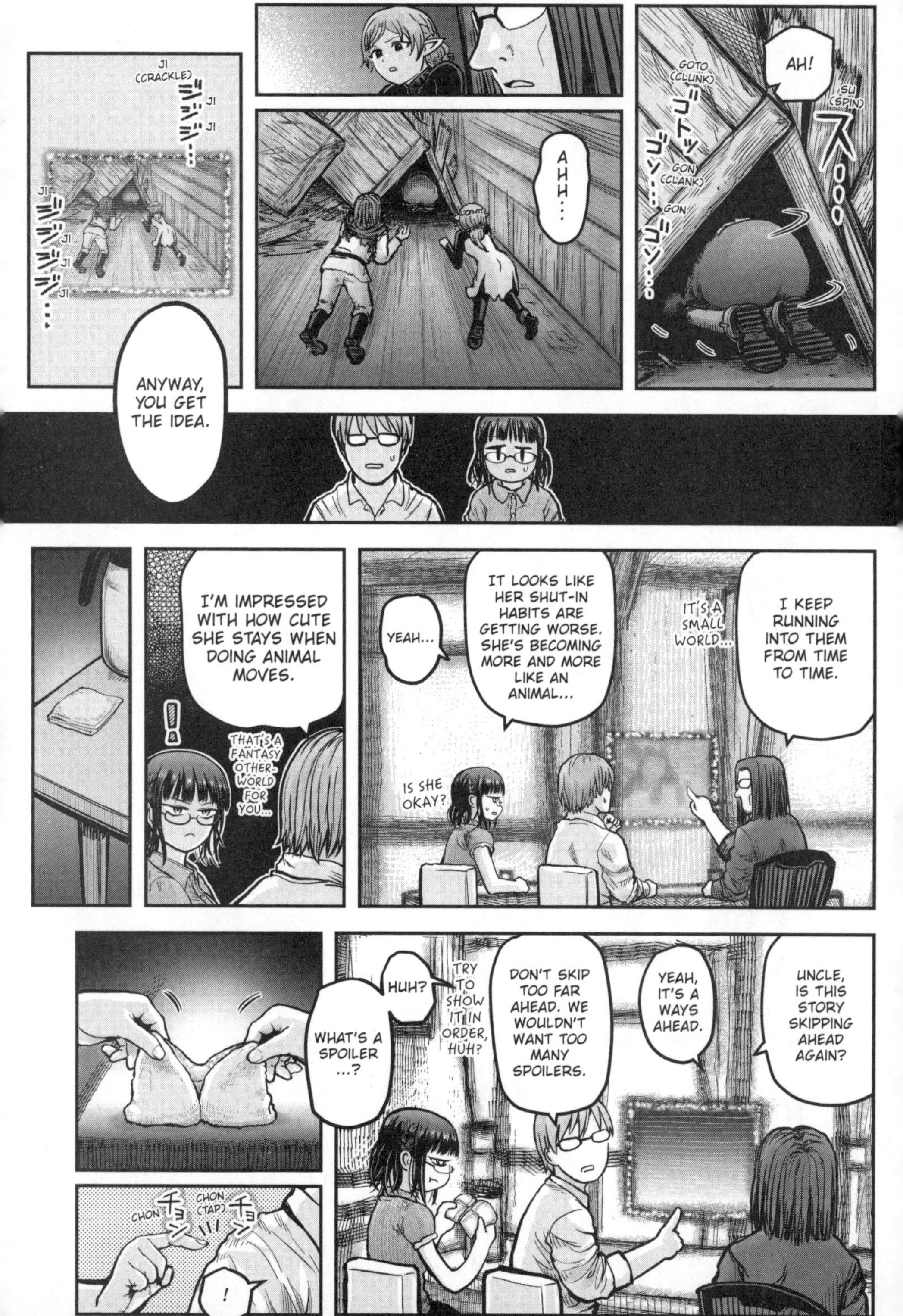
AH!
GOTO (CLUNK)
ゴトッ
GON (CLANK)
ゴン…
GON
ゴン…
SU (SPIN)
スーーー
AHH…
JI (CRACKLE)
ジジジジ…
JI JI JI JI JI
ジジジジジ…
ANYWAY, YOU GET THE IDEA.
I KEEP RUNNING INTO THEM FROM TIME TO TIME.
IT'S A SMALL WORLD…
IT LOOKS LIKE HER SHUT-IN HABITS ARE GETTING WORSE. SHE'S BECOMING MORE AND MORE LIKE AN ANIMAL…
YEAH…
IS SHE OKAY?
I'M IMPRESSED WITH HOW CUTE SHE STAYS WHEN DOING ANIMAL MOVES.
!
THAT'S A FANTASY OTHER-WORLD FOR YOU…
UNCLE, IS THIS STORY SKIPPING AHEAD AGAIN?
YEAH, IT'S A WAYS AHEAD.
DON'T SKIP TOO FAR AHEAD. WE WOULDN'T WANT TOO MANY SPOILERS.
TRY TO SHOW IT IN ORDER, HUH?
HUH?
WHAT'S A SPOILER …?
CHON (TAP)
チョン
CHON
チョン
!

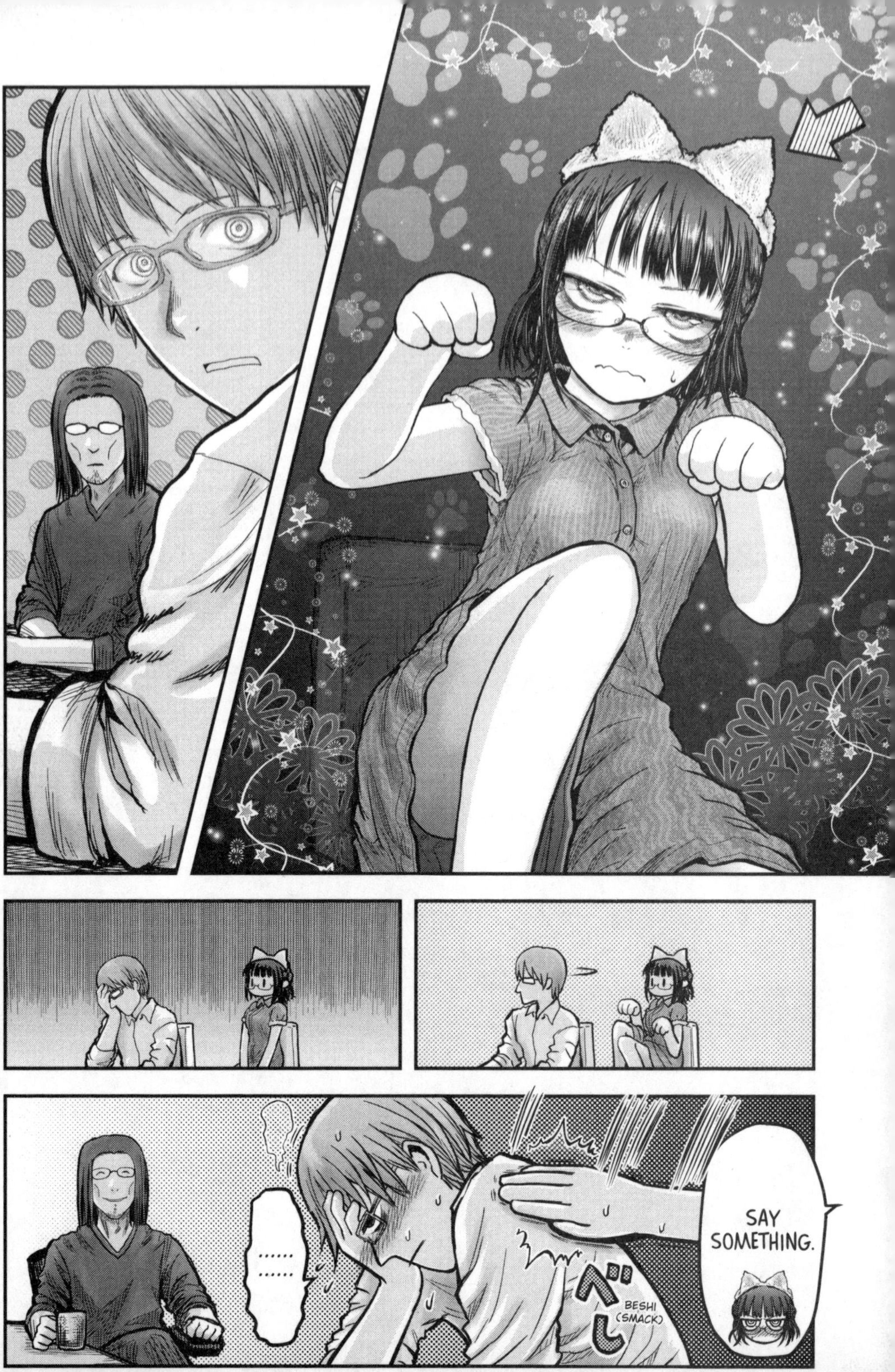
SAY SOMETHING.
……
……
BESHI (SMACK)

Translation Notes

COMMON HONORIFICS

no honorific: Indicates familiarity or closeness; if used without permission or reason, addressing someone in this manner would constitute an insult.

-san: The Japanese equivalent of Mr./Mrs./Miss. If a situation calls for politeness, this is the fail-safe honorific.

-sama: Conveys great respect; may also indicate that the social status of the speaker is lower than that of the addressee.

-dono: Roughly equivalent to "master" or "milord."

-kun: Used most often when referring to boys, this indicates affection or familiarity. Occasionally used by older men among their peers, but it may also be used by anyone referring to a person of lower standing.

-chan: An affectionate honorific indicating familiarity used mostly in reference to girls; also used in reference to cute persons or animals regardless of gender.

-senpai: An honorific for one's senior classmate, colleague, etc., although not as senior or respected as a *sensei* (teacher).

¥100 is approximately $1 USD.

A●ien Soldier, Uncle's favorite game, is an action title from 1995 known for its extreme emphasis on elaborate boss fights and for being impossibly ambitious in scope.

PAGE 3
Alt●red Beast is a 1988 beat-'em-up arcade game where you control a Greek hero revived from the dead by Zeus to fight an evil sorcerer and rescue Athena. The hero can gather power orbs and transform into different werebeasts with unique abilities.

PAGE 12
Bushi means "warrior" in Japanese and is commonly associated with samurai—though it doesn't refer solely to them.

PAGE 25
Yodob●shi is a electronics store chain in Japan that plays prerecorded in-store announcements throughout the day.

PAGE 39
Pu●seman is a 1994 platformer game by a company whose later monster-battling creation, *Po●ket Monsters* (1996), would spawn a global mega franchise.

The **M●ga Drive** was a 1988 16-bit home video game console released by Se●a that was touted for its "blast processing."

The attack mentioned, "**Volteccer**," is a reference to the anime *Tekkaman the Space Knight*. The version of the move seen in *Pu●seman* would itself be referenced in Po●ket Monsters as its iconic yellow mascot's signature technique, Volt Tackle (known as "Volteccer" in Japanese).

PAGE 47
YuY● Hakusho is a 1990 battle manga about a high school delinquent who becomes a spirit detective. **Territories** are domains wielded by psychics in battle. **Hi●i** is one of the hero's demonic foes who becomes an ally.

PAGE 58
Tsundere is an archetype common to anime and manga where a character either grows from hating someone to loving someone, or acts especially prickly toward a character they have feelings for.

PAGE 88
Wolfgunblood (one word) is a boss character from A●ien Soldier.

PAGE 93
NEET stands for "Not in Education, Employment, or Training." Originally coined in the United Kingdom, the term gained widespread use in Japan beginning in the 2000s.

PAGE 96
The firmness of hakata ramen noodles is cooked to customer preference (extra hard, **hard**, normal, soft, extra soft), somewhat like the difference between *al dente* and *ben cotta* for Italian pasta.

Chashu is braised pork belly, and is loosely related to the Cantonese barbecued pork dish *char siu*.

PAGE 100
Shaberi means "talk" or "gab" in Japanese.

PAGE 101
Cringe notepad doodles in Japanese is more literally "dark-history notebooks." Referring to embarrassing drawings and ideas for characters and video game ideas committed to paper from one's younger years, it's become something of a meme in Japanese online culture.

Dr. Eggman is a robotics scientist and main antagonist of a certain blue hedgehog mascot.

PAGE 106
Sawatdee Khrap is Thai for "hello." **Tom yum kung** is a variation of the hot-and-sour tom yum soup that uses prawns.

PAGE 108
Pan●er Dragoon is a 1995 3D shoot-'em-up where players take on the role of a dragon rider in a fantasy world.

PAGE 114
Kuroki Tenma is a character from A●ien Soldier. In him resides the evil Epsilon-1, the counterpart to the heroic player character, Epsilon-2.

PAGE 142
Guardian H□roes is a 1996 beat-'em-up game with elements of fighting games and role-playing games. It also includes branching story paths leading to multiple different endings.

The **Se●a Saturn** was a 1994 home console. While capable of 3D graphics, its original emphasis on 2D sprite graphics put it at a disadvantage against its competitors.

PAGE 155
Gi●n is the neighborhood bully from a classic manga and anime series about a blue robot cat from the future.

INSIDE COVER (FRONT)
Dari●s Gaiden is a 1994 2D shoot-'em-up arcade game (later ported to home consoles) that features massive mechanical bosses that resemble aquatic creatures. **Golden Ogre** is one such boss. A boss's arrival is preceded by a large warning message flashing on the screen.

B●nanza Bros. is a 1990 stealth-action arcade game where you play as thieves robbing various high-end places. The game eventually found its way onto home consoles.

UNCLE from ANOTHER WORLD

III

Hotondoshindeiru

TRANSLATOR: **Christina Rose**
LETTERER: **Phil Christie**

ISEKAI OJISAN Vol. 3
©Hotondoshindeiru 2019
©SEGA

First published in Japan in 2019 by KADOKAWA CORPORATION, Tokyo.
English translation rights arranged with KADOKAWA CORPORATION, Tokyo through TUTTLE-MORI AGENCY, Inc.

English translation © 2021 by Yen Press, LLC

Yen Press
150 West 30th Street, 19th Floor
New York, NY 10001

Visit us at yenpress.com ✦ facebook.com/yenpress
twitter.com/yenpress ✦ yenpress.tumblr.com ✦ instagram.com/yenpress

First Yen Press Edition: October 2021

Yen Press is an imprint of Yen Press, LLC.
The Yen Press name and logo are trademarks of Yen Press, LLC.

The publisher is not responsible for websites (or their content) that are not owned by the publisher.

Library of Congress Control Number: 2021932161

ISBNs: 978-1-9753-2396-7 (paperback)
978-1-9753-2397-4 (ebook)

10 9 8 7 6 5 4 3 2 1

WOR

Printed in the United States of America